The Origins of the English Legal Profession

The Origins of the English Legal Profession

Paul Brand

BLACKWELL
Oxford UK & Cambridge USA

Copyright © Paul Brand 1992

The right of Paul Brand to be identified as author of this work has been asserted in accordance with the Copyright, Designs and Patents Act 1988.

First published 1992

Blackwell Publishers
108 Cowley Road
Oxford OX4 1JF
UK

Three Cambridge Center
Cambridge, Massachusetts 02142
USA

All rights reserved. Except for the quotation of short passages for the purposes of criticism and review, no part may be reproduced, stored in a retrieval system, or transmitted, in any form or by any means, electronic, mechanical, photocopying, recording or otherwise, without the prior permission of the publisher.

Except in the United States of America, this book is sold subject to the condition that it shall not, by way of trade or otherwise, be lent, resold, hired out, or otherwise circulated without the publisher's prior consent in any form of binding or cover other than that in which it is published and without a similar condition including this condition being imposed on the subsequent purchaser.

British Library Cataloguing in Publication Data

A CIP catalogue record for this book is available from the British Library.

Library of Congress Cataloging-in-Publication Data

Brand, Paul.
  The origins of the English legal profession / Paul Brand.
    p.   cm.
  Includes bibliographical references and index.
  ISBN 0–631–15401–9
  1. Lawyers – England – History. I. Title.
  KD460.B7   1992
  349.42 – dc20
  [344.2]   91–36250
                                                                                CIP

Typeset in 10 on 12 pt Erhardt by Graphicraft
Printed in Great Britain by TJ Press (Padstow) Ltd, Padstow, Cornwall

This book is printed on acid-free paper

Contents

Preface		vii
1	Anglo-Norman England: a Land without Lawyers	1
2	Creating a Demand for Lawyers: the Transformation of the English Court System, 1154–1307	14
3	Creating a Demand for Lawyers: Changes in the Process of Litigation and in the Rules Governing the Use of Legal Representatives, 1154–1307	33
4	From Proto-professional to Professional: the Emergence of the Professional Lawyer in England, 1199–1272	50
5	The English Legal Profession in Edward I's Reign (I): the Size of the Profession	70
6	The English Legal Profession in Edward I's Reign (II): the Profession at Work	86
7	The English Legal Profession in Edward I's Reign (III): Training and Entry into the Profession	106
8	The English Legal Profession in Edward I's Reign (IV): Regulation	120
9	The Other Legal Profession: Canon Lawyers in England before 1307	143
Conclusion		158
Notes		161
Index		219

Preface

I would never have begun work on this book but for the encouragement and stimulus provided by two good friends. The late Denis Bethell, while we were colleagues at University College Dublin, suggested to me that I write a book on the beginnings of the lay professions in Western Europe. This is not that book, nor even a first instalment of it, but it was Denis who started me working on the origins of that profession about which (as an English legal historian) I knew most. The second scholar to unwittingly provide me with a stimulus to work on the same topic was Professor Robert C. Palmer. A by-product of his own work on the English county court was an article on the origins of the English legal profession which I encouraged him to publish in *The Irish Jurist*. There was and is much of interest and value in the article, but I disagreed and disagree with its overall argument. I soon found myself working on a detailed refutation of his argument and on the development of an alternative hypothesis that would restore the central royal courts to their correct position as the focus of the birth and early development of the English legal profession. It was then Virginia Murphy who provided the necessary encouragement for me to turn what was originally envisaged as a long article into a book.

It may be helpful if I state here at the outset the working definitions I have adopted in this book for those notoriously slippery concepts, the 'professional lawyer' and a 'legal profession'. For me a 'professional lawyer' is someone recognized by others as having a special expertise in legal matters and who is willing to put that expertise at the disposal of others, who is paid for doing this and who spends a major part of his time in this professional activity.*

---

* My definition is close to that of Professor Robert Palmer though not quite identical with it: R. C. Palmer, *The County Courts of Medieval England, 1150–1350* (Princeton, 1982), p. 89.

A 'legal profession' exists when professional lawyers start being singled out for special regulation in their professional activity. This may take the form of measures restricting the numbers allowed to offer their professional services to litigants in particular courts or imposing certain minimum standards of competence on those wishing to do so. It may also take the form of measures subjecting professional lawyers to particular standards of behaviour in their professional activity and to special punishment for infractions of those standards. I do not consider it necessary that the 'professional lawyers' who form a 'legal profession' enjoy any degree of autonomy or self-regulation.

The research for this book was conducted primarily in two institutions: the Public Record Office (Chancery Lane) and the British Library. My thanks go to the staff of both for their help and kindness over the years. If I single out Dr David Crook of the Public Record Office for special mention this is only because his kindness and helpfulness over the years have far exceeded anything that might reasonably have been expected even of an erstwhile colleague and fellow-medievalist. Like many other scholars I also owe a special debt of gratitude to the Institute of Historical Research in London and its ever-helpful staff, not just for providing ready access to a wide range of scholarly materials but also for its important role in facilitating social contact and intellectual interchange with my fellow historians.

While working on this book, various institutions have offered me the opportunity to present work in progress to their seminars and meetings and I have benefited from the suggestions and criticisms of many of those who heard such papers. They include: in England – the Oxford Medieval Society; the Early and the Late Medieval and the Law and Society Seminars of the Institute of Historical Research in London and the Anglo-American Conference of Historians held at the Institute; the London programme of Wake Forest University School of Law; the History Workshop; the Eighth British Legal History Conference held at Cardiff in 1987; in the USA – the History Department and the Law School of Cornell University; the Law School of the University of Chicago; the Law School of Harvard University; the Law School of Boston University; the History Department and Law School of the University of Kansas; the Law School of UCLA; the History Department of UC Santa Barbara; the University of Cincinnati College of Law; the University of Illinois College of Law; the New York University School of Law; the History Department of the University of Washington; in Canada – the Pontifical Institute of Mediaeval Studies and the Law Faculty and the History Department of the University of Toronto. Some of the work on this book was done while I held a Golieb fellowship at New York University Law School and I am very grateful to the Law School for its support.

On a more personal level there are many individuals whom I should like to thank for stimulus, support and encouragement during the writing of this book. They include: John Baker, Jim Bolton, Chris Brookes, Jim Brundage,

David Carpenter, Michael Clanchy, Peter Coss, Edwin and Anne DeWindt, Charlie Donahue, John Gillingham, Anthony Gross, Michael Haren, Dick Helmholz, Clive Holmes, Jim Holt, John Hudson, Barbara Kern, Lou Knafla, Andrew Lewis, Janet Loengard, Donald Logan, Mavis Mate, Bill Nelson, Alexandra Nicol, James Oldham, Nial Osborough, Russell Osgood, Bob and Pat Palmer, John Parsons, Seymour Phillips, Wilf Prest, Alice and Frank Prochaska, Susan Reynolds, Eleanor Searle, David Seipp, Bob Stacey, John Styles, David Sugarman, Sue Sheridan Walker and Scott Waugh. I owe my introduction to English legal history to the late Derek Hall, who was a meticulous and encouraging supervisor of my postgraduate work and whose own published work reflects his own exacting standards of scholarship. While an Assistant Keeper at the Public Record Office I greatly benefited from having the late C. A. F. Meekings as a colleague. I owe a special debt of gratitude to Joseph Biancalana for his willingness to discuss English legal history with me on his regular trips to London. My friendship with Paul Hyams goes back to the period when we were both graduate students working under Derek Hall and I owe more than he may realize to his encouragement and criticism over the years. This is not the book he would have written nor yet the book he thinks I should have written but I hope he knows how much it owes to him. My greatest debt, however, is to my wife Vanessa. She has supported me financially as well as emotionally during the writing of this book. She has also done her best to improve its prose style and its clarity. Without her it would not have been written; the remaining faults are all my own.

Paul Brand
London, 1991

1

Anglo-Norman England: a Land without Lawyers

THE ANSTEY CASE

Richard of Anstey took the first steps in asserting his claim to the inheritance of his uncle, William de Sackville, not long after Henry II finally made good his own claim to the throne of his grandfather, Henry I, in 1154.[1] William had not been in the first rank of English landowners, but had possessed seven Essex manors and the lordship of ten and a half knights' fees in Essex and three neighbouring counties. Mabel de Francheville, Richard's opponent, was William's only child and she had been accepted as his heiress by the various lords of whom he had held lands. But there was a flaw in her title: she was the daughter of a marriage which had late been annulled and so Richard claimed that she was illegitimate. As the eldest son of William's sister Agnes, he claimed to be William's closest surviving legitimate relative and thus his rightful heir. Richard started the litigation late in 1158. Initially his claim was heard in a royal court over which Richard de Lucy, one of Henry II's two chief justiciars, presided. When Richard raised the question of Mabel's illegitimacy the case was transferred to the court of the archbishop of Canterbury. From there it went by way of a hearing before papal judges delegate to be decided at the papal curia. Judgment was eventually given at Rome that Mabel was illegitimate. The case then returned to the king's court. After several adjournments judgment was given in Richard's favour in July 1163.

Richard subsequently compiled a detailed memorandum giving particulars of the money he had spent during the course of the litigation. It is from this that we derive most of our knowledge of what happened in the 'Anstey case'.[2]

Richard's total expenditure came to around 350 pounds. For that part of the litigation which was heard in the English ecclesiastical courts he obtained expert assistance from two Italian canon lawyers who were in the service of the abbey of St Alban's and of the bishop of Lincoln, master Ambrose and master Peter de Meleti.[3] They acted as his advocates. He also took their advice about the drafting of letters from the archbishop of Canterbury and the judges delegate to the pope about the litigation. Richard paid master Peter ten marks and gave him a gold ring worth half a mark for his services. The memorandum does not record what master Ambrose was paid, though his fee was probably included in the total of 11 marks paid to 'pleaders and clerks giving me assistance in the court of the archbishop'. Richard also took care to ensure that he had the company of others for his appearances in the church courts. He was accompanied not just by 'clerks'[4] and witnesses but also by 'friends' (*amici*), probably meaning kinsmen, and 'helpers' (*auxilia*), perhaps friends in the modern sense.

For that part of the litigation which took place in the king's courts the memorandum mentions no comparable expert involvement. Nothing is said about sending for named experts when the case was to be heard and the memorandum provides no evidence that experts were regularly present in court to speak on Richard's behalf.[5] It does mention the expenditure of 12 and a half marks in cash and in kind in respect of unnamed *placitatores* who regularly came to hearings of the case. Might these have been expert lawyers? Probably not, for we are also given one further crucial piece of information about them: they were drawn from his neighbours. This suggests that they were simply men willing to spend time keeping Richard company on his way to and from the court and to appear in court with him (and perhaps, when required, to bear witness for him): the people whom elsewhere he calls his *auxilia*, rather than a group of legal experts. Some may, indeed, have had more experience than others of legal matters and may have been able to give him useful advice, but they were present primarily as friends, advisers and supporters, not as experts.

The Anstey case thus shows that a litigant who was willing to spend considerable sums of money to secure a valuable inheritance was able in the early years of Henry II's reign to obtain expert, paid assistance for his litigation in the ecclesiastical courts, but that, despite his links with a royal justiciar, there were no comparable expert advisers for him to pay for their assistance in his litigation in the king's courts.[6]

The absence of professional legal advisers early in the reign of Henry II might have been a short-term phenomenon associated with the disorders of the Anarchy (1135–54). But I think it was more than that. My reading of the somewhat exiguous evidence of the period between the Norman Conquest and the end of the reign of Henry I (1066–1135) is that there were no legal experts in that period either, and certainly no professional lawyers of the kind we find in England in the thirteenth century.[7] England before the middle of the twelfth century was a country without professional lawyers.

Well before 1300 there had come to be legal experts in England who were paid for providing their services to litigants both in the king's courts and elsewhere and who seem to have been engaged in such activity on a full-time basis: men whom we may reasonably call professional lawyers. By the last quarter of the thirteenth century there are even reasons for beginning to see these professional lawyers as members of a nascent English legal profession. It will be the argument of this book that the emergence of this group was a response to the changed legal environment created by a number of separate but linked developments in the English legal system which took place in and after the reign of Henry II. In the remainder of this chapter I want to sketch some of the main features of the English legal system prior to these changes as it can be glimpsed in the surviving evidence of this period and to see why these might have discouraged the earlier emergence of professional lawyers.

THE ENGLISH LEGAL SYSTEM BEFORE HENRY II'S REIGN:
(I) THE NATURE OF LITIGATION

Litigation during this period started with a plaint setting out the plaintiff's claim or grievance. Professor Milsom has suggested that this was the element in legal proceedings which required the greatest degree of skill, since it had to be made 'in settled formal terms' and had 'to be composed and spoken correctly'.[8] This, however, probably overstates the formulaic nature of the plaint. The *Leges Henrici Primi*, our most detailed source on English legal custom during the Anglo-Norman period,[9] does not mention the possibility of a count being rejected for failure to conform to particular fixed verbal formulas. Nor does there seem to be any trace in surviving accounts of litigation of counts failing because they had not followed a prescribed form. The author of the treatise does, it is true, talk of the prevalence of *miskenning* in London and the suspect (but contemporary) charter of Henry I purports to abolish *miskenning* in the city courts.[10] Some thirteenth and early fourteenth-century evidence identifies *miskenning* as a penalty payable in the case of a defective count or as a fine payable to emend such a count.[11] There is, however, no twelfth-century evidence for *miskenning* existing outside London and Bristol; and other thirteenth-century evidence suggests that it was a fine payable for variation or self-contradiction in making a count rather than for failure to adhere to a standard formula.[12] The position in Anglo-Norman England was probably close to that described by Brunner as typical of French customary law in the thirteenth century. A plaintiff would normally need to show a recognized cause of action (a claim or grievance for which customary law considered a legal remedy appropriate) in his count and to make an offer of proof. He might also need to use certain specific phrases and formal expressions in doing this, but he did not have to follow a set formula for the whole of his complaint.[13] The main difficulty for a plaintiff lay not in the need to adhere to a fixed formula but in the need to avoid contradicting himself and to spell out clearly and exactly the nature and content of his complaint, since judgment would be given on the basis of what he had actually said in court and not what he had meant to say. Anything he had once said could not subsequently be unsaid by him.[14]

Milsom's description of the form the defence took under the 'ancient pattern of law-suit' by contrast suggests that this required much less skill: indeed, little more than a reasonably good memory. Normally, he suggests, a defendant would do no more than make 'an equally formal denial, recapitulating and denying the claim point by point'.[15] The only possible alternative was for the defendant to rely on the authority of a third party and vouch him to warranty. It would then be up to the warrantor to make a similar blank denial.[16] This was then followed by one of the parties swearing to the justice of his cause and his oath being put to the proof by compurgation, ordeal or trial by battle. Because it was God who was judging between the parties, there was no need for the defendant to make any other kind of defence. God would not be misled in the way that a jury later could be by factual situations which seemed to support the plaintiff's claim but actually exonerated the defendant.[17]

The making of defences was, however, perhaps more complex than Milsom's picture might suggest. Brunner's work on thirteenth-century French custom is again relevant. This indicates that even within a system of customary law in which jury trial was not in use it was possible for the defendant to make exceptions, showing why he should not be required to make a formal defence to the complaint or claim as it had been stated by the plaintiff.[18] There are passages in the *Leges Henrici Primi* which indicate that this was also already a possibility in early twelfth-century England.[19] Accounts of litigation from the Anglo-Norman period certainly show defendants pleading exceptions. When William of St Calais was on trial for treason in 1088, he claimed that he could not be made to answer the allegations against him until the possessions of his bishopric had been restored to him.[20] In the 1140s the abbot of Battle answered allegations made against him by the archbishop of Canterbury by claiming that the legislation of Henry I on wreck, on which the archbishop was relying, was no longer in force.[21]

The pleading of exceptions of this kind opened the way to reasoned argument and when a court gave judgment on such exceptions it was certainly doing more than simply adjudging proof. In other litigation we can see a different kind of variant on the straight denial. In answer to the claim of the monks of Thetford to the body of Roger Bigod, we see the bishop of Norwich (in litigation heard in the king's court in 1107–8) not simply denying they were rightfully entitled to the body but counter-asserting that Roger had given his body to the church of Norwich even before there had been monks at Thetford.[22] In the 1121 case of Modbert against the prior and monks of Bath, we see the prior answering Modbert's claim not with a blank denial but with the counter-assertion that the land concerned had long ago been given to the church of Bath and had never been held by military tenure; and that the previous tenant had himself acknowledged on his death-bed that he was only life-tenant of the land.[23] Thus there seems to have been rather more room for reasoned argument at this stage of the proceedings than Milsom suggests.[24] But what is less clear is whether such reasoned argument required any great degree of legal skill. Professor Stephen White has suggested with respect to legal proceedings in Western France during this same period that legal norms or rules were not clearly distinguished from rules with only moral or customary status at this time and were not in any case clearly articulated.[25] If the same was also true in England (and it seems likely) this would mean there was little place for specialists with particular legal expertise at this stage in the proceedings since there was little for them to be expert about.

Overall, then, we can probably agree with Professor Milsom's judgment that 'what happened actually in court did not call for much specialist expertise'.[26] Litigation in the Anglo-Norman period was perhaps not quite as formulaic as Milsom's account would suggest but was none the less a process which required considerably much less expertise and knowledge than was later to become the case. This may then have been one significant factor in inhibiting the development of any effective demand for the services of legal experts.

THE ENGLISH LEGAL SYSTEM BEFORE HENRY II'S REIGN:
(II) THE NATURE OF THE COURTS

The right to hold a court for their tenants was a right enjoyed not just by the king's barons but also by many other lords; indeed, thirteenth-century evidence suggests that any lord who had enough tenants was entitled to hold one.[27] The seignorial courts of the Anglo-Norman period belonged in general to one of two main types: the purely local manorial court (often called the 'hallmoot') which was attended by the lord's peasant tenants and the 'honorial' court which was attended by his more important non-peasant tenants.[28] It was later believed that seignorial courts had met every two weeks during Henry II's reign, but there seems to be no contemporary evidence as to their frequency in the Anglo-Norman period and it is possible that they met rather less frequently.[29] In any case it seems likely that in this period (as later) seignorial courts were only held on a periodic basis. The lord's reeve seems normally to have presided at the manorial court; the lord himself at the honour court.[30] The primary responsibility for making judgments appears, however, to have rested not with the lord or the lord's reeve but with the lord's tenants.[31] Neighbouring landowners or friends of the lord might also be added to their number, apparently at the lord's discretion, and perhaps only to deal with particularly sensitive cases.[32] But even with such reinforcement these remained essentially 'lay' courts, run by non-professionals (most of whom were themselves subject to the court's jurisdiction) who possessed no particular legal expertise.

Hundred or (in some Midland and Northern counties) wapentake courts represented the lowest level of public or quasi-public justice in the English countryside.[33] Each county was divided into a number of hundreds or wapentakes and every hundred or wapentake, at least in theory, possessed its own court.[34] As a general rule these courts probably met once every four weeks.[35] Regular attendance was expected only from the more substantial landholders resident within the hundred or wapentake.[36] When they were away from home, their duty of attendance might be discharged by their stewards and, in the absence of both landowner and steward, by the reeve, priest and four men of each village held by the landowner.[37] It was probably from arrangements to allocate the burden of attendance as between members of this latter group that the later link between suit of hundred court and the holding of specific tenements developed.[38] In the thirteenth century it was the hundred bailiff who normally presided over the hundred court but it was the landholders owing the duty of regular attendance at the court who made judgments there.[39] During the Anglo-Norman period the duty of making judgments in the hundred court seems likewise to have been incumbent on those who had the duty of regular attendance.[40] Judgments were made, then, not by a group of experts chosen specially for legal skill or knowledge but simply by some or all of the more substantial landowners of the hundred or wapentake.

A similar position also obtained in the county court. Each of the counties of England possessed its own court.[41] By the early thirteenth century most county courts were meeting at least once a month and the 1217 reissue of Magna Carta found it necessary to stipulate that they should not meet more often. The pre-Conquest practice seems to have been for county courts to meet only twice a year but it allowed for additional meetings where this was necessary. Legal historians have generally thought it probable that county courts were already meeting on a monthly basis by the early twelfth century.[42] The author of the *Leges Henrici Primi* gives a comprehensive list of those obliged to be present. All fall into one of two categories: major landholders and holders of public or quasi-public office.[43] Additional confirmation that regular attendance was required from all those who held landed property of a certain minimum value is provided by a royal writ of William II's reign concerning the attendance of tenants of the abbey of Bury St Edmund's at county and hundred courts.[44] This duty of regular attendance might be fulfilled in the lord's absence by his steward or, failing that, by the reeve, priest and four men of each village.[45] The *Leges Henrici Primi* also suggests that it was the 'barons of the county' who held free lands there who gave judgments at the county court.[46] These are probably the same as the major landholders who were required to attend its meetings. In the county court, as in the hundred court, then, judgments were made on a periodic but relatively infrequent basis by a non-specialist group of substantial local landowners who were themselves subject to the court's jurisdiction.[47]

A much less well-defined element in the legal system of the Anglo-Norman period were the various *ad hoc* courts created by the appointment of particular individuals or groups of individuals to act as royal justices for the hearing of particular cases. The documents which tell us of these commissions refer in varying terms to the position of the justices thus appointed: requiring pleas to be heard 'in their presence' or for them to 'preside in place of the king' or simply instructing them to 'make' or 'hold' justice.[48] In many instances we are told enough to make it clear that such commissioners were expected merely to preside at the plea, not to make the judgments there, and that it was those who regularly made judgments at the county court (in some instances at particular hundred courts) who were to make judgments. The distinction between the two roles is reflected in a royal order of Henry I's reign addressed to Swein of Essex. This tells him to respect the bishop of London's freedom from various dues, as the bishop had proved was right at Writtle before the king's 'justices' (*ante justiciarios meos*) by charters and writs at a session where Swein himself had been one of the 'judges' (*ubi tu ipse fuisti unus ex judicibus*).[49] A later reference to the plea between the bishop of Worcester and the abbot of Evesham which the bishop of Coutances was commissioned to hear some time between 1079 and 1083 describes the plea as being heard before the commissioner and others but 'with the whole county judging and attesting'.[50] We find Henry I commissioning Hugh de Buckland, sheriff of Berkshire, and Aubrey de Vere in connection with various complaints made by the abbot of Abingdon, but for part of the business specifying that they were to act 'by the just judgment of the county'.[51] In essence these *ad hoc* sessions held by royal justices were special sessions of county or hundred courts meeting under a different presiding officers and with special business to transact; but any judgments were made by the usual judgment-makers of the county or hundred court concerned.

By the early twelfth century there had also come into existence a different and more permanent kind of royal justice, the local 'justiciar', appointed to act in a particular area.[52] His functions, as defined in the suspect but contemporary royal writ in favour of London, were to 'keep the pleas of the king's crown and to plead the same'.[53] The local justiciar did not make judgments in his court. A charter from the very end of Stephen's reign in favour of the bishop of Lincoln, granting him the office of local justiciar within the county of Lincolnshire and in Lincoln, makes clear that, although it is the bishop who will decide when he is going to hold sessions, it is the men of Lincoln and Lincolnshire who will attend those sessions 'to hold the king's pleas and make the king's judgments'.[54] Those who attended such sessions were probably much the same as those who attended sessions of the county court: indeed, in one passage the *Leges Henrici Primi* suggests that the sessions over which the justiciar presided could simply be described as sessions of the county court.[55]

The reign of Henry I, and more particularly the latter part of his reign, first saw the emergence of itinerant royal justices: justices appointed by the king to hear a wide range of pleas in several different counties in turn.[56] There were several ways in which these itinerant justices differed from the itinerant justices of the later twelfth and thirteenth centuries. In the present context, perhaps the most important is that they, too, do not seem to have made judgments at their sessions but merely to have presided over them. Judgments were made by others: the judgment-makers of the county courts.[57] In essence, then, these courts, too, were no more than special sessions of the county court: another variation on the general type of non-professional and non-expert local court.

There was also a central king's court or *curia regis* over which the king himself normally presided.[58] Even here judgments were generally made not by the king nor by expert royal justices whom he appointed but by the king's barons, the tenants-in-chief of the crown. In some cases the records themselves stress the size and comprehensiveness of the group who made the decision.[59] More commonly we hear only of a case having been heard before the king and his barons. Thus we have no way of knowing how many barons were present for the hearing of the plea other than a minimum figure derivable from the list of those who were said to have witnessed the proceedings.[60] There is also some evidence of the existence of a *curia regis* of a rather different kind: one in which decisions were taken and judgments given by a small core group of 'barons' and in the absence of the king. Already before the end of the eleventh century we read of the abbot of Westminster proving his right to certain lands before a group of the king's barons consisting of no more than five named and prominent individuals.[61] This group seem to have been the forerunners of that better-attested group which existed in the reign of Henry I whose members became the viceregal court during the king's absences and who also acted twice yearly as the 'barons of the Exchequer' when the Exchequer met to audit the royal finances: a group of *curiales* whose chief functions were administrative but who might sometimes act as 'judges' of the king's court.[62] This group looks rather more specialized than the much larger group of royal tenants-in-chief who normally formed the *curia regis* but their expertise was in politics and administration, not in law; and they were in part drawn from the ranks of prominent tenants-in-chief and shared their outlook.[63] This seems to be the closest we come in the Anglo-Norman period to a group of 'specialists' making judgments in a court; but the evidence seems to suggest that they heard little legal business.

The courts of Anglo-Norman England were thus almost all of the same type. In none were judgments given by small groups of judges chosen for their special expertise. In most, judgments were given by substantial landowners, themselves subject to the court's jurisdiction. Most courts held sessions only once a month or at irregular intervals, so there was little possibility that their judges would become legal experts because they spent so much of their time hearing litigation. Most courts were local, with jurisdiction only over the inhabitants of a single restricted area. Even those courts which were not local (honorial courts and the king's court) still exercised jurisdiction only over restricted groups of people. The constitution of the courts thus also played a significant part in diminishing any potential demand for the services of legal experts. As long as judges were men without any special legal expertise, litigants did not need the assistance of legal experts in their dealings with the courts. Such expertise as was needed was well within the grasp of the ordinary landowner. Courts may have followed their own customary procedures and rules but these were as well known to litigants as to judges, since they were part of the same local community or the same lordship and the litigants themselves on other occasions acted as judges. Thus there was no need for legal experts to advise litigants on legal rules and procedures.

The author of the *Leges Henrici Primi* advised litigants when they had a choice as to whether they should plead or put off a plea, that they exercise that choice in accordance with who was present in court and who absent.[64] The clear implication is that it is the presence of friends and absence of enemies rather than expert assistance that is one of the key factors, if not the decisive factor, in obtaining a favourable judgment. This may help to explain a number of agreements made between particular abbeys and powerful individuals by which the abbeys attempted to secure their friendship or alliance in any litigation involving the abbey. In the early twelfth century we hear of Picot son of Colswain holding lands of the abbey of Peterborough at Riseholme in Lincolnshire and of the origins of this tenure in an agreement between the abbey and his father, probably during the Conqueror's reign, under which Colswain was to 'maintain' the abbey's property and the abbot's men both in the county court and elsewhere.[65] Another agreement of the same general kind of the early twelfth century is recorded in the Abingdon chronicle. Nigel d'Oylly agreed that if the abbot of Abingdon had any litigation in the king's court, he would be on the abbot's side unless the plea was one brought by the king.[66] A third such agreement is that made in 1111 between the abbot of St Augustine's Canterbury and Hamo *dapifer* which granted certain lands to Hamo and his heirs on condition that Hamo when necessary 'advise, help and succour' the abbot, his successors and their church in pleas in the county court and the king's court against any baron other than those whose vassal Hamo already was.[67] These men were certainly powerful and influential individuals. Colswain and Picot were lords of the Lincolnshire barony of Brattleby and held other lands as tenants of other Lincolnshire tenants-in-chief.[68] Nigel d'Oylly was not only lord of the Oxfordshire barony of Hook Norton and constable of Oxford castle but also one of Henry I's constables and as such regularly in attendance at the king's court.[69] Hamo *dapifer* was not only sheriff of Kent (which would make his assistance in the county court of particular value) but also one of the king's stewards and as such regularly in attendance in the king's court.[70] The terms in which these agreements were couched suggest that it was influence rather than expertise that the abbots hoped to gain.

THE ENGLISH LEGAL SYSTEM BEFORE HENRY II'S REIGN: (III) RESTRICTIONS ON THE AVAILABILITY OF REPRESENTATION

The *Leges Henrici Primi* suggests that it was common practice for litigants to come to court accompanied by a group of supporters drawn from friends and relatives similar to the group which accompanied Richard of Anstey to his litigation.[71] Such a practice is also reflected in other evidence from this period.[72] This group were not merely passive spectators but there to give advice. In all cases other than those in which felony (the most serious type of wrongdoing) was alleged, it was a recognized part of court procedure that a defendant be given an opportunity to take such advice, once he had made an initial general denial of the plaintiff's claim or complaint.[73]

Another passage from the *Leges Henrici Primi* shows them doing rather more than this. The passage follows on from one referring to the right of defendants to take 'counsel' from their friends and relatives and which advises them to speak truthfully so that their advisers can see whether it is better to continue with the defence or to take steps to make peace with the plaintiff. It reads:

> It is best when anyone's advice [*consilium*] is given in a plea that it be said in advance that it is spoken subject to a right of correction, so that he is allowed to correct it if the speaker has said too much or left anything out. For it is often the case that somebody is less perceptive in his own case than in the case of another; and commonly what he could not change if he had spoken himself can be changed if spoken by another.[74]

In this passage we are obviously concerned with 'advice' of a quite different kind to that mentioned in the immediately preceding section. It is 'advice' given in the plea itself and it is better that it be given subject to a right of correction. Someone is speaking in a formal context in court where an error of omission or commission can have serious consequences. The context further suggests that the 'advice' referred to is the equivalent of what the litigant would have said himself if the speaker had not given it, for the author goes on to emphasize the benefits for a litigant in having an adviser speak for him as opposed to speaking himself. The passage seems to refer to someone acting in a way that resembles the activity of the 'pleader' of French thirteenth-century customary law in that what he says can be made subject to a right of amendment by the litigant.[75] But it seems much more doubtful whether this passage also implies that such a 'pleader' could be used by either litigant at any stage in the proceedings.[76] The context suggests that the author may have been talking only about defendants and there is no suggestion here or elsewhere that the plaintiff enjoys any similar right. Nor is it clear that the defendant enjoys the right to have his 'counsel' speak for him at every stage in litigation. It may well be that the defendant has to make the initial formal defence himself. Indeed, if the right to use a 'pleader' developed out of the right to take 'counsel' it seems not unreasonable to suppose that the use of a 'pleader' may initially have been restricted in just this kind of way.

Brunner argued that the agreement of German, Lombard and Franco-Norman sources on the main characteristics of the 'pleader' was so close that the institution must itself go back to the Frankish period; he used a thin line of evidence to trace the institution back to the seventh century.[77] What Brunner's evidence did not show, however, was that such 'pleaders' could be used generally by any litigant who wished to do so. Lass subsequently showed that the evidence of the Carolingian capitularies was that their use was limited quite narrowly to certain disadvantaged groups such as the sick, widows, orphans and the poor and to those of very high status – and then only in certain higher courts.[78] It cannot therefore be assumed that the ability of both parties to use 'pleaders' freely to speak on their behalf in court was any part of the Frankish institutional inheritance of the Normans which they brought with them to England. Nor can it be assumed that it was necessarily something which English courts inherited from the Anglo-Saxon past. It has been suggested that the 'pleader' who spoke on behalf of a litigant is to be found in Anglo-Saxon England from the reign of Alfred onwards.[79] Yet the evidence for regarding the Anglo-Saxon *forespeca* as a 'pleader' who spoke in court on behalf of others turns out not to be very convincing. In none of the formal documents which use the term is it used in this sense. Commonly, it means no more than 'protector' or 'mediator'. Only in the vocabulary ascribed to archbishop Aelfric compiled in the tenth century do we find *forespeca* given as an equivalent for *causidicus* or *advocatus* (both terms used on the continent and in classical Latin for those who speak on behalf of others in court, though *advocatus* also has a wider meaning) and *forspeca vel mundbora* given as the equivalent for *advocatus, patronus vel interpellator* and thus appearing to equate *forespeca* with 'pleader'.[80] But this may well be a case where the compiler used the nearest Anglo-Saxon equivalent for a term that literally had no direct equivalent and one that picked up its non-technical sense (of patron) rather than its technical one.

It is possible, therefore, that during the Anglo-Norman period litigants were restricted in the use they might make of 'pleaders' speaking on their behalf: that plaintiffs had normally to speak for themselves and defendants were only able to make limited use of 'counsel' to speak for them. When professional lawyers do emerge in England, speaking for litigants in court is one of their main areas of expertise and among the more important of the functions they performed for litigants. Restrictions on the use of 'pleaders' may thus have constituted a further barrier to the development of professional lawyers in this period.

A second important institutional base for the eventual emergence of a legal profession in England, as we shall see, was the existence of a rather different kind of legal representative: the attorney. The 'pleader' could only act on behalf of the litigant if the litigant was there in court beside him ready to avow or disavow what he said. The attorney's function was to appear in court in place of the litigant. Once validly appointed, his appearance counted as an appearance of the litigant who had appointed him; anything he said in court was treated as if spoken by the litigant himself and could not subsequently be disavowed by attorney or litigant. Richard of Anstey's memorandum makes no mention of the use of such a representative and indeed makes plain that Richard was himself present at each stage of the litigation. Was this a matter of choice on Richard of Anstey's part or may it again have been that he was compelled to do so by the existence of restrictions on the use of attorneys?

Some passages in the *Leges Henrici Primi* appear to show acceptance by early twelfth-century English legal custom of the representation of litigants by persons who in function prefigure the later attorney. These same passages, however, suggest certain important restrictions which would debar or might have debarred a litigant like Richard of Anstey from appointing one to act on his behalf. One passage concerns a landowner who has appointed a steward or other official to be in charge of his affairs and who has given proper notice that he has done so. When a landowner has done this, any summons against him may be served on the representative; it will then be this representative who appears in court on his lord's behalf.[81] This passage provides no warrant for supposing that a plaintiff may be represented in the same way. More significantly, perhaps, this representative is not someone appointed to act for a litigant only in connection with a particular piece of litigation; he only represents his principal in litigation because he in overall charge of his affairs.

Thus this passage does not suggest that it was possible to appoint a representative to act simply in one piece of litigation. It was, moreover, only major landowners (tenants-in-chief and honorial barons) who appointed stewards or other such officials to take charge of their lands. Perhaps only such men could enjoy the benefits of being represented in this way. A second passage appears to show English legal custom allowing the representation of a plaintiff in a single case.[82] But the context (where the plaintiff is lord of the court in which this litigation is being conducted) is a very special one. We know that in his own court the lord as litigant enjoyed other special privileges[83] and it seems unwise to assume on the basis of this passage that plaintiffs generally enjoyed any such right or that in other contexts litigants enjoyed the right to appoint representatives to act on their behalf in a single piece of litigation. A very limited scope for the use of attorneys would not be out of line with French thirteenth-century local custom as surveyed by Brunner.[84] In several areas of France this prohibited representation altogether other than in exceptional circumstances. In other areas it was the rule that the plaintiff could not appoint a representative other than by obtaining royal letters of grace (in effect trumping local custom by invoking royal power) but that the defendant could.

Restrictions on the use of representatives in litigation therefore provide us with a third possible contributing factor helping to explain the absence of professional lawyers in Anglo-Norman England. The next two chapters will examine changes in the English legal system beginning in the reign of Henry II which helped to create a much more favourable legal environment for the emergence of the professional lawyer.

2

Creating a Demand for Lawyers: the Transformation of the English Court System, 1154–1307

Richard of Anstey brought his litigation at the very beginning of Henry II's reign and before Henry and his advisers had begun making major changes in the English legal system. These changes and their continuation and further development in the reigns of Henry's successors created an environment which favoured the emergence of professional lawyers in England and a rapid growth in their numbers. In this chapter I discuss the relevant changes in the English court system; in the next I shall discuss changes in the way litigation was conducted and in the rules governing the appointment and use of representatives in litigation.

THE REIGN OF HENRY II

The beginnings of the General Eyre

Although legal historians have sometimes located the beginnings of the General Eyre in the reign of Henry I, credit for the invention of this institution more properly belongs to Henry II and his advisers.[1] The earliest countrywide visitation by groups of itinerant royal justices for which there is chronicle evidence began in 1176 and continued into 1177.[2] It was planned at a meeting of the king and his council at Northampton early in 1176. The country was divided into six circuits, each visited by a group of three justices. Instructions drawn up for them show they were to deal with all three types of business (civil, criminal and information-gathering) characteristic of the later

General Eyre. The instructions also make clear that the justices themselves were to make judgments at their sessions. Surviving final concords recording the settlement of litigation during this visitation show that sessions of the itinerant justices were regarded as sessions not of the county court but of the king's court. They also confirm the dominant role played by the justices. In almost all, only the justices are named and described as constituting the court before which the settlement was made.[3]

A further seven visitations took place before the end of the reign, so that on average there was a visitation every other year. Arrangements varied both as to the number of circuits (anything between two and five) and the number of justices allocated to each (anything between three and nine).[4] Final concords made at sessions follow the precedent set in the first visitation of describing the court where they were made as the king's court. They also show that the king's justices continued to play a dominant role in the proceedings.[5]

The beginnings of a central royal court at Westminster

An older generation of scholars traced the origins of the Common Bench to arrangements made by Henry II in 1178 appointing two clerks and three laymen of his household to hear and redress complaints from all over England. More recent scholarship has shown that the Common Bench developed gradually out of the Exchequer during Henry's reign.[6] Ordinary litigation may have been heard very occasionally at Exchequer sessions in the reign of Henry I.[7] Exchequer sessions at Westminster were once more hearing civil litigation by the mid-1160s and the first final concords recording the settlement of litigation there come from shortly thereafter. By the later 1170s enough copies of final concords survive to show that civil litigation was being heard at Exchequer sessions (in what was often described simply as 'the king's court at Westminster') on a regular basis twice a year.[8] This practice continued for the remainder of the reign.[9] The Exchequer did not possess a fixed complement of justices or barons at this time.[10] The smallest number mentioned as constituting the court is four,[11] the largest 14,[12] with an average of around eight.

Distinctive characteristics of these new royal courts

The Exchequer and the General Eyre differed in a number of important respects from the courts which had existed in England before Henry II's reign and set a pattern which was to be followed when other royal courts were created in the next century.

A common feature of virtually all the courts of Anglo-Norman England had been a division of responsibility between a presiding officer and a group of 'suitors' who made judgments. The latter were normally drawn from substantial landowners subject to the court's jurisdiction and possessed no special legal expertise. In the new royal courts small groups of royal justices not only presided but also made judgments, uniting these two hitherto separate functions. This created the possibility of courts being run for the first time by legal experts. There were no legal experts to be appointed to these new royal courts in Henry II's reign, but Henry and his advisers kept a 'core' group of royal judges in office over long periods of time, thereby developing and utilizing their legal expertise. The final concords show at least 70 different individuals sitting as justices in the Exchequer between Michaelmas 1165 and Henry's death. Half are recorded as sitting on one or two occasions only. A small group of no more than 12 individuals together with the justiciar account for about two-thirds of the total number of appearances of named justices in the surviving records. Three served for 20 years or more and another four for at least ten years.[13] A majority of the men known to have acted as justices in eyre during the reign (46 out of 84) likewise acted only on a single eyre visitation and a further 20 justices in only two visitations. But an inner group of 18 justices were active on three or more eyre visitations and two (Roger fitzReinfrey and Michael Belet) served on as many as six. Moreover, there was a significant degree of overlap between the two inner groups. Just under half the 18 'core' eyre justices (seven out of 18) were also 'core' justices of the Exchequer and they included the two eyre justices who served on the largest number of visitations.

A second major difference between these new royal courts and their older counterparts clearly visible in the thirteenth century is that the new courts held daily sessions over more or less protracted periods while the older courts did business only for a day at a time (at most) at more or less regular intervals. This difference almost certainly goes back to Henry II's reign, although the patchy survival of final concords before 1195[14] makes it difficult to demonstrate conclusively.[15] Continuous sessions made it possible for these courts to deal with a much greater volume of business than was feasible for the older courts. Continuous sessions were in turn only made possible by the fact that these courts were run by men who were (for a period at least) full-time judges in the king's service, not local landowners whose commitment to the legal system was at best part-time.

A third significant difference lay in the way these new courts kept a written record not just of their final judgments but also of the various intermediate stages in litigation, whereas the older courts had made no attempt to keep any such record of their proceedings. No plea-rolls of Henry II's reign now survive, but there are enough references in later plea-rolls and other sources to indicate that they were being compiled on a regular basis, perhaps from as early as 1176.[16] The new royal courts also issued written orders in the king's name to local sheriffs in connection with litigation; typically such writs also ordered that the writ concerned be returned to the court. The earliest evidence for the use of returnable writs is in the legal treatise *Glanvill*, dating from the last years of Henry II's reign, but it seems likely that their use goes back to at least the mid-1170s.[17] The first writs of this kind to survive come from the very end of the twelfth century and show that by then sheriffs were recording the action they had taken in response to the writ on its dorse.[18] A full record of proceedings was an essential tool in the efficient running of the courts. Some record of the appearance and non-appearance of litigants and of the orders the court had issued was vital once the courts were dealing with anything more than a small level of business. The writs issued by the courts ensured that sheriffs had a written reminder of the action they were to take. Making these writs returnable provided some assurance that the writs had actually reached the sheriffs and ensured that the court was informed of what action sheriffs had taken in response to them. Keeping a permanent record of final judgments in litigation ensured that they were final and their terms were not subject to subsequent dispute.

A fourth distinctive characteristic of the new royal courts as soon as we can see their operation in detail, and probably from the very beginning, was that they only heard, and could only hear, such litigation as they had been specifically authorized to hear by royal writ. This normally took the form of an 'original' writ (generally following the formulas of one of a limited number of standard types of writ) addressed to the local sheriff instructing him to summon the defendant to answer a specific plea at a specific court on a specific date[19] and then to 'return' the writ to the court where the plea was to be heard.[20] Although some litigation had been initiated by royal writ before Henry II's reign there is no indication that this was a necessity in any kind of court; most litigation had probably been initiated orally by making an informal complaint to the presiding officer of the court concerned.

A final characteristic of these new courts which set them apart from almost all pre-existing courts was that they were national courts. This is obviously true of the Exchequer which heard litigation from all over England. It is less obviously true of the individual sessions held by the justices of the General Eyre in particular counties, but they, too, are best seen as individual local sessions of a national court. Sessions of the eyre justices were regarded as sessions of the king's court (not of the local county court); they were run by justices who held sessions in a whole series of counties and the visitations were part of a scheme of countrywide visitations run by justices with an identical remit and jurisdiction.[21] The existence of national courts and, in particular, of national courts run by a small core of long-serving royal justices, helped make possible the emergence of a national law and custom of England common to all the new royal courts: the English law that produced its first great treatise in *Glanvill*, written towards the end of the reign.[22] But as the treatise itself reminds us, that national custom was also in part a deliberate legislative creation. Royal courts followed the same procedures and rules in part because they were following the same national legislation.

The imposition of royal control over seignorial courts and the county court

Henry II's reign also saw the establishment of a considerable measure of control by the king's courts over the more important of the various pre-existing types of local court.

Seignorial courts By the time *Glanvill* was written it had become the rule that 'no-one is obliged to answer in the court of his lord for any free tenement without the order of the king or of his chief justiciar'.[23] Legal historians have disagreed (and continue to disagree) about the origins of this rule, but there is no dispute that its effect, so far as seignorial courts was concerned, was to require that any litigation about title to free land brought in a lord's court be initiated by royal writ.[24] In the short term, the effect of this rule was mainly symbolic. Such litigation was basic to the seignorial court and represented its most important area of jurisdiction. Any lord hearing such litigation was now treated as a royal commissioner and he could only act if he had specific royal authorization to do so. In the longer term, however, as we shall see, it was to have quite different and much more serious effects on the jurisdiction of seignorial courts and on the ability of those courts to compete for business with royal courts.[25]

Procedures were also put in place to make it possible to remove certain kinds of litigation out of seignorial courts into the new royal courts. Indirect removal became possible in land litigation through use of the procedure known as *tolt*. All a plaintiff had to do was to complain to the sheriff that his lord's court had failed to do justice on his claim. The sheriff would then send a subordinate to the court at the next day appointed for a hearing, together with four or more knights. The demandant could then 'prove' the default of justice by his own oath and the oaths of two others who had been present at the court without the lord being allowed to rebut the allegation. The procedure was probably created *c.*1164 though modified in detail thereafter.[26] *Tolt* only removed litigation into the county court, but the plaintiff could then have it removed into the king's court (the Exchequer or the Eyre) by acquiring the royal writ *pone*.[27] Direct removal into the king's court on the initiative of the defendant occurred when he opted to defend his right to land through the verdict of the 12 knights of the grand assize rather than battle.[28] This procedure was probably created in 1179 when the grand assize itself was first made available to litigants and represented a compromise between the claims of lords and the king.[29] Both procedures had the effect of draining litigation out of seignorial courts into the king's court.

Royal control over seignorial courts was also demonstrated through the availability of the action of false judgment in respect of judgments given in such courts. It is possible that as early as Henry II's reign this action allowed litigants to enlist the help of royal courts in ensuring that seignorial courts followed 'the law and custom of England' (its later function). If so, there is little hint of this in *Glanvill*. Its author seems to regard battle (preferably, he says, between the man who actually pronounced the judgment and the complainant), rather than a detailed examination of the proceedings by the king's court, as the normal procedure in this action.[30] Of much greater importance, it seems, in ensuring uniformity was the procedure followed when a case was being heard in a seignorial court and a legal difficulty arose which the court felt unable to determine. *Glanvill* tells us that there is a standard procedure in such a situation allowing the lord to transfer the case temporarily to the king's court to obtain the necessary expert advice; once it has been given, the case returns to the lord's own court for judgment.[31] Such a procedure also neatly symbolizes the general superiority of the king's courts over seignorial courts in Henry II's reign: when seignorial courts were in difficulty it was to the king's courts that they turned for help.

County courts Much was also done to turn county courts into junior and clearly subordinate partners in the operation of a system of royal justice. Side by side with their existing jurisdiction over matters brought to them by the complaint of aggrieved parties we find them beginning to exercise a jurisdiction specifically authorized by individual royal writs. These writs were of a set form and bore a generic similarity to the original writs which initiated litigation in the king's courts.[32] At least eight such viscontial writs existed by the final years of the reign.[33] Although they were addressed solely to the sheriff, they did not in practice authorize him to act on his own in hearing such litigation. As with other litigation heard in the county court, he presided at the session where the litigation was heard but it was the county court's usual judges who made any judgments.[34] The subordinate position envisaged for the county court in the system of royal justice emerges clearly when we examine the mechanism for the transfer of litigation initiated by royal writ out of the county court into one of the king's courts. This was achieved by the purchase from the king's chancery of the writ *pone*. *Glanvill* indicates that this writ could be acquired by either party to the litigation (or both). It was not necessary for them to show that the county court had failed to do right to the litigant(s) concerned or any other cause.[35] The case was, moreover, pleaded again from the beginning without reference to anything that had previously been said or done in the county court.[36]

FROM THE DEATH OF HENRY II TO THE DEATH OF EDWARD I (1189–1307)

During the period of almost a century and a quarter between the death of Henry II and the death of Edward I, successive English monarchs and their advisers built on the institutional legacy of Henry II.

The General Eyre

The General Eyre visited the counties of England on average once every second year during the reign of Richard I (1189–99).[37] John's reign (1199–1216) saw only two visitations, the second of which reached only about half the country, but the exceptional political conditions of the reign explain this relative infrequency.[38] During the reign of Henry III (1216–72) there were just seven completed or almost completed countrywide visitations or on average an eyre visitation of each county only once every eight years. Political circumstances led to the abandonment of eyre visitations before their completion in 1232 and again in 1263[39] but other factors must account for the relative infrequency of visitations during the reign as a whole.[40] The immediate explanation is a reduction in the number of groups of justices coupled with an increase in the amount of time the justices spent in each county on their circuit (itself in part a reflection of the growing infrequency of visitations), which meant that individual eyre visitations took much longer to complete. The length of eyre visitations (and consequently the length of the interval between visitations) was also adversely affected by the practice of covering most of the country in a series of continuous sessions but leaving a minority of counties to be visited up to one and two years before or after the main sessions. But the underlying explanation is that frequent eyres had ceased to be necessary. On the crown pleas side, the regular appointment of justices of gaol delivery to try the prisoners detained in local gaols removed the need for frequent eyres, though also important in this context was the institution of the office of coroner (in 1194). On the civil side, the commissioning of justices to hear petty assizes ensured that the most urgent and most common type of business was expedited without the need to wait for the next eyre from the 1220s onwards.[41]

Before 1278 each eyre visitation was planned separately. There was no continuity from one visitation to the next and justices drawn from the Common Bench constituted a core element in the judiciary of the eyre.[42] In 1278 two permanent groups of itinerant justices were established and the concept of separate countrywide visitations abandoned. This coincided with a substantial expansion in the jurisdiction of the General Eyre, giving it responsibility for testing the titles of all franchise-holders, for hearing and determining plaints and for receiving and determining presentments made under a substantially enlarged list of chapters of the eyre.[43] The work of the itinerant justices was suspended as a result of the Welsh wars between 1282 and 1284 and again as a result of the king's absence and of the upheavals within the judiciary which followed his return between 1289 and 1292. It was also external circumstances (the outbreak of war with France) which brought a further suspension of the eyre circuits in 1294. Thereafter only individual

Table 2.1 Average number of justices appointed to individual eyres, 1189–1307

Period	Total number of eyres	Average numbers
1189–99	126	6
1200–16	52	6
1217–28	69	5
1229–38	48	5
1239–49	75	4
1250–60	36	6
1261–77	58	4
1278–89	34	5
1290–1307	11	5

eyres were held (in 1299 and 1302) and Edward's successors effectively abandoned the holding of regular eyres altogether.[44]

The real importance of the reduction in the frequency of eyres which began under Henry III and was continued under Edward I lies in its effects on the Common Bench, the central court at Westminster. As long as eyres were being held every other year, litigants facing a choice between litigating in the Common Bench or in the Eyre might well choose to wait a little longer but to litigate more conveniently and less expensively in their own county at the next eyre session. Once eyre sessions became much less frequent and much less predictable, the balance of advantage changed significantly in favour of the Common Bench. This was a major factor in what we shall see to have been a dramatic growth in the volume of litigation coming to the Common Bench in the course of the thirteenth century.[45]

Throughout these changes and vicissitudes the General Eyre retained two of its most important characteristics. Its sessions in each county continued to be seen as sessions of the king's court; and those sessions were dominated and run by the small number of royal justices appointed to each of the circuits. There was some variation in the average number of justices allocated to eyre circuits as is shown in table 2.1, but it was a small one, with average numbers between four and six. The final concords (which survive in an almost unbroken sequence after 1195) and the plea-rolls (whose survival rate is much less impressive prior to the reign of Edward I) also allow us to see much more clearly than in Henry II's reign that the itinerant justices held continuous (or almost continuous) sessions in each county they visited. By the reign of Edward I, at least in the largest counties, the amount of business they were hearing required sufficiently long visitations for the justices and their clerks to divide up their sessions (and the record of those sessions) into a series of terms just like the Common Bench and King's Bench, with vacations in between.[46]

The Common Bench

It was in the last decade of the twelfth century that the ordinary judicial work hitherto dealt with by the Exchequer came to be performed by a recognizably separate institution, the Common Bench.[47] The most important immediate consequence was that the hearing of litigation at Westminster ceased to be tied to sessions of the Exchequer. From the mid-1190s the Common Bench heard litigation on a regular basis during four terms each year rather than two (adding Hilary and Trinity terms to the existing Easter and Michaelmas terms).[48] This helped to make the court a more attractive forum for litigants, since it meant that litigation could be initiated with rather less delay and could proceed through the court with shorter adjournments between stages. It also made possible the emergence of a more specialized judiciary. Hitherto the men who had run the judicial side of the Exchequer's activities were also, it seems, the men who ran its financial side. The new institution was manned by men whose responsibilities were solely judicial. This made it possible to appoint men with experience and knowledge only of legal matters.

During John's reign the very existence of the newly independent institution came under threat and for a period of almost five years it ceased to function. But the chief long-term significance of the episode was that it led to baronial demands that it should not be allowed to happen again: in itself an indication of the court's popularity. The result was King John's concession in clause 17 of Magna Carta in 1215 that 'Common pleas shall not follow our court, but be held in some fixed place ...'. The same formula was repeated in subsequent reissues of Magna Carta and amounted to a legislative guarantee of the continued existence of the court.[49] The clause was not, however, at first interpreted to mean that the Common Bench had to be in session for four terms every year. In practice, its sessions were suspended for one or more terms during every major Eyre visitation before 1250, apparently because all competent royal justices were then busy holding eyres.[50] After 1250 sessions were only suspended when political circumstances made it impossible to hold them.[51] Nor was the clause taken to mean that sessions could only be held at Westminster. During Edward I's reign the court was moved to Shrewsbury for Trinity and Michaelmas terms in 1277 and again from Michaelmas term 1282 to Trinity term 1283 and to York from Hilary term 1299 to Trinity term 1304.[52] The ending of the practice of suspending Common Bench sessions while the Eyre was in progress was a second development which enhanced the attractiveness of the court to potential litigants. It meant that litigants no longer ran the risk that litigation which they had started there would be delayed by the suspension of the court or even adjourned indefinitely until the Eyre had reached the relevant county.[53] Moving the court was an inconvenience for most litigants and those whom they employed, but an inconvenience which could be dealt with: for litigants from the north of England (and particularly from Yorkshire itself) the court's stay in York seems even to have enhanced its attractions.

Making the Common Bench a more attractive court to litigants, though probably never a conscious policy, was important for the court's longer term growth. The court did not enjoy a monopoly in any area of jurisdiction. A note in a register of writs from the later years of Henry III's reign shows that litigants could then only obtain writs to initiate litigation in the Common Bench without special payment if the writ belonged to a fairly restricted group.[54] For any other form of action the litigant would have to pay a premium which he could avoid by initiating the litigation in the county court or in the eyre. Even in the case of those writs for which no special premium was payable the litigant always had a choice between bringing his case in the Common Bench or bringing it before the justices in eyre when they next came to his county. This had probably been the rule for most of the reign of Henry III and perhaps even longer. It thus required a positive choice on the part of litigants to initiate litigation in the court and they would often need to make an additional payment to be able to do so. This gives particular importance to those institutional changes which helped make the Common Bench more attractive to potential litigants or decreased the attractiveness of the general eyre to them.[55] In fact the Common Bench seems to have been remarkably successful in attracting litigants for there was a continuous and dramatic expansion during the thirteenth century in the amount of business it handled. One obvious, albeit fairly crude, indication of this is the number of plea-roll membranes needed to record the court's business. Table 2.2 indicates there was a doubling of the business dealt with by the court between 1200 and 1242–3; another doubling of business between then and 1260; a further doubling between 1260 and 1280; a 78 per cent increase between 1280 and 1290; and roughly a further doubling between 1290 and 1306.

As table 2.3 shows there was a steady decline in the complement of justices serving in the court from an average of seven during the reign of Richard I to just three during the final years of Henry III's reign.[56] This decline is at first sight somewhat surprising, given the steady increase in the amount of business dealt with by the court. However, until the court began to divide up to hear business in separate sections there was no particular advantage to having large numbers of justices and it is possible that a smaller group of justices was able to function more efficiently. This long-term decline was reversed in Edward I's reign and by the end of it the normal complement of justices had crept back up to six. This was probably connected with the beginning of the practice of dividing the court into separate sections for the expedition of its business.[57]

Table 2.2 Quantities of business in the Common Bench as measured by the number of plea-roll membranes, 1200–1306

Year covered	Number of membranes
H1200–M1200	49
H1203–M1203	49
H1206–M1206	41
H1220–M1220	89
M1228–T1229	51
M1230–T1231	81
M1242–T1243	100
H1250–M1250	108
H1260–M1260	207
H1275–M1275	352
H1280–M1280	415
H1290–M1290	737
H1300–M1300	1056
H1306–M1306	1520

Notes
1 Wherever there was a choice I have used the rolls of a single calendar year; otherwise I have simply used whatever consecutive sequence of four rolls happened to survive. I have not used obviously heavily defective rolls.
2 To make the comparison a fair one I have excluded those membranes of the early rolls which simply record essoins; later rolls do not have such a section because essoins had been removed to a separate roll.

The creation of new royal courts

The same period also saw the creation of further royal courts of the type first created during Henry II's reign. A royal court accompanying the king as he travelled round England had existed at times in the reign of Henry II and in John's reign had for a five-year period replaced the Common Bench. There was, however, no direct institutional continuity between these courts and the court of King's Bench which was created in or perhaps a little before 1234.[58] Although this court also travelled round the country with the king it differed from its predecessors in continuing to function while the king himself was out of England and in exercising a jurisdiction much more clearly, though still not totally, differentiated from that of the Common Bench. Clause 17 of the Magna Carta barred it from hearing 'common pleas' and it came to specialize in pleas that could plausibly be represented as of special interest and concern to the king.[59]

Table 2.3 Numbers of justices active in the Common Bench, 1189–1307

Period	Average number of justices	Total
Richard I's reign (H1190–H1199)	7	57 (40)
John's reign (E1199–E1215)	6	41 (27)
Henry III's reign		
period H1218–M1228	5	34 (21)
period H1229–M1238	5	9 (18)
period H1238–M1249	4	15 (14)
period H1250–M1260	3	7 (16)
period H1261–M1272	3	15 (15)
Edward I's reign		
period H1273–T1278	5	12 (12)
period M1278–M1289	5	7 (7)
period H1290–T1301	5	8 (8)
period M1301–T1307	6	8 (8)

Notes

1 The average number of justices given for each period is derived from computing the total number of justices present in the Common Bench (or in the earliest period the Exchequer) for a majority of the final concords for each term within the decade and then averaging these termly totals over the decade.

2 The first total figure gives the total number of justices mentioned in final concords of the period as present at the making of one or more concord in the Common Bench. The figure in brackets immediately succeeding it is the total number of justices, excluding such justices as were not present for a majority of the final concords of at least one term during the period.

For certain periods of Henry III's reign (before 1240 and again from Michaelmas term 1251 to Easter term 1253) King's Bench possessed only a single full-time justice and its normal complement of full-time justices during Henry's reign did not exceed two. For most of the period the stewards of the royal household made up the numbers in the court by sitting with its full-time staff of justices as required. During the 'period of baronial reform' between 1258 and 1264 the court was also afforced by holders of the revived office of chief justiciar.[60] In Edward I's reign the minimum number of justices was two and the average complement of justices working in the court was three.[61] The stewards of the household continued to play some part in the work of the court in the early part of the reign; but this had come to an end before 1290, a development perhaps connected with the creation of a new court associated with the royal household, the court of the marshalsea, with which the stewards were now closely associated.[62] The court was henceforward manned wholly by full-time justices.

As already noted, from the 1220s onwards it was increasingly common for petty assizes (assizes of novel disseisin and mort d'ancestor) to be heard locally before justices specially commissioned for this purpose.[63] Between 1220 and 1241 such commissions went most commonly to four men from the locality concerned (often four local knights). Thereafter it became the norm to commission a single justice or two justices from the pool of central-court justices and royal servants with judicial experience with power to choose local associates. In 1259 and again in 1271 there were attempts to limit the number of individuals to whom commissions might be issued but these were effective only for short periods of time; on neither occasion was there any attempt to assign those who were eligible for commissions to particular counties.[64]

At the very beginning of Edward I's reign it was decided to divide England up into a series of circuits (initially six) and two justices were assigned on a permanent basis to each circuit to hear petty assizes in the counties of their circuit.[65] This marks an important stage in the development of the assize courts: it is the first time that something like permanent assize courts with their own justices and their own specific areas of jurisdiction were established. As yet, however, the system remained fluid. In 1274 the six circuits were reduced to four. Subsequent piecemeal alterations had raised the number of circuits by 1284 to eight or nine.[66] Chapter 30 of the statute of Westminster II (1285) envisaged a continuation of the existing practice of assigning specific justices to hear assizes in circuits but stipulated that the two sworn circuit justices were in future to take one or two local knights as their associates in each of the counties they visited, a partial return to the pre-1241 arrangements. It also stipulated that in future assizes were to be heard only during three specific periods of the year (or three terms): between 8 July and 1 August; between 14 September and 6 October; and between 6 January and 2 February.[67] In practice, although there was a substantial reorganization of the circuits in August 1285, the first of these changes remained a dead-letter. Nine circuits were established, each now manned by three or four justices.[68] The second change (limiting the period when assizes could be heard) does seem to have been effective, though it remained possible to obtain authorization for specific assizes to be heard at other times.[69] A further reorganization took place in 1293. Eight of the 12 assize justices appointed in 1273 had been justices of the central courts, able to act only in vacations. This had been reduced to just one in 1274; but the 1285 reorganization had seen a return to the practice of using central-court justices (and central-court clerks) on assize commissions and the timing of the sessions laid down in the statute may have been fixed to allow them to take assizes during their vacations. In 1293 it was decided to appoint full-time permanent justices with no other responsibilities to take assizes. This allowed a reduction in the number of circuits to four and also allowed a reduction in the number of justices assigned to each circuit to two. In order to make full use of the services of these full-time justices the provisions of the statute of Westminster II about the timing of sessions was repealed at the same time.[70]

Chapter 3 of the Statute of Fines (1299) made a major addition to the duties of these full-time assize justices by giving them responsibility for gaol deliveries (trying criminal suspects in gaol or on bail) in each of the counties of their circuit.[71] Special gaol-delivery sessions had formed part of the judicial system since at least the 1220s, but for most of the thirteenth century commissions were issued separately for each gaol and the commissioners were drawn mainly from the local gentry.[72] Circuit panels of gaol-delivery justices do not seem to have emerged before 1294 (20 years later than the similar development of assize circuits). The merging of the assize and gaol-delivery justices in 1299 was not in practice permanent and the link between them had been broken again by the end of the reign; but it prefigured and perhaps suggested the permanent merger of the two which took place early in the reign of Edward III.[73]

By the end of the reign of Edward I the assize courts had become a reasonable facsimile of the other royal courts. They possessed a uniform jurisdiction and applied a single national common law. They kept full records of their business and only heard such business as they were specifically authorized to do by individual royal writs. They were also now run by expert justices on something like a full-time basis.

The development of an expert professional judiciary

We have already noted the existence in Henry II's reign a small 'core' group of long-serving justices in the king's courts who acquired a considerable degree of legal expertise simply from the length of their service.[74] Such men were not, however, legal specialists for they served the king in other capacities as well.[75] Long-serving, professional justices who made a career out of judicial service to the king are a thirteenth-century phenomenon and become more significant as the century progresses. The first royal justice to be a career judicial specialist is Simon of Pattishall, a justice of the Common Bench and of the Eyre under Richard and of those courts and of the court of King's Bench under John, with a continuous judicial career lasting some 26 years.[76] During Henry III's reign we find several more long-serving career justices of the same type. Gilbert of Preston served continuously in the Common Bench and in eyres for over 30 years between 1240 and 1273.[77] Three other justices (Robert of Lexington, Roger of Thirkleby and Henry of Bath) had careers of 20 years or more. A further eight judges had careers of between ten and 20 years in the royal courts.[78] But Edward I's reign produced a proportionately much larger number of long-serving career justices.[79] Two royal justices had judicial careers of over 30 years. William of Bereford acted as a justice in eyre and as a justice of the Common Bench between 1292 and 1326. Ellis of Beckingham served as an assize justice from 1273 to 1285 and then as a justice of the Common Bench from 1285 to 1306. Four other justices who began their careers under Edward I (or the major portion of whose careers lie in Edward's reign) held judicial office for 20 years or more.[80] Edward's reign also produced no less than 14 justices whose careers spanned ten years or longer.[81]

The effects of this increase in the number and proportion of long-serving career justices are to be seen most clearly in the Common Bench. Only 26 justices sat in the court during Edward's reign. Seventy-nine justices had sat in the same court at some point during the much longer reign of Henry III, 41 justices during John's reign and 57 during the reign of Richard I. Adjusting both for the different lengths of the various reigns and for the different complements of justices sitting in the court at different periods, we find that the average length of service of a Common Bench justice under Richard I was little more than a year; that under John this rose to a little over two years and under Henry III to a little over three years; but that under Edward I it rose to over six years. Under Edward I the longer-serving justices also came to play an even more predominant role in the Common Bench than had previously been the case. Over the reign of Henry III as a whole the longer-serving justices (those whose careers lasted for ten years or more) between them accounted for around 60 per cent of all judicial service in the court. Thus already a fairly small group of long-serving justices had become dominant in the court. The comparable figure for Edward I's reign shows them not merely dominant but predominant. During Edward's reign they accounted for around 85 per cent of all judicial service there.

Another significant aspect of the increasing professionalization of the royal courts during this period was the beginning of the practice of appointing justices who had acquired knowledge and experience of legal matters before their appointment. The earliest of such experts acquired this through service to their predecessors. Two of the royal justices of John's reign (master Eustace de Faucunberg and master Godfrey de Lisle) had served as clerks to their predecessors.[82] In Henry III's reign we find serving as royal justices Martin of Pattishall, who for most if not all of John's reign had served as the clerk of Simon of Pattishall;[83] his clerk William of Raleigh;[84] and Raleigh's clerks Roger of Thirkleby and Henry of Bratton.[85] Another royal justice, William of York, had served as a clerk in the Common Bench in a position which foreshadowed that of the later keeper of writs and rolls for more than a decade before his appointment.[86] Roger of Whitchester in turn served as clerk to William of York and then as keeper of writs and rolls himself before his appointment.[87] Starting in the 1250s Ralph de Hengham served a long apprenticeship as a clerk to Giles of Erdington but also in the service of various other royal justices before his appointment as a royal justice in the early 1270s at the end of Henry III's reign.[88]

At least six of the Common Bench justices of the reign of Edward I had gained legal experience as clerks in the courts before their appointment.[89] The same is true of three of the justices of King's Bench[90] and three of the more senior Eyre justices.[91] Edward's reign also saw the beginning of the appointment of men who had gained their knowledge of the law and legal procedure through acting as serjeants. This was true of four of the justices appointed to the Common Bench in this period (though none was appointed before 1290)[92] and the appointment of Gilbert of Thornton as chief justice of King's Bench in 1290 brought a professional lawyer to the highest judicial office in England. Among the itinerant justices of the 1280s we find another professional lawyer, Richard of Boyland. By the end of Edward I's reign it was becoming uncommon, if not yet unthinkable, for someone to be appointed a justice of one of the major royal courts who did not have a background which equipped him with suitable expertise in the law of the courts.

Royal control of seignorial courts and the county court

Seignorial courts We have already noted that it was in Henry II's reign that the king managed to impose the rule that no litigation concerning title to land held freely could be heard without the authorization of a royal writ. During Henry's reign this may not have represented a particularly burdensome restriction on seignorial courts, for many litigants were content to claim land through the action of right initiated by the writ of right in the lord's court. Lords were only debarred by the rule from hearing claims of recent dispossession or claims based on the seisin of a close ancestor at the time of his death. These were in effect reserved for the king's courts. During the thirteenth century the king's courts came to offer a much wider variety of remedies, many of them based on isolating some specific flaw in the tenant's title (writs of entry). Plaintiffs came to prefer them if only because they offered a speedier resolution of their claim and one which did not offer their opponent the choice between trial by battle and jury trial as the writ of right did.[93] Seignorial courts were debarred by the royal monopoly of the authorization of such litigation from offering their own competing remedies and this condemned their jurisdiction over land other than villein land to a slow, lingering death.[94]

By c.1230, moreover, the king's courts had extended the purview of the rule (and the royal monopoly) to cover any litigation which might have a significant effect on the defendant's free tenement. This was now interpreted to include litigation about the lord's entitlement to the services he claimed from his free tenants.[95] Here there was no royal writ which initiated litigation in the lord's own court[96] and the overall effect was to ensure that such litigation came either to the county court (from which it could be removed in to the king's court) or directly to the king's courts. This in effect brought a large body of litigation into those courts from seignorial courts.

A further reduction in the competence of seignorial courts came in the last quarter of the thirteenth century when a new rule was introduced in relation to litigation concerning debts or title to movable property (chattels). Henceforward any such litigation concerning a debt of 40 shillings or more or movable property of an equivalent value had to be initiated by royal writ.[97] Again, the effect was to bring all such litigation either to the county court (from which it could be removed to the king's court) or directly to the king's court, for no such writ was available to initiate litigation in seignorial courts.

Also important, however, were the procedural constraints which the king and his courts managed to place on the operation of seignorial courts. From at least the early thirteenth century (and perhaps from the reign of Henry II) the king insisted that he alone had the power to authorize the compulsion of free men to serve on juries.[98] For certain kinds of minor criminal justice, this right was delegated on a permanent basis to certain holders of private courts,[99] but otherwise the right was given only to the sheriffs and the county court (and then probably only when they were hearing business initiated by royal writ) and to the justices of the king's courts. By the thirteenth century increasing numbers of litigants wanted to have their cases decided by jury verdict instead of wager of law, the older method of proof. This meant they had to begin their litigation by royal writ and in the county court or in a royal court. In practice, it was also the king's courts alone which enjoyed the right to follow litigants (and those incidentally involved in litigation) from one county to another in the course of process in personal actions to secure their appearance or to enforce judgments. This gave them a significant advantage over all other courts including local county courts. Seignorial courts were even more restricted than county courts in this respect, for they could only execute process within the area of the lord's own fee.[100]

The county court The position of the county court as a junior partner with the king's courts in the provision of royal justice was enhanced during the same period by an extension of the number of standard writs available to litigants for the initiation of litigation in the county court. Already before 1236 a further seven or eight standard writs had been added to those found in *Glanvill*; one of the *Glanvill* writs had been made less specific and thus of wider use; and only one of the *Glanvill* writs had dropped out of use.[101] By the end of Henry III's reign at least another four writs had been added;[102] and the reign of Edward I saw the beginning of a further new category of such writs, viscontiel writs of trespass.[103]

One change which took place early in the thirteenth century actually slightly reduced the possibility of litigation initiated by writ in the county court being removed by *pone* into one of the king's courts. In the later years of Henry II's reign it appears to have been the case that either party could obtain a *pone* to remove such litigation without needing to show any specific cause for doing so.[104] Before 1236 it had become the position (certainly in the case of writs of right and probably in the case of all other types of litigation brought by writ in the county court) that although the plaintiff could obtain the writ *pone* for such a transfer as a matter of course, his opponent could only obtain such a writ for good cause or as a special favour.[105] The so-called *Hengham Magna*, probably a work of the 1260s, explains the logic of the different treatment accorded to the two parties. The plaintiff can readily obtain the *pone* because his purchase of the writ will be likely to cause additional delay and this will normally only benefit his opponent.[106] The defendant is not normally allowed ready access to the writ because delay favours him, rather than his opponent.

In Glanvill's day it may have been possible to remove litigation which had not been initiated by royal writ out of the county court into the king's court.[107] Subsequently, it became established that such pleas could not be removed. The rule (if such it can be categorized) was apparently already being disregarded by some sheriffs and litigants in the 1260s[108] and in a register of writs of the early 1270s we find a form of *pone* writ specifically intended for use in removing a replevin case brought without writ from a county court.[109] In 1275, as Robert Palmer has shown, there began the use of the writ *recordari facias* for the removal of certain kinds of plea brought without writ from the county court. Initially the new form of writ could be used for the removal of pleas not just of replevin but also of trespass, debt and detinue, but after the early 1290s it became restricted to pleas of replevin.[110] Litigation removed by *recordari* was not repleaded from the beginning, but simply from the point it had reached in the county court, and typically allowed the use of jury trial in the Common Bench for a case which would otherwise have had to be determined without the use of a jury.[111]

The review of judgments in seignorial and county courts Although nothing in what *Glanvill* says about the writ of false judgment suggests that it was available against the county court as well as seignorial courts, it had clearly become available as a means of challenging judgments in both by the beginning of the thirteenth century.[112] It also becomes clear in the thirteenth century that trial by battle, although a theoretical possibility, had ceased in practice to be used as a means of determining such cases, which typically now revolved around a detailed examination of the record produced and the flaws in procedure and judgment it could be made to disclose.[113] It was also possible to challenge judgments given in these courts in other, less direct ways. From at least the late twelfth century onwards the assize of novel disseisin could be used to challenge a dispossession which resulted from a court judgment in a seignorial court or a county court and thus allowed a review of the judgment.[114] By the last quarter of the thirteenth century the action of replevin (which allowed someone who had been distrained by seizure of his movables to challenge the justice of that distraint) was also being used to challenge various other kinds of judgment given in the course of litigation in lower courts.[115] The availability of these different methods of challenging the judgments of lower courts helped to undermine them in the eyes of litigants and encouraged them to go instead directly to the king's courts. Thus they too played a part in the increase of business in the Common Bench and in other royal courts.

THE CONSEQUENCES OF THESE CHANGES

Cumulatively the effect of these changes was to create a legal environment that was much more favourable to the professional lawyer. The new royal courts were run by judges whose continuous activity in these courts gave them a judicial expertise of a new kind. That expertise was developed and enhanced (in the case of a steadily increasing proportion of royal judges) by the length of their judicial careers. Such judges were, moreover, increasingly recruited from men who had already gained knowledge of the law from service as clerks or as professional lawyers: they were already legal experts at the time of their appointment.

The employment of expert, professional lawyers to represent litigants made much more sense in courts run by such men than it had in a world of courts run by non-professional judges. It was also significant that the new royal courts were 'national' courts, run by judges who applied a single 'law and custom of England', but one which was subject to constant change and modification as new cases were decided. This meant that litigants needed expert assistance in dealing with a set of rules and procedures with which they were not and could not be familiar: the assistance of legal experts who were familiar with them. The success of the new royal courts in attracting litigation, moreover, had the effect of concentrating the potential demand for legal services in a relatively small number of courts and more particularly in the Common Bench at Westminster. Such a concentration of demand made it much easier for professional lawyers to develop to meet the demand.

3

Creating a Demand for Lawyers: Changes in the Process of Litigation and in the Rules Governing the Use of Legal Representatives, 1154–1307

THE PROCESS OF LITIGATION

With the new royal courts came new ways of conducting litigation. One major change has already been mentioned: litigation in these courts was normally initiated by a royal writ returnable into the court.[1] Only a limited number of standard forms of original writ, each corresponding to a type of litigation which the king's courts were prepared to hear, were made available to litigants. These numbered no more than 15 by the end of Henry II's reign.[2] This was still sufficiently small to pose no real problem for litigants. There was, however, a major expansion in the number of original writs during the period of rather over a century between Henry II's death and that of his great-grandson, Edward I, in 1307.[3] Our best sources of information on this process are the various surviving registers of writs.[4] The register known to legal historians as CA, which belongs to the period before the enactment of the statute of Merton (1236), marks only a small advance on the number of writs found in *Glanvill*, containing some 19 writs for initiating litigation in royal courts[5] together with a further 14 for the initiation of county-court litigation (all of which could be removed into the kings courts by *pone*).[6] By the time of the compilation of the register CB in the 1250s the number of writs for the initiation of litigation in the king's court had grown to around 40 and there were a further 19 for the initiation of litigation in the county court.[7] When the Luffield Register (CC) was compiled in the last years of Henry III's reign, the number of writs available for the initiation of litigation in the king's court had risen to over 65; the number of county-court writs to over 20.[8] A register of writs now in the British Library (MS. Harley 408) from the end of Edward I's reign shows that by then there were well over 100 different writs for the initiation of litigation in the king's courts and at least 30 county-court writs.

One consequence was to make it much more difficult for litigants to know which writ was best suited to the circumstances of their own particular case. By the end of Henry III's reign, for example, someone bringing litigation for the recovery of land faced a choice between an almost bewildering variety of writs. These ranged from the petty assizes of novel disseisin and mort d'ancestor through the various types of writs of entry (both within the degrees and in the post), the congeners of mort d'ancestor (aiel and cosinage), the writs of intrusion, escheat and formedon to the two different types of writ *precipe* and a number of different kinds of writ of right. Even where there was less choice, as for example in the case of the litigant wishing to assert his right to present to a vacant church (where the choice lay between the assize of darrein presentment and the action of quare impedit), a litigant might still be puzzled as to which of the two writs was appropriate to his particular claim. Thus the purchasing of a writ to initiate litigation had come well before 1307 to be something which required expert advice and assistance. Making the right choice was important. Bringing the wrong writ would probably cost a plaintiff both time and money; it might also prejudice his right to bring subsequent proceedings using the right writ and thus leave him without a remedy. Chancery may have offered litigants some advice but the sensible litigant would also have consulted a legal expert.

The procedural rules in actions of right for land or for the advowson of a church in the king's court in the final years of Henry II's reign appear to have allowed extensive opportunities for delay. A defendant could sit out three successive summonses before an order would be given for the seizure of the property or advowson and only if he then failed to 'replevy' it within a fortnight of its seizure (by finding sureties for appearance in court) would seisin be adjudged to the plaintiff.[9] Alternatively, a defendant could excuse his absence on three successive occasions by alleging that he had fallen sick on the way to the court (the essoin *de malo veniendi*) or that he was sick in bed at home (the essoin *de malo lecti*). It was only after receiving three such excuses and adjourning the litigation three times that the court would require him (in the case of the essoin *de malo veniendi*) to appear or send a representative to answer for him or (in the case of the essoin *de malo lecti*) send four knights to see if he was seriously ill. They could adjourn the litigation for a year and a day if they found him seriously ill; if he was not, they would resummon him.[10] When he appeared in court he could ask for a view of the land (an inspection of the property in dispute) and secure an adjournment while this was done; he was then also entitled to another three essoins before having to appear.[11]

Further delay could be secured by vouching a third party to warrant the property in dispute, since both defendant and the warrantor could enjoy three essoins before having to appear or losing the land.[12]

There are, however, reasons to doubt whether the rules were quite as tolerant of abuse for the purposes of delay as they appear. A defendant who sat out the first three summonses was required, when he did appear, to deny on oath (and supported by 11 compurgators) each of the summonses he had received; if he admitted receiving them or failed in his denial, he would lose seisin of the property in question. Many defendants may not have been willing to perjure themselves; perhaps the more so as at this date the summoners themselves were apparently still required to appear in court to attest having made the summonses.[13] Nor was the making of essoins quite as easy as it appears. The plaintiff against whom an essoin *de malo veniendi* was cast could apparently demand that the person making the essoin for the defendant (the essoiner) prove on the spot that the excuse was genuine.[14] The alternative was for the plaintiff to allow the essoiner to find a surety or take an oath that he would produce his principal to warrant the essoin as genuine. If the defendant failed to appear, measures could be taken not just against him but also against the essoiner.[15] If the defendant appeared he would be required to swear on oath to the truth of the essoin which had been offered on his behalf.[16]

Subsequent changes reduced the opportunities for delay, at least in theory. The three summonses preceding a seizure of land when the defendant was absent without excuse had already been reduced to just one by 1194.[17] By 1200 the number of occasions on which a defendant could essoin himself *de malo veniendi* without appearing in court had also been reduced to just one;[18] and the number of occasions on which a defendant could essoin himself *de malo lecti* before knights were sent to see him had been reduced to one (though he was also allowed a first essoin *de malo veniendi*).[19] But if essoining was more difficult than it seems in *Glanvill*'s day these changes may have been comparatively unimportant; indeed, their effect may well have been more than outweighed by another change which took place around the same time. The courts began to take a much more liberal attitude towards the use of the essoin *de malo veniendi*. The possibility of the plaintiff requiring the essoiner to prove the excuse he had proffered for his principal had either fallen into disuse or been expressly abrogated by the time of the earliest surviving plea-rolls (the end of the twelfth century). By the time the relevant part of *Bracton* was written its author was quite clear that although the essoiner had to say that he was ready to prove that his principal was unable to appear for the reason he had given, it was not up to him to prove the truth of what he had said.[20]

Another possibility which had disappeared by the time *Bracton* was written was of action being taken against an essoiner when his principal failed to appear to warrant his essoin.[21] A third change relates to the warranting of the essoin by the defendant. In one passage *Bracton* seems doubtful whether the court could waive the requirement without the consent of the litigant's opponent; elsewhere the author is clear that this is a matter in the court's discretion and that the prompt despatch of business will mean that it is normally waived.[22] The consequence of these changes was that essoins *de malo veniendi* could now be incorporated into a fairly complicated framework of delaying tactics. The major part of the legal treatise known as *Hengham Magna* composed in the early 1260s is written round this very framework;[23] and its author was probably reflecting a fairly widespread attitude when he mentioned the possibility of the defendant appearing to warrant his essoin before judgment had been given on it or being found in court at this stage and being made to answer. This he characterized as foolishness (*fatuitas*) on his part, since by so appearing he had lost all the established possibilities of delay.[24]

Other developments made procedural rules more complex. In *Glanvill*'s day the only rule about the view seems to have been that it was not available if the defendant held only the lands claimed by the plaintiff in the village concerned.[25] By the time the relevant portion of *Bracton* was written there were much more complicated rules about when the view was available in each form of action[26] and these rules went on developing down to the end of the century, partly through judicial decision-making, partly through statutory enactment.[27] Only an expert would know whether or not the view was available in any particular instance. Basically the same procedures were used to secure the attendance of the defendant in the various new forms of action about title to land (writs of entry, escheat, formedon, cosinage, aiel, etc.) as were used in the action of right. But there were some modifications. One in particular stands out: the fact that in none of these newer actions were defendants allowed the use of the essoin *de malo lecti*.

These various developments made it desirable, perhaps even necessary, for the defendant to take expert advice if he was to use to the full the possibilities of delay open to him and not to make any fatal mistakes in doing so. Faced with delaying tactics of this kind from his opponent, it was also increasingly desirable for the plaintiff to employ expert assistance himself. An agent could save the litigant the repeated journeys to court necessary for putting in an appearance at the day fixed for the litigation and suing out the next stage of process against his opponent; if that agent was also an expert he might also catch any mistakes the defendant made in deploying his delaying tactics and thus win the case for his principal.

The procedural rules in the petty assizes afforded few opportunities for delay. No essoin was allowed to delay the assize of novel disseisin, nor was the defendant in it allowed a delay to produce a warrantor; and whether or not the defendant was present the assize gave its verdict on the day for which it had been summoned. This was the position in *Glanvill*'s day and had probably been so from the creation of the assize. It remained the position both in the thirteenth century and later.[28] In the other petty assizes (mort d'ancestor, utrum and darrein presentment) in *Glanvill*'s day the defendant was allowed two essoins but the assize would then pass, whether or not the defendant appeared; *Glanvill* says nothing about any other possibilities for delay (other than the minority of the defendant).[29] What *Glanvill* tells us elsewhere about essoining, moreover, may suggest that as yet it was difficult to use essoining simply as a delaying tactic.[30]

The rules had been recast by the time *Bracton* was written in the second quarter of the thirteenth century. Only one essoin was now allowed, but the relaxation of the rules governing essoins probably made it easier for the defendant to use his essoin simply as a delaying tactic.[31] The defendant was also now allowed to absent himself without an essoin on the first day for which an assize had been summoned: he would simply be resummoned to appear at a second day when the assize would be taken whether or not he appeared.[32] In the assizes of mort d'ancestor and utrum the defendant had also gained the additional possibilities of delay associated with vouching to warranty: an adjournment was allowed for the production of a warrantor and that warrantor might himself enjoy one essoin before appearance.[33] The new rules allowed more opportunity for delay; they certainly introduced more complexity into the procedural rules associated with the assizes and more need for expert advice for the parties involved.

When *Glanvill* was written, mesne process (the measures taken to secure the defendant's appearance in court) in personal actions (all actions other than the assizes and actions concerned with title to land and other forms of real property) began either with three summonses or with three attachments (under which the defendant was required to find sureties for his appearance).[34] If the defendant still did not appear, the court would then proceed to one further, and much more drastic, measure to ensure his appearance. Clearly *Glanvill* envisaged that this would be successful or would effectively satisfy the plaintiff's claim.[35] Changes had already occurred by the time of the earliest surviving plea-rolls. By the mid-1190s there had developed a standard mesne process for all kinds of personal actions which commenced with a single summons and then went on to two attachments. There was also a standard fourth and final stage of process in which the sheriff was ordered to produce the defendant's body in court (*habeas corpus*). Two further stages were added at the end in the early 1220s: one ordering the defendant to be distrained by his lands and chattels (seizure by the sheriff of his lands and chattels); the second repeating this order but adding that the sheriff was to ensure that the defendant retained no control over them. In the mid-1240s, the fourth stage of process (*habeas corpus*) dropped out, but from around 1250 a further stage was added at the end, requiring the sheriff to distrain the defendant by all his land and chattels and to answer for their profits to the king.[36] The overall effect of these changes was to increase the number of stages of process that most plaintiffs had to go through before they could ensure the appearance of their opponents. This must again have enhanced the attractiveness for plaintiffs of the use of agents who could turn up at the court on their behalf on the days to which the case was adjourned in order to put in an appearance for them and sue out the next stage of mesne process against their opponents.

In the case of defendants it is less clear that the lengthening of mesne process had any such effect; though it is possible that by hiring local legal assistance at an early stage, defendants were able to get advice on how long they would be able to sit out the process against them without major inconvenience and also acquire an intermediary who might help ensure the diminution of the effectiveness of the actions of the sheriff and his subordinates against the defendant.

At the end of Henry III's reign, under legislation enacted in 1263 and re-enacted in 1267, the standard mesne process was reduced by the omission of the two stages of distraint before the final grand distress, and the first hesitant steps taken towards allowing judgment to be given by default against recalcitrant defendants in certain kinds of action.[37] This was followed in 1275 by further legislative reform of the mesne process which abolished the second of the two attachment stages[38] and in 1285 by a limited extension of judgment by default.[39] Edward I's reign also saw the beginning of the use of outlawry against recalcitrant defendants in certain forms of action.[40] The overall effect of these changes was a certain simplification of the standard process, but the introduction of an even greater amount of variation between the different kinds of process possible. Expert assistance to litigants in the preliminary stages of such litigation remained desirable, even necessary.

When the parties both appeared in court, the plaintiff made a count setting out his claim or complaint. By the end of Henry II's reign this was beginning to lose some of its older flexibility. *Glanvill* indicates that set formulas had begun to be used in actions of right initiated by the writ *precipe*, though it does not suggest that their use was as yet obligatory.[41] We also see the beginnings of a different kind of constraint on the count, requiring it to be consistent with the original writ in the specific facts which the latter contained.[42]

Counts subsequently became more standardized and more complex. Take for example the count in the action of right for land. The usual basis for a claim in this action was seisin of the property being claimed by a particular ancestor of the plaintiff. Until the later part of John's reign the plaintiff was not required to trace how the right to the property had descended from that ancestor to himself but simply asserted that he was his father or grandfather or other relative without precisely tracing the relationship.[43] Originally, it may not even have been necessary for him to name the ancestor on whose seisin he was relying. The specimen count in *Glanvill* suggests this;⁴⁴ and the fact that such a change had only recently taken place might explain why several litigants in the early thirteenth century failed in their claims as a result of making counts in which their ancestor's name was omitted.⁴⁵ How the right had descended to the plaintiff is recorded in a few cases from 1200 onwards,⁴⁶ but it was only after 1208 that this became a standard and clearly obligatory feature of the count.⁴⁷

Nor did the development end there. By the time the relevant section of *Bracton* was written there was evidently disagreement about who had to be included. Some thought it was only necessary to mention those to whom the right could have descended (allowing the omission, for example, of sons who had died in the lifetime of their fathers). The author's line was that it was necessary to mention all those to whom the right had descended or through whom the right had passed but not, for example, sons who had died in the lifetime of their fathers without issue.⁴⁸ The eventual rule was that all those to whom the right could have descended had to be mentioned, irrespective of whether or not they had died without issue.⁴⁹ These were not the only changes. In *Glanvill* we find the plaintiff claiming simply that he (or the ancestor on whose seisin he was relying) had been seised of the property he was claiming 'in demesne as of fee'.⁵⁰ The early plea-rolls, however, show a variety of characterizations of the nature of the seisin relied on.⁵¹ It was only in 1220–1 that it became the normal practice for counts to characterize the seisin as being 'in demesne as of fee and right'. Thereafter this phraseology became absolutely standard.⁵²

A second form of action demonstrates a similar movement towards a more complex but also more standardized count. This is the action of replevin which was used for challenging the use of distraint by lords and others.⁵³ Enrolled counts in early cases vary considerably but seem in general to have just two features: a non-specific allegation that the defendant had taken animals or chattels belonging to the plaintiff and an allegation that the defendant had subsequently detained the distresses taken against gage and pledge. The first change was that plaintiffs, from the 1220s, began regularly to specify in their counts precisely what had been taken in distraint: the number and kind of animals or the number and description of chattels. Around 1250 a whole series of further details begin to appear regularly in the enrolled counts. They now specify the date on which the distresses were taken, the village where they had been taken, the village where they had been impounded and how their release had been secured. Further details still appear in the counts of Edward I's reign: the precise location where they had been taken and not just the name of the village and the date when the distresses were released, as well as when they were taken. These seem to be more than just changes in enrolment practice and reflect changes in the detail included in the count.

Counts became more complex and also more standardized during the thirteenth century. This may in part have been a consequence of the fact that counts had become the province of specialist experts; it must certainly also have had the consequence of making it more necessary to employ specialist experts to make them. A defective count could lose a case for a litigant. If he was lucky he would simply have to begin the litigation anew. If he was unlucky he might be barred from doing so and find himself losing all claim to the property concerned in perpetuity. In the action of right, for example, by the mid-thirteenth century it had become the rule that omission of any of the persons who should have been mentioned in the descent (whether or not the omission was material) not only lost the plaintiff his case on this occasion but also barred him from renewing it in the future.[54]

Once the plaintiff had made his count the defendant had to make a formal defence. In Henry II's reign (as later) this probably took the form of an short, simple denial in fairly general terms of the complaint or claim made by the plaintiff. The defendant would then ask the court's permission to 'imparl' (withdraw to speak with his advisers). On his return he would repeat his formal denial and add a promise to repeat this denial 'where and when he ought'. It was at this point that in the thirteenth century it became common for the defendant to make a series of 'exceptions', objections to answering the claim or complaint, which would then give rise to legal argument between the two parties or their legal representatives. *Glanvill* suggests that this may have been much less common in Henry II's reign. His discussion of the action of right for land initiated by the writ *precipe* – the action to which he devotes most attention – suggests that such cases were normally decided by battle or the verdict of the grand assize and that the defendant would normally choose one of these two immediately without any preliminary attempt to defeat the plaintiff's claim by an exception.

He only mentions one kind of circumstance where further argument might ensue. This was when the plaintiff in response to the defendant putting himself on the grand assize said that the assize should not proceed because they were both descended from the ancestor on whose seisin the plaintiff had counted. Here the appropriate method of deciding the question of entitlement was not the grand assize but the court's judgment as to which was the 'closer heir' of the ancestor concerned. If the two parties disagreed about their family tree, their mutual kin and, if necessary, a local jury were to be summoned to ascertain the facts.[55] On the other hand, in his discussion of the action of right initiated by the writ of right *Glanvill* does show us that exceptions could be made on such grounds as error in one of the names contained in the writ or in the service it specified as owed for the land sought.[56] This suggests that his discussion of the writ *precipe* may be a little misleading, for such exceptions must also have been available in litigation initiated by this writ. However, it is probably right to conclude that the making of exceptions was still comparatively rare in most forms of action and thus that there was as yet comparatively little legal argument in most cases.

The one major qualification to this generalization seems to have been the petty assizes. Here no formal defence needed to be made by defendants but *Glanvill*'s discussion indicates that they had already begun to make full use of exceptions and we can assume that this led to regular exchanges of legal argument between the parties.[57] There were special reasons for this. Since the jury was summoned in the petty assizes to give its verdict on a question or series of questions formulated in general terms in advance, it was clearly thought proper for the defendant to be given an opportunity to show why the jury's answers might be misleading.

Glanvill's discussion of the use of exceptions in the assize of mort d'ancestor shows that these were of several different kinds. Some claimed, in effect, that even though the answers to all the questions might favour the plaintiff there were none the less additional facts which meant that the defendant was rightfully in possession of the land. It might thus be true that the plaintiff's ancestor had died in seisin of the land within the time limit of the assize and that the plaintiff was his closest heir but that the plaintiff had been in possession of the land since the ancestor's death and had granted it to the defendant. Here, even if the plaintiff disputed the truth of such a claim, the assize answering the questions formulated was not an appropriate way of deciding the dispute between them. The defendant could also make an exception of villeinage or bastardy against the plaintiff. This was apparently because the assize was not considered the appropriate way of proving or disproving villeinage or bastardy. Villeinage was proved by suit of kin; bastardy by a certificate from the bishop. Simple distrust of the jury seems to be manifested in the allowing of an exception to the effect that the ancestor concerned had died seised but only by way of holding the land in gage (as security for a debt). Here the appropriate way of discovering whether or not this was the case was a jury, but one specifically charged with deciding whether the ancestor had died seised as of fee or of gage. Yet other exceptions show the invocation of specific legal rules by the defendant: for example, a rule which bars the assize from passing in connection with land in towns held by burgage tenure, perhaps because such land was commonly left by will.

From the late twelfth century onwards the use of exceptions also became widespread outside the assizes. The plea-rolls of the king's courts, for example, show a variety of exceptions now being made in the action of right. In Hilary term 1214 we see a defendant successfully excepting to the jurisdiction of the Common Bench on the grounds that he had letters patent of protection privileging him against being impleaded except before the king or his chief justiciar and that neither of them were present in the court.[58] As early as 1205 we find a defendant excepting to a writ because it stated that the land was in one village when it was in fact in another. The plaintiff then received permission to withdraw from his claim.[59] In 1228 a defendant asked for judgment against a count in which land was claimed on an ancestor's seisin in Henry I's reign on the grounds that it was the rule that no one could bring a claim on a seisin more ancient than the day of Henry I's death.[60] We also find defendants excepting to counts on the ground that they varied in significant respects from the details given in the plaintiff's writ: for example, in a case of 1203, in seeking 16 bovates of land when the writ had mentioned only nine.[61] By the time the relevant part of *Bracton* was written the author could devote a substantial section of the treatise to the exceptions which could be made in this very action.[62]

By the 1270s the defendant was positively encouraged by the rules which governed pleading to make exceptions. Provided his exceptions related to matters of law that could be determined by the judgment of the justices, he could make as many such as he liked and, if the first was quashed, he could then simply go on to make a second one and so on.[63] But care still needed to be taken in making exceptions, for there had come to be detailed rules about when and in what order they could be made. *Bracton* tells us that in land actions in which the defendant was able to ask for a view, certain exceptions had to be made before the view was requested[64] and this rule is also mentioned in a case of 1231.[65] A King's Bench case of 1241 shows us that making a peremptory exception (one that, if proved true, would be a final answer to the plaintiff's claim or complaint) constituted a renunciation of any kind of merely dilatory exception (one that merely quashed the writ or caused a delay in the hearing of the case).[66] By 1268 there are also indications of the existence of a set order among dilatory exceptions.[67] The existence of such an order is asserted by a serjeant in a report of a case from the 1293 Kent eyre; his assertion was accepted by one of the justices. The serjeant also asserted (and the justice similarly accepted) the corollary that making an exception lower down in the list barred the defendant from subsequently making one of the exceptions higher up in it.[68]

In these developments we again see the creation of additional opportunities for professional lawyers. The ordinary litigant might well have been able to manage a straight denial leading to battle or the grand assize or wager of law or the verdict of a jury, but he was at a distinct disadvantage in the making of exceptions. This was a technical matter requiring the skills of a professional lawyer attuned both by prior study and by his own experience to discovering defects in writs and counts and to presenting exceptions in the correct order. He would know the right way to present the exceptions he made and support them by arguments which would sound convincing to the justices. And because such exceptions needed to be rebutted by the arguments of the plaintiff or his legal representatives, the use of exceptions, indeed the positive encouragement of that use by the courts, also created opportunities for professional lawyers in the service of plaintiffs.

CHANGES IN THE RULES GOVERNING THE APPOINTMENT AND USE OF LEGAL REPRESENTATIVES

Thus far we have been concerned with ways in which the process of litigation changed during the century and a half between the beginning of Henry II's reign and the end of the reign of Edward I: changes which made litigation more technical and complex and thus increased the demand for the services of experts who could assist litigants in dealing with these complexities. We now turn to look at those changes which made it possible for litigants to employ expert legal representatives to assist them in their dealings with the courts.

Attorneys

By the time *Glanvill* was written, there had been a dramatic change in the rules governing the use of attorneys. An attorney (what *Glanvill* terms a *responsalis*) might now be appointed by either litigant in any type of litigation and at any stage in the proceedings. He had normally to be appointed by the litigant in person before the justices of the court. The attorney was also himself required to be present unless he was known to the court.[69] An attorney might also be appointed out of court by a defendant or a vouchee either in writing or verbally, though in the latter case the person appointed had to be someone known to have close connections with the litigant. This option, however, was available only in a limited range of actions and only where the litigant was unable to come to court because of illness.[70] *Glanvill* does not suggest there was any difference between attorneys appointed in these two rather different ways in respect of the powers they exercised. Both possessed full power to 'win or lose' in place of their principal in the litigation for which they had been appointed.[71]

It had thus now become possible for any plaintiff to appoint someone to represent him in litigation. One journey to court would be necessary to appoint the attorney but only one. Subsequent court appearances, of which a number were normally necessary, could be made by the attorney. The plaintiff also had the additional security that he could at any stage in the proceedings remove the attorney he had appointed and act himself or appoint someone else.[72] The defendant, too, now had a way of appointing whomever he liked to act for him. No longer could he be represented only if he had appointed a bailiff or steward to take charge of his affairs. Nor did he have to be represented by his bailiff or steward, even if he had made such an appointment. Indeed, *Glanvill* is careful to point out that even if a litigant has such an official, and this fact is known to the court, the litigant must still specifically appoint him if he is to act for him in a particular piece of litigation.[73]

Glanvill gives us a coherent and apparently comprehensive picture of the legal rules governing the appointment and use of attorneys at the end of Henry II's reign but provides us with little evidence as to how and when those rules had come into existence. The Battle abbey chronicle suggests that it had in fact become possible as early as the 1160s for either party to litigation to appoint someone to represent them and that they did not have to appear before the king's court to do this at this time. The abbot of Battle was bringing litigation in the king's court against Hamon Pecche. The chronicler tells us that the abbot sent a monk named Osbert to act for him since he was 'unwilling or unable to tire himself by attending on the day and at the place fixed'. Hamon sent his son Geoffrey to excuse his father's absence and empowered to speak and act on his behalf. On neither side is there the slightest hint that these representatives had been formally appointed by their principals before the justices of the court.[74]

In a passage from the *Dialogue of the Exchequer* written in the late 1170s the author considers what happens when an Exchequer official is involved in litigation in another court. If this occurs while the Exchequer is in session and the official is the plaintiff, he is said to have a choice between deferring the litigation and acting through a representative ('*per procuratorem*'); if he is the defendant he will simply be excused from appearing. If, however, the litigation takes place while the Exchequer is not in session and even if the day set for his appearance is such as to make it impossible to appear at the Exchequer for the beginning of the session, then he will simply have to appoint a representative ('*procuratorem vel responsalem*').[75] This also suggests that it had become comparatively easy for either party to appoint a representative or attorney, though it does not tell us anything about the method of appointment.

The evidence of the Battle abbey chronicler suggests that at some date between the later 1160s and the time *Glanvill* was written it became more difficult, for some litigants at least, to appoint an attorney. The evidence of the final concords suggests a probable date. None earlier than 1182 contains any reference to either of the litigants being represented by an attorney. Thereafter a number do record that one of the parties was being represented by an attorney.[76] The most likely explanation is not that parties before 1182 were never represented by attorneys but that it was only in 1182 that such an appointment became a matter of direct concern to the court. It was perhaps at the same time that it was decided that such appointments should normally be made in court and be enrolled on the court's rolls. Such appointments certainly were so recorded by the time of the earliest surviving rolls. The comparative informality of the appointment of attorneys by defendants out of court in the special circumstances where this was allowed may be a survival of the older methods, allowed to survive only when exceptional circumstances made it difficult to insist that the defendant come to court to make an appointment. The change ensured that the appointment of an attorney in England would normally henceforth be an oral act recorded in the formal records of the court, not a private transaction taking place out of court of which the main evidence was a written private deed – as was to become the practice elsewhere in Western Europe.

Some changes that took place during the first half of the thirteenth century reduced the availability of attorneys. By the end of Henry III's reign it had become the general rule that no defendant could appoint an attorney in a case that might end with his imprisonment. This prevented the defendant appointing an attorney in pleas of prohibition (concerning the bringing of litigation about lay matters in ecclesiastical courts), pleas concerning the breaking of the terms of a final concord, criminal appeals and pleas where a breach of the king's peace was alleged.[77] But no such restriction applied to the appointment of attorneys by the plaintiffs in such cases. Less significant was the restriction imposed in 1227 which prevented defendants in the assize of novel disseisin from appearing by attorney because it still remained possible for a third party to appear in court and present arguments on behalf of a defendant as the defendant's bailiff. All he could not do was to compromise the case or give the case away by confessing to the disseisin.[78]

More significant, however, were other developments which made it easier for litigants to appoint attorneys. By 1202 it had become possible to appoint an attorney in chancery, which then notified the appropriate court.[79] This was only useful, however, if chancery happened to pass through or near a litigant's home county. By the later part of Henry III's reign it had also become possible to make such an appointment before a commissioner who would go to the litigant's place of residence to receive the appointment and report back to chancery, which would then notify the appropriate court of the appointment.[80] Initially, its use seems to have been restricted to litigants who were sick and it was always an expensive option.[81] It thus did little to make it easier for the bulk of litigants to appoint attorneys. But other changes did have such an effect. In *Glanvill*'s day appointments had to be made in open court while the court was in session. By 1219 attorneys were being appointed before one of the justices of the Common Bench (and local associates) out of term and in the countryside.[82] By the early 1260s any justice of the Common Bench could receive the appointment of an attorney locally by himself.[83] By the end of Henry III's reign the senior justice of the Common Bench was authorizing specific individuals to receive the appointment of attorneys for litigation in his court[84] and the Common Bench was also accepting the appointment of attorneys before the justices of other royal courts, apparently without advance authorization.[85] Under Edward I the procedures for the admission of attorneys became even more liberal.[86]

The relatively informal procedure for the appointment of attorneys by a sick litigant out of court survived into the thirteenth century but by the time of the earliest plea-rolls its use had become much more restricted.[87] It had also become the case that if such a representative gave an answer on behalf of his principal that would lead to a decision of the litigation, such as waging battle or putting himself on the grand assize, the court would not accept his action until it had been specifically ratified by his principal and the latter had appointed the representative as his attorney.[88] This procedure seems to have been in operation by 1206.[89]

As we have seen, *Glanvill* describes a legal agent who is in all important respects identical with the later attorney but calls this agent a *responsalis*. Nor is the term *attornatus* (attorney) used in the earliest surviving plea-rolls. We find instead the rather clumsy adjectival phrase *positus loco X* ('put in place of X'). The neater *attornatus* is first found in Michaelmas term 1200 and soon came to supersede the older phrase.[90] We also find continued use of the term *responsalis*, but restricted to the attorney appointed by a litigant outside court and without official approval, who no longer possesses the full powers of the attorney.[91] The verb *attornare (loco suo)*, meaning 'to appoint (in one's place)', is found much earlier than the noun *attornatus*. It occurs in the final concords of 1182 and 1183, the earliest surviving final concords to mention the representation of a litigant, though not in later ones. It is also used in one of the specimen final concords given in *Glanvill*.[92] *Attornare* is derived from the French verb *attorner* meaning primarily 'to turn', but in a more extended sense, 'to assign or depute for a particular purpose'.[93] The more classical *ponere* and the more colloquial *attornare* and their connected families of words (and their French equivalents) existed side by side with much the same meaning. It was *attornare* which eventually triumphed. But not wholly, for even at the end of the thirteenth century the phrase used to record the appointment of an attorney was simply that *X ponit loco suo Y ad lucrandum vel perdendum*.

It should be emphasized that the changes which made it possible for litigants to appoint attorneys to represent them in litigation and which subsequently made it easier for litigants to make such appointments did not in themselves create the professional attorney. When it became possible to appoint legal representatives on an *ad hoc* basis this created an opportunity for the emergence of a professional group which would specialize in acting for litigants in this capacity; but it remained possible long afterwards for litigants to appoint friends, relatives or servants to act for them as their attorneys. Without the creation of this form of representation the emergence of the later professional attorney would not have been possible; but the creation of this form of representation is not sufficient in itself to explain that emergence.

Serjeants

There is comparatively little evidence from Henry II's reign of the use by litigants of 'pleaders' to speak on their behalf in court: men who spoke on behalf of litigants but subject to disavowal by them. Nowhere in *Glanvill* is there any mention of the 'pleader' and the counts which he puts into the mouth of litigants are all in the first person singular: the form appropriate to a litigant speaking in person and perhaps to an attorney but not to the 'pleader' or serjeant, for whom a count in the third person is the appropriate form.[94] In the litigation about Thurlow church of which we are given a detailed account in the Battle abbey chronicle, it was evidently the monk Osbert whom the abbot had sent in his place as his attorney who spoke in court on behalf of the abbot and Geoffrey Pecche, the attorney of his father Hamon, who was expected to speak on his father's behalf.[95] Likewise in litigation between Battle abbey and Alan de Beaufou over the church of Mendlesham which was heard in the king's court at Winchester it was Robert the philosopher, appearing as the abbot's attorney, who spoke in court as did the abbot's opponent Alan, who was appearing in person.[96] It is, however, the same chronicle which indicates that by the late 1150s it had become possible for a plaintiff to make his count through a 'pleader'.

The litigation in question was a land case heard in the king's court at Clarendon. The chronicler makes it clear that although the abbot was present, the count explaining the abbot's case and also complaining of the long delay in hearing it was made by two men. One was his monk Osbert, who had acted as the abbot's attorney in the Mendlesham case. The other was a local knight, Peter de Criol. Gilbert de Balliol's defence, however, was made in person.[97] This evidence stands alone in suggesting that it was possible for a plaintiff to use a 'pleader' or 'pleaders' to speak on his behalf in Henry II's reign; the lack of confirmatory evidence suggests that the use of such a 'pleader' by litigants was as yet neither common nor widespread.

From the early thirteenth century we begin to get much clearer evidence that the king's courts accepted the use by litigants at all stages of legal proceedings of representatives able to speak on behalf of litigants though not formally empowered to do so who were thus also subject to disavowal by their principals. The earliest evidence of the use of such representatives (whom for the sake of simplicity I shall hereafter call serjeants, though this term is not used till later in the thirteenth century)[98] comes from what can be presumed to be a small minority of cases where the official record notes that a particular serjeant has been disavowed by the litigant for whom he has been speaking. Thus a laconic entry on a 1204 *coram rege* plea-roll notes that Alard of Westcote has been amerced twice: once for discussing a settlement in an assize of novel disseisin without the permission of the justices, a second time for saying something that was then disavowed. We are not told for which of the parties he had been acting.[99] From another note on a 1207 Common Bench plea-roll we learn that Bertram of Hornby had been amerced because Richard de Linz had disavowed something he had said for him.[100]

Fortunately there are also entries where we are told rather more. In a case of 1228 we see William of Cookham disavowing his serjeant John de Planaz when he had made an initial count for him on an action of right. We can even see why he did so. John had made a count which spoke of William's ancestor having been seised of the land in the reign of king Henry, the grandfather of king John. This was an obvious error since king John had no grandfather with such a name. William then emended the count to speak of his ancestor having been seised in the time of the king Henry who was the grandfather of the grandfather of the present king (Henry I).[101] Other entries which show serjeants making counts include one of 1236. This shows the defendant asking the plaintiff whether he avowed the count made by his serjeant and the plaintiff then doing so;[102] and another of 1244 where the plaintiff was amerced in an action brought by a writ of *precipe in capite* because he had avowed the count made for him by Richard de Hotot and thereby contradicted his writ.[103] In a 1222 case we see a serjeant speaking on behalf of a plaintiff at a rather later stage of the proceedings, after the formal count and defence and in the course of legal argument, and only then being disavowed.[104]

The earliest clear evidence of a serjeant speaking in court on behalf of a defendant comes from a case of 1207 where Abel son of William was amerced for speaking on behalf of the defendants and being disavowed.[105] Other similar evidence can be found in cases of 1221[106] and 1253.[107] A case from 1261 which does not involve a serjeant shows that by then it was clearly accepted that a serjeant could make the initial formal defence as well as engage in subsequent pleading on the defendant's behalf. In it the defendant's attorney in responding to the plaintiff's count failed to make the necessary formal defence and simply put himself on the grand assize. The court held that as the defendant's attorney he could not disavow himself. Since he had made an insufficient defence he had left his principal 'undefended'. The plaintiff therefore recovered. The implicit comparison is with what was clearly the more common situation where such a defence was made by a serjeant and the defective defence could have been disavowed.[108]

The term normally used during the first half of the thirteenth century to refer to persons speaking on behalf of litigants in the king's courts is *narrator*, meaning 'one who makes a count' and referring to one, but only one, of the functions performed in court by such agents. The earliest use of the term seems to be in Michaelmas term 1220 when John Bucuinte was so described when being amerced.[109] In Hilary term 1222 we find another (this time anonymous) serjeant so labelled when being disavowed by his client.[110] The French equivalent (*le cuntur*) is the term used in the pleading manual *Brevia Placitata* which was compiled around 1260 as also in the so-called *Hengham Magna* of about the same date.[111] The more classical term *advocatus* was the term used for persons carrying out the equivalent function in the ecclesiastical courts. It is also found at least once in the records of the royal courts in the entry recording the disavowal of John de Planaz in 1228.[112] It is also one of two terms used in London legislation of 1244[113] and the only term used in further London legislation of 1264.[114] There is also some evidence of the use of the terms *placitator* and *causidicus* to refer to serjeants, though not in the royal courts.[115] The earliest evidence of the use of the term *serviens* ('serjeant'), which was to become (in its Latin and French versions) the standard term in the second half of the thirteenth century and thereafter is in connection with an order for the payment of the king's serjeant, Laurence del Brok, in 1252, but it seems to refer to the position he held rather than to the function he performed.[116]

4

From Proto-professional to Professional: the Emergence of the Professional Lawyer in England, 1199–1272

THE PROTO-PROFESSIONAL LAWYERS OF THE REIGN OF KING JOHN

Lady Stenton thought that it was the reign of king John that saw the 'emergence of the professional attorney' even though the 'office of attorney' was then 'still in the early stages of development' and 'more often than not a man appointed a kinsman to represent him, a son, a brother, a husband or a wife'.[1] It is a view that demands respect, for it was based on an extensive knowledge of the early plea-rolls.[2] There are, none the less, good reasons for questioning whether it is correct. At no stage did Lady Stenton make clear her criteria for distinguishing the professional attorney from the non-professional. The nearest she came to doing so was in a passage in which she said that 'a number of men can be seen, as the rolls are carefully read, appearing on behalf of more than one client whose cases concerned land in different shires. When a man is seen acting as an attorney for litigants whose lands lie as far apart as Yorkshire, Devon, Norfolk, Essex and Kent, a professional relationship must be assumed'.[3] But this seems altogether too generous a definition of the 'professional' attorney. If we are to distinguish the full professional attorney from the semi-professional and from the amateur who acted on behalf of more than one friend or relative in litigation from more than one county, we need to look for individuals appointed as attorneys with sufficient frequency to suggest that they spent most of their time acting as attorneys and gained a major part of their income from doing so. In fact, none of the attorneys we find on the rolls in John's reign are sufficiently active for them to be classified as fully professional in this sense, even if we make allowance for appointments recorded on rolls now lost.

There can none the less be little doubt that a number of individuals did act as attorneys over a number of years between 1199 and 1216 for a number of different litigants with whom they had no other known connection. They are commonly also to be found acting as sureties for baronial essoiners and for the waging of law or of battle in a way characteristic of their later fully professional counterparts. It may well be that as a result of their activities they had at least some of the specialist expertise later associated with the professional attorney. They were probably also being paid for their work, though perhaps not enough to provide them with a living. They certainly have some claim to being considered as precursors of the professional attorney, if not professional attorneys themselves.

These proto-professional attorneys belong to one of three general types. Some were office-holders in the courts or in the Exchequer, for whom activity as an attorney was no more than a profitable sideline. At least four of the 15 'minor professional men in the courts of justice' to whose work Lady Stenton accumulated references, belong to this group.

Stephen Boncretien is the most impressive both in terms of the quantity of appointments he received and the length of time during which he acted.[4] He was first appointed as an attorney in 1200. Thereafter he was appointed at least once and sometimes as many as three times a year and reached a peak of activity with five appointments in 1214. After the civil war he was again appointed as attorney in a number of cases between 1219 and 1223. He does not reappear as an attorney until 1231 though he acted as a surety in 1224 and 1225. Stephen was apparently a court clerk. In 1200 Amfrid de Dene appointed him as his attorney for litigation in the Common Bench and the plea-roll gives his name as Stephen Boncristien; but when in the following term he put in an appearance for Amfrid he was simply called Stephen the clerk. A significant number of his clients seem to have been persons who were holding or had held posts within the royal administrative machine or with close connections to such individuals: a pattern best explained by his having come into contact with them in the course of his other official duties.[5] The other three members of this group are *William of Buckingham*,[6] who was certainly a clerk in the courts,[7] *Richard Ducket*,[8] whom Lady Stenton noted was 'attached to the staff of the Justiciar Geoffrey fitz Peter' and subsequently passed into the service of Geoffrey's successor in office, Hubert de Burgh,[9] and *Robert of Rockingham*,[10] whom Lady Stenton herself again specifically noted was a clerk.[11]

Four of these 'minor professional men in the courts of justice' belong to a second group of individuals of no particular local standing and only small or no traceable property holdings who did not hold positions in the courts or in royal administration. *Aubrey Buc of Barking* probably came from Barking in

Essex.¹² Between 1202 and 1208 he was appointed an attorney in 13 different cases. His busiest year was 1207 (which accounts for just under half the total); in other years his total of appointments was never more than one or two. Four of his 13 appointments were for cases from his home county of Essex and a further two in cases from the neighbouring county of Middlesex. His one appearance as a surety is in 1209. It is impossible to be certain where *Thomas de Ho* came from.¹³ He occurs once in 1194 as an essoiner and 16 times as an attorney between 1198 and 1214. His busiest years were 1212 and 1214 when he was appointed in as many as six and five cases. In 1212 he also acted on six occasions as a surety for essoiners in the court of King's Bench. *Thomas Tutadebles of Therfield* was a free tenant at Therfield in Hertfordshire.¹⁴ He was appointed an attorney only four times between 1203 and 1214.¹⁵ He also acted three times as a surety between 1196 and 1200.¹⁶ In 1205 he acted as essoiner of the attorney of the abbot of Ramsey. The abbot was a major landowner at Therfield.¹⁷ *Thomas Beivin* came from Feering in Essex and part of his activity in the courts can be directly connected with the lord of the manor of Feering, the abbot of Westminster.¹⁸ In 1204 and 1205 he was the attorney of Godfrey of Eye, a tenant who resisted a dower claim on the grounds that he was the abbot's tenant in villeinage; in 1205 he was the essoiner of an attorney of the abbot and in 1212 one of the sureties of the abbot's essoiners. Much of the rest of his activity was connected with his own home county of Essex. On seven occasions between 1204 and 1221 he was appointed attorney by litigants with cases from the county and three times between 1214 and 1224 he stood surety for people from the county. A fifth man in this category not mentioned by Lady Stenton is *Reiner de Gloz*. Reiner is probably to be identified with the man of that name against whom the prior of Longueville sought an acre at Weston Longville in Norfolk in 1229.¹⁹ There is certainly a marked Norfolk bias to his legal activity. He was appointed an attorney for Norfolk pleas nine times between 1207 and 1214.²⁰ Of the other three cases in which he was appointed, one is from the neighbouring county of Suffolk and the other two seem to involve litigants with Norfolk connections.²¹ On two of the three occasions when Reiner acted as a surety it was in connection with Norfolk litigation.²²

The remaining category consists of two much more substantial individuals with easily traceable property holdings who can be found acting as attorneys for a number of different litigants but who are also to be found subsequently or contemporaneously acting as serjeants. *Matthew of Bigstrup* drew his surname from a village whose name is now preserved only in a farm in the parish of Haddenham in Buckinghamshire and he can be 'securely placed' as a member of a rural Buckinghamshire knightly family.²³ The main holding he inherited from his father was half a knight's fee at Moreton in Oxfordshire, a hamlet close to Bigstrup,²⁴ but he may also have inherited a hide at Forest Hill in the same county.²⁵ Matthew acted as an Oxfordshire knight on various occasions between 1206 and 1232[26] and can also be seen acting as a Berkshire knight between 1229 and 1235, although he is not known to have held any land in that county.[27] His first appointment as an attorney was in 1200 and his busiest period was between 1211 and 1214.[28] As Lady Stenton noted, his clients in this period included many 'of high position' who 'would be satisfied only with the best attorneys available'. His pattern of activity changed significantly after the civil war. Between 1219 and 1223 Matthew was appointed an attorney in litigation in the Common Bench ten times, but in six out of ten cases he was acting for Faukes de Breaute and in a seventh for Gilbert de Breaute. This fits well with evidence showing Matthew to have been a member of the household of Faukes at this time.

Thereafter there is a complete break in the record of his activity as an attorney until 1229–30 when he is again to be found acting for one particular client, Peter fitz Herbert.[29] This break may be connected with the downfall of Falkes de Breaute but one possible explanation is that Matthew had now become a serjeant and largely abandoned acting as an attorney. He was certainly acting as a serjeant in the 1228 Suffolk assize of mort d'ancestor in which he was disavowed.[30] His pursuit of a career as a serjeant might explain why he does not appear as an attorney after 1230 but was apparently present in the Common Bench and thus able to act as a surety for licence to make a concord in 1233 and in connection with an appeal in 1235.[31] The other point of interest about him is the evidence noticed by Lady Stenton which suggests that he had received an academic training. He is described as master Matthew when acting as attorney for the first time in 1200 and again in a case brought against him in 1204.[32]

John Bucuinte was of the same general type.[33] He came from a London merchant family, perhaps of Italian origin, whose name may point to a certain inherited verbal dexterity (it seems to mean 'oily mouth').[34] He was probably the son of Geoffrey Bucuinte and married Juliana the daughter of William Renger who came from another London patrician family. John held property in Holborn, in Smithfield and in the city of London proper.[35] He is also to be found quitclaiming land at Tottenham Court in the parish of St Pancras, as tenant of a messuage at Westminster and holding land at Hughenden in Buckinghamshire.[36] His most substantial property, however, seems to have been a holding at Edmonton in Middlesex which he acquired before 1198 but later sold to Gundreda de Warenne.[37] John acted as a Middlesex knight on several occasions between 1201 and 1211. He was appointed attorney in some 31 cases in the Common Bench between 1198 and 1220. He also acted as a surety in cases of 1201, 1202 and 1220, and as a serjeant at the same time as he was being appointed an attorney. The Crowland chronicler's account of litigation between his abbey and the priory of Spalding shows him acting as a serjeant at the very beginning of John's reign.[38] It was also as a serjeant failing to produce suit in support of his allegation, that he spoke on behalf of the prior of Shouldham though not his attorney in a case of 1204[39] and that he advised a litigant to put herself on a jury in another 1204 case. In 1220 he was amerced 'because he sat at judgment and was a serjeant in the case'. This probably means that he participated in some way in the making of a judgment in a case where he had previously acted as serjeant. It should probably be linked with evidence from the previous Easter term of part of the plea-roll being ascribed to him and two others, perhaps as deputies to the justices of the Common Bench for hearing some of the litigation before the court.

John Bucuinte is not the only man recorded on the plea-rolls during John's reign as having acted as a serjeant, but all the others so described appear to have been only amateurs. Certainly none of them appears elsewhere on the rolls as an attorney or even as a surety. Nor were any of them men of any great substance or position. Take for example the *Abel son of William* amerced in the Common Bench in Hilary term 1207 'because he spoke for [the defendants] and they did not warrant him'.[40] It is not possible even to locate where he came from, let alone know whether he was a property-owner in that or any other area. About the *Richard of Inland* amerced at a Norwich session of pleas and assizes in 1209 'because he was not warranted for his count' in an assize of mort d'ancestor concerning a holding of four acres at Gateley in the same county we can say a little more.[41] He was probably a neighbour of his 'client' for there is a locality within Gateley called Inland. It is also reasonably certain that he was not a major landowner either there or elsewhere.

THE SERJEANTS OF THE COMMON BENCH DURING HENRY III'S REIGN

During the course of Henry III's reign (1216–72) it becomes clear that it has become the norm for litigants in the Common Bench to have serjeants to speak on their behalf. The specimen counts given in *Glanvill*, as we have seen, are all in the first person singular: the form appropriate to a litigant speaking on his own behalf.[42] The same is also true of two of the counts given in *Bracton*.[43] A majority, however, are in the third person: the form appropriate to a serjeant speaking on his client's behalf. This is also the form used throughout the pleading manual *Brevia Placitata* which was composed shortly before 1260.[44] It cannot be assumed that the third person speaking on the litigant's behalf is necessarily a serjeant rather than an attorney, but the dangers of using an attorney to speak in court as well as to appear for the litigant, which are graphically illustrated by the case of 1261,[45] provide good reason for thinking that most litigants employed a serjeant as well as an attorney and thus that the third-person formula used in the count in almost all cases does represent a serjeant speaking.[46] It may also be noted that the author of *Hengham Magna*, a brief legal treatise written during the 1260s, assumes as a matter of course that when a defendant in the action of right for land appears at Westminster to ask for a view of the land in dispute, he will employ a serjeant.[47]

Even if most litigants at Westminster now used the services of a 'serjeant', was that serjeant always a professional, someone making a career and a living out of speaking for litigants in the court? In the early 1220s there is certainly some evidence of men acting as serjeants who seem to be amateurs. They are men who come from the same area as the litigants for whom they act and who are not otherwise recorded acting as attorneys or sureties. The *Robert of Sudbury* who was amerced for 'speaking falsely and lying' in Trinity term 1220 had probably been acting as serjeant for the man who stood surety for the amercement. He was probably being penalized for attempting to deceive the court in the interests of his 'client'.[48] There are no other references on the rolls to Robert, but he probably came from the Sudbury in Suffolk which is only eight miles north of Pebmarsh, the village where the litigant was seeking property. Equally obscure is the *Ralph of Bardfield* recorded as having spoken for the defendant in a dower case concerning land at Finchingfield in Essex in Michaelmas term 1221. He was amerced 'for speaking foolishly'. Again it was the client who stood surety for the amercement; what was being penalized was the client's decision to change from pleading against the claim to vouching to warranty.[49] Once more we may suspect a purely local connection between the parties. Great Bardfield is the next village to Finchingfield. The absence of later evidence for the use of such 'amateur' serjeants in the Common Bench does not prove that they were never used there but it does suggest that their use had become uncommon. All our later evidence shows what seem to be regular professional serjeants acting in the court and it may well be that as early as the 1220s it had become the normal practice for litigants to employ their services.

Identifiable Common Bench serjeants of Henry III's reign

Of the first half of the reign (1216–44) In his account of Hubert de Burgh's trial before the king's council in 1239, Matthew Paris, the St Alban's chronicler, speaks of Hubert being forced to rely on his steward, master Laurence of St Alban's, because the king had already obtained for himself the services of 'all' of the serjeants of the Common Bench.[50] This suggests that by 1239 there was a recognizable group of regular and presumably professional serjeants practising in the court. It also suggests that this group was a fairly small one. We have already encountered two of the professional serjeants who practised in the court during the first half of Henry III's reign: Matthew of Bigstrup and John Bucuinte.[51] Incidental references on the plea-rolls allow us to identify another three professional serjeants of the period with reasonable certainty and to suggest that two others were probably members of the group.

In 1228 *John de Planaz* was amerced when his client disavowed the count which he made for him in an action of right.[52] John was appointed an attorney in the Common Bench in 1225, 1228, 1230 and again in 1242[53] and the pattern of his activity as a surety between 1230 and 1242 is also congruent with a career as a professional lawyer between those dates.[54]

It was *Richard de Hotot*'s client who was amerced in 1244 for avowing the count which Richard had made for him.[55] Richard is likewise to be found acting as an attorney in the Common Bench in cases of 1226, 1230 and 1239,[56] and the pattern of his activity as a surety in that court and in the court of King's Bench between 1223 and 1244 suggests he may have pursued a career as a professional lawyer between those dates.[57] Indeed, his position among the witnesses to a quitclaim in favour of the clerk Robert of Thornborough made during the course of the 1247 Buckinghamshire eyre suggests that he was still then in practice, for the other witnesses include three of the four eyre justices and at least two other professional serjeants.[58]

The evidence is less conclusive in the case of *Stephen of the Strand*. In 1220 Stephen was amerced for 'speaking foolishly'.[59] This was not an offence committed only by serjeants but a series of other references link him with activity in the court and suggest he may have been a professional serjeant. Between 1219 and 1234 he was appointed on at least 19 separate occasions to act as an attorney for litigants there, commonly to receive final concords for them or to hear judgment on their behalf.[60] He was even more active during the same period as a surety.[61] He is also to be found among the 'official' witnesses to a deed enrolled on the plea-roll in 1230 in favour of the Common Bench justice, Robert of Lexington.[62] But Stephen was more than just a professional lawyer. In 1226 he was one of the royal envoys sent to Rome[63] and was appointed to take measures against Flemish merchants.[64]

A similar pattern of legal activity suggests that at least two others not specifically identified as professional serjeants of the Common Bench may have been so. *Peter of Bramford* (*'Brumford'*) was appointed an attorney on at least 11 occasions between 1221 and 1230[65] but thereafter is to be found so acting only in 1237 in the rather special role of king's attorney.[66] Peter was certainly present in the court on at least four occasions between 1230 and 1242 when he served as surety for litigants there.[67] He also appears first among the 'official' witnesses to a deed of *c.*1245 in favour of the Common Bench clerk, John Weyland,[68] and among a similar group of witnesses to a grant by Richard of Havering, a serjeant, to Thomas of Ramsden, also probably a serjeant, and his wife Isabel of *c.*1253.[69] *Reyner* or *Reynold*[70] *of Bungay* was likewise appointed as the attorney of litigants in the Common Bench on at least 20 occasions between 1219 and 1234[71] and during the same period acted on many occasions as a surety.[72] He continued to stand surety for litigants in the court for some years after he had ceased to be appointed as an attorney, down to 1241 at least, probably while acting as a serjeant.[73] Other evidence consonant with his having been a serjeant includes the pension of 40 shillings a year he received from Canterbury cathedral priory between 1231 and 1246[74] and another pension of similar value he was being paid by Ramsey abbey in 1242–3.[75]

It is possible to trace local connections for all these men. *John de Planaz* was in possession of the manor of Tolworth in Surrey in 1242–3 and seems at one stage to have also held lands at Shoreham in Kent and at Shawford in Surrey.[76] *Richard de Hotot*'s acquisitions, presumably financed from the profits of legal practice, feature prominently in the two volumes of his son Thomas which have been edited by Edmund King.[77] Richard's father was a senior member of the northern Northamptonshire and Rutland gentry but Richard was probably a younger son of his second marriage. Richard became a substantial landholder at Clapton in Northamptonshire and Turvey in Bedfordshire. His biggest single purchase was one at Clapton in 1248 which cost him 160 marks; his total expenditure on purchases, as recorded by his son, came to just over 400 pounds.[78] *Stephen of the Strand*, as his name suggests, came from the Strand area between London and Westminster. In 1218 he acquired a messuage and other land there and in 1219 he and his wife acquired a further messuage there and five messuages and one acre of land at Aldwych.[79] He is also to be found acquiring rents at Westminster and at Hendon and lands at Tyburn and at Lisson, and may have had an interest in other lands elsewhere in Middlesex.[80] His local connections may explain why he became involved in 1233–4 in supervising the construction of the house of Jewish converts at London.[81]

About *Peter of Bramford*'s property holdings it is difficult to discover much. His initial appearance as an attorney on behalf of Rose of Bramford, wife of Hubert of Bramford and co-heiress to a third of the barony of Southoe in Huntingdonshire, suggests that like Hubert he probably came from Bramford in Suffolk; in 1260 we find his son Richard releasing claims to land there.[82] *Reyner* or *Reynold of Bungay* does not seem to have held any land in Suffolk (the county from which his surname derives) but he is known to have held lands at a number of places in Middlesex.[83] Reyner's wife Phillippa was the co-heiress of Nicholas Duket, who died in possession of a messuage in London (in Vintry) which passed to Reyner and Phillippa.[84] It was also perhaps as a result of his marriage that Reyner became an alderman of the city of London,[85] a sheriff of London and Middlesex[86] and mayor of London.[87] Reyner also seems to have acquired an interest in lands in Wiltshire through his wife.[88]

Of the second half of Henry III's reign (1245–72) More plentiful sources of information allow us to identify a much larger group of professional serjeants from the second half of Henry III's reign, though it is still not possible to trace their careers in any detail or to find more than occasional references to them acting or being described as serjeants.[89] *Nicholas of Lynn* is specifically described as a serjeant (*narrator*) in a pardon granted in 1257 to a man who had been involved in an attack upon him.[90] Nicholas had been appointed to act as an attorney in the Common Bench on at least six different occasions between 1230 and 1242[91] and acted as a surety on a number of occasions between 1230 and 1257 both in the Common Bench and elsewhere.[92] He is also to be found among the 'official' witnesses with connections with the courts who witnessed a deed in favour of the Common Bench clerk John Weyland *c*.1245, among a similar group of witnesses to the 1247 deed in favour of Robert of Thornborough, the *c*.1253 charter of Richard of Havering in favour of Thomas of Ramsden and his wife, and the 1257 charter of William de Stuteville in favour of Castleacre priory.[93] His name is also used by the compiler of the mid-thirteenth century pleading manual *Brevia Placitata*, perhaps in jest, as that of the lord of whom land is held.[94]

Richard of Havering is specifically described as a serjeant in a royal grant of February 1258, probably in order to distinguish him from a contemporary of the same name who was not a serjeant.[95] He is to be found acting as surety in 1250, 1253 and 1261.[96] His status as a 'man of the court' may also be reflected in the unusual amercement entered in a 1262 assize roll against him which is assessed not as usual in money but in the form of 12 partridges.[97] Other evidence of his legal activity comes from an agreement made probably in the course of the 1262 Essex eyre by which Stratford abbey granted him a pension of one mark from the abbot's chamber and four ells of grey cloth for 'diligent regard to their business'.[98]

Robert de Coleville was in trouble in 1267 for having assaulted Robert of Fulham, one of the justices of the Jews, while he was crossing Westminster Hall; the more forthcoming of the two entries that record this episode and its sequel specifically describes him as one of the serjeants of the Common Bench.[99] Robert is also to be found acting as an attorney for a final concord made in 1260 and as surety for the law waged by a litigant in cases of 1261 and 1277.[100]

William de Thornegg is described as a king's serjeant (*serviens regis*) in royal letters patent of 1269.[101] The expression is ambiguous but that William was a serjeant of the Common Bench in the king's service is shown by his appearance with a number of other professional lawyers among those listed as being paid a pension by Ramsey abbey during the 1260s. In 1268 and 1270 he is to be found in company with others (including some of his fellow-serjeants) acting as a surety for persons accused of serious criminal offences.[102] **John of Houghton** is likewise described as a king's serjeant in 1271 when a life exemption from service on assize juries was granted at his request.[103] Again this seems to mean a serjeant of the Common Bench in the king's service for he is to be found suing there on behalf of the king in 1270.[104] **Richard of Boyland** is similarly described as a king's serjeant when a pardon was granted at his request in 1272.[105] Again there is good evidence for him acting as a serjeant on the king's behalf in the Common Bench (though only between 1273 and 1277).[106] He is almost certainly the R. of Boyland mentioned in the report of an unidentified case of *c*.1268–72.[107] Richard had previously acted as an attorney for John of Gaddesden in the 1255 Kent eyre and as the attorney of litigants making final concords in 1259 and 1260.[108] In 1254, 1261 and 1270 he acted as a surety.[109] He, too, was in receipt of a pension of a mark a year from Ramsey abbey during the 1260s and in 1269 was suing the dean and chapter of Chichester for 100 shillings arrears of an annuity of 20 shillings a year, both presumably paid for his services as a serjeant.[110] *John Giffard* appears in a number of law reports belonging to the later part of the reign.[111] He is perhaps the John Giffard of Westminster described as a king's serjeant at whose instance a pardon was granted in 1272.[112]

There is no direct evidence of *John of Pakenham* being described as serjeant but he was suing on the king's behalf in the court in cases in 1262, 1268 and 1270 and in a case in the 1268 Yorkshire eyre, something commonly done by serjeants.[113] He may also be the serjeant mentioned in the report of a case heard in Michaelmas term 1270.[114] In 1260 John claimed a case in King's Bench for hearing in the court of the abbot of Bury St Edmund's and in 1261 he was one of the sureties of the essoiner of the abbot's attorney in the Exchequer.[115] In 1270 he was one of two general attorneys appointed by Adam of Jesmond before setting off on crusade.[116] He, too, is to be found among those in receipt of pensions from Ramsey abbey during the 1260s and also among those in receipt of pensions from Durham priory *c*.1265–72.[117]

Andrew Croc is mentioned in a note included in *Casus Placitorum* in a context which the editor of that text took to refer to him as a litigant. The note refers to the situation which could occur (and according to the note had occurred) in the action of right when the serjeant has omitted part of a count and the litigant has then specifically avowed it. However, Andrew was probably the serjeant who made the mistake and who was avowed and thereby lost the land for his client.[118] Andrew was first appointed as an attorney in 1243.[119] In 1249 and 1250 he was appointed an attorney for the making of final concords and in 1250 twice acted as a surety for litigants waging their law.[120] He is also among the 'official' legal witnesses to the 1247 deed in favour of Robert of Thornborough, among the witnesses to the *c*.1253 grant by Richard of Havering to Thomas of Ramsden and his wife, and among the legal witnesses to a 1258 release by Baldwin de Rivers of certain claims against the abbey of Cirencester.[121] Andrew is also among the group of professional lawyers and others who were in receipt of pensions from Ramsey abbey during the 1260s.[122]

Roger of Boyland, perhaps the father of the serjeant Richard of Boyland, can be found acting as an attorney in the Common Bench on at least 11 occasions between 1232 and 1244. During the 1240s his clients included the king, the royal justice Roger of Thirkleby and the earl of Norfolk.[123] His period of activity as a surety or pledge lasted from 1241 until at least 1250 and took in certain other courts as well. This may suggest that he became a serjeant once he had finished acting as an attorney or that he continued acting as a serjeant after he had stopped acting as an attorney.[124] Other evidence consonant with his having been a serjeant includes his receipt of a pension of 40 shillings a year from Ramsey abbey in 1242–3 and his presence among other 'official' legal witnesses to the 1245 charter in favour of the Common Bench clerk John Weyland and the c.1253 charter of Richard of Havering in favour of Thomas of Ramsden and his wife.[125]

Thomas of Ramsden himself can only be found acting as an attorney in the Common Bench on three occasions between 1233 and 1238, in each case in connection with litigation from his own home county of Essex.[126] I have only noticed him acting as a surety on two occasions, both for the same individual (Thomas fitzAucher) and again both in connection with Essex litigation.[127] But he does appear c.1245 among the 'legal' witnesses to a charter in favour of the clerk John Weyland and c.1240–7 among the witnesses to a charter in favour of the clerk Robert of Thornborough with the serjeant Richard de Hotot, as well as a number of obviously local witnesses.[128] He was also in receipt of an annuity of ten shillings from Ralph of 'Ginges' for whose arrears he sued in the 1254 Essex eyre: litigation that was settled by final concord.[129] *William of Wandsworth* can only be traced acting as an attorney for John of Gaddesden in several pleas in 1243 and for an individual making a fine with the first king's attorney (or serjeant), Laurence del Brok, in 1247.[130] His record as a surety is not much more impressive, though he did act as such on at least four separate occasions between 1242 and 1250.[131] He does, however, also occur among the 'official' legal witnesses to a deed of c.1245 in favour of John Weyland; among a similar group of witnesses to the grant of Richard of Havering to Thomas of Ramsden and his wife of c.1253; and among the witnesses to the grant of an annuity by Stratford abbey to Richard of Havering, probably of 1262.[132] *John of Ramsey* occurs as a serjeant in a number of reports of cases from the earlier part of the reign of Edward I.[133] That he was already a serjeant in the latter part of Henry III's reign is suggested by the fact that he was in receipt of an annual pension of two marks from Canterbury cathedral priory from 1257–8 onwards and of a pension of 20 shillings a year from Ramsey abbey from 1262 onwards.[134] Other evidence consonant with his being a professional serjeant includes his acting in 1268 as surety for an essoin made for Amice countess of Devon.[135]

Nothing is known of the property holdings of three of these men (John Giffard, John of Houghton and William of Wandsworth); though John Giffard perhaps came from Westminster and William from Wandsworth in Surrey.[136] Several other members of the group seem never to have been more than small-scale landowners. The fact that *Robert de Coleville* is described in 1273 and again in 1277 as being of the county of Middlesex suggests that he may be the Robert de Coleville of Westminster who in 1269 acquired a messuage in Westminster with his wife Alice and against whom a messuage in Westminster was unsuccessfully sought by assize of mort d'ancestor but subsequently recovered by writ of entry in 1276.[137] He was probably also the serjeant described in 1265 as being of Buckinghamshire when acting as a surety and who in 1276 was suing with his wife Alice against the earl of Cornwall for her dower from a previous marriage from land in that county.[138]

Nicholas of Lynn seems to have been a minor Norfolk landholder. He held a small area of land at Ickburgh and acquired small areas of land at Wiggenhall.[139] In the 1257 Norfolk eyre he was unsuccessful in an assize of novel disseisin for a plot of land in King's Lynn.[140] The only property his wife Margery is known to have brought him is a rent of half a mark a year at Warham in the same county.[141] The toponymic surname of *Roger of Boyland* was derived from a locality called Boyland now in the parish of Morningthorpe in Norfolk. He had certainly once held land there, for after his death his widow claimed a dower moiety of 15 acres there and at Fritton, also now in the parish of Morningthorpe.[142] Otherwise we know only of an agreement reached in 1250 between him and Henry the chaplain, the brother and heir of John of Stradbroke (in Suffolk), by which Henry granted Roger and his wife Alice one third of the inheritance of his brother John, except for the chief messuage of Stradbroke. However, we do not know how much land was involved and the terms of the grant suggest that the land had still to be recovered by litigation. It seems likely that the grant was made specifically in order to obtain Roger's advice and assistance in the litigation.[143] All we know about another East Anglian serjeant, *William de Thornegg*, is that in 1269 he was in possession of the Suffolk manor of Brookshall, close to Ipswich.[144] *Andrew Croc* paid 20 shillings in 1247 to acquire a messuage in High Wycombe in Buckinghamshire and in 1248 acquired for an unknown consideration six acres of wood there.[145]

Other serjeants of this period, however, were landholders on a more significant scale and seem to have acquired property during the period they were professionally active and perhaps from the profits of that activity. *Richard of Boyland* had begun accumulating property by 1257. In the Norfolk eyre of that year he acquired a small holding at Hapton and Shotesham.[146] In 1260 he added a rather more substantial holding at Wacton[147] and in 1262 a rent of ten shillings at Tasburgh.[148] His first really major acquisition was in the 1268 Suffolk eyre where he and his first wife Helen reached an agreement with Richard of Heacham concerning two messuages and three carucates in eight Suffolk villages. Under the terms of the agreement they were to get immediate possession of part of the tenements and the possession of the remainder at Richard of Heacham's death. The price recorded in the final concord is 200 marks.[149] In 1271 Richard paid out a further 50 marks to acquire a holding at Long Stratton in Norfolk.[150] By the end of Henry III's reign Richard was well on the way to becoming a substantial landholder.

John of Pakenham also appears to have been a substantial landowner though it has proved impossible to recover full details of his holdings. In 1265 he was granted rights of free warren in his demesne lands at Pakenham in Suffolk and in the neighbouring village of Thurston.[151] Earlier (in 1261) he had sued the abbot of Bury St Edmund's for the right to present to the church of Pakenham and in 1270 he claimed the right to present to the church of Dersingham.[152] In 1267 he paid 200 marks to acquire a substantial holding in Hertfordshire.[153] *John of Ramsey* came from Ramsey in Essex and was acquiring lands there in 1257.[154] In 1264 he is mentioned as tenant of a seignory in the neighbouring village of Wrabness[155] and after his death (in 1287–8) his widow sought a dower share of a messuage and a carucate in these two villages against his son.[156] In 1268 he also acquired a messuage at Ipswich in Suffolk.[157] His first wife Agnes was one of six heiresses of Robert de Grymylles and brought him one sixth of the Suffolk manor of Saxmundham and various other properties in that county.[158] The messuage in Southwark which they sold for 60 marks in 1272 was perhaps a joint acquisition rather than property she had inherited from her father.[159]

Richard of Havering, sometimes known as Richard de Ulmis, needs to be distinguished from two contemporaries of the same name who were themselves father and son. Richard de Ulmis of Havering, the serjeant, first appears in the records in 1234 when his title to 44 acres of land at Havering was challenged by quo waranto brought in the name of the king. On showing insufficient title the land was taken into the king's hand and the land then granted out again at the request of Henry III's sister, Eleanor countess of Pembroke, to her servant Richard of Havering, one of the serjeant's contemporary namesakes.[160] Not much later he acquired the remainder of a 40-year lease of a messuage and half a virgate at Havering from the lessee and then the reversion from the lessor.[161] It may have been the same land (though differently described) that Richard subsequently granted together with a rent of 36 shillings to Thomas of Ramsden and his wife Isabel by a deed witnessed by two royal justices and several other Common Bench serjeants amongst others.[162] The same land may also have been involved when in 1253 Richard settled a substantial holding in Havering on them in return for a grant of a messuage and a carucate of land at three places in Somerset.[163] However, this transaction was subsequently called into question. In February 1258 the king agreed that if he could prove his right to the land which Richard of Havering *narrator* had formerly possessed in Romford (part of Havering) and which Richard had given to Thomas of Ramsden, he would give the land to William de St Ermine and his heirs by charter. There is an endorsement on the 1253 final concord noting that it had been cancelled by order of the king because the land was part of the king's demesne.[164] To judge from the dower claims made by his widow Christine after Richard's death in 1277, the bulk of the holding (and perhaps of other lands Richard had once held in Havering) seems to have ended up with the master of Hornchurch whom she sued for a dower third of property once held by her husband in Havering and in the neighbouring village of Rainham.[165] The land acquired by Richard in Somerset in 1253 was probably augmented through a further final concord of 1256 but in 1258 he exchanged these lands for life tenure of other lands at Long Crichel in Dorset.[166] Christine's dower claims after Richard's death indicate that at some stage Richard may also have held a rent at Kingston on Thames and a sizeable holding at Lambeth in Surrey.[167]

Thomas of Ramsden certainly held lands in the Essex village from which he derived his name; but our only real evidence as to their extent is the dower claim of his son's widow in 1284 which claimed a third share of a sizeable holding not just in Ramsden itself but also in three other neighbouring villages.[168] It is impossible to be certain whether or not the son had added to (or indeed subtracted from) his father's holding; but it seems possible that his father's holding in these villages was of about the same size. We can certainly see from 1240 onwards Thomas's steady process of accumulation of property in the Essex countryside. In the 1240 Essex eyre he paid 60 marks to acquire rents amounting to just under five pounds a year in eight Essex villages and in the 1240 Sussex eyre a further ten marks to acquire 20 acres in the village of Downham.[169] In 1244 he is said to have paid only 40 shillings to acquire a holding of a messuage and 110 acres in five Essex villages, together with rents amounting to 25 shillings and sixpence in a further three villages.[170] Before 1248 he had also acquired a holding of 30 acres at Shenfield.[171] In 1248 he acquired for nine marks a rent of one mark at Little Waltham in the county.[172] In or before 1253, as we have already seen, he acquired lands at Havering from Richard of Havering in exchange for lands in Somerset. Some of these lands may have been recovered by the king; others seem to have passed before 1271 to Roger Loveday.[173] In 1255 he made what seems to have been his last substantial acquisition, this time in Hertfordshire, when he paid 28 marks to acquire a holding of two-thirds of a messuage and 80 acres at Shenley.[174] Thomas is also of interest as the only one of these later serjeants to have held local government office, serving as sheriff of Essex from 22 November 1256 to 3 April 1257.

The professional serjeants active in the Common Bench had become a recognizable and cohesive group by the final years of the reign. This much is clear from the sequel to the assault made by Robert de Coleville, one of their number, on Robert of Fulham, one of the justices of the Jews.[175] The assailant was eventually persuaded to appear as a humble suppliant before the treasurer and barons of the exchequer and the justices of the Common Bench to make a full and total submission to his victim. Honour having been satisfied, the two men were then reconciled by a kiss of peace. The mediators who were responsible for bringing the two men together and ensuring their reconciliation were not some *ad hoc* group of peacemakers but Robert de Coleville's fellow-serjeants, his colleagues (*socii*) as the record calls them, apparently acting together as a body.[176]

Professional serjeants in other royal courts

Less can be discovered of the activity of professional serjeants in other royal courts during Henry III's reign. We have already noted evidence that the king employed the services of the serjeants of the Common Bench when bringing charges against Hubert de Burgh before the king's council in 1239 and that Hubert was forced to make do with the services of his own steward. This suggests that there was no separate corps of professional serjeants in King's Bench or other royal courts.[177] Evidence from 1253 suggests that major litigants in King's Bench were then still using the services of non-professional serjeants. In that year Abel de St Martin was amerced when disavowed by his brother Laurence de St Martin, bishop of Rochester, in the course of litigation brought against the bishop by the archbishop of Canterbury.[178] There is no reason to suppose that Abel regularly acted for litigants in the court but he did act as his brother's agent on a number of occasions both before and after 1253 and it was clearly as such that he spoke for his brother on this occasion.[179]

The court of King's Bench was, however, also the main place of operation of the first professional lawyer to be employed on a regular basis by the English Crown, **Laurence del Brok**.[180] Laurence was granted a salary of 20 pounds a year 'for suing the king's affairs of his pleas before him' in August 1247.[181] Thereafter he was paid ten pounds twice a year, normally in January and in June or July of each year, until July 1262.[182] Although Laurence's main sphere of activity was King's Bench he also acted on the king's behalf in the Common Bench not just before his permanent retainer by the king in 1243 but also between 1259 and 1263 and perhaps also at other times.[183] Laurence has commonly been described by legal historians as the king's attorney, for he is recorded on the rolls as suing on the king's behalf in a way reminiscent of other attorneys who sue on behalf of their clients. It seems probable, however, that Laurence was more than just an attorney and also acted as the king's serjeant in those cases in which he represented the king.[184] It seems possible that he was also employed as a serjeant by other litigants. Certainly he was in receipt of retainers from a number of patrons of the kind that serjeants commonly received: of as much as 100 shillings a year from the abbey of Glastonbury; of perhaps 20 shillings a year from Ramsey abbey and of 40 shillings a year from Durham cathedral priory.[185] Also consonant with an extensive private practice as a serjeant is the large amount of money he had available for the purchase of land. The total sum specifically recorded in the various deeds and final concords recording those acquisitions between 1241 and 1271 amounts to over 1,000 pounds.[186]

Professional serjeants were also being employed by litigants in the General Eyre during Henry III's reign. It can have been no coincidence that when the clerk Robert of Thornborough wanted witnesses to a deed made in his favour during the 1247 Buckinghamshire eyre he was able to secure not just two of the justices holding the session but also at least three Common Bench serjeants. They were clearly not there just to witness his deed.[187] The earliest surviving deed of retainer of a Common Bench serjeant, that between Richard of Havering and the priory of Stratford, was probably made during the 1262 Essex eyre. From it we can certainly deduce his presence at the eyre. It can also be assumed that his services were available to litigants there.[188] A Peterborough chronicler writing about the 1263 Lincolnshire eyre speaks of the large expenses and great liberalities the abbot of Peterborough was put to in respect not only of the justices but also of the serjeants and others of the county.[189] For the following Lincolnshire eyre, which took place at the end of Henry III's reign in 1272, we have two surviving law reports. One was printed by Dunham in *Casus Placitorum* and does not identify the serjeants who are speaking.[190] The other identifies two of the speakers. They are (Gilbert of) Thornton, subsequently prominent as a serjeant in the Common Bench and as a king's serjeant on eyre, and 'Pageman', probably the John of Pakenham who was a Common Bench serjeant in the latter part of Henry III's reign.[191]

PROFESSIONAL ATTORNEYS IN THE KING'S COURTS DURING HENRY III'S REIGN

The professional attorney is a much more elusive figure during this period. By *c.*1260, at the latest, however, he is observable in the record of appointments of attorneys in the Common Bench plea-rolls. At least eight attorneys who can reasonably be described as 'professional' were functioning in the court at this time.[192] *Richer* (sometimes *Richard*) *of Colchester* was appointed as an attorney in three different cases in Michaelmas term 1258, in another three cases in Hilary term 1259, in one further case in Hilary term 1260 and in two cases in Easter term 1260.[193] Four out of the nine cases come from his own home county of Essex. He is also to be found around the same time acting for a litigant making a final concord with the abbot of St John's Colchester and a little earlier (in 1256) being appointed one of two attorneys of the bishop of Lincoln for litigation with the king in the court of King's Bench.[194] *John of Easton* was appointed as an attorney in three cases in Michaelmas term 1258, in two cases in Hilary term 1259, in four cases in Hilary term 1260 and in five cases in Easter term 1260.[195] Five of these 14 cases come from Norfolk; a further three from Suffolk. Other evidence of his activity in the courts comes from the 1257 Norfolk eyre where he acted as surety for a litigant's champion and the 1262 Essex eyre where he was amerced in company with the future serjeant, John of Quy.[196] In 1270 he was appointed as a general attorney of Richard de la Rokele when Richard went on crusade.[197] *John fitzWilliam* was appointed as an attorney in five cases in Michaelmas term 1258, in another five cases in Hilary term 1259, in two cases in Hilary term 1260 and in five cases in Easter term 1260.[198] There seems to be no particular regional or county bias in his activity. At around the same time he is also to be found being appointed by a litigant to hear judgment for him in a case in the court of King's Bench.[199]

Another professional attorney is *John of Harpley*. John was appointed attorney in two cases in Michaelmas term 1258, in two cases in Hilary term 1259, in one case in Hilary term 1260 and in six cases in Easter term 1260.[200] Unlike the other professional attorneys John was also active in other central courts. He was appointed attorney for one case in the court of King's Bench in Michaelmas term 1260, for one case in the Exchequer of Pleas in Hilary term 1260 and for two further cases there in Easter term 1261.[201] Whenever it is possible to read the county from which these cases come, it is John's home county of Norfolk. *William of Skutterskelfe* is another of this small group of professional attorneys. He was twice appointed as an attorney for litigation in Michaelmas term 1258, appointed once in Hilary term 1259, four times in Hilary term 1260 and twice in Easter term 1260.[202] He also appears as an attorney in the Exchequer of Pleas, once in Hilary term 1261 and once in the following Easter term.[203] Four of these appointments are for litigation from his own home county of Yorkshire, a further two for litigation from the neighbouring county of Nottinghamshire. Final concords also show him acting for John of Everingham in connection with a Lincolnshire final concord in 1255 and for a number of clients for Yorkshire final concords between 1260 and 1265.[204]

John of Wandsworth also appears from the frequency of his appearances to have been a professional attorney. In Michaelmas term 1258 he was appointed to act in four cases, in Hilary term 1259 in another four and in Easter 1260 in some seven cases.[205] John was still being appointed as an attorney in Trinity term 1272, in Hilary term 1277, in Easter term 1278, in Michaelmas term 1278 and as late as Easter, Trinity and Michaelmas terms in 1282.[206] *Reginald* (sometimes *Roger*) *of St Alban's* was appointed attorney in four cases in Michaelmas term 1258, two cases in Hilary term 1259, three cases in Hilary term 1260 and two cases in Easter term 1260.[207] He also appears once as an attorney in the Exchequer of Pleas, in Easter term 1260.[208] *Robert of Wolmersdon ('Wolmereston')* is the final member of this small group. He was appointed attorney in one case in Michaelmas 1258, in three cases in Hilary term 1259, in one case in Hilary term 1260 and in five cases in Easter term 1260.[209] Four of these cases are from his own home county of

Somerset. Other evidence of his legal activity is to be found in his appointment to act as an attorney for a Somerset litigant at an assize session held before Bratton at Lambeth in 1254 and in his presence among 12 mainpernors of a man who was to be tried at the king's suit in Michaelmas term 1261.[210]

PROFESSIONAL LAWYERS OF HENRY III'S REIGN OUTSIDE THE KING'S COURTS

Outside the royal courts there is clear evidence of professional lawyers only in the courts of the city of London. As early as 1244 legislation was enacted prohibiting those who had spoken on behalf of litigants in the city courts (*advocatus aut placitator*) from subsequently taking any part in the making or giving of judgments in such cases.[211] However, it is not absolutely clear that we are dealing here with professional lawyers. Subsequent legislation enacted in 1259 certainly is.[212] One clause made it illegal for any serjeant (*causidicus*) who practised in the city courts to agree to act for a litigant in return for a share of the tenement or land that was at stake. The penalty on conviction was for the serjeant not just to lose the share thereby acquired but also to be suspended from office. A further clause of the same legislation, as it is reported by the London chronicler, Arnulf fitzThedmar, provided that litigants would not in future need to have a serjeant in any plea in the city courts, except pleas of the crown, pleas about land and pleas of replevin. Litigants were to make their claim or their defence in person and in their own words and the courts were to give judgment accordingly. FitzThedmar seems here to be conflating the legislation and its intended results. What the legislation probably said was simply that in all types of litigation, other than those specifically excepted, the formalities of pleading hitherto observed were no longer to be required, though perhaps only if the parties actually spoke for themselves. It was merely the intended result that the use of serjeants should in future become unnecessary. In practice, the serjeants of London seem to have survived the blow. As will be seen, they were clearly a well-established and well-accepted feature of the city courts in Edward I's reign.[213] One other piece of London legislation from Henry III's reign seems to indicate a wish to draw clear boundary-lines between the different parts of the fledgeling legal profession. A provision enacted in the hustings in 1264 forbade any serjeant (*advocatus*) from acting as an essoiner, whether in the husting or in other courts of the city.[214]

Another piece of evidence may show the existence of local professional serjeants in East Anglia as early as 1242. In this year the accounts of Ramsey abbey record a payment of 13 shillings and four pence (one mark) to two serjeants at Norwich.[215] However, what is not made clear is in which court the two serjeants had been acting. Conceivably, it was the city court of Norwich.

More plausibly it was the Norfolk county court. Just possibly it was a royal court: a session of assize justices or the like. In any case the evidence is too unclear to allow us to draw any firm deductions.

EXPLANATIONS FOR THE EMERGENCE OF PROFESSIONAL LAWYERS IN HENRY III'S REIGN

The disappearance of such restrictions on the use of serjeants as may have existed in the early twelfth century enabled litigants to use professional serjeants but did not in itself make them or even necessarily encourage them to do so. The changes that made it possible for litigants to appoint whom they liked as their attorneys were likewise clearly an essential preliminary to the emergence of the professional attorney but did not in itself cause that emergence. The emergence of a recognizable group of professional serjeants in the Common Bench early in Henry III's reign is probably to be related in part to some of the special characteristics of the new royal courts in general, in part to the special characteristics of this particular court. The new type of royal court in which almost all litigants were 'outsiders', both in the sense of having no social or family links to the judges and in the sense of their being ignorant of the law and custom followed in and constantly being reshaped by the court, created a demand for individuals who could act as intermediaries between litigants and the court: men who were in regular attendance at the court and so were familiar with its rules and customs (and perhaps also with its justices) and who were able to advise litigants and represent them in court, particularly at the most difficult stage in legal proceedings: the pleading stage. Thus the most pressing demand initially was for serjeants, men able and willing to speak for litigants in court. Litigants had to make a deliberate choice and pay extra to bring their litigation in the Common Bench. Thus the litigants of the court were a self-selected group of wealthier litigants able and willing to pay for better justice. This court constituted the ideal market for specialist lawyers offering a service to the wealthier litigant. Its continuous or almost continuous existence (particularly after 1249) and its permanent location at Westminster also gave it an obvious advantage as the focus for the growth of a group of specialist lawyers over the eyre. The eyre was continually on the move, was constantly being organized in new circuits and was by no means always in session. Thus the natural tendency was for the serjeants to be organized and think of themselves as Common Bench serjeants who also offered a service in some eyres rather than eyre serjeants who also offered a service in the Common Bench.

The early emergence of professional serjeants in the courts of the city of London is more difficult to explain. It may have been due to the close proximity of the city courts to Westminster. The Common Bench offered an obvious model, and its serjeants could easily have made their services available in the city courts as well as in the Common Bench. A number of the early serjeants came from the London area and were in a good position to benefit from this connection. The London courts may also have resembled the Common Bench in offering a considerable pool of wealthy litigants keen to take advantage of the services of serjeants, and in being courts which most litigants themselves did not regularly attend.

The emergence of a recognizable group of fully professional Common Bench attorneys was probably retarded by the fact that service as an attorney was for long not commonly seen as requiring any particular professional skills. An agreement of 1228, for example, between Essex litigants that brought a peaceful end to one piece of litigation between them and contemplated the cooperation of the parties in other litigation against an unnamed third party, envisaged that if an attorney was appointed for this litigation it would be from among the men of those making the agreement, not some professional stranger, though clearly both parties were interested in winning the litigation.[216] There were good reasons for litigants to appoint attorneys, particularly if they were plaintiffs in litigation. For most litigants a journey to court at Westminster was slow, inconvenient and possibly dangerous. A single piece of litigation would normally require a number of such journeys. But as long as the job was not seen as requiring any special skill there was no reason for litigants to use a professional rather than a relative or servant.

The emergence of the professional attorney may also have been retarded, initially, at least, by the willingness of the professional serjeants to act on occasion when required as attorneys. This seems only to have ceased to be the case during the second half of the thirteenth century. But two other factors were crucial to the emergence of the professional attorney in the Common Bench by c.1260. One was that there should be enough litigation from particular areas of the country for a professional attorney who came from one of these when offering his services to several clients to be able to offer a significantly cheaper service than his amateur competitor. It was the increase in business in the Common Bench (the probable quadrupling of business there between 1200 and 1260) that helps to explain the emergence of the professional attorney there. Certainly, as we have seen, of the very small group of attorneys active in the court c.1260, four out of eight took a majority of their business from their own home county or that county and one other neighbouring county; John of Harpley seems even to have taken all his business from his own home county. The second factor was a growing recognition by litigants of the value of having the assistance of a professional attorney to deal with the complexities of the processes of the court.

5

The English Legal Profession in Edward I's Reign (I): the Size of the Profession

The reign of Edward I brings a massive increase in the amount of information available about professional lawyers. In this chapter I begin a general survey of the Edwardian legal profession by looking at the numbers of professional lawyers practising in England in this period.

THE COMMON BENCH

Serjeants

The first surviving Anglo-Norman reports of litigation in the Common Bench (forerunners of the Year-Book reports) belong to the final years of the reign of Henry III.[1] Similar reports constitute one of our two main sources of information (and before 1293 the main source of information) on the serjeants practising in the court during the reign of Edward I.[2] For the period before 1290 most of these reports are as yet unprinted though I am currently in the process of editing them for publication by the Selden Society.[3] The limited quantity of surviving reports and their uneven chronological spread means there is little point in attempting to compile a year by year list of serjeants practising in the court for this period.[4] What is feasible is the compilation of lists of serjeants known to have practised in the court over rather longer periods. These show that at least 12 and perhaps as many as 14 serjeants were active during the period before Thomas Weyland became chief justice of the court (1273–8);[5] at least 12 men were active as serjeants between the time of Weyland's appointment in the summer of 1278 and the end of 1284;[6] and a minimum of 19 and perhaps as many as 23 men were active as serjeants between 1285 and the end of 1289.[7]

From 1290 there is a sizeable increase in the number of surviving reports. Some were edited by A. J. Horwood for the Rolls Series in the second half of the nineteenth century but most still await the work of an editor who will match the undated reports with the corresponding plea-roll enrolments and check the dated reports in unedited collections with the terms to which the manuscripts assign them.[8] Not long after 1290 we also gain a second major source of information on the serjeants practising there. When two parties to litigation wanted to make a final concord (an agreement made under the auspices of the court and recorded in a tripartite chirograph of which the third section was kept for safe-keeping in the royal treasury) they required royal permission to do so. The court's plea-rolls had long recorded the payment proffered to the king for that permission and accepted on the king's behalf by the justices. During the course of Michaelmas term 1293, in around mid-October, the entries recording the proffer and acceptance of these fines suddenly began to include an entirely new clause, noting that the parties had their chirograph by (*per*) a particular named individual who is their serjeant (*narratorem suum*). Thereafter the new clause is commonly (though not at first invariably) included as part of such entries.[9] From 1290 onwards it becomes possible to provide figures for the total number of serjeants operating in the court each year and these are given in table 5.1. Except in those years where the figures are clearly incomplete (1290, 1291, 1293) the totals vary only over a fairly restricted range, from a low of 25 in 1299 to a high of 35 in 1296; the average (excluding the years where the figures appear to be incomplete) is just over 30.

Overall, then, the picture seems to be one of a surprising degree of stability in the size of the body of Common Bench serjeants. The comparatively low figures for the numbers of serjeants in the court before 1285 (maxima of 14 and 12) are probably no more than a reflection of the imperfections of our evidence during these periods, though they may also indicate that a rather smaller group of serjeants then practised in the court. The maximum of 23 for the period 1285–90[10] is close to the minimum figure for the period after 1290 and suggests that although there may have been some growth in the numbers of serjeants after 1290 it was not a large one.

Attorneys

Although there are a few specific references on the plea-rolls of the Common Bench to professional attorneys practising in the court[11] there are no comprehensive lists of them. Our only reliable information, both on their numbers and as to the pattern of their professional activity, is that which can be derived from the separate sections of the plea-rolls which record individual

Table 5.1 Total number of serjeants active in the Common Bench, 1290–1307

Year	Total number of serjeants
1290	13[1]
1291	15[2]
1292	27
1293	21[3]
1294	32
1295	34
1296	35
1267	32
1298	31
1299	25
1300	30
1301	29
1302	29
1303	29
1304	29
1305	33
1306	30
1307	28

Notes
1. Figures probably incomplete: based on 10 identified reports.
2. Figures probably incomplete: based on 23 identified reports.
3. Figures probably incomplete: based on 28 identified reports and final concord references for part of Michaelmas term only.

appointments of attorneys for particular litigation by clients. Reading and analysing all the recorded appointments for the reign would be a massive (and very tedious) task. I have attempted to gain a general picture of attorney appointments by analysing the appointments recorded on the rolls for two complete years, one near the beginning of the reign (1280) and the other close to the end (1300). The disadvantage of using 1280 is that it is a year when the General Eyre was in progress. This means that litigation from counties where the eyre was being held or had recently been held is under-represented on the rolls, and probably means that several professional attorneys specializing in work from the counties concerned who might otherwise have appeared are excluded. This makes direct comparison with 1300 difficult and in certain respects misleading. On the other hand 1280 is representative of many years in the earlier part of the reign precisely because it does show us the Common Bench at a time when a General Eyre was in progress. The year 1300 is also problematic, but in a different way. It was when the court was holding sessions at York rather than at its more normal home of Westminster. Almost certainly this means that a higher proportion of business was coming from the north of England than was true when the court was based at Westminster. It probably also means that more business was going to northern attorneys. Again, however, it is not atypical of its period, for the court was at York for almost six years between Hilary term 1299 and Trinity term 1304.

It was certainly still possible as late as 1300 for a litigant to appoint as his attorney for litigation in the Common Bench someone who was not a professional attorney. The attorney sections of the plea-rolls for both 1280 and 1300 yield examples of wives appointing their husbands as their attorneys and even the occasional husband appointing his wife; of mothers and fathers appointing their sons and occasionally their daughters; of other litigants appointing as their attorneys persons who from their names appear to be close relatives; and of the heads of religious houses appointing monks or canons belonging to those houses. In all these cases we are clearly dealing with non-professional attorneys. Such appointments, however, constitute only a small minority of the total. In 1280 they represent no more than about 3 per cent of the total and by 1300 only just over 1 per cent.

These are the easy cases, the obviously non-professional attorneys. Equally easy to categorize are the indubitably professional attorneys. In 1280 three attorneys each had 60 or more appointments to his credit[12] and there are a further six men for whom 40 or more appointments are recorded.[13] Between them these nine men account for around 10 per cent of all the appointments recorded. By 1300 the top two attorneys each had over 70 appointments to their credit[14] and there were now also a further 11 men for whom 40 or more appointments are recorded.[15] Between them these 13 men again account for just over 10 per cent of all appointments recorded in this year: the growth in their number of appointments simply reflects the growth in litigation in the interim.[16]

Such men were exceptionally busy, even for professional attorneys: for to these cases, if we are to gauge the total case-load of each attorney, must be added those cases still continuing from previous years. Also fairly clearly full-time attorneys and professional lawyers are the much larger group of individuals appointed to act in ten or more cases in each of these years. In 1280 there were nine further attorneys for whom a total of between 30 and 39 appointments are recorded (who between them account for around 7 per cent of all recorded appointments); 26 attorneys for whom a total of between 20 and 29 appointments are recorded (who between them account for around 13 per cent of all recorded appointments); and 57 attorneys for whom a total of between ten and 19 appointments are recorded (who between them account for around 16 per cent of all recorded appointments). The comparable figures for 1300 are 26 attorneys for whom a total of between 30 and 39 appointments

Table 5.2 Numbers of persons appointed as attorneys for fewer than ten cases in the Common Bench in 1280 and 1300 who are not readily identifiable as close connections of their principals

Number of appointments	Numbers appointed (percentages of all attorneys appointed in brackets)	
	1280	1300
9	12 (2)	15 (2)
8	16 (3)	18 (2)
7	22 (3)	26 (3)
6	17 (2)	20 (2)
5	30 (3)	43 (2)
4	51 (4)	46 (3)
3	86 (5)	84 (4)
2	203 (9)	160 (2)
1	883 (18)	607 (9)

are recorded (accounting for around 13 per cent of all recorded appointments); 51 attorneys for whom a total of between 20 and 29 appointments are recorded (accounting for around 18 per cent of all recorded appointments); and 120 attorneys for whom between ten and 19 appointments are recorded (accounting for around 24 per cent of all recorded appointments in this year). In all, the 102 attorneys recorded in 1280 as being appointed in ten or more cases between them account for less than half (46 per cent) of all appointments recorded on the rolls. By contrast their 210 counterparts of 1300 account for almost two-thirds (65 per cent) of the total.

Our real difficulty comes with the men who were appointed in fewer than ten cases. This is a large group, though one whose membership is heavily weighted numerically in both 1280 and 1300 towards those appointed in only one or two cases, as table 5.2 clearly demonstrates. Are all or some of these men to be regarded as professional attorneys? There is certainly some evidence to suggest that a dividing line between professionals and semi-professionals and amateurs drawn at ten appointments in one particular year may be too high. The Robert of Burton appointed as an attorney in 1300 in only four cases is probably the man of the same name who was supended from acting as a professional attorney in the Common Bench in 1292 but who subsequently returned to professional practice[17] while the William of Cottenham who was appointed only five times as an attorney in 1300 was enough of a professional to have been paid a salary in 1303 by the executors of no less a figure than the bishop of London for his services as an attorney to the bishop and his executors.[18] The John son of Robert of Marske appointed as an attorney only five times in 1300 is also to be found suing a client in 1305 for money owed for his services.[19] Our group also contains a number of individuals who were sufficiently active as attorneys in other royal courts to leave little doubt that they were professional attorneys: thus William of Grantchester, who was only appointed once as an attorney in the Common Bench in 1300, was appointed no less than 35 times as an attorney in the Exchequer in the same year and is thus indubitably a full-time, professional attorney. But if we are to try to draw any kind of dividing line between professionals and semi-professionals, it is probably as well to draw it at a point that is a little too high rather than too low; and ten appointments in the course of the year seems as good an arbitrary point to do this as any other, subject to the caveat that it is not intended to imply that those below this line were not professionals, merely that we can be reasonably certain that those above this line were. Our overall figure of 102 for the number of professional attorneys active in the Common Bench in 1280 and 210 for the number of professional attorneys active in the same court in 1300 should therefore be taken as a minimum figure for the number of professional attorneys at both dates.

By 1300 a majority of those attorneys who were indubitably professional drew a majority of their business (but not all of it) from a single county. Such a pattern is typical of almost two-thirds of such attorneys.[20] In 1280 such a pattern of activity was much less common: only around one-third of the indubitably professional attorneys drew a majority of their business from a single county.[21] This figure may, however, be somewhat distorted by the absence of Yorkshire business. Only a small number of attorneys drew all their business from a single county. It is difficult to calculate the figures for 1280 with any certainty because damage to individual membranes of the plea-rolls means it is not always possible to know to which county a particular appointment should be assigned. Erring on the generous side, however, still provides us with no more than about 7 per cent of the total number of clearly professional attorneys whose business is or may be drawn from a single county.[22] The proportion had grown only marginally (to around 8 per cent) by 1300.

The author of *Hengham Magna*, writing in the 1260s, had advised litigants that they should always appoint two attorneys to avoid the serious consequences of a single attorney falling sick, dying or deceiving his client.[23] In 1280 almost half the litigants appointing attorneys took this advice, but around the same proportion, despite the possible dangers, only appointed one. By 1300 there had been a decisive shift against the practice and almost 70 per cent of all entries record the appointment of a single attorney. The overall figures mask a considerable variation in practice from county to county. In

1280, for example, there is a marked bias towards the appointment of single attorneys for litigation from Norfolk, Cumberland and Devon, while there is a marked bias in the opposite direction for litigation from Suffolk, Lancashire, Middlesex and Oxfordshire. Even more noticeably in 1300 the normal preference for the appointment of just a single attorney is reversed when it comes to litigants from the western counties of Cornwall and Somerset and the northern counties of Cumberland and Westmorland who, unlike the general body of litigants, more commonly appointed two attorneys to represent them than just one. At both dates it was uncommon, but not wholly unknown, to appoint more than two attorneys. Such appointments account for around 3 per cent of all recorded appointments in 1280 but less than 1 per cent in 1300.[24]

THE COURT OF KING'S BENCH

Serjeants

Not enough reports survive from the court of King's Bench to allow us to follow year by year the serjeants active there. Nor are there any alternative sources of information that will enable us to do this. Of the two reports of cases in this court belonging to a date before 1290, one shows us men acting as serjeants found in other reports acting as serjeants of the Common Bench or of the Eyre[25] but the other shows two serjeants who are not known to have so acted in other royal courts.[26] Both are identified in the report solely by their surnames (Cave and Ashbourne). These are names borne by more than one attorney active in the court during this period and we may assume that it is two of the erstwhile attorneys who are acting as serjeants in this case.[27] However, it is unclear whether the individuals concerned had ceased to act as attorneys and had become full-time serjeants or whether they acted in both capacities at the same time.[28] It was also before 1290 that William of Wells was hired to act for clients in this court.[29] He is not someone encountered among the serjeants active in other courts, nor was he one of the court's regular attorneys.

At least 15 reports survive of cases heard in King's Bench during the period after 1290.[30] Nineteen individuals appear as serjeants in them. Without exception they are also men who appear during the same period as serjeants of the Common Bench.[31] It is possible that other serjeants continued to act in the court but that the surviving reports do not reflect this fact. It seems more probable that the reports reflect the underlying reality that by the second half of the reign the serjeants of the Common Bench had come to dominate, perhaps even in practice to monopolize, the provision of service to clients in King's Bench.

Attorneys

In King's Bench as in the Common Bench there are no lists of professional attorneys practising in the court and the names of professional attorneys have to be derived from analysis of attorney appointments recorded on the plea-rolls. To allow comparison with the Common Bench such appointments were analysed for two similar specimen years: 1280 (as in the Common Bench) and 1299 (chosen in place of 1300, since two of the King's Bench plea-rolls for 1300 are missing).

The proportion of obviously non-professional attorneys appointed in King's Bench seems to have been marginally higher than in the Common Bench in both years: around 6 per cent (as compared with only 3 per cent) in 1280; around 2 per cent in 1299 (as compared with 1 per cent in 1300). The number was still very small. As for the clearly professional attorneys, as we might have expected given the lower volume of business in the court, none of the King's Bench attorneys in either year was quite as busy as their Common Bench counterparts. In 1280 the two busiest attorneys were appointed in 43 and 37 cases respectively,[32] some way behind the busiest attorneys in the Common Bench, three of whom were appointed in 60 or more cases. These two alone between them, however, accounted for around 10 per cent of all attorney appointments. By 1299 the top professional attorney in the court (Geoffrey of Lakenham, for whom 69 appointments are recorded) was still appointed in fewer cases than the two leading Common Bench attorneys, but he was much closer behind them. There were also now a further five attorneys with 40 or more appointments to their credit[33] and these six men between them accounted for just over 30 per cent of the total number of appointments. These were, as in the Common Bench, just the most active of the clearly professional group of attorneys. Its other members in 1280 include two attorneys appointed in 20 or more cases (who between them account for around 6 per cent of all appointments) and seven attorneys appointed in ten or more cases (who between them account for around 13 per cent of all appointments). By 1299 this group had grown. There were now two attorneys for whom 30 or more appointments are recorded (who between them account for around 7 per cent of the total number of appointments); eight attorneys for whom 20 or more appointments are recorded (who between them account for around 22 per cent of the total number of appointments); and ten attorneys for whom ten or more appointments are recorded (who between them account for about 15 per cent of the total number of appointments). Overall, in 1280 the group of 11 clearly professional attorneys with ten or more appointments accounts for a smaller share of all appointments than their counterparts in the Common Bench: 29 per cent of all appointments (as opposed to the 46 per cent of their Common Bench counterparts). By 1299–

Table 5.3 Numbers of persons appointed attorneys for fewer than ten cases in King's Bench in 1280 and 1299 who are not readily identifiable as close connections of their principals

Number of appointments	Numbers appointed (percentage of all attorney appointments they account for in brackets)	
	1280	1299
9	0	0
8	3 (5)	1 (1)
7	3 (4)	0
6	1 (1)	1
5	3 (3)	1
4	5 (4)	4 (2)
3	8 (4)	9 (3)
2	49 (8)	23 (5)
1	271 (34)	120 (13)

1300 the position had been reversed and the 26 attorneys accounted for 74 per cent of the total (as compared with the 65 per cent accounted for by their Common Bench counterparts). As table 5.3 demonstrates, King's Bench also resembles the Common Bench in the way that both in 1280 and in 1299–1300 by far the largest group of persons who were appointed attorneys consisted of persons who were appointed only once; the number appointed only twice is also comparatively large. The figures also resemble those for the Common Bench in demonstrating a major decline in these numbers between 1280 and 1299 (as also in the percentage of all attorneys appointed that they represent).

None of the clearly professional attorneys of King's Bench in either 1280 or 1299 drew all of his business from a single county. Indeed, in 1280 none of the group seems even to have drawn a majority of his business from a single county. By 1299 this was the case with rather under half of the group (10 out of 26).[34] In King's Bench as in the Common Bench there was also a significant shift between 1280 and 1299–1300 towards the appointment by litigants of only a single attorney. In 1280 this practice was rather more common in King's Bench than in the Common Bench (accounting for 54 per cent rather than just under 50 per cent of all appointments); by 1299 the number of such appointments had increased to account for no less than 83 per cent of the total (as compared with only just under 70 per cent in the Common Bench). There is no county where the appointment of two attorneys is more common than the appointment of just one.

THE GENERAL EYRE

Serjeants

Just over 120 surviving individual reports of cases heard on the northern eyre circuit of 1278–88 can be identified in manuscript collections, and I have found corresponding plea-roll enrolments for around two-thirds of them. However, the survival rate of identifiable reports varies considerably from eyre to eyre. No less than 31 identifiable reports survive from the 1285 Northamptonshire eyre while only a single report has so far been identified from the 1287 Gloucestershire eyre and none at all from the 1287 Bedfordshire eyre. Taking the circuit as a whole it is possible to identify with reasonable certainty some 16 individuals as having acted as serjeants in one or more eyres on this circuit[35] and another seven individuals as possibly having done so.[36] A number can be tracked from county to county on the circuit.[37] Others can only be traced in a single county or two counties.[38] Thus it seems probable that nowhere near 16 serjeants were available to litigants in any one county. In the well-attested 1285 Northamptonshire eyre at least seven serjeants were available (and perhaps as many as 11 or 12); in the 1286 Cambridgeshire eyre probably no more than eight, though maybe as many as 11 or 12. A clear majority of the 16 are also known to have acted as serjeants in the Common Bench before 1290, suggesting a considerable overlap between Common Bench and Eyre serjeants.[39]

Far fewer reports survive from the southern eyre circuit of the same period: only just over 20. Almost all come from the first and the last eyres on the circuit (the 1278 Hertfordshire and 1289 Wiltshire eyres). These reports together with certain other sources give us a total of 17 names of men who acted as serjeants on this circuit.[40] Seven of the 17 are also men who are known to have acted as serjeants on the northern circuit and a further two are among the possible serjeants of that circuit.[41] Ten of the 17 are known to have acted as serjeants of the Common Bench before 1290 and a further two may have done so; another three did so after 1290. In addition to the serjeants mentioned in the reports there are incidental references in two cases heard in the Common Bench to two other individuals who acted as serjeants in the 1286 Norfolk eyre, neither of whom is mentioned as a serjeant in any other source.[42]

For the remaining eyres of Edward I's reign a much greater quantity of reports survive. Those from the northern circuit eyres of 1292–4 do not survive in collections that allocate them to particular eyres, so, pending the necessary editorial work matching particular reports and plea-roll records, they have to be treated as a group. The 62 reports give us the names of some 21 serjeants. Of these, 16 or 17 are also known to have acted during this period as Common Bench serjeants.[43] For each of the five completed eyres of the 'southern' circuit of 1292–4 there survive separate collections of reports assigning cases to the individual eyres.[44] These show a total of 22 serjeants who participated in one or more eyres on this circuit. Sixteen are also known to have acted at around this time as serjeants in the Common Bench.[45] But by no means all 22 acted in each eyre of the circuit. The reports suggest that in no eyre were more than a maximum of ten serjeants active. Only four serjeants (Huntingdon, Howard, Kinsham and Spigurnel) appear in the reports of each eyre on the circuit, while a fifth (Lowther) appears in the reports of all except the final Middlesex eyre. All five were Common Bench serjeants before and after the eyre circuit. Only two or possibly three men are to be found acting as serjeants on both circuits.[46]

After 1294 only isolated eyres were held. Reports survive for both the 1299 Cambridgeshire and the Isle of Ely eyre and the 1302 Cornwall eyre.[47] Twelve serjeants are mentioned in the reports as participating in the former. Of these ten are known to have been Common Bench serjeants.[48] Ten serjeants are mentioned as participating in the latter. Of these nine are known to have been Common Bench serjeants.[49]

Overall, then, our evidence suggests that the majority (and by the end of the reign the overwhelming majority) of eyre serjeants were drawn from the serjeants of the Common Bench: thus indicating that certainly by 1290 and perhaps before that date a single corps of serjeants served clients in the Common Bench, in King's Bench and in the General Eyre, with serjeants who acted only in the eyre being in a small minority.

Attorneys

Some form of sampling is again a necessity when it comes to estimating the numbers of professional attorneys active in the eyre. Since there was no eyre in 1300 and only a single isolated eyre in 1299 I have analysed only the appointments recorded on the plea-rolls of the eyres in session in 1280.

On the northern eyre circuit two eyres took place wholly or in part during the year 1280: the eyre of Yorkshire, which had started in May 1279 and was not completed till February 1281, and the eyre of Nottinghamshire which took place during November and early December 1280. For the Yorkshire eyre I have analysed all the appointments of attorneys, whether they took place in 1280 or in 1279 and 1281, because it is not entirely clear when appointments were made and any sort of division seemed to be artificial. The proportion of attorneys appointed in the Yorkshire eyre who are clearly non-professionals (relatives and the like) at 8 per cent of the total number of appointments is relatively high. The busiest of the professional attorneys were extremely busy (though in comparing their workloads with those of their contemporaries in the Common Bench it must be remembered that these

Table 5.4 Numbers of persons appointed attorneys for fewer than ten cases in Yorkshire eyre of 1279–1280 who are not readily identifiable as close connections of their principals

Number of appointments	Numbers appointed (percentage of all attorney appointments they account for in brackets)
9	7 (1)
8	12 (2)
7	20 (3)
6	24 (3)
5	24 (3)
4	43 (4)
3	73 (5)
2	99 (4)
1	547 (12)

figures cover more than just a single year): at least three were appointed to act in 100 or more cases in the course of the eyre[50] and another ten men were appointed to act in 40 or more cases.[51] These 13 men between them account for about 20 per cent of all attorney appointments in the eyre. However, the total number of attorneys appointed to act in ten or more cases during the course of the eyre was much larger: a total of 83 in all. Between them they account for around 50 per cent of all attorney appointments in the eyre. As table 5.4 shows, the largest group of attorneys in this eyre (as in other contemporary royal courts) were those attorneys appointed for only a single case whom we can fairly certainly classify as non-professionals, but they account between them for only some 12 per cent of all attorney appointments. Also fairly certainly non-professional are those in the next two largest categories: those of individuals appointed just two or three times, who between them account for just under 10 per cent of all appointments. A comparatively high proportion of litigants (just under 60 per cent) chose to appoint two attorneys to represent them, a significantly higher proportion than in the Common Bench or King's Bench. There was also a significantly larger group (5 per cent of all litigants) who chose to appoint three representatives to act for them.

The 1280 Nottinghamshire eyre was of much shorter duration. An even higher proportion of litigants than in the Yorkshire eyre chose to appoint clearly non-professional attorneys to represent them. Such attorneys account for over 11 per cent of all attorneys appointed in this eyre. Because of the short duration of this eyre it is hardly surprising to find that only two individuals were appointed to act in more than ten cases (and between them these two account for only around 6 per cent of all appointments).[52] Again the largest group of attorneys is that composed of individuals appointed for only a single case. It consists of 128 individuals (who between them account for about 36 per cent of all appointments). Also probably to be excluded from the professionals are the 19 individuals appointed to act in only two cases (who between them account for about 11 per cent of attorneys appointed). Given the short duration of this eyre all men appointed three times or more can be considered as potential professional attorneys: this adds 24 men to our group of professional attorneys (and between them this group of men appointed in between three and eight cases account for around 33 per cent of all attorney appointments).[53] Here, too, we find a clear majority of litigants choosing to appoint two attorneys to represent them (59 per cent of all litigants appointing attorneys) but only around 2 per cent of all litigants chose to appoint three (and one litigant alone chose to appoint four).

On the southern eyre circuit three eyres were held during 1280: the Dorset eyre in January and February; the Somerset eyre from late May to late July and from October to early November; and the Hampshire eyre which started in mid-November and lasted to early December and then resumed in early January 1281 and continued till early March. Again I have included all the attorney appointments made during the Hampshire eyre in the analysis which follows since it is difficult to distinguish between appointments made in 1280 and those made in 1281. The number of attorney appointments which went to clearly non-professional attorneys at just under 10 per cent of all attorney appointments in the three eyres is very much in line with the proportion of such appointments in the Yorkshire and Nottinghamshire eyres. Even taking all three eyres together, no individual attorney was anywhere near as busy as the busiest attorneys in the Yorkshire eyre. The most active was William Poleyn appointed in a total of 63 cases;[54] but there were also another two attorneys (Hugh de la Hele and Peter of Denston (Denardestone)) appointed to act in 40 or more cases.[55] Between them these three men account for just under 6 per cent of all attorney appointments in the three eyres. Including these three men there were 37 men in all who were appointed to act in ten cases or more in these three eyres; and between them they account for just over 30 per cent of all attorney appointments.[56] This is a markedly lower proportion of the whole than was achieved by their counterparts in the two northern-circuit eyres. As a glance at table 5.5 demonstrates, attorneys appointed only once were by far the largest numerical group of all attorneys, just as they were in the two eyres of the northern circuit; and between them they account for around 18 per cent of all appointments (a figure that falls between the figures for the two northern-circuit eyres). Also fairly clearly non-professional were those appointed only two or three times, a group accounting for a further 20 per cent of all attorney appointments. This leaves only 86 individuals (between them accounting for around 16 per cent of all appointments) in the uncertain borderland between the clearly professional

Table 5.5 Numbers of persons appointed attorneys for fewer than ten cases in Dorset, Somerset and Hampshire eyres of 1280–1281 who are not readily identifiable as close connections of their principals

Number of appointments	Numbers appointed (percentage of all attorney appointments they account for in brackets)
9	4 (1)
8	6 (2)
7	9 (2)
6	10 (2)
5	16 (3)
4	41 (6)
3	78 (9)
2	137 (11)
1	463 (18)

and the clearly non-professional. The proportion of litigants choosing to appoint two attorneys to represent them was markedly lower on this circuit than in the two eyres of the contemporary northern circuit: overall in all three eyres only just over 50 per cent of all litigants (as compared with 60 per cent and 59 per cent in the Yorkshire and Nottinghamshire eyres): though this overall figure does mask some variation between individual eyres (and in the Dorset eyre as many as 57 per cent of all litigants appointed two attorneys). Overall less than 1 per cent appointed more than two attorneys.

PROFESSIONAL LAWYERS IN LOCAL COURTS

The reports of cases in the Warwickshire county court discovered by Professor Robert Palmer show some five or six professional serjeants practising there in the early fourteenth century.[57] Reports of two cases also survive apparently from the county court of Cambridgeshire of around the same date which show that pleading there was also in the hands of experts who were probably professional serjeants.[58] Isolated pieces of evidence demonstrate the activity of paid serjeants in a number of other county courts and it seems reasonable to assume that by the end of the reign, if not before, they were to be found in all county courts and may well by then have been playing a dominant role in legal proceedings there.[59] It is conceivable that by the end of the reign there were also professional attorneys practising in the county court. Robert Palmer has shown that by 1333 it was common for litigants in the county court of Cornwall to appoint attorneys to represent them, but he was not able to show whether or not the attorneys who were appointed were professionals.[60] From the evidence of an almost contemporary county-court roll from Bedfordshire he was able to point to the activity of at least one clearly professional attorney active in that county court and to five other individuals who were possibly professional.[61] But this evidence, exiguous as it is and coming as it does from a quarter of a century after the end of Edward I's reign, is hardly sufficient to allow us to assume that there must have been professional attorneys in the county court in our period in the absence of any confirmatory evidence.

An ordinance of 1280 created a monopoly of regular paid employment as a serjeant in the city courts of London for those specially admitted to that office.[62] The numbers seem to have been small. Four men were admitted in 1289[63] and five in 1305.[64] On the second occasion at least the wording of the relevant entry suggests that these five were to be the only serjeants practising in the city and not simply an addition to the ranks of existing serjeants.[65] The same London ordinance of 1280 also regulated the conduct of attorneys but did not control those allowed to practise in the city courts.[66] The 1289 memorandum on the admission of serjeants is, however, followed by a note giving the names of six other men 'admitted and elected' by the four serjeants. These seem to have been attorneys and the note suggests that by 1289 there may also have been a closed order of professional attorneys in the city courts, entry into which was controlled by the serjeants.[67] When a further admission of serjeants took place in 1305 a space was left blank for a similar entry of the admission of attorneys but for some reason this was not completed.[68] The surviving plea-rolls of the city courts for the later part of Edward I's reign indicate the existence of a core of professional attorneys in the city courts throughout this period but one which varied in size from as many as 13 in 1298–9 to as few as seven in 1307.

A serjeant who was in receipt of a regular annuity from one of his clients is known to have been present in the town court of King's Lynn in the early 1280s, for it was his alleged refusal to give legal assistance to the client although present in the court that was cited by the client's successor in litigation of 1295 as reason for non-payment of arrears of that annuity.[69] Other stray evidence allows us to see a paid and presumably professional attorney in another town court: that of Shrewsbury in the early 1290s.[70] A King's Bench conspiracy case of 1297 tells us of one Thomas Marshal of Oxford who acted as a serjeant in the city court of Oxford and who frequently acted as an expert assessor in that court with the town's bailiffs but who was accused of conspiracy and maintenance in an assize heard before royal justices. Thomas himself claimed to be a 'common serjeant pleader who acted before the justices and elsewhere wherever he was hired to do so'.[71] However, it is not entirely clear that we can take him at his word and regard him as a specialist serjeant. The Oxford city-court roll of 1292–6 shows him acting as an attorney, as an essoiner and as a surety during those years though not as a serjeant.[72] Probably he performed all these roles. It is also possible to identify from that roll at least one other putatively professional lawyer acting in the same combination of roles during those years: Richard de St Martin. The entry on the roll that shows he had been acting as a serjeant suggests a reason. It shows Richard disavowing himself on a count that he had made for a client.[73] This indicates that in the Oxford city court, at least, it was possible to combine the roles of attorney and serjeant, with the attorney being allowed to disavow what the serjeant had said. We may reasonably assume that by end of the reign there were small groups of professional lawyers (who may or may not have been specialist serjeants) in the courts of each sizeable town. By Edward I's reign professional serjeants were also to be found offering their services to litigants in the fair court at St Ives and this was probably also the case in other fair courts.[74]

Paid, and perhaps professional, serjeants can also occasionally be glimpsed at work in seignorial courts[75] and in at least one hundred court.[76] If we could assume that every time we encounter a *narrator* in one of these lower courts he was necessarily a professional serjeant then we could say with confidence that the use of professional serjeants in these lower courts was widespread.[77] But such an assumption does not seem to be justified. If there were still non-professionals (friends, relatives and perhaps even servants) speaking on behalf of litigants in the courts in Edward I's reign, it is in these lesser courts that we might expect to find them; and *narrator* would be a perfectly adequate term to describe them, for it would simply be saying what function it was they were then performing. In the absence of clearer evidence it seems best to remain agnostic: the number of professional serjeants practising in these courts must remain uncertain.

6

The English Legal Profession in Edward I's Reign (II): the Profession at Work

This chapter surveys the world of the working professional lawyer during Edward I's reign. It looks at how clients made contact with lawyers and how they appointed them to act on their behalf. It also examines what services lawyers performed for their clients and how lawyers were paid. Much of our information on these matters comes from the plea-rolls of the Common Bench and from reports of litigation heard there and relates specifically to lawyers practising in that court. As we have seen, this was the court with the largest group of professional lawyers, so this material is of immediate relevance to a significant proportion of the Edwardian legal profession. But there is also some reason to suppose that the practices and procedures followed in this court were not markedly dissimilar from those followed in other royal courts and thus that this material may also be relevant to the working lives of professional lawyers practising in other courts. There is also some direct evidence about lawyers practising elsewhere and this has been used where relevant in the following discussion.

ATTORNEYS

Terminology

The term 'attorney' (*attornatus*) continued to be used for any person appointed by a litigant with power to win or lose litigation on his behalf, whether the person appointed was a professional, an amateur or anything in between. From the early 1290s onwards, however, we also begin to find two specific terms being used on occasion in the Common Bench to distinguish the professional from the non-professional: 'general attorney' (*generalis attornatus*)¹ and 'common attorney' (*communis attornatus*).² The former term is also used at least once of a professional attorney active in the court of King's Bench.³

Functions

The primary function of the attorney was to attend court in place of his clients. Whenever the client's name was called out in court by one of its criers, he answered for the client, affirming that he was present through his attorney. In the 1260s it was still apparently an official of the court (the keeper of rolls and writs) who took the initiative in having the crier call the parties in Common Bench.⁴ By the 1290s it seems to have been the attorney himself who did so.⁵ But the change may be more apparent than real, for even in the 1260s the keeper of rolls and writs may normally only have acted after being prompted. If the attorney's client was the plaintiff, several such appearances over a number of terms would normally be necessary before the court's mesne process secured the defendant's attendance. At each the attorney had not just to attend court and answer for his client but also to ask for the court's judgment on the default and ensure the court ordered the next stage of mesne process against the defendant.⁶

When the defendant or his attorney finally did appear it was again the plaintiff's attorney who would ensure that the case was called for hearing. The attorneys of both litigants would then normally come up to the bar of the court to hear what was said by the serjeants for their clients.⁷ However, this did not invariably happen, for at least two separate reports show attorneys claiming not to have heard what had been said by serjeants because they were too far away from the bar at the time.⁸ The attorney had the power and responsibility to avow or disavow what the serjeants said.⁹ It was also the attorney, rather than the serjeant, who was treated by the court as its channel of communication with the litigant. When law was waged on the litigant's behalf, the attorney was instructed to tell his client to appear in person to take the oath. In a case brought against the bishop of Norwich in 1300, chief justice Mettingham instructed the bishop's attorney to tell his client about a deed of his client produced in pleading by the bishop's opponent and to advise him that the chief justice placed great weight on it and that they should reach a settlement in the case before St John's day next.¹⁰

After pleading had taken place the plaintiff's attorney would commonly need to put in several further appearances to seek judgment on defaults made by the defendant and also by the jurors before a verdict could be obtained and a judgment awarded on the basis of that verdict. Alternatively, for tactical reasons and perhaps on the advice of his client's serjeants, he might decide to be non-suited.¹¹ In the real actions concerned with title to land and other real property, final judgment in favour of his client might be secured by the plaintiff's attorney without any pleading taking place at all, simply on the basis of the repeated defaults of the client's opponent.[12]

By the later part of Edward I's reign the professional attorney had also come to perform a number of other functions for clients. Several cases show the plaintiff's attorney acquiring the original writ needed to initiate litigation[13] and it seems likely that attorneys commonly advised litigants on the choice of original writ even when they did not obtain the writ for them.[14] During the preliminary stages of legal proceedings, when only the plaintiff's attorney was present, he seems to have been responsible for ensuring that his own appearance and the absence of the defendant were recorded on the plea-rolls,[15] that one of the clerks made out the appropriate judicial writ authorizing the next stage of mesne process,[16] and that this writ reached his client, who was then himself responsible for ensuring that it was delivered to the appropriate sheriff.[17] When the two parties agreed to an adjournment of the case it was again the attorney who was responsible for having the appropriate entry made on the roll.[18]

It may also commonly have been the attorneys of the two parties who engaged serjeants to act on their behalf. In at least two cases we hear of serjeants being paid through the litigant's attorney, the kind of arrangement that would have been appropriate if it was he who had initially approached the serjeant on his client's behalf.[19] Also significant is the casual way in which the reporter of an early fourteenth-century case referred to the plaintiff's attorney (rather than the plaintiff) as the serjeant's 'client'.[20] It may also have been the attorney who normally briefed serjeants about the main facts of the cases. In a 1281 case, litigants in King's Bench seem to have briefed their serjeant themselves[21] but in a 1294 Common Bench case the briefing seems to have been through the plaintiff's attorney. Chief justice Mettingham suspected that the court was being deceived and gave the plaintiff's serjeant a formal warning. He said that the facts as stated in his count were as given him by the plaintiff's attorneys, and they in turn confirmed they had received them (apparently in writing) from their client.[22] When Thomas Palmer of Cornhill was sworn attorney of the city of London in the court of King's Bench in 1303, among his duties was that of instructing and informing the serjeant of the city as often as was necessary.[23] Attorneys were also entrusted with deeds and other muniments required in litigation. In 1291 Arnold Purdeu complained that his attorney was detaining the transcripts and other muniments he had handed over to him, a charge the attorney denied. In 1294 Henry of Guildford sued his attorney for damage to a bond he had entrusted to him for the prosecution of a case the attorney claimed had become damaged in court due to the press of persons at the bar.[24] In 1305 Thomas Charles sued his attorney for the return of a bond delivered to him in connection with litigation in the court of Great Yarmouth.[25]

After pleading had taken place it was also apparently the attorney's duty to check the plea-roll enrolment of the case on his client's behalf. Enrolments were sometimes challenged by litigants[26] and entries changed with the consent of the parties.[27] Attorneys expected to have ready access to the rolls. In 1298 Reginald de Kernyek, a Cornish attorney, insulted a servant of Henry of Hales, a leading clerk of chief justice Mettingham, who had custody of the rolls, because he was not able to inspect them after dinner in the church of St Andrew's York. Reginald subsequently attempted to seize them from a clerk who was writing judicial writs and threatened the servant.[28] It was also the litigant's attorney who would challenge individual jurors on any panel returned by the sheriff before the jury gave its verdict.[29]

A professional attorney might also perform yet other services for clients. A 1295 case shows one Herefordshire attorney arranging for a defendant to secure judgment against his opponent on the grounds of want of prosecution, without that defendant having formally to appoint him as his attorney at all.[30] This and other cases from the 1290s indicate that it was commonly the professional attorneys of the Common Bench who arranged for their clients to be essoined.[31]

Appointment

To appoint an attorney a litigant appeared in person before a competent official and gave the name of the individual(s) whom he wished to appoint, the name of his opponent and (in general terms) the type of litigation concerned. He might still do this in what had once been the only permissible manner: during term-time and before the full court. But by the beginning of Edward I's reign, as we have seen, a number of alternative possibilities existed.[32] These included appointment in chancery or before a commissioner authorized by chancery and appointment before one of the justices of the court in one of the counties through which he passed during the vacation. A litigant might also arrange to appoint an attorney locally before a particular individual empowered to receive the appointment by one of the justices of the court. In 1277 we hear of one of one of the puisne justices of the Common Bench (master Ralph of Farningham) authorizing such an arrangement[33] and in the 1279-81 Yorkshire eyre similar arrangements were authorised by each of the puisne justices of the eyre.[34] By the early fourteenth century the right to authorize such arrangements seems to have become confined (in the case of the Common Bench) to its chief justice but in Michaelmas term 1306 we find him authorizing as many as eight different individuals (many of them clerks of the court) to receive appointments.[35]

A further possibility was appointment before a justice of one of the other royal courts, again while he was in the litigant's home area. This was more problematic. In a 1276 case it was alleged that an attorney appointed before the royal justice Solomon of Rochester had not been validly appointed because Solomon 'had no power to receive the attorney because he was not a justice of the Common Bench'. The court accepted this assertion but excused the litigant, as the fault in accepting the attorney lay with Solomon.[36] But by 1300 attorneys were being admitted for litigation in the Common Bench before each of the three justices of the court of King's Bench, before the treasurer, three of the barons and one of the remembrancers of the Exchequer and before five different assize justices,[37] By 1306 the list of officials receiving appointments had lengthened still further to include a number of senior chancery clerks as well as a number of senior clerks belonging to the Common Bench itself.[38]

In 1307 legislation was enacted restricting the right to receive attorneys. In future the justices of the king's courts and the barons of the Exchequer were only to be allowed to admit attorneys in respect of litigation in their own courts. The statute also prohibited the admission of attorneys by the servants and clerks of justices, though it specifically preserved the right of the chancellor and chief justice(s) to grant others the power to receive attorneys on an *ad hoc* basis. The legislation was published on 15 January but only took effect from the octaves of Trinity following.[39] The Common Bench plea-roll for that term certainly shows a much reduced body of individuals admitting attorneys but still includes individuals who were not justices of the court and were not said to be acting with the permission of the chief justice. These include the chief justice of King's Bench and his junior colleague Henry Spigurnel, an Exchequer baron, a senior royal clerk and two senior Common Bench clerks.[40]

Although the actual appointment of an attorney was a purely oral matter it appears to have become normal by the 1290s for litigants in the Common Bench to provide a written bill recording the appointment and giving exactly the same facts as were given in the oral appointment. This was probably still complementary to that appointment, an *aide-mémoire* for the enrolling clerk, and not a replacement for it.[41] It was also normally necessary for the appointment to be entered on the plea-rolls of the court or that the appointment be notified to the court by a writ that was then filed in its writ-files before the attorney attempted to act. Cases involving the challenging of attorneys show this was the general rule but indicate some degree of flexibility in its interpretation. In a 1281 case a plaintiff challenged the right of one of the defendants to appear as the attorney of his co-defendant (his wife). It turned out that he had indeed been appointed before a commissioner authorized by chancery and the appointment been notified to the justices of the court by a writ dated prior to the hearing; but this notification was still sitting in the hanaper of chancery awaiting sealing when the challenge was made and had not reached the court till later. No judgment is recorded but the point was evidently an arguable one.[42] In a 1291 case a litigant tried to vouch the chief justice of King's Bench (Gilbert of Thornton) to prove that he had validly appointed an attorney before him. His opponent claimed he needed to be able to vouch either a record of the appointment on the rolls or a writ on the writ-files of the court and that Gilbert's record of the appointment was not sufficient. Again no decision is recorded.[43] In a third case of 1305 the court decided that an attorney whose appointment was notified to the court by a writ dated before the day the attorney appeared in court, but only brought to the court after that appearance, possessed valid authority to act for his client, though only in the rather special circumstances where the great seal had been out of commission between the date of the writing of the writ and its delivery into the court.[44]

Contracts between attorneys and their clients

The formal appointment of an attorney was preceded by some sort of agreement between attorney and client over the services to be provided by the attorney and the remuneration he could expect for providing them. Such agreements are normally mentioned in surviving records only when they are relevant to some subsequent dispute between lawyer and client. Evidence of this kind clearly demonstrates the existence of a number of different kinds of agreement.[45]

It appears to have been comparatively uncommon for attorneys to be retained for life by particular clients. Litigation of 1312 shows that John of Swinburn had made an agreement with John of York in 1285 for the latter to act as his attorney both in the Common Bench and elsewhere for life in return for an annuity of 20 shillings and one robe. The agreement was in writing and its existence was common ground to both parties. The only point on which they differed was whether or not the attorney had forfeited his right to the annuity through failure to act in a specific plea in 1291.[46] But this seems to be the only such agreement mentioned in the records. In May 1298 William of Grantham was appointed attorney of the city of London in King's Bench for an indefinite term for a salary of 20 shillings a year, and on 1 August following he was granted the freedom of the city and retained for life for the same salary. But this life-retainer was said to be 'at the will of the aldermen', and seems to mean that the city could require his services for life but might dispense with them at any time if it thought fit.[47] This was a form of life-retainer but without the security normally implicit in such agreements.

A second type of agreement committed an attorney to acting for a particular client in all his litigation in a particular court in return for a fixed annual payment but only for a limited time period. Eustace le Hansere later claimed he had made an agreement of this sort with the city of Lincoln in 1295 to act for them in the Common Bench and perhaps more generally to give them legal advice for a period of five years in return for a payment of five marks a year.[48] A variant was for the attorney to agree to act in a particular court for a fixed annual fee but for an unspecified period of time or simply until further notice. Thomas of Hayton claimed to have made such an agreement with a client in 1299. He had acted for the client in the Common Bench for three years but had not been paid the one mark a year agreed.[49] Thomas le Sok alleged he had made an agreement in 1295 with the Bedfordshire baron, Roger de Beauchamp, to act as his attorney in the Common Bench and to provide him with advice for an annual pension of six shillings and eight pence. Thomas sued him for non-payment of the pension in respect of four and a half regnal years and for other moneys paid for writs and serjeants during that period.[50] William of Grantham's successor, Thomas Palmer of Cornhill, was appointed on 1 January 1303 to act for the city of London in King's Bench for an indefinite term but at a higher salary[51] and Harsculph of Whitwell was appointed the city's attorney in the exchequer as from Michaelmas 1306 at the rate of 40 shillings a year, again for an indefinite period.[52]

A third type of agreement committed attorneys to acting in all a client's litigation for an indefinite period but on a pro rata basis. In 1305 John son of Robert of Marske claimed six marks as due to him under an agreement he had made with a client in 1299 under which John agreed to act as his attorney for any litigation involving him in the Common Bench in return for a payment of half a mark a year per case. However, the client denied ever having made any such agreement and successfully made his law in affirmation of this denial.[53]

A fourth type of agreement required the attorney to act for the client only in one specific case or group of cases in return for a single compound payment. In 1286 Walter of Grainthorpe claimed he had made an agreement with clients in 1281 to prosecute a particular case for them till it was over in return for a payment of four marks, that he had done this but that they were now refusing to pay him.[54] Richard de Bretteville sued a client in King's Bench in 1285, alleging that he had agreed to act for the client in a particular case for a payment of five marks but that the balance owed him had never been paid.[55] A Common Bench case of 1291 tells us of William Tebaud, a professional attorney in the court, agreeing to represent a client in a particular case there for five marks.[56] In 1293 Osbert Motekan sued two sureties of a former client for the 40 shillings he claimed were owed him under an agreement for his services in a particular plea in the 1281–4 Lincolnshire eyre.[57]

Most of these agreements seem to have been purely verbal and clients were simply able to deny ever having made them. However, in 1297 a bipartite indenture was used to record an agreement between Roger the rector of Britwell Salome in Oxfordshire and the attorney John of Carswell under which Roger agreed to pay John eight marks in specific instalments at specified dates in return for John suing a writ of cosinage until the plea was duly determined (and apparently also finding all the incidental costs of the litigation). Roger claimed that the case had been lost through John's failure to continue suing it, but when the contrary was proved from the plea-rolls the money was awarded to John with damages.[58] The largest sum mentioned in litigation between a professional attorney and a client is the 20 marks Philip of Burgate claimed in a case heard in the 1280 Somerset eyre that clients had agreed to pay him for suing a plea on their behalf at his own expense. However, Philip's claim did not succeed because he failed to produce either written evidence or witnesses present at the making of the alleged agreement.[59] A variant was for the payment to be in the nature of a contingency fee.[60] In the 1279 Sussex eyre Henry of Burne complained that a client had agreed to pay him 40 shillings if he sued a writ with a second individual till the plea was determined and the client recovered anything of the land that was at stake, but that the client had made an out-of-court settlement with his adversary under which he had recovered part of the land and was now refusing to pay him. The client did not deny the terms of the agreement but claimed that Henry's own subsequent actions had disentitled him to the payment.[61]

The remaining possibility was for the attorney to insist on a separate payment for each stage of the case. In 1299 litigation William Pollard of Fulbeck in Lincolnshire claimed that he had made an agreement with William of Welby in 1286 under which the latter was to act as his attorney in a particular case for the sum of two shillings per appearance, with a further payment to cover the cost of serjeants, but that the attorney had subsequently deserted his service and caused him to lose his land.[62] Thomas of Brampton made two separate agreements with a client in 1306. Under one of them Thomas was to act for the client in two pleas in the Common Bench for 40 pence a day; under the other, Thomas was to receive a lump sum of 40 shillings for suing at his own cost a separate plea of debt for the same client. In 1310 Thomas alleged he had only been paid 40 pence for the first day of one of the pleas and was still owed the full 40 shillings and another 40 shillings for appearing for 12 days under the first agreement.[63]

As some of these cases suggest, professional attorneys might have difficulty securing the payments owed to them for their services. One possibility was to ensure payment by means of a penal bond. In a case of 1303 Richard Fox of Shrewsbury claimed to have been the stakeholder of a bond for ten pounds in his possession which Stephen son of Alan of Ross Hall was trying to recover. Richard claimed the debtor named in the bond had made it when he appointed Stephen to act on his behalf in litigation about a tenement in Ross Hall; and that the bond was made as a security for his expenses and was to be held in escrow till attorney and principal had accounted for those expenses. The plaintiff, however, claimed that the bond had been delivered to him unconditionally.[64] Attorneys may also sometimes have required payment in advance. This was probably the position when Hugh Fraunceys of Eynesbury in Huntingdonshire wanted to appoint Warin of Northampton of St Neot's to act as his attorney in a trespass plea in the Common Bench in 1292. Hugh certainly claimed this in litigation of 1293 although Warin asserted that the money was paid for his services in an earlier case that was by then concluded.[65]

It seems to have been quite common for agreements between litigants and their attorneys for service in the Westminster (or York) courts to be made not at Westminster or York but in the country and normally in the litigant's own home county. We have evidence of such agreements being made at Britwell Salome in Oxfordshire;[66] at Eaton Socon in Bedfordshire;[67] at East Somerton in Norfolk;[68] at Grantham[69] and Lincoln[70] in Lincolnshire; at Richmond in Yorkshire;[71] and at Swinburn in Northumberland.[72] The only agreement made at York while the Common Bench was there involved a Yorkshire attorney and a Yorkshire litigant[73] and the 1294 agreement for William of Tykesore to represent master Nicholas of Huntingdon in a prohibition plea in the Common Bench made at London in a tavern near Woolchurchhaw perhaps reflects the normal place of residence of the litigant rather than the proximity of the court at Westminster.[74] By the end of Edward I's reign a litigant could normally make his initial contact with a professional attorney in his own home county and, if he wanted, could probably conduct the whole of the litigation from that county without ever coming to court.

SERJEANTS

Terminology

The term normally used for serjeant on the plea-rolls of the king's courts during Edward I's reign is *narrator* ('one who tells a story'), the same term as was most commonly used for them on the plea-rolls in Henry III's reign. The French equivalent (*'le countour'*) is the term used for them in the pseudo-statutory *Modus Levandi Fines*[75] and in chapter 11 of the *Articuli super Cartas* of 1300.[76] The main alternative term was the Latin *serviens* and the corresponding French term *serjant*. As we have seen, this term seems first to have been used of the king's serjeant, Laurence del Brok, in 1252,[77] and the term *serviens regis* was regularly used in official records of this period to refer to those serjeants whom the king retained.[78] There is also at least one reference on the plea-rolls in 1292 to a professional serjeant of the Common Bench not employed by the king as being a *communis serviens ... in curia*.[79] *Serjant* is the normal term for serjeant in reports of cases[80] and is also the term used in the late thirteenth-century treatise *Britton*.[81] The portmanteau terms *serviens narrator* and *serjant contour* were also in occasional use. The latter is found in 1275 in chapter 29 of the statute of Westminster I;[82] the former in the late thirteenth-century treatise *Fleta*.[83]

There is little difficulty about the literal meaning of the term 'serjeant': it means 'one who serves'. The problem is in explaining why this term come to be used for the serjeant in the later thirteenth century and why it managed, if only partially, to replace the older term 'counter'. John Baker has suggested that the term may have come into use because of the frequency with which serjeants were retained by individual clients in return for pensions, for this meant they became seen as the 'servants' of those clients. More significant, he argues, was the process by which the serjeants became a closed order. The serjeants now became, or projected themselves as being, a group whose function was to 'serve' the whole of the king's people and who came to take an oath that they would do this and it was this which justified their monopoly of practice in the Common Bench.[84] It may be doubted, however, whether the receipt of a pension was enough in itself to turn a serjeant into the 'servant' of his client or into being seen as such, and there is little trace of any theory of popular service being used to justify the monopoly of paid professional activity in the Common Bench which its serjeants already enjoyed. Nor is there any trace of the serjeant's oath in this period. Thus alternative explanations for the use of the term merit consideration. It may be that the term is much older than its first recorded use and reflects the presuppositions of a much older world as to the theoretical basis of the activity of the serjeant in court: that he really was the 'servant' of the litigant and subject to his master's disavowal for precisely that reason. More plausibly, the term may have come to be applied to the serjeant because of the perceived analogy between the way in which he was liable to disavowal by his client for what he had said in court and the way in which a lord whose servants had performed a particular action without his express prior approval were subject to a similar right of avowal or disavowal after the deed.[85] In any case John Baker is almost certainly right in the suggestion that part of the explanation for the use of the new term was that the term 'counter' had by this time come to seem a not wholly appropriate one since 'counting had started to be a less important part of the countor's employment than pleading and advocacy in general'.[86]

The functions of the serjeant

Our main evidence about the functions performed by serjeants comes not from the plea-rolls, which continue to mention serjeants only in exceptional circumstances, but from reports that mention the serjeants involved in litigation as a matter of course. However, they are mainly concerned with the pleading of cases to issue in the Common Bench or in the Eyre and thus it is on this part of the serjeant's activities that they shed most light.

Proceedings started with one serjeant making a count for the plaintiff, explaining his claim or complaint, and a second serjeant making a formal defence for the defendant. For the next stage in proceedings, the making of exceptions by the defendant and their rebuttal by the plaintiff, it was advantageous to have the assistance of as many serjeants as the litigant could afford or obtain and there seems to have been no limit on the numbers he could use. It was common for a litigant to have two serjeants speaking for him and not uncommon for him to have more. In one exceptional case of 1296 a plaintiff had as many as five.[87] Occasionally the reports show serjeants who had not been engaged by either party also participating and speaking simply as *amici curie*.[88] When pleading in a case, the serjeants seem to have stood within the bar of the court: for sometimes we are told what the serjeant said subsequently 'outside the bar'.[89]

The use of a group of serjeants meant they needed to concert tactics in advance. Serjeants also needed to be briefed beforehand on the main facts relevant to their client's case. This led to the practice of holding preliminary meetings of the serjeants involved in a case. We learn only incidentally of the existence of such meetings from occasional mentions in the reports. At the end of one report of a case heard in 1304, a note tells us of a series of questions of facts relevant to the case that had been asked *in consilio narratorum* ('in the serjeants' advisory session'), presumably before the case began.[90] At the end of another report of a different 1304 case we are given details of what had been said in what was clearly a preliminary session (though all we are told is that it was *in secreto*) which had involved three serjeants. Pashley had opened by arguing in favour of adopting a particular line of defence in the case on the basis of what he had discovered through prior discussion with the 'client'. Scotter argued against using this tactic and pointed out its dangers. Pashley replied. A third serjeant (Mutford) intervened at the end.[91] In a report of a 1306 case we are told at the end what Warwick the serjeant had said *in consilio* and of how unnamed others had agreed with him. Again we are probably being told what he had said in the preliminary session.[92] It was perhaps also a similar meeting of the serjeants involved in the case together with the attorney(s) and/or the litigant which would take place when a serjeant sought permission to 'imparl' in the course of pleading.

The reports have rather less to tell us about the role of serjeants at the stage of jury trial in a case: normally (except in the case of petty assizes) a subsequent stage of the case which might take place locally before justices at a nisi prius session. A report of an assize of darrein presentment heard in the Common Bench, perhaps of 1302, shows one serjeant (Tothby) challenging the jurors of the assize for his client, alleging that they had been bribed by the plaintiff, and another serjeant (Willoughby) intervening in an attempt to ensure that the assize was taken without delay.[93] A number of reports show serjeants addressing the jury between the time the jury was sworn and the time it gave its verdict. Willoughby addressed a grand-assize jury in 1297 on behalf of his clients, the dean and chapter of Southwell, and produced for them the charter by which Ralph de Frescheville's father had granted the dean and chapter the advowson of the church of Bunny and the letters of institution of the first rector admitted to the church after the grant. Tothby demanded sight of these deeds and they were shown both to the court and to the opposite party. Ashby then addressed the grand jury on behalf of Ralph and told them of an assize of darrein presentment brought by the dean and chapter against Ralph's guardian in Henry III's reign which had found in favour of Ralph and a subsequent attaint brought by the dean and chapter which had simply affirmed the previous verdict and produced a piece of parchment containing a record of the cases. The grand assize then gave its verdict (in favour of Ralph).[94] In a report of a case in the 1293–4 Yorkshire eyre a jury was charged with giving its verdict as to whether the defendant (Gilbert de Gaunt) was tenant of the whole of the manor of Hunmanby on the day Robert of Tattershall acquired his writ against him and then John of Tilton spoke to the jury on behalf of Gilbert, though his 'evidence' (here merely an argument, not a demonstration of the truth of what he was saying) was in fact disallowed.[95] A report of an assize of darrein presentment heard in the Common Bench in 1305 shows serjeant Tothby deliberately choosing not to counterplead the assize. The reporter suggests this was because if he had, the plaintiff might have recovered without the verdict of the assize. However, Tothby did make a brief presentation of his client's title to the assize jurors after they had been sworn; serjeant Pashley answered for the plaintiff, showing a quitclaim and other deeds of the former owners of the advowson and the ordinaries of the diocese.[96]

Serjeants might also intervene between the giving of a verdict and the rendering of judgment. In the 1305 darrein presentment case already mentioned, the assize found in favour of neither of the parties. Tothby, for the defendant, none the less attempted to secure damages for his client for having been troubled by the plaintiff, but was rebuffed by justice Bereford. In an early fourteenth-century assize of novel disseisin which revolved around the question of the legitimacy of the defendant's father, the assize justice Spigurnel elicited relevant information from the assize jurors and serjeants Tothby and Mutford argued on behalf of their clients on the basis of the information supplied by the jury. Spigurnel none the less adjourned judgment till the next session.[97] Earlier, in a report of a case of trespass concerning the destruction of a fold from the northern eyre circuit of the 1280s, we again see a jury giving a verdict that supplies the relevant facts, and then the serjeants Kelloe and Selby arguing on the basis of those facts for judgment for their clients but judgment being adjourned by the justice.[98]

Serjeants also played an important role when a final concord was to be levied in one of the king's courts, whether the final concord was to bring genuinely hostile litigation between two parties to an end or simply to secure an agreed transfer of property between them. It was the serjeant who asked the justices for permission to concord; agreed with them the sum to be paid to the king; and recited to the court the terms of the proposed concord. Only one serjeant appears to have been required, not separate serjeants for each party to the concord.[99] An undated report belonging to the later part of Edward I's reign shows that this serjeant was also responsible for drawing up the form of the agreement. In it justice Bereford asked serjeant Hedon why the fine mentioned an advowson separately from the moiety of a manor. Hedon then went away to change the draft in accordance with Bereford's suggestion.[100] Of the serjeant's wider role in advising his clients on matters of law we see comparatively little. One suggestive piece of evidence, however, is a report of an assize of novel disseisin probably from the Yorkshire eyre of 1293–4 which tells us about the background to the assize. An assize of mort d'ancestor had been brought by the defendant against the plaintiff but the defendant had been unsuccessful. He had then, however, followed the advice of two serjeants (Roger of Higham and John de Lisle) in disseising his opponent, thereby giving rise to the current assize.[101]

The authorization of serjeants: avowal and disavowal

No prior authorization was required before a serjeant spoke for a client because, as we have seen, it was the *raison d'être* of the serjeant that he was an agent who spoke for the litigant but without any specific authorization to do so.[102] In many, perhaps most, cases serjeants spoke for their clients without any question being raised as to whether what they had said was acceptable to those clients. However, it was possible for an opponent to ask specifically whether something that had been said by a serjeant was 'avowed' by his client (or his client's attorney) and the client or the attorney had then to avow or disavow the serjeant. Such a challenge seems normally to have been made only when the opponent believed that the serjeant had made a serious formal error either of omission or commission. Thus in a 1293 covenant case a defendant (or more probably his serjeant) asked whether the plaintiff avowed the count his serjeant had made; the plaintiff's attorney did so; the defendant then successfully sought judgment of a discrepancy between the date of the deed recording the agreement mentioned in the count and the date on which the serjeant had said in the count that the agreement had been made.[103]

In a 1302 replevin case the defendant's serjeant had justified a distraint as made for damage caused by the plaintiffs' cow in the defendant's meadow. In reply the plaintiffs' serjeant claimed the plaintiffs had the right to put a cow in the meadow concerned from Good Friday till the first day of August and claimed that they and their ancestors had been seised of this right since time out of mind. The defendant's serjeant then asked for this answer to be avowed. It was. He then asked what proof they had that they were entitled to this right. Their answer was that they claimed it as a right attached to their holding in the same village. He sought judgment of their answer since they had initially claimed the right as a separate entity not as a right attached to other property and had thus contradicted themselves.[104] However, it was not possible to demand that a serjeant be avowed for everything that he said in the course of pleading. We learn this from a report of a warranty of charter case of the 1290s in which the plaintiff's serjeant (Warwick) asked for the defendant's serjeant (Lisle) to be avowed. Lisle said the exception he had made was one of law and such exceptions did not need to be avowed. Warwick did not disagree but said that this was not properly an exception in law since it was not something which could be decided by the judgment of the justices but something which could only be decided by inspecting the record of the rolls.[105]

We have already mentioned two cases in which the justices asked whether the litigants' attorneys avowed a count or what had been said for clients in the course of argument but the latter claimed not to have heard what had been said.[106] In another report of a 1296 case a justice asked the defendant whether he was willing to avow what his serjeants had said; the defendant, who had previously disavowed what had been said by another serjeant, carefully avowed only what Howard had said on that day.[107] It was also Howard, now a justice, who in a report of a 1299 replevin case was careful to ensure that when the plaintiff's serjeant disclaimed holding of the defendant this answer was avowed by the plaintiff's attorney, since such a disclaimer would be the basis for an action by the defendant to recover the land in demesne.[108]

It was also possible for the attorney or the litigant to disavow his own serjeant without being specifically asked to do so by someone else. This was apparently what had happened at an earlier hearing in the same term of a debt case recorded on the plea-rolls in 1292. Hartlepool, the serjeant acting for Stephen of Cornhill, had made a formal defence and then sought and obtained a hearing of the writ. He had then requested that the plaintiffs who were executors prove themselves to be such and subsequently requested that they show what evidence they had of the debt they claimed (and was shown a bond). When he sought permission from the court to imparl, his defence was immediately disavowed by his client's attorney.[109] It was important not to leave disavowal too late. In a 1292 prohibition case the defendant, master Giffred de Vezano, made a formal denial and then requested permission to imparl. He subsequently challenged the count for variation from the writ, because in the count the plaintiff had alleged that he had both held and sued a plea in court christian contrary to the prohibition, whereas in the writ he was said only to have held the plea. The plaintiff then attempted to disavow his serjeant and to make a different count but was not allowed to do so.[110]

Robert Palmer has suggested that the avowing of a serjeant took the form of a ritual action or gesture.[111] This is incorrect. The text he cites concerns the gesture appropriate to the offering of a wager of law, not one appropriate to the avowing of a serjeant.[112] The avowing and disavowing of serjeants seems to have been a purely verbal act by the attorney or litigant: perhaps no more than a 'yes' or 'no' in answer to a specific question.

The retaining of serjeants

The beginnings of the practice of retaining serjeants for life in return for an annual pension can be traced back to Henry III's reign[113] but the surviving evidence seems to indicate that it was only in Edward I's reign that it became common.[114]

The only surviving original deed of retainer I know is the bipartite chirograph of 1262 by which the abbot and convent of Stratford granted Richard of Havering an annual pension for life in return for his homage and service, and Richard's agreement to pay a diligent regard to their business both far and near whenever his services were needed.[115] But complete or almost complete contemporary transcripts survive of the 1275 deed of Thomas Cantilupe, bishop of Hereford, in favour of Hamon de la Barre;[116] the 1285 deed of the abbot of Barlings confirming (and increasing) an annual pension to Gilbert of Thornton;[117] the 1300 deed of the abbot of Peterborough granting an annual pension to Roger of Higham;[118] and the c.1280 deed of John son of John l'Estrange granting an annual pension to Adam of Kinsham.[119] In a more modern transcript at least one example also survives of the kind of deed a serjeant might make in favour of the client who was granting him an annuity.[120] More common are extracts from such deeds or references to them in the course of litigation brought by serjeants or their executors for arrears of pensions. Many such cases were settled in or out of court without full pleadings between the parties and here it is only the names of the serjeants that allow us to identify the litigation as probably concerned with an annuity granted to the serjeant in return for his professional services. Also problematic, but in a slightly different way, is evidence showing institutions paying pensions to men we know to have been serjeants. Such evidence survives for the abbey of Peterborough;[121] Canterbury cathedral priory;[122] Westminster abbey;[123] Tynemouth priory;[124] Norwich cathedral priory;[125] Durham cathedral priory;[126] and the city of Norwich.[127] It seems reasonable to assume that the payments were being made to the serjeants concerned under formal contracts of retainer made to secure their professional assistance and also that the retainers were for their lifetimes, since these seem to have been the normal practice: but neither assumption can actually be proved.

Of the purely monetary retainers paid to serjeants active in the king's courts (the most common type) the sums most frequently mentioned are 20 shillings and 40 shillings, with retainers of one and two marks also being fairly common.[128] The smallest retainer is the half a mark mentioned in litigation brought by John of Bromholm against two clients in 1280;[129]

the largest the ten pounds owed to Roger of Higham by the abbey of Peterborough under a deed of 1300.[130] Some retainers were paid solely in kind,[131] while others took the form of money payments together with liveries in kind.[132] These annuities were usually payable from the client's chamber without being secured on particular lands but there are a few examples of annuities secured on specific lands.[133] There is also at least one example in Edward I's reign of a serjeant being retained not by a pension but by a lifetime grant of land.[134] In the case of serjeants active in local courts, the sums mentioned seem to be at a slightly lower level: the most common payments were one mark a year or 20 shillings. The lowest found is again half a mark,[135] the highest 40 shillings together with two robes.[136] It is not clear whether or not the serjeant was entitled to a further fee if he acted in litigation for a client who paid him a retainer. The Westminster abbey accounts reveal at least two instances of serjeants who were paid annuities also being paid further specific sums for their services; but it is not clear whether they were entitled to such sums or were merely receiving further remuneration from a grateful client.[137]

Annuity deeds are usually vague about the service required in return for the annuity. Many said simply that the annuity had been granted in return for the serjeant's 'homage and service' or for his 'homage, service and counsel' or for his 'service and aid'. In later deeds it became more common to refer to the service or the aid or counsel or some combination of these three words already performed and to be performed in the future as the reason for the grant. But some deeds were more precise. The 1277 deed of William rector of Field Dalling in favour of Nicholas of Calveley, who appears to have acted as an advocate in local ecclesiastical courts as well as a serjeant in local secular courts, stated that the grant was 'for the service (*patrocinium*) already performed and to be performed in future by Nicholas to William in his litigation'.[138] It goes on to specify that Nicholas is obliged to act both within and without the diocese of Norwich as William sends him 'for the expedition of causes' at William's expense.[139] The 1286 deed of Ralph de Tony in favour of Adam of Kinsham specifically required Adam to be intendant to all pleas and business (*negocia*) touching Ralph in the Common Bench, the eyre and in all other places.[140]

Also more precise, but in a different kind of way, was the 1285 deed of the abbot of Barlings in favour of Gilbert of Thornton.[141] This required him to 'attend to the business of our house wherever he might be'. This probably meant that if Gilbert was acting as a serjeant in the eyre, the abbot could not require him to act on his behalf in the Common Bench or vice versa. The service the abbey could require of him was also limited in another respect. Since Gilbert was a king's serjeant, the agreement was subject to a reservation specifically safeguarding 'the faith and service of the king and his heirs'. There is also a second reservation, this time in favour of Gilbert's other prior clients 'to whom he was obliged before he received a fee from our house'. The 1278 deed of the serjeant John de Lisle in favour of his client William of Swinburn was also fairly precise.[142] John promised to be faithful to William and his heirs and to 'stand' with them (act for them in court) and help them with advice and aid to the best of his ability wherever he was or anywhere he could reach, once given notice. This was evidently not his first pension for he was also careful to make a reservation in favour of previous clients; but the deed goes on to make clear that when such clients had litigation with William, John would still not be allowed to act against William but would be obliged to act for neither side.

However unspecific the terms of the grant, those who granted such annuities could in fact expect as a minimum that the annuitant would not assist any opponent of theirs in litigation against them. They might also be entitled to demand that the annuitant act for them. The annuitant's legitimate expectations are the subject of a series of annuity cases heard in the Common Bench. In 1294 Hugh of Lowther sued John of Lancaster for two years arrears of an annuity. John attempted to justify the withdrawal on the grounds that the reason for giving the annuity had been to secure Hugh's aid and counsel but that Hugh had refused to assist him in a plea in the recent Lancashire eyre. Hugh does not seem to have denied this, but the court found that the annuity had not been forfeited since the reason for the grant had not been expressed in the deed.[143] In other pleas of the same period, however, mere refusal to act was considered sufficient cause for the withdrawal. In a 1291 case it was Robert Duffhus's failure to come to the assistance of Maud de Merk when she was indicted in the 1286–7 Suffolk eyre which was adjudged sufficient justification for the loss of that part of an annuity attributable to her.[144]

In 1295 it was Robert of Ringstead's failure to come to the assistance of the prior of Coxford's predecessor when he was impleaded at King's Lynn in 1283 which was pleaded by the prior as justification for stopping payment of an annuity whose arrears were claimed by Robert's executors; it was the truth of this assertion that was denied by the executors.[145] Some doubt about the matter seems to be revealed in a debt plea of 1302 brought by the executors of John de la Chapele against the abbot of Shap. The abbot attempted to bar the annuity by citing John's refusal to act when asked to do so in a plea in the county court of Westmorland but the executors in replying felt it necessary to deny not only this but also that he had ever aided the abbot's opponents in the plea against the abbot.[146]

In an annuity plea of 1307 brought by Robert of Herriard against Nicholas de Vilers the court seems to make a distinction between deeds that spoke of service that had been and would be performed and those that spoke only of future service. In the case of deeds of the former kind the annuity could not be barred by mere failure to serve, but only by the annuitant acting against the client in litigation.¹⁴⁷ A series of cases do indeed show clients alleging annuitants had acted for opponents and citing this as justification for not paying the annuity. There was never any doubt that this warranted ceasing payment.¹⁴⁸ Indeed, as Robert Palmer has pointed out, it was a justification not just for stopping payment of the annuity but also for refusing to pay any arrears that had accumulated before the date when the right to the annuity had been forfeited.¹⁴⁹

When Gilbert of Tothby was sworn of counsel of the city of London in 1298 at a fee of four marks a year, it seems probable that he was being retained as a serjeant in the service of the city for that annual sum.¹⁵⁰ However, it may well be that this retainer was not for life but merely for as long as the city wished to keep his services; as we have seen, the city's attorneys were engaged on such terms.¹⁵¹ It was certainly on similar terms that the king retained serjeants.¹⁵² G. O. Sayles states that the 'first appointment of king's serjeants, regularly paid to make his interests their principal concern, took place in the autumn of 1278'.¹⁵³ This is probably true but misleading. The king's serjeants are mentioned as an established group in the answer to a petition that seems to belong to a date before (though not much before) the autumn of 1278.¹⁵⁴ These earlier serjeants were certainly not regularly paid, though since no royal servants were paid on a regular basis during the first six years of Edward's reign this is hardly surprising. In any case, as Sayles himself noted, at least one of them (Alan of Walkingham) was paid in 1280 for his service as a king's serjeant for the preceding six years (thus taking his paid service to the Crown back to 1274).¹⁵⁵ Earlier still, in the second half of Henry III's reign, as we have seen, the King retained Laurence del Brok to act for him mainly (though not exclusively) in the court of King's Bench between 1247 and 1262 and he appears to have united in his person the functions of attorney and serjeant for the Crown;¹⁵⁶ and there are a number of other references to king's serjeants, though not to them being paid for acting as such.¹⁵⁷

The year 1278, however, clearly marks an important turning-point. In 1278 the king began to pay regular retaining fees to more than one serjeant for the first time, and to retain serjeants principally to act on his behalf before the justices in eyre.¹⁵⁸ The latter move is presumably connected (as Sayles suggests) with the extension of the jurisdiction of the eyre justices to cover claims to franchises and the resulting quo waranto pleas, as also with an expansion in the number of suits brought on the king's behalf to establish his claims to land and other property.¹⁵⁹ Between 1278 and 1294 (when the war with France brought an end to the general eyre) two serjeants were retained on a regular basis at an annual salary of 20 pounds, one on each eyre circuit.¹⁶⁰ From 1290 to 1299 the king paid a regular retainer of ten pounds a year to Richard de Bretteville who seems like Laurence del Brok to have combined the functions of king's serjeant and king's attorney in King's Bench. Although his successor, John of Chester, was paid a similar sum, he seems only to have acted in the latter capacity.[161] From 1292 until the end of the reign the king also retained Nicholas of Warwick for 20 pounds a year to act as king's serjeant in the Common Bench.[162] Although these retaining fees are significantly higher than those paid by private individuals, the king did not obtain an exclusive right to the services of his serjeants. All continued to act for private clients during the time the king retained them, though we can assume that the king had first claim on their services.

The ad hoc engagement of serjeants

A significant number of litigants secured the services of serjeants through permanent retainers but the majority probably obtained them on an *ad hoc* basis through their attorney. This must normally have been arranged in advance of the actual hearing, if only to allow enough time for the serjeant(s) to be briefed on the main facts of the case and for different serjeants to concert tactics with each other.[163] The reports, however, do show us that on occasion a serjeant was engaged only after the hearing had begun. In 1296 a serjeant came up while a case was being pleaded and was engaged on the spot to act for the defendant.[164] In 1306 the judge hearing a case advised the plaintiff's serjeant to go away and seek assistance and the latter subsequently returned with two fellow-serjeants.[165] The serjeants of the Dublin Bench could be assigned by the court to the service of particular litigants if they requested assistance in finding a serjeant.[166] They were perhaps always a smaller group, which might make finding a serjeant more difficult than it was at Westminster. There certainly seems to be no evidence of the same practice being followed at Westminster and indeed fairly strong negative evidence that it was not. In one of the complaints made against the justices during the so-called 'State Trials' Thomas of Denham complained he had been unable to find any serjeant willing to act for him in the Common Bench because two of the justices of the court (Weyland and Brompton) favoured his opponent. But he does not say that he had asked for the court to assign him a serjeant and that this request had been ignored or refused.[167] By the 1290s the justices in eyre were probably assigning serjeants to the service of poor clients and perhaps requiring them to provide gratuitous service. In a bill presented in the 1292 Shropshire eyre a complainant who claimed to be poor asked the justices to 'grant' him a serjeant, 'so that his right is not lost'.[168]

In a mid-fifteenth-century year-book case it was argued (and perhaps also accepted by the court) that in the absence of any specific agreement in advance to the contrary, 40 pence was the sum payable 'as of common right' to a serjeant of the Common Bench for his services.[169] Forty pence is also the sum known to have paid on a number of occasions to various different serjeants acting in the king's courts in Edward I's reign.[170] But we also find serjeants receiving rather larger payments for their services: half a mark (twice the 40 pence fee);[171] one mark;[172] 20 shillings;[173] 30 shillings;[174] 40 shillings[175] and as much as 100 shillings[176] or even ten marks.[177] This suggests that 40 pence was not a standard fixed fee but at most a minimum fee and also therefore (as later) the fee payable if no agreement had been made to the contrary in advance.

7

The English Legal Profession in Edward I's Reign (III): Training and Entry into the Profession

In this and the following chapter I shall examine evidence indicating that it was in Edward I's reign that professional lawyers in England began to behave and to be treated as members of a profession. This evidence relates to the imposition of controls over entry into practice, the development of arrangements for the education of future practitioners and the enunciation and enforcement of rules of conduct for members of the profession.

SERJEANTS

Entry into the profession: a 'closed' profession?

By the end of the fourteenth century members of an 'order' of serjeants at law enjoyed a monopoly of practice in the Common Bench. This 'order' was a small group, consisting of around 12 members at most. Entry into the 'order' was by means of an elaborate ceremony which included the giving of gold rings, the taking of an oath, the making of a count by the newly created serjeant and much feasting. Members were normally admitted into the 'order' in batches and the king's council decided who should take the 'degree and status' of serjeant at law at these 'calls'.[1]

The serjeants who practised in the Common Bench in Edward I's reign were certainly subject to the disciplinary control of the court and the measures at its disposal included the suspension of individual serjeants from practising there.[2] It is tempting to extrapolate from this to the existence of a more general control by the court over who was allowed to offer their services to litigants. But the inference is not necessarily a legitimate one. As John Baker notes: 'it is possible to allow men the freedom to follow any calling, or a multiplicity of callings, without prior examination, and yet to discipline them by punishment if they go wrong'. Baker argues that control of this kind is no more than 'perhaps ... the natural first stage' in the development of more general controls over the practice of a particular profession.[3]

But there are other, better reasons for believing that by the 1290s the Common Bench did exercise some kind of general control over who was allowed to practise in the court. Serjeants who practised there on a regular basis were certainly recognized by the court as possessing some sort of special status. In 1292 Richard Newman of Suffolk submitted a petition to the king's council in which he complained that Adam of Kinsham had dragged him by his hood away from the bar of the court, had knocked him down and had then trampled him underfoot. The council referred the petition to the justices of the court. Under questioning Richard changed some of the details of his story. He still claimed that Adam had dragged him away from the bar of the court and now added that this had been when he was about to plead. But he also now said it had been two other men who had knocked him down and trampled him underfoot. No defence by Adam is recorded. The justices decided that Adam had done no wrong in behaving as he had done and dismissed the case. The precise reason for this judgment is not clear but we do know that the justices considered Adam's action to be justified because he was a 'common serjeant' in the court (*'qui communis serviens est in curia hic'*): that fact is expressly mentioned in their judgment.[4] The implication is that he was justified in taking this action but that someone who was not a serjeant would not have been.[5] This case does not show how individuals attained such a privileged status. Formal admission by the court is one possibility, but not the only one. As will be seen, the 'common attorneys' of the court do not seem to have been specially admitted to practise there by the court but to have acquired this status simply by virtue of the fact that they regularly acted for clients there.[6] The same might also have been true of the 'common serjeants'.

The final concord evidence may take us a little further. As we have seen, a new clause was added to plea-roll entries relating to the making of final concords in the court from Michaelmas term 1293 onward which noted that the parties had their final concord through a particular serjeant.[7] The purpose may have been no more than that of showing which serjeant bore responsibility for the form and content of the fine in question. If so, it would simply have served to reinforce the court's existing disciplinary jurisdiction over serjeants. But it seems rather more likely that its purpose was to ensure that one of the serjeants of the court was associated with the making of every final concord and had received his fee for this. This implies recognition by the court of a specific group of serjeants and the court's willingness to modify its procedures in their interests. It is possible that members of such a group might have gained recognition simply through speaking for clients in the court on a regular basis. But it seems more likely that they would have become members only through some sort of process of admission or recognition by the court. Thus the addition of the new clause provides some reason for thinking that by 1293 there may have existed a specific group of serjeants practising in the Common Bench who possessed a monopoly over at least one of the functions of the serjeant in the court and whose members probably entered the group through some sort of formal admission procedure. If this is the case, then it seems unlikely that they did not also enjoy a monopoly in other areas of the serjeant's work, for there is no reason to suppose that their role in the making of final concords was any more taxing than their role in the transaction of other kinds of business; and there is no obvious reason why members of the group should have enjoyed a monopoly in this area of the serjeant's work and not in other areas.

However, the strongest evidence for thinking that by the 1290s regular practice in the Common Bench had come to be a monopoly in the hands of a group of professional serjeants formally admitted to practise in the court by its justices is to be found in the numbers of serjeants found in regular practice in the court between the early 1290s (when we first begin to find something like complete figures for the numbers of serjeants practising in the court) and 1307. These never rose above 35 and are more commonly around 30.[8] Such stability might have been the product of 'natural selection', the workings of the market within what was still an open profession, as John Baker has suggested, but this seems unlikely.[9] The amount of business coming to the court doubled during the same period. In free-market conditions such a doubling ought to have created openings for sizeable numbers of additional serjeants. It did not. It seems even less likely that the free market alone could or would have produced the phenomenon clearly observable in 1293 and 1299 of a whole group of serjeants taking up practice together at almost exactly the same time.[10] This implies the existence of restrictions on entry and probably means that in both these years there was a 'group call' of serjeants similar to the much better attested 'group calls' of the fourteenth century, when a whole group of men were admitted to the 'order' of serjeants at the same time.[11]

Other more circumstantial evidence for the existence of a 'closed' order of serjeants in the Common Bench by the end of the thirteenth century is to be found in the clear separation of attorneys from serjeants[12] and the emergence of a group of 'apprentices' of the king's court.[13] As John Baker notes: 'In the absence of control over admission there will be no clear line between men of different degree. There will be no demarcation between learners and practitioners, nor between attorneys and countors'.[14] Evidence of the existence of such distinctions is in itself presumptive evidence of the existence of such control.

John Baker's main argument against the existence of a closed group of Common Bench serjeants during the reigns of Edward I and Edward II is that a number of individuals appear as serjeants on the plea-rolls or in the reports during this period for only a short period of time or only in a few references. He sees these men as the unsuccessful competitors in a free market: 'the beginner who did not succeed, or the man who tried his luck at the bar before moving on'.[15] Some of the individuals he cites seem to be well-known serjeants under alternative names;[16] others may not have been Common Bench serjeants at all.[17] But clearly there is a residue of men whose brief appearance in the records cannot be explained on either of these grounds. There remain two explanations, neither of which is inconsistent with the existence of controls over practice in the Common Bench. As yet the number of serjeants admitted to practise at any one time was comparatively large, certainly when compared with the figures for the mid-fourteenth century and later. It may therefore have been possible for a man to pass whatever tests were imposed to secure a reasonable standard among those admitted to practise but still to fail in the subsequent competition for clients. The serjeants of the Common Bench, moreover, are also known to have been active during the same period in a number of other royal courts: King's Bench, the General Eyre, the Assize courts.[18] It is quite possible that some men gained admission to the ranks of Common Bench serjeants, perhaps as the only available professional qualification and with a view to impressing potential clients, but who always intended to practise primarily in one of these other courts or found it easier to make a living there and did so.

This does not mean there was as yet necessarily anything quite like the ceremonial admission of new serjeants found later in the fourteenth century.[19] Nor is there any reason to believe that the king or his council as yet had any part to play in deciding who should become serjeants or in pressuring certain individuals into taking up the 'status and degree' of serjeant at law. This seems to be a development of the later fourteenth century.[20] But there must have been some kind of admission procedure: and admission probably depended in some way on the justices of the court being satisfied about the competence of those they were admitting.

There is no evidence that a 'closed' group of serjeants enjoyed a similar monopoly of practice in any other royal court, though lack of evidence comparable to that available for the Common Bench means we cannot entirely exclude such a possibility. In any case, as we have seen, by the latter part of the reign it was the serjeants of the Common Bench who dominated practice in King's Bench and the Eyre, so admission to the elite in the Common Bench was in practice also admission to practise in those courts as well.

A separate 'closed' group of serjeants enjoyed a monopoly of practice in the courts of the city of London. This was specifically authorized by a city ordinance of 1280.[21] It purports to have been made at the request of the skilled serjeants currently in practice in the city. But there is reason to doubt whether all its clauses were in fact their suggestions and it seems possible that their 'request' was a mere formality and that the real impulse for the legislation came from elsewhere. The existing situation, as depicted in the preamble to the ordinance, was that anyone could offer his services as a serjeant in the city courts. As a result, it was claimed, litigants were losing their cases and in some instances suffering disinheritance through reliance on the services of men who called themselves serjeants but who did not possess the requisite skills. There are also other problems which the makers of the ordinance believed were associated with the existence of a free market in legal services. These included the use of abusive language by serjeants in court and the perversion of justice in the city courts through the practice of serjeants sitting as assessors to the judges of those courts. The ordinance is careful to safeguard the individual litigant's right to use the services of relatives and strangers in individual cases, but lays down that only those with the requisite legal skills are to be allowed to offer their services as serjeants in the city courts on a regular basis. It also requires all such practitioners to take an oath to observe certain specified rules of conduct. The ordinance insists that in future no serjeant should act as an attorney or as an essoiner. This is part of a more general scheme of total separation of the three groups, with the members of each group performing only the functions of his own group.[22] Subsequent evidence shows that the 1280 ordinance was enforced in practice down to the end of the reign and controlled those allowed to practise in the city courts.[23]

Training and education

In the late 1280s we begin to hear of the existence of a group of 'apprentices of the Common Bench'. The earliest reference so far noted is one of 1289 to Nigel of Amcotts, then living in York, and to an unnamed fellow-apprentice. The context is a legal one but does not show them undertaking legal work or gaining legal experience. They were in trouble with the law for having stolen ginger, canvas and swords at Boston fair.[24] Further references to apprentices of the court occur in 1292,[25] 1293–4,[26] 1298,[27] 1301,[28] 1302,[29] 1303[30] and 1305.[31] There are also other undated references which seem to belong to the same period.[32] The term 'apprentice' simply means 'learner'[33] and these men seem to have acquired their name from the fact that they were studying to acquire the skills and legal knowledge required to become a serjeant of the Common Bench.

One important element in their studies was regular attendance at the court. Here they could listen to the serjeants and justices at work.[34] By the end of Edward I's reign and perhaps for some time before, the court was giving them official encouragement. We first hear of the 'crib', a special enclosure set aside for their use, in a petition from the apprentices to the king dating from early in Edward II's reign. This asks him to allow them to set up a second 'crib' on the other side of the court. Since the petition gives no hint that the first 'crib' had only recently been erected we may deduce it was already in existence by the later years of Edward I's reign.[35] The petition specifically describes the 'crib' as being for the education of the petitioners (*'pur lour esteer a lour aprise'*). The justices of the court explained matters for the benefit of the apprentices present in court. The earliest evidence of this is a 1302 case where chief justice Hengham explained the general rule involved specifically for their benefit at the end of a case.[36] The apprentices, moreover, seem to have done rather more than just sit and listen. Different theories have been put forward about the identity and motives of the compilers of the early year-book reports. The most plausible remains that long ago advanced by Maitland, who saw in them the work of the apprentices and who suggested that they compiled the reports for their own instruction.[37] They learned their law and mastered the technical skills of the serjeant not just by attending the court but also by recording what they heard for subsequent study.

Apprentices evidently also learnt their law in other ways. By the early fourteenth century reports had come to play a dual role in the education of lawyers. They were compiled in court, perhaps by the more senior apprentices, as part of their own education. But they were also used, again perhaps by those more senior apprentices, to teach law to others, probably their own more junior colleagues.[38] There are several indications of this in the surviving manuscripts. In many reports there is an explanation of the factual situation underlying the dispute either at the beginning or at some other relevant point. This was certainly not the work of a listener taking down what he had heard in court, for no such clear account of the underlying factual situation was ever given in court except sometimes at the jury stage of litigation: a stage the reporters normally ignore. It is conceivable that the reporters gained the knowledge that allowed them to write the explanatory paragraph as a result of being present in court at the jury-verdict stage or perhaps because they had been present at the preliminary briefing session between one of the litigant's attorneys and his serjeants.[39] But the paragraph seems to owe its position and form to the demands of the classroom. The teacher using the report finds it necessary to provide a summary of the underlying factual situation in order to explain what happened in court and why the pleading took the form it did. We also find what seem to be superfluous notes embedded in reports making specific points related to the matters being discussed but going beyond what was actually said in the course of pleading by either serjeants or justices.[40] Again, these look like the work of teachers using the reports as a way of teaching law to junior colleagues. Even more characteristic of the pedagogue is the summary at the end of the report of the various points of interest or significance the student should note.[41] By the end of the reign there may also have been lectures in the form of commentaries on the statutes, a forerunner of the later 'readings' associated with the inns of court.[42] The most likely audience for such lectures is the junior apprentices; the most likely teachers, the senior apprentices or serjeants.

Another element in the educational system were formal disputations that bear a distant resemblance to the formal disputations of contemporary universities. The evidence for them comes from around 23 different *questiones* or *questiones disputate* to be found in as many as nine different early fourteenth-century manuscripts.[43] Most follow the same basic pattern. The *questio* starts with a brief statement of facts. This is followed by a question of law related to these facts. This in turn is followed by alternate paragraphs of arguments for two contrary viewpoints on the question of law.[44] At first sight these *questiones* bear a resemblance to year-book reports of real litigation. However, what is distinctive about them is that they never give names to either of the 'parties' involved (other than A and B) nor any other circumstantial detail; they are generally concerned with a single question of law and never cover more than three closely related points (unlike the year-book reports which almost always raise a number of unrelated points); and they never tell us of a presiding judge's opinion expressed during the course of the argument or of his final judgment on a disputed point (something always of interest to the reporter in real cases).[45]

Some of these *questiones* may represent a boiling-down of material from real cases for educational purposes: an abstraction of an argument out of its original context in order to present it as starkly and clearly as possible.[46] Others may have arisen in the kind of circumstances of which we are told in a report of an assize of novel disseisin case heard while Mettingham was chief justice of the Common Bench (1290–1301). Mettingham had given judgment in the case but then argued the principle involved with one of the serjeants in the case. The reporter introduces the argument with the words 'after the judgment the opposite was argued for the sake of disputation' (*post judicium arguetur ad opositum causa disputacionis*).[47] But this does not seem to be true of most of them. They read like wholly artificial disputations in an academic setting between two or more individuals. It seems possible that they were a regular part of the training of apprentices. Indeed, it is just possible that it was through proficiency in them that an apprentice manifested his fitness to become a serjeant.[48] There is also some evidence to suggest that there may have been learning exercises to give future serjeants practice in making counts and defences and engaging in the subsequent oral argument that was typical of the contemporary English courtroom. An undated report in British Library MS. Additional 31826 appears to show serjeant Inge presiding at such an exercise and giving his critique both of the count made and of the subsequent defence (made by the future serjeant and Common Bench justice, Doncaster).[49]

Private reading also seems likely to have played some part in their education. By the end of the thirteenth century *Bracton* was becoming seriously out of date on many points but chief justice Mettingham in 1294 clearly expected the serjeants arguing before him to have ready access to it and to know it well enough to find passages dealing with particular topics there;[50] it seems reasonable to assume that the treatise would also have been read by at least some apprentices. They are also a possible market for the treatises based on *Bracton: Britton* and the much less successful *Fleta* and *Thornton*, both probably the work of men who had themselves been serjeants.[51] The apprentices are also the probable market for the various works produced during the reign of Edward I which dealt with counting and the making of exceptions: the three different collections of specimen counts (and related defences) which have been edited as *Novae Narrationes*;[52] the Latin treatise *Articuli qui narrando indigent specificari* (also known by a variety of other names) which sets out the main elements needed in counts in the most common types of action;[53] the Latin treatise *Excepciones contra brevia* which sets out some of the more common types of exception to a variety of different actions[54] and (just possibly) the Latin treatise *Excepciones ad cassandum brevia*, though this is at such a basic level that it may well belong to the more elementary educational treatises whose probable market was young men wanting to become attorneys.[55] However, it is difficult to be absolutely certain whether the main method of transmission of these treatises was in writing rather than oral teaching. It is possible that their proper place is with the evidence for the instruction of apprentices.

Most Common Bench serjeants of Edward I's reign I can be shown to have acted as attorneys in the court before becoming serjeants. Some did this only for a relatively short period of time and had comparatively few clients.[56] Others were in practice with many clients for much longer periods.[57] Practice as an attorney would have been a valuable training in itself for the future serjeant. It was the attorney who was responsible for briefing serjeants for his clients. The questions which they asked and he had to answer must have provided him with a valuable practical education in the legal rules relevant to the cases concerned and perhaps also gave him an insight into the various possible litigation strategies which might be adopted by serjeants.[58] He was also commonly present in court to hear the serjeants pleading for his client and ready to avow or disavow what they had said.[59] If faced with a decision about the avowal or disavowal of the serjeant he was probably able to take advice from other serjeants employed by his client and from the serjeant himself, but it seems unlikely that he would not also have been paying attention to what had been said against just such an eventuality. This too was an excellent preparation for a future serjeant who needed to learn how to make counts and defences of the correct form and the rules of pleading.

Many of these future serjeants who acted as attorneys at an earlier stage in their careers may well have thought of themselves as apprentices of the

Common Bench helping to support themselves by acting as attorneys rather than as full-time professional attorneys. The existence of such a group seems to be assumed in the legislation of 1292 which attempted to restrict practice as a professional attorney in the court to county quotas of attorneys.[60] This stipulated that those selected by the justices to make up these quotas were to be drawn from the 'better and more respectable and the better learners'; and that it was specifically apprentices that the king and his council had in mind is demonstrated by the fact that the relevant entry on the parliament roll refers to itself as being concerned with apprentices as well as attorneys. It was probably not intended to restrict practice solely to apprentices but it was clearly the intention that room should be found in the county quotas for those apprentices who also acted as attorneys. Additional evidence that apprentices sometimes acted as attorneys is provided by litigation of the same year in which a defendant sought to escape liability for negligence in suing a plea on the grounds that he was not a professional attorney.[61] The instructions sent to the justices of assize before whom the jury was to give its verdict told them to proceed to judgment if the jury found that the defendant was not an 'attorney of this court or apprentice'; but to remit the case to the Common Bench for judgement if they found that he was. So, too, in a case of 1301 we find an apprentice of the court, Thomas Torel, being sent to prison for the year and a day laid down by statute for serjeants (and subsequently extended by judicial rulings to professional attorneys) for deceiving the court in litigation conducted on his own behalf, but at the end of his term being ordered not to meddle with the prosecution or defence of any pleas in the court, again clearly assuming that as an apprentice Thomas would normally act for others as their attorney.[62]

We have no information about the education and training of the serjeants who practised in the courts of the city of London. However, we do know a little about the training of the serjeants who practised in county courts. Several of the Warwickshire county-court serjeants at the end of the reign had been active as attorneys in the Common Bench over considerable periods of time.[63] As we have seen, service as an attorney could in itself be a good preparation for acting as a serjeant. It is also possible that some of these men took advantage of the educational opportunities available to the apprentices of the Common Bench while acting as attorneys and may even themselves have been apprentices. The serjeants of other county courts were probably educated in the same way. A report of a trespass case apparently heard in the Cambridgeshire county court around 1300 shows both serjeants arguing by analogy from the way trespass cases were dealt with in the Common Bench and thereby indicating that they, too, both had a detailed knowledge of the court which was presumably gained from having studied there.[64] By the end of the reign there may even have been a lecture course in London intended for the aspiring local serjeant. The treatise *Curia placitata* (or *Chescun manere de trespas*) survives in at least five different manuscripts and two rather different versions and seems to derive from lectures given in the early fourteenth century.[65] The treatise starts as a guide to preliminary process in trespass pleas in local courts but goes on to give specimen counts and defences in a range of types of plea that might be heard in such courts. The local detail that occurs in one of these versions suggests a London connection. An agreement to lend oxen for ploughing is rather implausibly said to have been made in the house of Edmund Peacok in the suburb of London in a street called Fleet Street.[66] A little more plausibly a replevin avowry justifies a distraint made against the tenant of a messuage and a virgate in Holborn close by.[67]

ATTORNEYS

Controls on practice: the 1292 ordinance on the attorneys of the Common Bench

An ordinance of 1292 purported to limit the number of professional attorneys practising in the Common Bench, and to give the justices of the court power to decide who should be allowed to practise there.[68] The justices were instructed to establish a separate quota for each county and were advised that the king and his council considered that a countrywide total of around 140 would be about correct. They were, however, given the freedom to fix the total at under or over this figure. The quota for each county was to be filled with the 'better, the more respectable and the more willing to learn' ('*de melioribus et legalioribus et libentius addiscentibus*') of the existing attorneys and apprentices.[69] Only those who had been admitted to the quota were to be allowed to stay around the court and do business for others there.[70] The ordinance empowered the justices to deal as they thought fit with those infringing its terms; but a related royal mandate issued later that same year instructed the justices to notify the king of their names, so that he might deal with them.[71]

The motive for making this ordinance seems to have been concern at evidence of widespread misconduct by professional attorneys. The royal mandate of 2 June 1292 speaks of their 'numbers, and the fraud and malice of many of them' which 'often leads to the unnecessary disturbance of numbers of people' as the reason for its enactment. G. O. Sayles has plausibly connected the ordinance with evidence of a general enquiry into the misconduct of attorneys, the results of which were recorded in 'rolls of the indictments of attorneys' which no longer survive.[72] The underlying theory seemed to be that excessive numbers of attorneys lead to unnecessary litigation, as attorneys tried to make a living not by serving a pre-existing demand for their services by creating it themselves.[73] The theory may also have been that excessive numbers meant that some attorneys could survive only by 'fraud and malice' though this is less clear. It may be that 'fraud and malice' on the part of attorneys were simply seen as a consequence of the courts failing to exercise any control over who was admitted to the ranks of professional attorneys.

The ordinance of 1292 sounds impressive and legal historians have generally taken it to mark a major stage in the development of the legal profession. Maitland thought that 'by this measure' both branches of the profession were placed under the control of the justices and 'apparently a monopoly was secured for those who had been thus appointed'.[74] Plucknett believed that the ordinance placed 'legal education under the direction of the court' and succeeded in turning 'the attorneys' branch' of the legal profession into 'a closed profession, reserved for those who had been educated to it and admitted to it, in the official course'. Thereafter, he believed, 'each county had its group of attorneys who confined their activities to business arising within their county'. He also thought that it might have had a similar effect on the other branch of the legal profession (the serjeants).[75] However, there is no reason to suppose that the ordinance had, or was intended to have, any effect on the serjeants' branch of the legal profession. When ordinance and writ are read in conjunction with each other it becomes clear that the apprentices are only mentioned in the ordinance as constituting a special group among the attorneys whom the framers of the ordinance wished to single out for special (and more favourable) treatment when the county quotas were chosen, not because there was any intention to control who became apprentices. Nor was there anything in the ordinance to suggest it was intended to bring legal education under the control of the court: the passage that Plucknett appears to have understood to mean this seems rather to have been concerned with ensuring that only those admitted to the quotas offered their professional services as attorneys to clients.

Plucknett and Maitland were right in thinking that the legislation was intended to turn the professional attorneys of the court into a closed group, with separate groups allocated to each county, but they were wrong to assume that the ordinance was carried into effect. If county quotas were established in 1292 (and there is no other evidence that they were), they had soon fallen into disuse: there is no evidence of new attorneys being admitted in the place of those who had retired or died or in place of those apprentices who had been promoted to become serjeants, something that should have been recorded on the plea-rolls of the court. Nor is there any evidence of either justices or the king taking measures to prevent persons not admitted to the quota from practising in the court or punishing them for doing so. Moreover, as we have seen, the number of professional attorneys practising in the court in 1300 (only eight years after the ordinance) seems to have been at least 210, well in excess of the 140 envisaged in the ordinance.[76]

Just why the measure should have turned out to be so ineffective is much less clear. Perhaps the outbreak of war with France in 1294 distracted the attention of king and council from its enforcement. Perhaps it was just that it soon became clear that it was difficult, if not impossible, to enforce. There was no clear dividing line between amateur and professional attorney and no easy way of distinguishing one from the other. As long as litigants were allowed to appoint their relations and their friends as their attorneys, it was difficult to stop individual attorneys who were practising for hire from getting themselves appointed by litigants. At the moment of appointment, they looked no different from the amateur attorney and, once appointed, they could only be prevented from acting for their client by leaving the client without an attorney to represent them: something that might cause the litigant considerable inconvenience and delay.

The control of practice by professional attorneys in other courts

Only in the city of London is there evidence of any similar attempt to restrict professional practice to a small group of attorneys. The ordinance of 1280, which introduced the monopoly of a small group of serjeants, did not attempt to introduce a similar monopoly for a similar group of attorneys, though it did debar attorneys from acting as essoiners as well as serjeants.[77] However, the 1289 memorandum on the admission of serjeants under the provisions of the ordinance gives the names of six individuals 'admitted and elected' by the serjeants who seem to have been attorneys and who may have been intended to enjoy a monopoly of professional practice in the city courts.[78] The monopoly, if such it was, may only have been short-lived. When the next group of serjeants were admitted and sworn in in 1305, space was left for noting the names of the attorneys admitted to practise but it was left blank.[79]

The education of professional attorneys

Although there is no evidence that those wanting to practise as professional attorneys in the Common Bench or elsewhere were required to satisfy the justices of the court or any other authority as to their professional competence, it seems clear that there was a market in the second half of the thirteenth century for elementary legal instruction and probable that among the persons comprising this market a considerable number were intending to practise as professional attorneys.

Proof that such a market did exist is provided by the surviving evidence of attempts made to satisfy it. By 1278 at the latest, lectures were being given, probably at Westminster, to provide beginners with a basic introduction to common-law litigation. These started with a general analysis of the different kinds of action and then looked in more detail at each of the more common types, explaining the different kinds of complaint or claim that could be made through each of them, giving the wording of the appropriate original writ (but translated into French) and reproducing a specimen count and defence for each type. The earliest manuscript to contain these lectures (British Library, MS. Lansdowne 467) fortunately preserves many of the asides and connective passages that provide the main evidence for seeing the work as a student's report of a series of lectures given by a teacher rather than as a elementary treatise which only ever circulated in written form.[80] Two further manuscripts now both at Harvard (Harvard Law School, MSS. 24 and 33) appear to record the lectures of the same teacher a few years later, revised to incorporate references to cases heard on the northern eyre circuit in 1278 and 1279 and changes made by the statute of Gloucester of 1278. Neither manuscript contains as much connective material as Lansdowne 467 and, had it not been for the evidence supplied by the latter, it would not be possible to be certain that they were also derived from lectures.[81]

There is no evidence that our anonymous teacher of the late 1270s went on updating his course or found any successors who taught a similar course during the 1280s, but what we do have from this period are two treatises that offered a different kind of introduction to the more common types of remedy available in the king's courts. *Modus Componendi Brevia* was composed in Latin c.1285 and provides a brief analysis of the various kinds of action about title to land and to advowsons, explaining the different circumstances in which each was appropriate.[82] It also discusses the uses of the three different kinds of remedy available in the case of disputes about liability to feudal services; it gives an account of the different remedies available in pasture-right disputes; and concludes with a brief introduction to different kinds of exception. It does not give any of the actual writs or specimen counts and defences in the various different kinds of action. The treatise purports to be the work of senior chancery clerk writing for the use of junior colleagues, but it reads as though it was composed with the needs of the law student as well as the junior chancery clerk in mind. The manuscripts in which it is found normally also include a number of other contemporary legal treatises, suggesting that it went into general circulation as a fairly basic treatise containing information that was useful to law students at an early stage in their careers and perhaps to non-experts, too. It is conceivable that it was derived from what was originally a lecture but more probable that it was only ever a written treatise.

The second treatise, composed in French a little later (but not long after 1285), is the first of the various treatises to bear the name *Natura Brevium*.[83] This explains the functions of the most common types of action (a much wider range of actions than are discussed in *Modus Componendi Brevia*) and the mesne process appropriate to each. It does not reproduce the writs themselves or give any specimen counts or defences. Internal evidence suggests that this 'treatise' may have started life as a lecture or series of lectures[84] but its subsequent textual transmission was probably as a written treatise.[85] A third treatise composed between 1285 and 1290 was *Hengham Parva*.[86] This covered four separate topics: the different kinds of essoin; the different kinds of dower action; the rules about the viewing of land in land actions; and the working of the assize of novel disseisin. All are discussed with particular reference to the relevant statutes relating to each topic. The choice of topics suggests that the intended market or audience for the work was those who wanted to become professional attorneys or perhaps those beginning to act as such. It is conceivable that derived from lectures given by chief justice Hengham during those years.

By 1300 the register of writs may have formed the subject of an organized educational course run by senior chancery clerks and geared to the needs not just of their juniors but also of law students. This is suggested by the content of the notes and rules accompanying the writ formulas in surviving registers and the sheer number of such notes and rules.[87] Professional attorneys needed to know about the various different kinds of original writ that were available to litigants in order to advise their clients about which writs they should purchase and indeed to purchase them for clients themselves.[88] A detailed knowledge of the formulas appropriate to each writ might also save their clients time and money when chancery clerks made some blunder in their writing. Since this was so, attendance at such a course was perhaps already part of the preparation necessary or at least desirable for any would-be professional attorney.

8

The English Legal Profession in Edward I's Reign (IV): Regulation

During Edward I's reign professional lawyers began to be treated as members of a distinct occupational group to whose behaviour special rules applied. Legislation established certain norms and provided penalties for their infraction. Courts enforced and interpreted this legislation and enforced other norms of professional behaviour.

THE LEGISLATION

National legislation

The first legislation specifically concerned with the behaviour of members of the nascent English legal profession was chapter 29 of the statute of Westminster I of 1275.[1] Its main focus was on serjeants practising in the king's courts.[2] Any serjeant convicted of conduct amounting to deceit or collusion (irrespective of whether it was the court itself or a litigant who was being deceived) was to be imprisoned for a year and a day and permanently barred from practice. Similar misconduct by others was to be punished by a similar term of imprisonment and the king was to impose a stiffer penalty in any case where the gravity of the offence seemed to require it.[3] The legislation seems to have been badly drafted or to have been amended without due care. The use of the term 'other' appears to suggest that the statutory punishment awaited the non-professional attorney or litigant convicted of misconduct. In practice, however, only professional serjeants and attorneys received such punishment and it seems probable that this was in accordance with the intentions of the legislators.

The statute said nothing about professional lawyers practising outside the king's courts.[4] This may again be a drafting error or it may be that this was because they were as yet so few in number as to be easily overlooked. But there are also other possibilities. The regulation of lawyers practising in city courts could perhaps safely and more appropriately be left to city authorities.[5] Local regulation might also have been thought appropriate for lawyers practising in county courts. However, the first part of chapter 33 of the same statute provided that no sheriff was to allow any 'baretour' to 'maintain' (*'meintenir'*) cases in the county court.[6] 'Maintenance' covered at least some of the functions normally performed by professional lawyers[7] and 'baretour', though perhaps more precisely a term for dishonest lawyers,[8] may have been used here simply as a pejorative term for professional lawyers in general. If so, this part of the chapter was in effect an attempt to prohibit professional lawyers practising in the county court altogether.

No other general legislation of the reign was concerned solely with the conduct of professional lawyers. They were singled out for special mention in the so-called *Statute of Conspirators* of 1292, whose main purpose was to prevent the stirring up of 'false' litigation, by which the framers probably meant avoidable or unnecessary cases.[9] This was clearly a phenomenon then causing some general concern, for it was also cited as one of the motives for the abortive legislation of the same year to restrict the number of professional attorneys allowed to practise in the Common Bench.[10] The statute identified 'champerty', the practice by which lawyers and others acted for litigants or gave litigants other forms of support in return for a share of whatever was at stake in the case, as the main cause for this. But the prohibition of champerty contained in the statute was a general one and the punishment (three years imprisonment and a fine) the same for professional lawyers as for others. G. O. Sayles has described this 'statute' as 'rightly placed among the flotsam and jetsam of legal pronouncements which the editors of the *Statutes of the Realm* consigned to their apocrypha of 'Statutes of Uncertain Date'.[11] There is certainly no evidence of the three-year term of imprisonment ever being imposed and it seems possible that the 'statute' may be merely a legislative draft that came to be copied into books of statutes as though it had been duly enacted. But it is also possible that the statute was briefly in force but was soon superseded by the *Ordinance of Conspirators* of 1293. This dealt with a wider range of misconduct than the earlier statute (though it included champerty) and left the punishment of 'conspirators' (including those convicted of champerty) to the discretion of the justices.[12] Champerty was also mentioned in chapter 11 of the *Articuli super Cartas* of 1300.[13] This asserted (mistakenly) that only royal officials were prohibited from the practice (under chapter 25 of the statute of Westminster I of 1275)[14] and so extended the prohibition to make it of general applicability. Professional lawyers were not singled out for special mention or special treatment, except by a saving clause making it clear that the legislation was not intended to prohibit payment for their services.

Local legislation

The only local legislation known to survive from the same period comes from London. In 1280 the city authorities enacted what amounted to a general code of conduct for the professional lawyers practising in the city's courts.[15] The code reflects a variety of concerns. Worry about the unnecessary stirring up of litigation is the probable motive for the prohibition of champerty.[16] Concern about corruption and the betrayal of clients lies behind the prohibition against receiving money from the opponents of clients ('ambidexterity'). Concern about undue influence exercised on the courts by lawyers on behalf of clients underlay the prohibition against either serjeants or attorneys leaving their proper places in the courts to sit as assessors with those presiding over the sheriffs' courts, or sitting with them on a more informal basis unless specifically requested to do so and on condition that the lawyer concerned swore not to support any of the parties with cases before the court.[17] A wish to ensure that city courts conducted their business with due decorum explains the requirement that serjeants should refrain from abusing their opponents while pleading there. A similar concern with decorum and a desire to uphold the prestige and dignity of the city and its courts led to a prohibition against serjeants impugning the judgments of those courts or their records other than by bringing an action of error in due form before the mayor of the city and to a prohibition against them seeking to overturn the decisions of the city community.

The serjeants admitted to practise in the city courts were required to take an oath to observe these provisions. No such requirement was imposed on the city's professional attorneys, probably because they were not obtaining a monopoly of professional practice. But observance of the code was also ensured through a sliding scale of penalties. Abuse of an opponent, sitting with a judge without being specially requested or impugning the judgments or record of the court were the least serious. If they took place in the sheriffs' court the punishment was suspension of the serjeant for eight days or half a mark's fine; if in the husting court, the minimum punishment was suspension of the serjeant for three sessions. Ambidexterity was punished by suspension of the serjeant (and perhaps also of the attorney) for three years and also, though this part of the ordinance is not very clear, the payment of damages equivalent to double the amount received. Permanent suspension from practice awaited the serjeant who sought to overturn the decisions of the city community and the serjeant or attorney who was convicted of champerty. In addition, and even though due diligence was not something specifically mentioned in the code of conduct, attorneys who lost their clients' cases

The Regulation of the Legal Profession 123

through negligence were threatened with imprisonment 'in accordance with the king's statute', presumably for the year and a day stipulated by chapter 29 of the statute of Westminster I.[18]

ETHICAL REGULATION IN PRACTICE

The serjeants of the king's courts

The enactment of chapter 29 of the statute of Westminster I suggests that misconduct by the serjeants of the king's courts had been a major problem before 1275 though there is in fact no other independent evidence to support this conclusion. It might therefore have been expected that there would have been a flood of cases against errant serjeants after 1275 and that these would have helped to clarify the chapter's meaning and establish clear guidelines for the conduct of serjeants. In practice, however, such cases were rare and there are only two possible instances of the statutory penalties being imposed on a serjeant between 1275 and 1307.

Misbehaviour in a serjeant's own litigation and business dealings Both cases concerned a single individual, Matthew of the Exchequer. Matthew was associated with William of Gisleham in suing pleas on the king's behalf in the 1286 Suffolk eyre. He also seems to have assisted him in the 1287 Hertfordshire eyre[19] but he does not appear among the serjeants of the Common Bench in the surviving reports of this period, nor is he mentioned in any of the surviving reports of cases from contemporary eyres. His legal knowledge and close acquaintance with the treatise known as *Bracton*, however, are attested by his probable authorship of *Fleta*. Although this is in large part an epitome of *Bracton* it also shows knowledge of recent legislation and other legal material.[20] One complaint alleged that when Matthew had levied a final concord with the complainant by way of assurance for a lease, he had tricked the complainant into giving him permanent title to the lands leased and to certain other lands as well. The other alleged that he had knowingly sued a default against the complainant after that complainant had been essoined. Matthew was convicted on both charges and sent to the Fleet prison for two successive terms of a year and a day.[21] These cases show that a serjeant convicted of fraudulent behaviour in his own dealings (particularly if they involved the courts) or in his own litigation (even though he was not acting in a professional capacity) was subject to the statutory punishment appointed for professional misconduct.[22]

The duty of loyalty to clients In 1282 the men of the manor of South Petherton brought litigation in King's Bench against William of Wells who had acted as their serjeant in earlier proceedings in the court against the lord of their manor.[23] They claimed they had paid him part of the fee for his professional assistance but that he had failed to give it and had gone over to their opponent without their permission. They also alleged that he had changed sides after he knew their *'consilium'* (perhaps here to be translated as their strategy for the litigation) and that he had reported their *'consilium'* to their opponent. They were not suing him for breach of contract but prosecuting him for breach of his professional obligations. His behaviour evidently constituted 'deception' within the terms of the statute of 1275. In his defence, William claimed that he had left their service only because they had refused to pay him more than the first instalment of the money promised and had told him they no longer needed his help. He also claimed he had never helped the other party. The factual disagreement was submitted to a jury. Although no verdict or judgment is recorded, the case is significant for its revelations about the general rules of conduct which both parties, and probably the court itself, assumed were applicable in the serjeant-client relationship. A serjeant was not entitled to leave the service of his clients before the conclusion of litigation unless they told him they no longer needed him or unless they failed to pay him the money promised. If he did leave a client's service, he was not entitled to enter the service of his opponent unless he had specific permission to do so.

A report of an unidentified case of the late thirteenth or early fourteenth century shows that Walter of Risley and his wife had been summoned to the Common Bench to acknowledge what right they claimed in lands whose reversion had been granted to a third party by final concord.[24] Both grantor and grantee of the reversion claimed that Walter's wife was only life-tenant of the lands. She claimed to hold them in fee simple. The court did not think it could allow issue to be joined on this point in such proceedings and so put the case *sine die*. The grantee subsequently brought a second action against the same husband and wife. Their serjeant objected that they had previously gone *sine die* in a similar case. No immediate judgement was given. When the case came on for rehearing their serjeant refused to speak for his erstwhile clients. He had discovered in the interim that they were only entitled to a life-tenancy of the land but were reluctant to admit this because of their prior claim to the fee simple (since such a claim was grounds for them forfeiting even their life-tenancy). The court did not find such behaviour reprehensible. A serjeant, it seems, was entitled to desert his clients even in the middle of a case in circumstances such as these, when by continuing to represent his clients he would be engaging in conduct intended to deceive the court.

A 1292 case shows that the serjeant's obligations towards his client did not end once the litigation for which the serjeant had been engaged was over. John of Mutford, a leading serjeant, was about to act for the earl of Norfolk in litigation the earl was bringing in the Common Bench against John Weyland claiming the Suffolk manor of Blaxhall. His right to do so was challenged because in previous, connected litigation in the court of King's

Bench John had acted for John Weyland and thus already knew John Weyland's 'secrets' (the strengths and weaknesses of his case). Judgment was given that he should act for John instead and he then did so.[25] The serjeant's duty of loyalty subsisted beyond the original plea and obliged him not to appear against that client in any subsequent related litigation; the court itself would enforce the obligation if necessary. There is no hint that Mutford was disciplined, perhaps because the rules were still being clarified and it seemed unreasonable to penalize a serjeant for breach of rules that were themselves only just being written.

Duty not to deceive the court

Other cases flesh out some details of what was involved in the serjeant's duty not to deceive the court and of possible defences to such a charge. In 1294 Robert of 'Hakebech' brought litigation against the abbot of Crowland, alleging that he had been distrained by his plough-animals when other animals were available for distraint, contrary to a statute of 1275.[26] Robert said that 14 of his plough-oxen had been taken by the abbot on 19 May 1291. The abbot's serjeant alleged there had been previous litigation between them about the distraint of 14 oxen by the non-statutory writ of replevin, although in that case eight of the oxen were said to have been taken on 26 May and six on 29 May; the abbot had made a successful avowry justifying his distraint and had secured judgement for the animals' return. He said Robert should not be allowed to contest the same distraint a second time. Robert's serjeant, Simon East, pointed out that the dates assigned to the distraint in the two actions were different, implying that they were about different events. The abbot's serjeant claimed his client had only made the two distraints mentioned in the previous case and that the plaintiff had simply assigned a different day to the distraint (the day of the distraint was not normally material to the action) in order not to be seen to infringe the rule against bringing a second action on the same facts as the first. Chief justice Mettingham then intervened. He warned East of the danger he was in if he was responsible for advising his client of this way of attempting to evade the rule against litigating twice about the same set of facts: '*Simon, parnet garde qe co ne seit mie vostre fet pur le peril*' ('Simon, take care that this is none of your doing: for you are in danger'). The implication is that he will incur the penalty laid down by the statute for attempting to deceive the court if this is the case.

East, however, was able to turn at once to his client's attorneys who were present in court. They confirmed they had given him the facts on which he had based his count, thereby absolving him of responsibility. They in turn were then given a warning by the chief justice for they, too, were in peril under the provisions of the statute. But they also claimed that the facts they had supplied East were the facts given them by their client and thus not their idea of a way of evading the bar.[27] A deliberate attempt to deceive the court by making a statement containing facts the serjeant knew to be untrue (perhaps particularly if made simply to evade the rule against reopening *res judicata*) might incur the statutory punishment for deception of the court. But it was a defence to such a charge to show that the serjeant had merely been following the instructions of his client and had not himself suggested the idea.

A more direct attempt at reopening *res judicata* is mentioned in a report of a 1307 case.[28] Robert Norman of Hedon had unsuccessfully made an argument for barring a widow from her dower before chief justice Hengham, who had then given judgment for the widow. Robert then attempted to reopen the case before a second justice, William Howard. He was suspended from acting as a serjeant by a third justice of the court, William of Bereford, 'because he began to plead again' ('*quia inde reincipit placitare*'). This suspension was only temporary.[29] Repleading a case already decided was not in this case behaviour serious enough to merit the full statutory punishment.

Other behavioural norms

Suspension might also be threatened for other behaviour unacceptable to the justices. In a 1305 case, serjeant Friskney persisted in a line of argument the justices did not find at all convincing.[30] Eventually he received a direct warning from the chief justice telling him he would be suspended if he continued. At this he finally backed down. The threat of suspension was perhaps also behind at least two instances where justices warned individual serjeants to speak 'in good faith'. One occurs in a report of a 1302 replevin case.[31] The defendant's serjeant avowed a distraint as made by virtue of various presentments at the defendant's leet (a minor criminal court). The plaintiff's serjeant, John of Mutford, then challenged the avowry on the grounds that the defendant had not shown that the individuals against whom the presentments had been made were residents within the court's jurisdiction. The justice told Mutford to answer over and also gave him a warning to speak 'in good faith'. He was probably being warned not to waste the court's time, but there also seems to be an implication that he was trying to trick the court.

A similar event occurred in a 1304 annuity case.[32] The annuity was payable until the plaintiff was presented to a suitable ecclesiastical living by the grantor or his heirs. The defendant's serjeants attempted various defences to the plea, culminating in a claim that the plaintiff had been presented to the deanery of Tamworth by the wife of the defendant's uncle at the defendant's request. This presentment had discharged the duty to pay the annuity. The plaintiff's serjeant (William of Harle) denied this sufficed for the purpose since the presentment had not been made by the grantor or one of his heirs. Justice Howard countered this argument but Harle simply repeated it. Chief justice Hengham then warned him about answering in good faith. Harle shifted ground by claiming that the presentment had been made for services to the lady concerned and not at the request of the defendant; and issue was joined on this.

One earlier suspension of a serjeant had occurred in 1276.[33] In the absence of a report to complement the somewhat bare plea-roll record it is impossible to be certain just why Adam of Kinsham was suspended. The note of the suspension occurs at the end of an entry in which the defendant had successfully sought and obtained judgment against a plaintiff on the ground that his count had been defective in not mentioning a specific day and year when the trespass he alleged had taken place. It must have been Adam who had made the count and he must have been suspended from having made it. Robert Palmer has suggested that suspension was the penalty for 'a particularly poor count he had made'.[34] This cannot be excluded. But there is another possibility. The case was one where the plaintiff claimed that he and certain third parties held pasture land as their several but that the defendant had grazed the land with his animals and flocks, claiming a right of pasture there. It was thus in effect a mixed suit, partly proprietary and partly trespassory. It was arguable that it was not necessary to specify in the count precisely when the alleged grazing had taken place since the real issue was whether or not the defendant had a right to graze his animals, not whether or not he had actually attempted to graze them on a particular occasion. It is conceivable that Adam was suspended in 1276 not for making an obviously defective count but because he made a controversial count and then supported the count he had made with too much vigour.

Conclusions

Chapter 29 of the statute of Westminster I imposed on the serjeants of the king's courts no more than a vague and unspecific obligation not to deceive either courts or litigants. In practice the courts developed and enforced detailed norms of behaviour for them. These covered their acceptance and relinquishment of clients. They also covered their behaviour in court and prohibited serjeants from knowingly misleading the court, persisting with lines of argument which the court had told them were unacceptable or wasting the time of the court by reopening decided cases. The establishment of these norms shows the courts treating serjeants as a distinct professional group, subject to court regulation in all the major areas of their professional life. Misbehaviour in the conduct of their own litigation or in their business dealings (where the latter directly involved the court) was also treated as an offence meriting heavier punishment than if committed by others. There was little that was distinctively 'professional' about the enforcement of such norms, apart perhaps from the relative informality of the procedures employed, and there is certainly no hint of any internal self-regulation. But the forms of punishment used (and threatened) were also distinctively 'professional' in nature: temporary or permanent suspension from professional activity clearly implies recognition of the 'professional' status of the individual being punished and is only appropriate as a punishment in the case of persons exercising an occupation on a full-time basis.

ETHICAL REGULATION IN PRACTICE

The professional attorneys of the king's courts

There is a much larger body of material on the existence and enforcement of both statutory and non-statutory norms of behaviour in the case of professional attorneys practising in the king's courts. But this is hardly surprising. They were a much larger group than the small elite of professional serjeants.

Conduct with respect to their own clients When the attorney's client was the plaintiff in litigation the attorney's main duties were due diligence in the suing process and ensuring that the defendant enjoyed as little opportunity for delay as was possible. He was also required to take full advantage of any possible benefits that might accrue from the defendant's defaults. Any neglect of these duties was liable to punishment by the courts. Such punishment varied in severity. In a 1291 case an attorney who had acted for a litigant in one action which had been dismissed was given money to purchase a new writ to renew the litigation. He assured her that he had done so and was prosecuting her case. When she came to court she discovered that he had not even obtained the second writ, let alone started the suing process against her opponent. She sued him for dereliction of duty. But all he was required to do was to pay her damages of half a mark together with a penalty of a similar amount to the king.[35]

In a 1294 case a professional attorney came to one of the clerks of the Common Bench at the end of term to have an adjournment 'at the request of the parties' ('*prece parcium*') entered on the rolls in a land plea where he was acting for the plaintiff. This would have had the effect of adjourning the litigation to the following term. Since neither the defendant nor his attorney was in court, the attorney could have secured judgment by default against them.[36] When this was discovered the attorney was remanded to the Fleet gaol where he remained till the following term. It was then decided that his offence did not merit the full statutory punishment since he had not succeeded in having the adjournment entered. He was merely suspended from acting as an attorney in the court for a year.

The full statutory punishment, however, was imposed in a third case of 1291. Here a Common Bench attorney was again in trouble for waiving a default which he could have used to secure judgment for his client.[37] The attorney claimed to have acted on his client's instructions. Under questioning, the client said the attorney had indeed told him that his opponent was in danger of losing but had also told him that he could accept payment for waiving the default and pleading the case on its merits. He had told the attorney to do what was in his best interests. He had known nothing of the waiver until he came to court but he had then made a ratification of the attorney's action in writing (clearly at the attorney's own request). The court, evidently more concerned than the client himself that he was being cheated (since it had been the attorney who had received the payment for the remission and the court considered it had been in the client's best interests to recover by default) sent the attorney to the Fleet prison for a year and a day. He also had to pay a small additional fine to leave prison at the end of that time.[38]

When the attorney's client was the defendant in land litigation the attorney would need to put in an appearance at some stage before judgment was given against his client by default. There are a number of cases in which it was alleged an attorney had failed to do this and at least one of them shows that this might be taken seriously. During the 1286 Norfolk eyre the knights of the county made a presentment against the professional attorney Simon of Cley.[39] He had been acting as an attorney in the Common Bench but had fraudulently transferred his loyalties to his client's opponent, absented himself from court and thus lost his client's land for him. Simon claimed not to have been the client's attorney; but a petty jury confirmed the truth of what the presentment jury had said and specifically stated that this had been contrary to the king's statute ('*et hoc contra statutum domini regis*'). Simon was therefore sent to prison. This was probably for the year and a day laid down by the statute though the enrolment does not specifically spell this out.[40]

It was common in land actions for defendants to put in an appearance and vouch some third party to warranty for the tenement in dispute. It was then up to the defendant's attorney to sue process against the warrantor to ensure his appearance. Any failure to do so would again lead to judgment being given against the defendant. This was also clearly considered a serious matter. In litigation of 1292 a defendant complained that his attorney had fraudulently failed to sue out the appropriate writs against his warrantors at the proper time, thereby leading to the loss of his land and the crop on it.[41] The attorney admitted he had been appointed to act in the case but claimed he had thought his only remit was that of procuring maximum delay in the case, as the supposed warrantors had no assets. The implication seems to be that inaction was as valuable to his client (if not more so) than suing the writs. The court did not find his explanation convincing or perhaps found that it indicated an intention of deceiving the court rather than his client. He had long been a professional attorney and so knew what he should have done.

He could not therefore plead ignorance as any excuse for his conduct.[42] His inaction was culpable and intended to deceive the court and the party: the appropriate punishment was imprisonment for a year and a day in the Fleet.[43]

The earliest clear evidence that the professional attorney (like the professional serjeant) was under a continuing obligation to former clients comes from a report of a conspiracy case heard in the 1299 Cambridgeshire eyre.[44] Gunnora de Valoines claimed she had made an agreement with William le Moyne and his son Thomas under which Thomas was to act as her attorney in land litigation and William was to ensure that the jury verdict passed in her favour. She had made a bond for 100 shillings in their favour. They had promised not to claim the money if she did not recover. Thomas, however, had then received a payment from her opponent to allow the assize to pass against her and they had then sued her for the 100 shillings. Thomas did not deny having received money from her opponent but did deny that he had received it to act against Gunnora. This was confirmed by the verdict of a jury which said that he had received it for acting in a different case. The two suits, however, were connected and the court concluded that Thomas had acted improperly in representing Gunnora's opponent in the second case. His punishment was imprisonment pending payment of a fine and banishment from the court for the remainder of the eyre: again a milder punishment than envisaged by the statute but one which may have reflected the fact that norms of professional conduct in such matters were only just emerging.

Conduct with respect to their clients' opponents Misconduct by attorneys towards their own clients sometimes also involved deceiving the court but often it did not. Misconduct towards a client's opponents almost invariably involved deception of the court and sometimes other serious wrong-doing as well.

In 1291 Peter of Luffenham, who appears to have been a professional attorney of the Common Bench,[45] was under indictment for having altered a plea-roll entry recording an essoin to remove all record of the fact that it had been properly adjudged and the case adjourned to a subsequent term.[46] Peter said he was not guilty and put himself on a jury of his colleagues in the court, apparently a jury of his fellow-professional attorneys. His colleagues then told the story of how he had committed the offence and why. Peter was sentenced on conviction to imprisonment in the Fleet for a year and a day. The judgment also specified that at the end of the term he was to be released only in return for a fine. The justices also seem to have imposed a further punishment when he was released. The record merely says that 'he was prohibited etc.'; but other cases where the same phrase was used but in a less abbreviated form indicate that he was prohibited from practising as an attorney in the court. Here for the first time we find evidence that in really serious cases the king's courts imposed not just the statutory punishment of imprisonment but also permanent suspension from practising in the court: a punishment the statute had envisaged being applied only to professional serjeants.[47]

In another case heard in 1291 it was alleged that an attorney had removed an original writ from the court's files to ensure that a case was dismissed for lack of the original writ warranting the proceedings.[48] The accused denied the charge, as did a second man allegedly involved. Both were professional attorneys and asked for a jury of their fellow-professionals to clear themselves. The keeper of rolls and writs also placed himself on the same jury to clear himself and his subordinates of any involvement. The jury found all of them innocent and provided circumstantial evidence that it had been the accuser himself who had removed the writ.

In a third 1291 case a defendant, or more probably his alert attorney, noticed that the jurors the sheriff was instructed to produce under a judicial writ issued by the court were not the same men as those whom he had returned for the panel of the jury on the previous return day.[49] Suspicion fell on the clerk who had written the writ and on the plaintiff's attorney. The clerk claimed the attorney had asked him to make out the writ and had shown him what he claimed to be a faithful transcript of the previous writ and attached a jury panel for him to do this. The attorney asserted that it was his client who had delivered the transcript to the clerk. The client denied having done this and said he had handed over a transcript of writ and panel to his attorney but told him to check them against the originals. A jury (which appears to have consisted of professional attorneys) confirmed the clerk's story. The clerk was briefly imprisoned and then released for a small fine. The attorney was sentenced to imprisonment in the Fleet for a year and a day.

In two 1295 cases attorneys were said to have been responsible for suing a default against their clients' opponents despite the fact that the opponents had been duly essoined. In the first the litigant himself was initially accused of responsibility.[50] He claimed that when he had come to the court it had been for the first time and he was wholly ignorant of its procedures. One of the professional attorneys from his home county had told him that he could secure the dismissal of the case for him. The attorney denied any responsibility in the matter or receiving any payment from the litigant. A jury of professional attorneys found that the attorney (notwithstanding his denial) had been responsible for suing the default but it cleared him of any wrongful intent in doing so. They said he had seen the essoin entry but it was only the bare entry without the essential additional memoranda showing that the essoin had been adjudged good by the court and the essoiner and his principal and the other party adjourned to a future term. As it stood, this was not a valid essoin. He had then gone round the greater part of the attorneys specializing in business from the area asking them if they were acting for the other litigant or if they knew anything of the essoin, apparently in an attempt to ensure that failure to complete the essoin entry was not just a result of a mistake or negligence on their part. This verdict seems to have cleared the attorney and his client, though the plea-roll breaks off without any formal record of acquittal. In the second case the litigant was again initially held responsible.[51] He denied all knowledge and responsibility, as did the second of his two attorneys; but the first attorney admitted his guilt and was sent to the Fleet prison.

The fraudulent recovery of land by default, where the defendant had no notice of litigation until judgment by default was being executed by the local sheriff, seems to have been a persistent temptation to litigants and a persistent problem for the courts. However, it was not something for which the plaintiff's attorney was or could normally be held responsible. Chief justice Mettingham tells us why in the report of a so far unidentified case in which a plaintiff sought to excuse herself on the grounds that it had been her attorney who had sued the default.[52] Mettingham explained that the attorney was only concerned with suing process in the court, not with the way that process was executed. There were none the less circumstances under which a professional attorney might be punished for his part in such a fraudulent recovery. In 1291 the plaintiff in such a case was initially accused of the deception.[53] He said that he had not initiated the plea but a man who claimed to be a professional attorney of the Bench (*'qui se gerit pro communi attornato curie'*) and it was the same individual who had then also taken seisin of the land in his name and had subsequently disposed of it. When the attorney came to court the following term he told a circumstantial story to exculpate himself but the jury who later gave their verdict did not believe him. It is not entirely clear what then happened to him.[54]

Conduct with respect to third parties and the court   In 1294 Alan Prat sued process against jurors to secure their attendance in court in a plea brought by his client after he had received word that his client's opponent was dead.[55] The jurors concerned complained to the court and when Alan admitted this he was suspended from practice for an indefinite period. In imposing sentence the justices were careful to point out that Alan was a professional attorney of the court (*'generalis ... attornatus in curia regis hic'*) and so ought to have known the correct procedure in such cases (*'nec ignorare debuit qualiter pro dominis suis secundum legem et consuetudinem regni placita sunt prosequenda'*). Alan was receiving appropriate punishment (suspension from practice) for professional incompetence.

When an attorney acted for a client without having been formally appointed there was little chance of this being detrimental to the client's opponent or to the client himself, as long as the client actually knew he was acting for him. It is not uncommon to find attorneys being challenged by their client's opponent for not having been properly appointed.[56] In at least one case, however, the challenge came from the court. This was in 1298 where the purported attorney had made an agreement on behalf of his clients with their opponents. As this agreement quitclaimed land to his clients, his activity was clearly not intended to defraud the party whom he had represented.[57] His behaviour was, none the less, treated as a serious offence. The Common Bench had transferred its sessions from Westminster to York but his sentence of a year and a day for deception of the court was served in the Fleet prison at London: at the end of the term he was prohibited from acting in the office of attorney in the court or in any other office from then on.[58]

Having a case which had already once been pleaded to issue repleaded was also behaviour that was subject to punishment if detected. In a 1291 case the attorneys of both litigants were arraigned by the court for having a case already pleaded before one division of the court repleaded a second time before a separate division 'to the burdening of the court'. But only the plaintiff's attorney was punished and he was given a choice between going to the Fleet for an unspecified time and paying a fine. When he chose the latter he was allowed to pay the fairly small sum of half a mark.[59] Collusion between the attorneys of the two litigants was also involved in a case probably of the early fourteenth century found in an undated report.[60] Judgment had been given by default in a dower case but the attorneys had then agreed to the crossing out of the relevant entry as though it was a clerical error (something apparently done with the cooperation of one of the leading court clerks) and for the case to be pleaded instead. This was detected and the attorneys and the clerk were sent to prison.

A different kind of deception and burdening of the court was in question in a case of 1292.[61] Roger of Lamport, a professional attorney of the Common Bench ('*communis attornatus in curia hic*'), had acted as the attorney of the defendant in a case in challenging jurors and awaiting their verdict; but when they returned to give that verdict they suddenly produced a writ showing that he had been removed and another man who had been with him but whom he had just sent away had been appointed in his place. Evidently he knew that the jury was about to give its verdict against his client and wished to ensure that the client lost his case by default rather than by the jury's verdict. Roger went to gaol partly for this but also because he already had a bad reputation.

In 1291 Robert of 'Greshope', a professional attorney from Cumberland, was accused of having docked part of a plea-roll membrane containing the appointment of attorneys of Michaelmas term 1290.[62] Realizing the potential seriousness of the charge, Robert first claimed clerical privilege and then acknowledged his guilt and explained his motives. A client whom he was representing had been in danger of losing his land. He had been afraid of going to prison if it could be proved that he was the client's attorney. He had therefore taken steps to ensure that the only evidence of this was removed from the roll. His offence was all the more serious because the portion of the membrane he had removed also contained a record of the appointment of a number of other attorneys and he was not in a position to restore the missing piece to the court. The judgment was that he should go prison to be held there at the king's pleasure. In practice he was kept in only for the statutory year and a day[63] but when he was released he was also debarred from future practice as an attorney.

Two attorneys were suspended from practising in the Common Bench in 1292 for being too late in suing defaults. Nicholas of 'Penskawen' had only acted at the very end of term 'after the proclamation'.[64] Robert of Burton should have sued a default at the return day of the quindene of Easter but had only done so two weeks later.[65] In both cases the suspension was apparently only temporary. It is less clear whether there was any element of deception or attempted deception involved or whether the disciplining of the attorneys was simply for professional negligence. The latter seems more probable. It was probably also mere negligence and not anything more serious that was punished in two other 1292 cases where professional attorneys were in trouble with the court (though not apparently with their clients) for failing to sue out the appropriate judicial writs to secure the appearance of a client's opponent or the jurors in the case, despite having secured the enrolment of an entry recording their default. In both cases some kind of temporary suspension appears to have been the only punishment; and in one of them even this was soon relaxed, albeit only on a temporary basis, once it became clear that if this was not done the client would be left without an attorney.[66]

Suspension from practice for an unspecified period was also the punishment meted out to a professional attorney of the court who was convicted on the testimony of credible witnesses of having said openly that Peter Mallore (one of the justices of the court) and all his colleagues were evil ('iniqui') and 'shrews' ('*shrewes*').[67] Many litigants and more professional lawyers appearing before the court might have agreed with the attorney's views: but it was punished as a contempt of the king and a defamation of the justices.

Conduct in their own litigation The norms of behaviour that applied to professional attorneys in their own litigation do not seem to have differed significantly from those that applied to other litigants, but any infraction of those norms was treated differently, as meriting special treatment and sometimes special punishment because of the status of the litigant concerned. In 1291 John le Chanu alleged that his uncle Wymund le Chanu[68] had used a forged writ of attaint against him in the court of King's Bench and thereby subjected John himself, the 12 jurors of the original jury and the 24 jurors of the attaint jury to considerable inconvenience.[69] He was careful to state in his plaint that Wymund was a professional attorney of the Common Bench and it was probably this fact alone that justified his taking action against his uncle through a plaint rather than by writ. Wymund denied that the writ had been forged but on questioning was unable to say precisely when the writ had been returnable into the court. He was committed to custody for not knowing this when the writ was of such importance. Somehow he managed to secure his release from custody. When he failed to return to the court to answer for his 'falsehood and deceit' his outlawry was ordered. He surrendered just before outlawry was pronounced against him, but then once more evaded custody and was only eventually outlawed in November 1293.[70] Here the defendant's status was important for the procedure followed in the case but probably not for its eventual outcome.

In a second case heard in Easter term 1295 we are again dealing with a serious offence: the forgery of a royal writ, though a very clumsy forgery. Suspicion fell from the start on the plaintiff but he attempted to clear himself by shifting the blame on to the shoulders of the sheriff of Warwickshire and his clerical staff. Eventually the plaintiff admitted that the forgery was his own work; that he had made it because there was a defect in the writ he had obtained from chancery; and that he had tricked a member of the sheriff's clerical staff into accepting the forgery in place of the original by asking to be allowed to have the original in order to make a transcript of it after it had been opened and subsequently handing back the forgery. It was only at the end of the record of the case that it became clear that the plaintiff was not just another litigant (though the fact that he got his own writ and then had the temerity to attempt to forge a substitute for it already suggests he had some legal expertise) for his sentence was imprisonment for a year and a day in the Fleet prison. Further confirmation of this is provided by his treatment at the end of his term of imprisonment. When he was released he was warned not to meddle with any business in the court in future and suspended from office (that is, practice in the court) in perpetuity.[71]

Conclusions

Our evidence demonstrates the existence and enforcement of detailed norms of behaviour governing the conduct of the professional attorneys of the king's courts in their conduct with regard to their own clients, the opponents of their clients, third parties and the court itself. 'Deception' of litigants and of the courts (the statutory offence) was given a fairly broad interpretation so that it was taken to cover even such matters as the docking or altering of plea-rolls. The courts can also be seen exercising a jurisdiction over their attorneys by disciplining them for matters such as negligence and defamation of the justices. Some of these norms were clearly also applicable to other, non-professional attorneys and to litigants bringing or defending suits in person, but others only applied to professionals or, perhaps more precisely, it was only professional attorneys who would be punished for their infraction. Thus even in the definition of punishable offences we find a clear distinction between professional attorneys and others and evidence that the professionals were regarded as a distinct group subject to different and higher standards.

Enforcement of the norms, as far as we can see, was something entirely for the courts or, more precisely, for the justices of the courts. There is no hint in our evidence of the existence of any kind of direct self-regulation. But there is evidence in the enforcement procedures for professional attorneys being treated as a distinct, if not a self-governing, group. From 1291 onwards the Common Bench was willing to entertain plaints (oral or written complaints of an informal nature) alleging misconduct against its professional attorneys, apparently because of their 'professional' status and the special relationship they had with the court in which they practised. When such plaints came to jury trial we see another feature which reflects the court's acknowledgment of the separate status of the professionals. Such juries are regularly composed of their fellow-professional attorneys. For matters of 'professional' misconduct such a jury made good sense. They were indeed the group most likely to know the truth of the matter. But there seems to be more to it than that. In some entries these jury members are referred to as the '*socii* ', the professional colleagues, of the defendant; and we may suspect that there is at least a hint here of the trial of the professional by his 'peers', his fellow-professionals.

Imprisonment for a year and a day was not the only form of punishment open to the courts, even if it is the only punishment mentioned in the statute. Punishments ranged from fines and brief periods in gaol to suspension from professional activity in the court for the remainder of an eyre or for a whole year to the statutory term of imprisonment and even to the statutory term together with permanent suspension from acting in the court. Those punishments which involved temporary or permanent suspension from working in the court are a clear acknowledgement of the professional status of the offenders concerned: a recognition that different punishments are properly applicable to them than those that might apply to non-professionals. And in the emergence of the last and most severe type of punishment (the statutory term of imprisonment plus permanent suspension) for professional attorneys by the 1290s, it may just be that we can see signs of the professional attorneys coming to be thought of as members of a single legal profession which embraced both them and the professional serjeants. Chapter 29 of the statute of Westminster I had envisaged that professional attorneys convicted of breaching its terms would suffer only imprisonment for a year and a day. By the 1290s they were receiving the same treatment as that intended for professional serjeants. Professional attorneys were now being treated on a par with professional serjeants.

ETHICAL REGULATION IN PRACTICE

Professional lawyers outside the king's courts

London Surviving records of the London city courts allow us to see how the 1280 code was enforced[72] and also the enforcement of other norms of professional conduct not specifically mentioned in the code. Our earliest evidence for the enforcement of professional ethical standards in the city comes from 1291. On 24 April the king sent a writ to the warden and sheriffs of London to enquire into the truth of certain allegations made by Laurencia widow of John Skip.[73] She claimed she had been suing Godwin le Felipper for her dower in the London hustings court. He had vouched the son and heir of her late husband to warranty and when making the voucher had said that John only held lands outside the city. He had therefore been told to sue a writ of warranty of charter against him in the Common Bench and the dower case had been suspended until this was determined. Godwin had then defaulted in the Common Bench and the court had ordered the seizure of the land claimed and the return of the case to the hustings. At the hustings court, Godwin and his serjeant, Robert of Sutton, had alleged that Godwin had been in prison at Cambridge when he was said to have made the default in the Common Bench. But the claim had been false, Laurencia said, and only further delayed her dower suit. If the warden and sheriffs found this to be true they were instructed to punish Godwin and his serjeant 'as the offence required and in accordance with the statute concerning serjeants and others who put forward false exceptions to the deception of our court and the [opposing] party'. The reference appears to be to chapter 29 of the statute of Westminster I and it suggests that by 1291 it was believed even in the royal chancery that the statute was applicable not just to the professional lawyers of king's courts proper but also to the professional lawyers who practised in London city courts. It also suggests that the making of false exceptions was covered by the statute as well as other kinds of deception: an interpretation of the statute's meaning which might have exposed many serjeants to the statute's penalties. A jury found that the serjeant had indeed falsely made this allegation and with Godwin's knowledge and full consent.

The roll does not record the punishment imposed but fortunately we learn something of this from another case heard in the same year.[74] A clerk of one of the sheriffs of London complained he had been insulted by Robert of Sutton while holding the sheriff's court because he had not allowed Robert to plead before him. He said that Robert had been 'suspended' from pleading by the warden of the city for 'a certain trespass' and was not at present allowed to plead there. Robert denied insulting the clerk, but as this was attested by the 'four benches' of the court he was sent to prison. Conviction on a charge of attempting to deceive the court in the previous case, it seems, had resulted only in a temporary suspension of the serjeant, not the permanent suspension envisaged by the statute; and if Robert had suffered any kind of imprisonment it was clearly for less than the statutory period of a year and a day.

In 1300 we find another city serjeant bringing a case against Thomas le Coffer for having made an allegation of unprofessional conduct against him in the course of litigation two days previously.[75] Robert of Kelsey had been acting for the plaintiffs in a case against Thomas and others. Thomas had alleged that Robert knew his 'counsel', had been paid 40 pence by him and should have been acting for him. Thomas did not deny having made the allegation against Robert but pleaded the truth of his allegation as justification. He said he had paid him the money in the course of a previous case against Robert's current client. This had been between the same parties and concerned the same property and so Robert knew his 'counsel'. He added that Robert had compounded his offence by having advised his current client to purchase his writ immediately after he had finished acting for Thomas. Robert admitted acting on Thomas's behalf in the previous litigation but only in challenging the jury. He had done this at the request of Gilbert of Tothby who had been acting as Thomas's serjeant in the case. He had never agreed with Thomas to act on his behalf. He also denied having advised his current client to bring the writ that initiated the current litigation. Eventually the two parties reached an agreement. Thomas withdrew his allegations and promised not to repeat them. This case demonstrates that the continuing obligation on serjeants not to appear against former clients in connected litigation was recognized in the London city courts as well as in the king's courts; but it also illustrates some of the finer points of interpretation to which such an obligation could give rise. Was a serjeant who had no contract with the 'client' for whom he had acted bound by this obligation? Was a serjeant who had merely challenged jurors for his client – something he could do without knowing the details of his client's case – obliged in the same way as a serjeant who had engaged in pleading for a client?

There is also one example, but apparently only one, of proceedings being brought against a London professional attorney alleging misconduct.[76] In 1298 John of Ugley alleged he had appointed Terry of Enfield to act as his attorney in land litigation. Terry, however, had proceeded to lose his writ and then defaulted in the plea, leading to the dismissal of the case for want of prosecution. Terry was unable to deny this and so he was sent to gaol: he was clearly being punished for professional negligence.

Other local courts From the early 1290s we find complaints being made against particular individuals at the eyre alleging what look like breaches of the norms of professional conduct; and some at least seem to be referring to the conduct of professional lawyers in local courts. In the 1292 Shropshire eyre, for example, Alice Kylot of Shrewsbury made a complaint against Adam de la Rue, claiming that he had agreed to purchase the necessary writs and sue for her as her attorney in litigation to recover certain property in Shrewsbury; that she had paid him five shillings for his services in the court of Shrewsbury (probably the city court) and in the eyre; but that as a result of his collusion with her opponents, her writ had been quashed.[77] But it is not entirely clear whether Adam can be classified as a professional attorney. Nor do we know whether or not Alice's complaint was justified since she was subsequently non-suited. It is not even clear precisely what she was alleging he had done, though perhaps he had shown her opponents some error in the writs he himself had purchased that allowed the writs to be quashed.

In the 1293 Staffordshire eyre, Lovekyn Semon of Stafford brought a plaint against John Organ of Newcastle under Lyme.[78] He claimed that he had supported John for three years in London 'so that he could help him if he had litigation' (*'par la reson ke il ly eidaut si il hut a pleder'*). Lovekyn had then brought litigation against Henry Meyler of Shrewsbury claiming a messuage in Shrewsbury; John had purchased the necessary writ and acted as Lovekyn's attorney in the plea for three and a half years. When it came to the crucial point in the litigation, John had taken ten marks from Lovekyn's opponent to defeat Lovekyn's claim and had apparently done so by making four pairs of false charters allegedly in the name of Lovekyn's ancestors (presumably granting and/or quitclaiming the property). All this had happened ten years before and had reduced Lovekyn to beggary (or so he claimed). Again there are a number of difficulties about interpreting this complaint. The first is that we have no way of knowing how much of it was true or justified, an important consideration made all the more difficult by our knowledge that Lovekyn did not pursue it. The second is that the complaint does not tell us where this litigation was taking place. Presumably it started in the town court of Shrewsbury. But did it continue there for three and a half years or was it removed into the Shropshire county court and from there into the Common Bench? And what are we to make of John's role in the litigation? Lovekyn at one point describes him as his '*atturne*' and his acting in this role seems to fit the mention of his purchasing a writ for Lovekyn and acting on his behalf for three and a half years. But subsequently he describes him as his '*pledour*' in the litigation: a term that more commonly seems to mean 'serjeant' than attorney. Perhaps it does not mean that here. However, we do seem to be dealing with something that can be seen as a kind of professional misconduct. The complaint is not so much that Lovekyn was defeated in litigation through the use of forged charters as that it was his own professional legal adviser that had assisted his opponent to win his case by actually forging these charters for him.

From the early 1290s onwards we also begin to find presentments at sessions of the general eyre and in sessions of the trailbaston justices against 'conspirators' and other individuals whose activities were seen as representing a threat to the proper workings of the judicial system. Many of these individuals seem to be local officials or others with power and influence in particular localities. But some sound as if they may be professional lawyers and the conduct complained of was misconduct by them in a professional capacity. Several were accused of 'ambidexterity': taking money from a client, and then later also receiving money from his opponent for some kind of treachery to the original client. In the 1292 Herefordshire eyre presentments of 'conspiracy' were made against some 34 individuals.[79] The petty juries that then passed verdicts on them said that nine of these men were maintainers of pleas in the king's court and took gifts (or money) from both sides. Such men could have been professional lawyers but probably were not. However, the William de la Haye who was said by the jury to have received 40 shillings to support John Ragon in a plea and then to have given advice to the opposite party, showing them how his writ could be quashed, and also to have acted similarly on other occasions, does sound much more like a local professional lawyer. In the 1293–4 Yorkshire eyre it was said that little Michael of Laton' was a serjeant and took from both parties for his 'office', perhaps again an allegation of ambidexterity on his part.[80] Another possibly professional local lawyer mentioned in a number of presentments in the 1305 Shropshire trailbaston sessions was Walter son of Reginald de 'Playssh' of Egerton.[81] Among the misdeeds ascribed to him was accepting payment in the form of two oxen from a client to act for him in a plea against the bishop of Hereford but then deserting him for the bishop, thereby causing his original client to lose his case. Again this sounds like a local serjeant deserting his client at the last moment for his opponent and leaving him without someone to speak for him in court. In the Herefordshire trailbaston sessions of the same year there was a presentment against John de la Barwe for deserting his client Roger of Hereford.[82] Roger had granted John an annual fee of two and a half marks to act for him in a plea against Robert de Tony on the manor of Yarkhill. He had then deserted Roger, who had lost the land. Once more this looks like a professional lawyer and perhaps more specifically a professional serjeant deserting his client for someone who offered him more money.[83]

A second kind of misconduct alleged against several of these putatively professional lawyers is 'champerty'. This is one of the charges made against Walter son of Reginald de 'Playssh' in the 1305 Shropshire trailbaston sessions and the indictment cites a specific case where Walter had acted for a share of the land at stake.[84] However, another indictment possibly referring to the same litigation suggests that the land in question may not have come to him by way of reward but simply have passed through his hands on the way to its being held by others as a defensive tactic.[85] In the 1306 Herefordshire trailbaston session John of Monnington was indicted for abetting Agnes the daughter of Richard of 'Badeschawe' in bringing litigation against John Smith of Monnington for land she had previously sold him and of 'maintaining' the plea at his own cost till John Smith handed over the property to John of Monnington in exchange for land of less value. He had then allegedly secured her withdrawal from the litigation.[86] The same man had also acted as the attorney of John of Willenhall for litigation which he again maintained at his own cost 'at champerty' and made his client enter into a bond not to settle the case without his advice and consent.[87] But we cannot be entirely certain that John of Monnington was a professional lawyer.

The third category of misconduct is one that shows just how far the jurors who made the presentments may still have been from accepting the activity of professional serjeants in their local courts. In the 1292 Herefordshire eyre we find a presentment against John Lightfoot for 'maintaining the party of his clients' ('*manutenet partem dominorum suorum*') both justly and unjustly.[88] This means no more than that he gave professional assistance to his clients, irrespective of whether or not they had justice on their side: something evidently not as yet seen as acceptable conduct by local jurors in late thirteenth-century England. Much the same accusation was also made against two local serjeants in the 1293–4 Yorkshire eyre.[89] John of Cave of Middleton was described in one jury verdict as a serjeant ('*narrator*') who supported ('*manutenuit*') a client against John de Thorni (presumably by acting as his serjeant) unjustly and who had also supported other parties, sometimes unjustly. Alexander of Kneton was described as a serjeant who 'speaks as willingly for the true party as the false'.[90]

CONCLUSIONS

Edward I's reign saw the first specific enunciation of norms of professional conduct for members of the nascent English legal profession. Legislation was enacted making deception of the king's courts or of parties to litigation in those courts by professional lawyers practising there an offence; other legislation outlawed 'champerty' both by professional lawyers and others. In London the city's own regulations laid down detailed rules governing the conduct of professional lawyers: banning champerty and ambidexterity, the abuse of opponents and attempts to undermine the authority of the city courts. In this legislation we can see an acknowledgement of the existence of a distinct and definable group of professional lawyers and also a clear attempt to enforce on members of that group special professional ethical standards. But the legislation is at best only an imperfect guide both of the norms actually enforced and of the variety of penalties imposed by the courts for breaches of them. The records of the king's courts and the reports allow us to see them enforcing a variety of rules on the professional lawyers who practised there covering matters such as the lawyer's continuing obligations to former clients (applicable to both serjeants and attorneys); professional negligence (apparently only a problem with attorneys); deception of the court (applicable in different circumstances to both serjeants and attorneys); and giving due respect to the justices (again perhaps applicable to members of both groups). Punishment varies from the minor (no more than a small fine) to the full statutory punishment, with the latter being inflicted on attorneys as well as on at least one serjeant. For neither group is there as yet evidence of any form of self-regulation or self-discipline, though in the trial of some professional attorneys by juries of their fellow-professionals we may see at least a step in that direction. The London court records also reveal the enforcement of similar norms on London's professional lawyers.

Other local courts are more obscure. Our only major source for the existence and enforcement of norms of behaviour on professional lawyers practising in such courts are the records of royal courts that penalized local lawyers for offences such as ambidexterity and champerty. But the royal courts did not treat these as distinctively professional offences and seem to have punished non-professionals for them as well. The presentments provide some evidence for supposing that as late as the final decade of the thirteenth century, professional activity itself was suspect in some localities. This suggests that even at the end of Edward I's reign, the legal profession and its professional norms were still to become established or fully accepted in the counties. The only local courts where they were well-established were the city courts of London: only a short boat ride away from the centre of the English legal profession, the Common Bench, at Westminster. It was in the king's courts and more particularly in the Common Bench that the English legal profession first developed; it was also there that distinctive ethical standards for members of the legal profession were first worked out.

9

The Other Legal Profession: Canon Lawyers in England before 1307[1]

I

INTRODUCTION

The history of the other legal profession active in medieval England, the canon lawyers, falls into three main stages.[2] During the first stage (before c.1190) there is some evidence for the study of canon law in England though not for its being taught in a university setting. There is also evidence for the activity of individual paid experts in canon law, but not for those experts being seen or seeing themselves as members of a distinctive or distinctively professional group. During the second stage (between c.1190 and 1274) canon law began to be studied and taught in the two English universities. Paid and expert canon lawyers also began to be treated as members of a profession both through the imposition of admission oaths on those who wished to practise professionally and by the enunciation of other professional standards for those in regular practice as professional canon lawyers. In a third stage (lasting from 1274 to the end of the period covered by this study and well beyond) specific educational requirements began to be imposed on those wishing to practise; some ecclesiastical courts imposed quotas on those allowed to practise on a regular basis before them; and for the first time all members of the profession were required to take an admission oath.

THE FIRST STAGE (BEFORE C.1190)

Although the *Decretum* of Gratian, the basic textbook of the academic study of canon law, was compiled at Bologna c.1141 and Gratian's compilation soon began to attract attention all over Western Europe, there is no clear evidence of academic interest in it in England before the 1160s. The first real sign of this is an anonymous *Summa de multiplici iuris divisione*, a canon-law textbook largely derived from the earlier *Summa* of Stephen of Tournai, which was compiled, apparently in England, some time in the 1160s. A number of other works attest to English interest in canon law during the period before *c*.1190; perhaps the most important is the anonymous *Summa Omnis qui juste* of *c*.1186, the most elaborate of all surviving commentaries on the work of Gratian before that of Huguccio.[3] This period also witnessed a major effort, associated with a number of English cathedral and other schools, to supplement the work of Gratian by assembling papal decretals which had been omitted from the *Decretum* or had been issued after its compilation (especially those sent in response to English queries, which were most readily accessible to the compilers) and to arrange these into some kind of order for reference purposes.[4]

There is some evidence for the teaching of canon law in England during the same period at the cathedral schools at Exeter and Lincoln and perhaps also at the abbey school at St Alban's. Canon law was probably also being taught at Oxford. Kuttner and Rathbone certainly thought it likely; so, more recently, despite the absence of any conclusive evidence, has Leonard Boyle. Boyle has even suggested that from the mid-1170s future canon lawyers were receiving instruction at Oxford not just in canon law but also in its close relative (and essential adjunct) Roman law.[5] However, it is clear that there was no organized university at Oxford at this time and the earliest conclusive evidence for canon-law teaching at Oxford comes from the period after *c*.1190 when the university itself began to emerge.[6] A much better education in canon law was available at Bologna; during the second half of the twelfth century and the first decade of the thirteenth there is plentiful evidence for Englishmen going there to study and (in a few cases at least) staying on to teach. Kuttner and Rathbone, however, emphasize the importance for English canon lawyers of the alternative (and much closer) French connection and discuss the careers of a number of Englishmen like Gerard Pucelle, Gilbert de Glanville, later bishop of Rochester, and master Honorius, who taught in France. They also note other evidence indicating that at least some English canon lawyers received their education there.[7]

As we have already seen, Richard of Anstey's memorandum recording his expenses in securing the inheritance of his maternal uncle indicates that as early as the late 1150s there were expert canon lawyers available to litigants bringing litigation in the English canon-law courts and wealthy and well-connected litigants were already making use of their services.[8] By the end of the century, Oxford had apparently gained a reputation as a place where canon lawyers could be found and engaged to act in litigation in the church courts: a reputation that may have preceded its reputation as an academic centre.[9] Such experts commonly seem to have borne the title of *magister*,

The Other Legal Profession: Canon Lawyers   145

though this was also a title borne by other products of the schools. But there is as yet little to suggest that those who practised canon law in England were regarded or regarded themselves as members of a distinct profession or professional group. There were, in particular, as yet no external controls over admission into practice and no kind of code of professional ethics for those who did practise canon law. Such distinctively professional features only appeared during the course of the thirteenth century.

THE SECOND STAGE (C.1190-1274)

It was during the period of just under a century between c.1190 and 1274 that a recognizable legal profession covering canon lawyers began to take shape in England as in the rest of Western Europe.[10]

Professional education

A university education in canon law became available in Oxford from some time in the late 1180s or early 1190s onwards.[11] We know the names and something of the careers of some of the earliest teachers of canon law there: Honorius of Kent (later archdeacon of Richmond), Simon of Southwell (later treasurer of Lichfield) and John of Tynemouth (later archdeacon of Oxford). We are also fortunate in possessing evidence of the teaching of these men and of some others of their near contemporaries in Gonville and Caius College, Cambridge, MS. 283/676, which contains *reportationes* or student notes of their glosses on the *Decretum*, and in British Library, MS. Royal 9.E.VII, ff. 191-8, which contains reports of their *quaestiones*. At the same time students intending to practise canon law were also receiving instruction in Roman law.

The study of Roman law was both then and later an essential complement to the study of canon law. The *Liber Pauperum* of master Vacarius was apparently used as the main textbook in the teaching of Roman law.[12] The major reorganization of the Oxford law school that took place c.1234, after the promulgation by pope Gregory IX of the *Decretals* (an official collection of papal decretals issued since the time of Gratian's *Decretum*), created two separate faculties of canon and civil (Roman) law.[13] The faculty of canon law now used the *Decretals* as well as the *Decretum* as its basic texts; the faculty of civil law abandoned the use of the *Liber Pauperum* and replaced it with lectures on the Code and Digest proper. However, although Roman law was now being taught in a separate faculty, it is clear that it was still being studied essentially as an adjunct to an education in canon law and not for its own sake. Its students, like those in the faculty of canon law, were being trained for careers as canon lawyers.

The university of Cambridge owed its foundation to a migration from Oxford in 1209 (during a dispute between the town and the university that led to a temporary suspension of teaching at Oxford) and to the encouragement given to the migrating masters by bishop Eustace of Ely. Professor Brundage has argued that there was probably a faculty of canon law at Cambridge from the time of the foundation of the university; and thus from the early thirteenth century there was a second English university helping to train canon lawyers for entry into the profession.[14]

It seems probable that most, if not all, professional advocates in practice in England during this period had received a university education: certainly those whom we can identify seem almost invariably to use the title *magister*, which indicates a university education and probably one in canon and or civil law. But we do not see in the period before 1274 any attempt to insist on a university education as a necessary formal requirement for practice in any of the English ecclesiatical courts.

Professional ethics

Admission oaths   As Professor Brundage has shown, admission oaths had been required of advocates in late antiquity, but were not revived in Western Europe until the thirteenth century.[15] The earliest local legislation to impose such a requirement on professional canon lawyers comes from France where two provincial councils of 1231, one held at Chateau-Gontier (for the province of Tours) and the other at Rouen (for the province of Rouen) required all advocates practising in those provinces to take detailed (but by no means identical) oaths setting out the standards of professional conduct by which they were expected to abide.

The first evidence for the imposition of a similar oath on professional canon-law advocates in England comes from 1237 when legislation enacted at a council in London held by the papal legate Otto included a chapter 29 requiring advocates to take an oath. This was much less complex and detailed than the corresponding French oaths. English advocates were only required to swear that they would serve their clients faithfully and that they would not unjustly delay their client's opponents or prevent them from getting justice if they had right on their side. Nor did the English legislation require all those appearing as advocates in the ecclesiastical courts to take the new oath. No advocate could appear in a case involving marriage or a contested election unless he had taken it; but in other kinds of litigation an advocate might act on up to three occasions in any particular case without doing so. If he was acting on behalf of his own church, for his lord, for a friend, for a poor man, for a foreigner or for some other member of a disadvantaged group, even this limitation was waived.[16] The new requirement was subsequently reiterated and reinforced by local diocesan legislation for the dioceses of Salisbury (*c*.1238–44), Worcester (1240) and Chichester (*c*.1245–52).[17] The 1237 legislation was also reinforced by being re-enacted (though apparently without the exceptions allowed by the earlier legislation) as part of the legislation of the papal legate Ottobuono in 1268.[18]

The synodal statutes of bishop Nicholas of Farnham for Durham (c.1241-9) show that not all bishops were content to follow the format of the legatine oath. Bishop Nicholas demanded that advocates wishing to practise in his diocese take an oath not to accept causes (particularly ones involving marriages) they knew to be unjust or believe to be so, once they been given an outline of the relevant facts. This was probably an oath to be taken in addition to that laid down in the legatine constitutions, though this is not specifically stated or made clear in the statutes.[19] At York, at some unknown date not long before 1279, we find another form of oath being required of advocates, again perhaps in addition to that laid down by the legatine constitutions. Advocates had to promise not knowingly to act in unjust causes and not to use false exceptions or false proofs to pervert the course of justice.[20]

Yet another variant form of oath was introduced in 1273 by archbishop Kilwardby for lawyers wishing to practise in the provincial Court of Arches in London; and for the first time, in England, this was an oath which had to be taken by proctors practising in the court (who performed a function roughly corresponding to that of the attorney of the common law courts) as well as its advocates. This was much fuller than any of the preceding English oaths and consisted of five separate clauses. Lawyers were required in the first part of the oath to promise faithful and diligent service to their clients. This was simply a more elaborate version of the oath required under the 1237 legatine constitution. The second part of the oath made them promise not to knowingly accept unjust causes and to relinguish such causes if they only discovered this after they had agreed to act. This took up and developed a theme of the Durham and York oaths. A third clause made them promise not to seek unjust delays nor to protract litigation unnecessarily. This again took up and developed part of the 1237 oath. A fourth clause, which seems to have no English precedents, required them to promise not knowingly or maliciously to infringe ecclesiastical liberties or to assist in their infringement. A final clause required them to promise to be moderate in their claims for payment from clients and to promise not to act in return for a share of what was at stake in litigation.[21]

Other ethical standards enunciated Concern with the ethical standards of those practising in canon-law courts in England preceded the 1237 legislation. As early as 1222 the provincial council of the province of Canterbury at Oxford had stipulated (in clause 4) the punishment of excommunication for all advocates who maliciously advanced or procured the advancement of exceptions in matrimonial suits which delayed such suits or which were intended to ensure the wrong outcome in them. Such advocates were not necessarily professional and there is nothing distinctively professional about their punishment. In a related piece of legislation, however, clause 45 of the same council required that, when in matrimonial litigation sentence was given in favour of the marriage, the advocate for the party opposing the marriage should be suspended from office for one year, unless the judge specifically excused him for probable ignorance or justified error.[22] Here it seems that we are definitely dealing with a professional and that he is being made subject to a specifically professional form of punishment: suspension from office for a limited period. The provisions of clause 4 of this legislation were subsequently incorporated into a large number of local diocesan statutes and reiterated at the 1279 provincial council of Reading.[23]

The 1237 legatine council itself enunciated certain ethical standards that were not specifically referred to in the new advocate's oath which it established. Subornation of the perjury of witnesses or the instruction of parties to suggest the false or suppress the true were to be punished on a first occasion by suspension from 'office' (activity as an advocate) and from any benefice the advocate held till he made satisfaction for his wrongdoing. Any repetition of the offence was to be punished by the 'due penalty' (unspecified). Here again we are clearly dealing with the professional advocate subject, initially at least, to the distinctively professional punishment of suspension from professional activity for an act of professional wrongdoing.[24]

Conclusion

It was during the period between $c.1190$ and 1274 that a legal profession comprising some, though not perhaps all, of those practising in the English canon-law courts began to take shape. What was to become the upper branch of that profession, the advocates, now commonly received a special university education to train them for practice in the church courts. Advocates came to be required to take an oath laying down some of the basic requirements of professional conduct before they were allowed to practise. They were also subject to certain other rules of professional ethics for whose breach they might be punished by the specifically professional punishment of suspension from professional activity. However, the provisions of the 1237 legislation suggest that at that date, and perhaps later as well, not all advocacy in the ecclesiastical courts was in the hands of professional advocates; and it is only at the end of this period, in the provisions of archbishop Kilwardby's statutes for the Court of Arches, that we can see professional proctors, members of what came to be regarded as the lower branch of the canonical legal profession, beginning to be regarded as members of the profession and thus subject to some of the same rules of professional conduct.

THE THIRD STAGE (1274–1307)

In the third stage of the development of the canonical profession, beginning in 1274 and continuing to the end of 1307 (and well beyond that date), we find further indications of professional canon lawyers being thought of and treated as members of a profession and much more evidence of professional proctors also being treated as part of that profession.

The imposition of specific qualifications for practice

As we have seen, it seems probable that even in the preceding period it was usual, and perhaps invariable, practice for professional advocates in English ecclesiastical courts to acquire their professional training through study of canon and or civil law at one of the English universities or perhaps occasionally elsewhere. However, it was only in the last quarter of the thirteenth century that we find this common practice being solidified into a specific rule which debarred those who had not qualified in this way from practising as advocates.

The first general rule enacted in England on this matter seems to be the 1281 canon of the provincial council of Lambeth which established that no one was to be allowed to practise as an advocate unless he had attended lectures in canon and civil law for a minimum of three years.[25] A still higher requirement was imposed by archbishop Winchelsey for advocates wishing to be admitted to practise in the provincial Court of Arches by statutes of 1295. They were required to have attended such lectures in a university for a minimum of four years or preferably five and also to have been in regular attendance at the Court of Arches itself for at least one year, presumably to learn the practice and customs of the court.[26] However, it was only $c.1342$ that archbishop Stratford imposed the requirement that advocates should at least have taken the degree of bachelor of canon or civil law.[27] In these latter statutes we also first find a preference being given for university law graduates in the competition for one of the limited number of places as proctor in the Court of Arches, though such a qualification was still not demanded as such for those wishing to practise to the court.[28]

The imposition of quotas

During the period around 1300 we first begin to have evidence of the imposition of quotas on the numbers of canon lawyers allowed to practise in particular courts in England: that 'professionalization' was beginning to take the form of securing a monopoly of regular practice in particular courts for particular practitioners.

Here, too, the provincial Court of Arches led the way. In the 1295 statutes of archbishop Winchelsey we find the archbishop limiting to 16 the number of advocates allowed to practise in the court and limiting to ten the number of proctors allowed to practise there. No particular reason was given for imposing these quotas and it is unclear whether or not it was at the request of the practitioners themselves. Practitioners admitted to the quota were required to pay a price for their monopoly rights. They had to be present at the court full-time and needed special permission to be absent in the service of their clients in other courts at a time when business was normally done in the court; nor could any of them agree to be in the sole service of one particular client. The proctors were also admonished to respect the traditional division of responsibilities between themselves and the advocates: none were to take on or prosecute business without advocates.[29]

These statutes may, however, merely have formalized or modified an arrangement which was already in existence. Other clauses in the same statutes seem to indicate that before 1295 problems had already arisen with powerful or ill-intentioned litigants in the court taking into their service so many advocates and proctors as to deprive their opponents of proper legal assistance; and with cases involving advocates and proctors practising in the court and officials of the court where their opponents had similarly found it impossible to find legal assistance. Measures were duly taken to deal with both kinds of situation.[30] Neither problem makes much sense if we assume that litigants might make use of the services of any of the professional canon lawyers practising in the country; both apparently assume that only a limited number of lawyers can practise in the court. Litigation in the Common Bench in 1298 between master John Lovel and the executors of bishop Roger Longespee of Coventry and Lichfield about arrears of annual pension granted by the bishop to master John in 1283 is also revealing.[31] This indicates that the pension was payable to master John for as long as he gave diligent and faithful service in the court of Canterbury (evidently the Court of Arches) in the office of advocate (*in officio advocacionis*) in business touching the bishop and his office. At the time this pension was granted, it looks as though master John was one of a limited number of advocates permitted to practise in the Court of Arches and that the bishop was granting the pension to retain his services there.[32]

There is, however, another piece of evidence which may suggest that if there was a closed shop for advocates before 1295, it covered not just the Court of Arches but all the main ecclesiastical courts in the city of London. This is provided by another pension case: this time between master Peter of Peckham and the prior of Lewes, heard in the exchequer of pleas in 1291, in which it was common ground to both sides that the pension was payable for the advocate's service to the prior as advocate in all causes in the city of London.[33] This must surely have included the Court of Arches, but it clearly also included other courts (particularly the consistory court of the bishop of London). Thus what may have been new in 1295 was an attempt to restrict the advocates of the Court of Arches to practise solely in that court and a similar restriction on its proctors.

The next court known to have imposed similar quotas was the corresponding court of the northern province, the consistory court of the archbishop of York. Statutes of 1311 imposed a limit of 12 on the number of advocates allowed to practise in the court and eight on the number of proctors there.[34]

In these regulations imposing quotas, we seem to see the beginnings of a major shift in the way in which the English canon-law profession was structured. Pension agreements between individual canon-law advocates and their clients during the second half of the thirteenth century generally seem to assume that the advocates would serve their clients wherever in England (and Wales) those clients have litigation and need their services: indeed some specifically spell this out.[35] Litigation about such pensions also shows clients expecting their advocates to travel around and appear for them in a number of different courts and claiming that the pensions have been forfeited as a result of their failure to do so.[36] In these provisions of the late thirteenth and early fourteenth centuries (and in later similar provisions) we seem to see a move towards a more localized and geographically fragmented profession, with particular advocates practising in specific courts rather than on a nation-wide basis.

The clear separation of professional canon lawyers from the beneficed clergy

Another indication of the way in which the profession of canon lawyer (or more precisely, the profession of being a practising canon lawyer in full-time private practice)[37] was coming to be seen as a distinct, full-time occupation in its own right is to be found in provisions intended to stop any of the beneficed clergy (who were supposed to be resident in the benefices of which they had the care of souls) also practising on a regular basis in the ecclesiastical courts. The earliest evidence of such a prohibition in England is found in the 1240 synodal statutes of bishop Walter de Cantilupe for his diocese of Worcester. It specifically exempted from the prohibition beneficed clergy acting on their own behalf, for their own churches, for their lords or for the disadvantaged. This was apparently in line with a recent ruling of pope Gregory IX on the subject.[38] There is then no further evidence of such an attempt to produce a complete separation between the beneficed clergy and professional canon lawyers till 1279 when archbishop Wickwane of York, on ordering his official to enforce the provisions of the Council of Lyons on the taking of annual oaths by advocates practising in the consistory court, also took the opportunity to make it clear that rectors, vicars and priests (whether or not beneficed) were not to be allowed to practise there.[39]

A similar provision (though phrased simply to exclude priests, whether or not they were beneficed) was included in the statutes of archbishop Winchelsey for the Court of Arches in 1295. Winchelsey was careful to make clear that the prohibition applied to the proctors as well as the advocates and specifically made an exception for priests acting on their own behalf, for their churches, for their lords and for the disadvantaged (provided in the latter cases they acted gratis).[40] The assumption may, none the less, have remained that practising canon lawyers would normally be in minor orders rather than laymen. This is certainly suggested by the 1287 synodal statutes of bishop Peter Quinel for his diocese of Exeter which actually excluded laymen from acting as advocates in his diocese on the grounds that church courts dealt with spiritual causes and it was improper for laymen to be involved in such matters.[41] It was also suggested by the way pension agreements between canon lawyers and their clients commonly (though not invariably) provided for the pension to be paid only till the client had provided the advocate to a suitable benefice.[42]

Ethical standards

Admission oaths In 1274 at the Second Council of Lyons the Church for the first time imposed a general requirement on all professional canon lawyers (both advocates and proctors) throughout Western Christendom to take an oath not just at their admission into practice but also at yearly intervals thereafter.[43] The oath promised that the lawyers concerned would put their best efforts into their work for their clients, but would abandon any case once they knew their client's case to be unfounded. No lawyer was to be allowed to practise without taking the oath and lawyers were reminded that any breach of its terms was tantamount to perjury. They were also threatened with more specific punishment for acting in any cause where they knew their client's case was unfounded: restitution of double the payment they had received and damages to the injured party.

Subsequently we find the archbishop of York in 1279 giving specific orders for the observance of the provisions of the legislation in his consistory court[44] and bishop Quinel ordering its observance in his diocese of Exeter through chapter 34 of his synodal statutes of 1287 (but also adding the additional penalty of suspension for one year for advocates and proctors who failed to take the initiative in offering to take the oath).[45] However, the Court of Arches continued to demand its own oath, which was more elaborate than that required by the Lyons legislation. Under the 1295 statutes of archbishop Winchelsea, advocates and proctors practising in the court were required to act diligently and faithfully in their office to the best of their ability (essentially a paraphrase of the Lyons oath); to observe the customs and statutes of the court; not (to the best of their knowledge) to make untrue or unjust claims or statements in court; to elicit the truth from their clients as far as possible; to warn them of the dangers awaiting them if they continued with their suits; and to refuse to take on or to abandon parties without just suits or defences.[46] A much fuller oath than that required by the Council of Lyons was imposed on the advocates and proctors wishing to practise in the consistory court

of Durham or in any other court of the bishop of Durham under statutes enacted by bishop Richard de Kellaw in 1312.[47]
Other ethical regulations The 1295 regulations of archbishop Winchelsey for the Court of Arches also laid down a detailed code of professional conduct for the lawyers practising in the court and a tariff of punishments for infractions of this code. This covered the malicious subtraction of proofs, the use of forged instruments, the suppression or alteration of genuine instruments, the direct or indirect subornation of witnesses, regular appearance in false cases, knowingly alleging untrue facts and procuring or exhibiting royal prohibitions in cases where such prohibitions were inappropriate. Conviction on any of these charges meant permanent suspension; suspicion of having committed them meant suspension from office till the suspect had cleared himself. Less serious was the impediment of the business of the court by lawyers who talked too much or who were discourteous to their colleagues or to the court. Punishment on any first offence was to be at the will of the presiding judge; permanent suspension the punishment only for incorrigible offenders. A similar punishment awaited those lawyers who were absent from the court without making arrangements with a colleague to cover for their absence when one of their cases came up from hearing; as also for advocates and proctors found to be regular haunters of taverns. Temporary or permanent suspension awaited those lawyers who made false and vain appeals to frustrate the passing of sentence by the court or the execution of such sentences.[48] Other ecclesiastical courts may have had similar rules of their own; but if so, none of them survive.

The Second Council of Lyons of 1274, in the same clause as the one that imposed a general requirement of an oath on advocates and proctors in ecclesiastical courts throughout Western Christendom, also laid down rules about the maximum payments that could be demanded by advocates and proctors. It enacted that lawyers who claimed in excess of the sums in question would not gain ownership of the money concerned and would be liable to a three-year suspension (if advocates) and a permanent suspension (if proctors) for doing this.[49] There is little evidence, however, that this part of the legislation was received or translated into action in England. The earliest legislation to lay down maximum fees for canon lawyers practising in any of the English ecclesiastical courts seems to be the legislation of 1311 regulating the consistory court at York which does not cite the Council of Lyons regulation at all. It imposed a maximum fee for any one cause per year of 50 shillings for advocates and ten shillings for proctors (figures that seem to bear no relationship to those of the Council of Lyons regulation). Any breach of this regulation was to lead to an order for the restoration of the whole of the fee and the suspension of the lawyer concerned. Suspension was to last until the president of the court lifted it, not for the three-year or indefinite period mentioned in the Lyons regulation.[50] The regulations of the following year promulgated by bishop Richard de Kellow of Durham make it fairly clear that there was no such scale of maximum fees in that diocese: the presiding judges of the bishop's courts were simply told to ensure that the advocates and proctors made themselves readily available to clients and did not hold out in the hope of extorting large salaries from them.[51]

The same Durham regulations of 1312 also bear witness to the enforcement in England of the professional ethical duty of canon lawyers to act for poor clients without payment.[52] In the consistory and other episcopal courts in Durham it was to be the duty of the presiding judge to assign advocates and proctors to act for such clients: one or more, if more were needed.[53] A similar provision also forms part of the 1295 statutes of the Court of Arches.[54]

Conclusions

The imposition on all advocates and proctors by the Council of Lyons of a standard oath which needed to be renewed annually made them (in some senses at least) part of a single, international legal profession; and the education that English advocates received (and that new minimum standards imposed during this period required them to have received) also provided them with a training not dissimilar to that of their counterparts in the rest of Western Christendom, with the common educational training of a Western European canon-law legal profession. But at the same time, as we have seen, there was also a movement away from even a national legal profession towards a regionally or locally fragmented canon-law legal profession, as certain courts begin to restrict practice before them to those admitted by the court and began to demand that advocates and proctors so admitted devote their time and energies to the service of clients in that particular court and not elsewhere.

A separate professional identity for practising canon lawyers was also enhanced in this period by the enforcement of older rules barring beneficed clergy and other ordained priests from practising at the canon-law bar; and the 'professionalism' of professional canon lawyers was further reinforced by the enactment of rules further regulating their behaviour in a professional capacity. The regulations imposed by the 1274 Council of Lyons also made clear that the new canon-law legal profession consisted not just of advocates but also of proctors. This soon came to be accepted more widely, as is suggested by the way in which, when quotas were imposed and standards of professional behaviour further elaborated, these quotas covered proctors as well as advocates and the standards were made applicable to them both.

II

The development of a canonical legal profession in England did not take place in total isolation from the world of the common law and its courts and lawyers. From Henry II's reign to the end of the thirteenth century, kings regularly recruited trained canon lawyers and trained Roman lawyers for their service and on occasion employed them among their judges. Of Henry II's judges, Godfrey de Lucy may have studied law at Bologna and master Jocelin, archdeacon of Chichester, probably studied canon law with his uncle bishop Hilary of Chichester.[55] Richard Barre, archdeacon of Ely, a royal justice in Henry's reign and in the reigns of Kings Richard and John, was also apparently a student of law at Bologna in the 1150s.[56] Of the royal justices of the earlier part of Henry III's reign, master Robert of Shardlow may well have been a canon lawyer by training.[57] In the second half of the reign master Simon of Walton had clearly practised as a canon lawyer before entering the king's service, for he was in receipt of a pension of five marks a year (later increased to ten marks) from Osney abbey for his legal services.[58] Master Simon was a regular royal justice in eyres and in the Common Bench for a decade between 1246 and 1256 before his election as bishop of Norwich in 1257. Master Roger of Seaton, chief justice of the Common Bench between 1274 and 1278 and before that a justice of the Common Bench and chief justice of an eyre circuit, appears to have been a trained canon lawyer, for in 1260 he acted as the official and commissary general of bishop Stichill of Durham.[59] Later in Edward I's reign we find master John Lovel, whom we have already encountered as a professional canon lawyer practising in the Court of Arches,[60] taken into the king's service. He was keeper of rolls and writs in the Common Bench between 1290 and 1292[61] and subsequently acted as an eyre justice between 1292 and 1294 and as one of the justices of the court of King's Bench, though only for a single term.

A number of the Common Bench serjeants of Edward I's reign had acquired a degree of expertise in Roman and/or canon law, presumably through attendance at one of the English universities. One of them, Edmund of Pashley, is specifically referred to in passing by one of the judges (Hervey of Stanton) as a 'legist',[62] a qualified Roman lawyer, though, in context, all he was expected to do as a consequence was to recognize a Roman law-tag cited by the judge.[63] Pashley also clearly knew some canon law.[64] The reports provide evidence of knowledge of Roman and canon law on the part of his colleagues Henry le Scrope[65] and William Inge,[66] and of the serjeants and Common Bench justices William of Bereford[67] and William Howard.[68] Some knowledge of canon law and its concept of *infamia* is also demonstrated by a number of other serjeants (Roger of Higham, John of Mutford, Nicholas of Warwick and Henry Spigurnel) in the report of a *quare non admisit* case of the 1290s.[69]

There is even evidence in at least one case of the mid-1290s of a professional lawyer in local practice who was expected by a client who was paying him a pension to represent him both in ecclesiastical and in lay courts. In 1294 Nicholas of Calveley was suing William, rector of Field Dalling, for

13 pounds arrears of an annual pension of 20 shillings a year. The pension had been granted to him by William in 1277 'for his service performed and to be performed for William in his litigation' ('*pro patrocinio suo causis suis ab eodem Nicholao eidem Willelmo prestito ac prestando*') both within and without the diocese of Norwich (a formula similar to that found in other pension agreements between advocates and their clients). William's defence to the claim was that Nicholas had forfeited the pension by refusing to act for him not just in a plea before the official of the bishop of Norwich but also in cases before Solomon of Rochester and his colleagues in the 1286 Norfolk eyre.[70] Issue was eventually taken on whether he had ever refused to give him assistance after being given due warning of William's need for his assistance in accordance with the terms of the writing.

The close relationship between the two worlds of the canon lawyer and the common lawyer is also demonstrated by a second annuity case of 1294 brought by William of Ormsby against Bartholomew, rector of Winterton, for 20 marks arrears of an annual pension of ten marks a year granted William for his service (*obsequium*) in 1286, probably at the time of the 1286 Norfolk eyre.[71] William of Ormsby was a common lawyer who appears to have been in practice in Norfolk during the 1280s[72] and who served as a royal justice in both England and Scotland in various courts (including the General Eyre and King's Bench) from 1292 onwards. Bartholomew's defence to the claim for arrears did not allege any default of service on William's part but did allege that William had assisted the bishop of Norwich with his aid and counsel in proceedings to deprive Bartholomew of his living in 1293. However, it turned out that William had not played any active role in the proceedings and had said nothing that could be heard by witnesses (*verba audita*). He had merely sat with the bishop during the proceedings and this had led Bartholomew to conclude that he was on the bishop's side against him. Since William was of good character (*probus et fidedignus*) and Bartholomew was still in possession of his church, the court concluded that the contrary presumption was to be made and that he had in fact assisted Bartholomew. So William recovered his annuity. Here we cannot see the common lawyer being expected to play or playing any active role in proceedings in the church court but both the bishop and the client seem to have thought his presence and his advice worthwhile and significant.

But showing that there were these and other channels of communication and potential influence running between the canon-law courts and the nascent canon-law legal profession and the common-law courts and the nascent common-law legal profession does not necessarily mean that the one exercised a significant influence over the development of the other. In fact, the two professions seem to have developed along separate lines which on occasion resemble each other but neither can be shown to have exercised a strong influence over the development of the other.

Thus the division of canon lawyers into two separate groups of advocates and proctors, comprising those who spoke in court on behalf of clients and those who merely attended court on their behalf, resembles the division among the common lawyers between serjeants and attorneys. But the church-court advocate was not a necessity in quite the way his common-law counterpart was, for the canon-law litigant who used a proctor would not be prejudiced by any purely verbal slips that the proctor made in quite the same way as the common-law litigant would be by the slips of his attorney.

Both sets of courts can be seen during the second half of the thirteenth century to be imposing controls on those allowed to practise before them. But here the first clear evidence comes from the lay courts, not the ecclesiastical. The 1280 London regulations controlling (though not as yet imposing a quota on) the admission of serjeants allowed to practise in the city courts, and the unsuccessful attempt to impose controls and a quota on the number of attorneys practising in the Common Bench in 1292, precede the earliest known attempt to impose such controls and a quota on the number of canon lawyers practising in the Court of Arches in 1295, though as we have seen there may in fact have existed some such controls before 1295. When the church courts imposed controls over the advocates allowed to practise before them, moreover, they had one obvious standard to apply: a requirement of a university education in canon and/or Roman law. Although several serjeants may have begun such an education and most, if not all, are likely to have participated in the educational programme that was available at Westminster or in London by the last quarter of the thirteenth century, there was no such obvious educational standard that could be applied to them, no clearly recognized qualification for advanced legal practice in the common-law courts.

Even in the matter of the imposition and enforcement of professional standards, the two systems took rather different paths. As early as the first quarter of the thirteenth century the church courts began to insist that canonical advocates take oaths that obliged them to observe some of the main standards of professional ethics; and from 1274 (as a result of the Council of Lyons) all canonical proctors as well as advocates were required to take such oaths. In the common-law courts, by contrast, it is only in London that we find any evidence of similar oaths being required during this period. There is no evidence that the main royal courts required such an oath either from serjeants or from attorneys. It is also only in London that we find any parallel (in the 1280 regulations) to the detailed regulation of professional conduct found in the 1295 Court of Arches regulations on the conduct of its practitioners.

Conclusion

In 1307 the English legal profession was still at an early stage in its development and a number of its characteristic features had yet to emerge. There were as yet no Inns of Court to organize the education of lawyers or provide accomodation for lawyers and students in London: these only developed from c.1340 onwards. Serjeants had begun to be appointed to judicial posts in the main royal courts but had not yet gained a monopoly of such appointments. Thus the fusion of bench and bar characteristic of the English legal system for most of its history had not yet been achieved. This, too, was a fourteenth-century development and one that was substantially complete by 1330. In 1307 apprentices were still no more than students and it was the serjeants practising in the Common Bench who also spoke for litigants in the other main royal courts. It was only during the fourteenth century that senior apprentices became legal practitioners in their own right, providing comparable services to those given by the serjeants in courts other than the Common Bench. This eventually led to the apprentices eclipsing their senior colleagues in importance, so the modern barrister traces his descent from them rather than from the serjeants. The solicitor only made his appearance in the fifteenth century, though the solicitor's branch of the modern English legal profession can legitimately be traced to the thirteenth century. It was created by the nineteenth-century fusion of attorneys and solicitors: the former, at least, were direct descendants of the professional attorneys whose origins have been discussed in this book.

Much had been achieved by 1307. The transformation of the English legal system during Henry II's reign and that of his successors, which brought into existence national courts manned by legal experts attracting large amounts of legal business, turned every part of the litigation process from the selection of a writ to initiate proceedings to the making of the plaintiff's count and the presentation of 'evidence' to a jury into matters requiring expert assistance. It provided the institutional basis for the employment of two different kinds of legal representative – the serjeant and the attorney – creating a demand for the employment of expert professionals to assist litigants and facilitating the meeting of that demand. By the end of Edward I's reign the demand was met by a group of around 30 full-time professional serjeants whose main base was in the Common Bench but who also offered their services to litigants in King's Bench and in the General Eyre. There were other groups of professional serjeants meeting the same demand in the county courts and in city courts around the country. In the Common Bench and perhaps in the other courts by 1307 these professionals also seem to have succeeded in excluding amateur competitors from any significant share in the business of the court. The demand for legal services was also being met by a larger body of professional attorneys: well over 200 in the Common Bench, 26 in King's Bench and around ten in the London city courts. The professional attorneys had apparently been rather less successful in driving out their amateur competitors, though by 1299–1300 almost two-thirds of the litigation of the Common Bench and almost three-quarters of the litigation of King's Bench was in the hands of obviously professional attorneys; the real figure may be even higher.

The reign of Edward I had also witnessed the first measures we may interpret as evidence of the treatment of professional lawyers as members of a professional group, of a recognizable legal profession. The imposition of controls over those allowed to practise as serjeants in the city courts of London and in the Common Bench manifest a concern for ensuring practice is in the hands of competent, qualified, honest professionals; while the unsuccessful attempt to impose similar controls over the professional attorneys allowed to practise in the Common Bench indicates a similar concern in their case but the difficulties in the way of translating that concern into an effective measure of control. The reign also saw the beginnings of a specific disciplinary code for the behaviour of professional lawyers and measures to apply that code in practice. It is also to the period before 1307 that we can trace the beginnings of a professional education for lawyers and the beginnings of a distinctive professional literature, much of it connected with legal education.

A second legal profession developed in England simultaneously: that of the English canon lawyers, though they were also in some senses part of a much wider Western European canonical profession. The practitioners and judges of the common law and litigants in common-law courts were clearly aware of developments in the ecclesiastical courts but it appears that these exercised little direct influence over the way in which professional lawyers and a legal profession developed in England. Those developments can be explained without any need to posit much in the way of external influence, either on the general overall way in which the profession developed or on specific details of that process. A detailed comparison indicates that the two professions developed along rather different lines.

The thirteenth-century legacy to the modern English legal profession has not been a wholly beneficial one. The division of that profession into two separate branches, an elite specializing in courtroom work, and a larger lower branch providing other kinds of legal services, goes back to this period and to the difference in functions and powers of the two different kinds of legal representatives allowed under thirteenth-century common law. Also in this period English legal education took on its characteristic form of a severely practical instruction in the details of common-law procedures and rules in a non-university setting almost wholly separate from the wider intellectual horizons of the Roman and canon law studied in the universities. Yet it would be wrong to blame the thirteenth century for the institutional inertia of the nineteenth and twentieth centuries which has prevented a merging of the two branches of the legal profession or for the intellectual blinkers of many succeeding generations of English lawyers and the fact that English lawyers were not exposed to the intellectual seductions of Roman law during their training was, as historians have long realized, one important factor in preserving the common law as a separate legal system.

Notes

Chapter 1 Anglo-Norman England: a Land without Lawyers

1 P. M. Barnes, 'The Anstey Case', in *A Medieval Miscellany for D. M. Stenton*, ed. P. M. Barnes and C. F. Slade (Pipe Roll Society, new series, 36 (1960)), pp. 1–23. Additional material on the case, including an identification of the lands over which the case was fought, will be found in P. A. Brand, 'New Light on the Anstey Case', *Essex Archaeology and History*, 15 (1983), pp. 68–83.
2 Barnes, 'The Anstey Case', pp. 21–3.
3 C. R. Cheney, *From Becket to Langton: English Church Government, 1170–1213* (Manchester, 1956), p. 55, n. 2; Barnes, 'The Anstey Case', p. 10, n. 6. Richard also sent once for the assistance of a third, English *magister*, master Stephen of Binham. He seems also to have used a second English canon lawyer, master Peter of Littlebury, in connection with the appointment of papal judges-delegate at Rome and may also have used him for the subsequent litigation at the papal curia.
4 Apparently a reference to his advocates rather than to his own staff of clerks who are mentioned elsewhere in the memorandum.
5 Towards the end of the litigation, when Richard hoped that his case would be heard in the king's court at Windsor, he sent his brother to secure the attendance of Ranulf de Glanville. In the light of Ranulf's later career as a royal justice and justiciar it might be supposed that Richard wanted his legal assistance. There is, however, no evidence that at this stage Glanville did possess any special legal skills and it looks as though Richard wanted him there simply to demonstrate how wide and influential a group of supporters he possessed. In the event, Richard's case was adjourned without a hearing because of other more pressing business and, when it was eventually heard and final judgment given, Ranulf de Glanville was not sent for and was probably not present. On Glanville's early career see J. S. Falls, 'Ranulf de Glanville's Formative Years *c*.1120–79: The Family Background and His Ascent to the Justiciarship', *Medieval Studies*, 40 (1978), pp. 312–27; R. Mortimer, 'The Family of Rannulf de Glanville', *Bull. Inst. Hist. Res.*, 54 (1981), pp. 1–16.

6 At one point in the memorandum he describes the justiciar Richard de Lucy as 'my lord'.
7 Professor Robert C. Palmer has argued for the existence of legal experts in England during this period in 'The Origins of the Legal Profession in England', *The Irish Jurist*, new series 11 (1976), pp. 126–46 at pp. 134–5. I have discussed the reasons for rejecting Palmer's view in 'The Origins of the English Legal Profession', *Law and History Review*, 5 (1987), pp. 31–50 at pp. 32–4.
8 S. F. C. Milsom, *Historical Foundations of the Common Law* (2nd edition, London, 1981), pp. 38, 39.
9 It was written during the second decade of the twelfth century and the most recent edition is *Leges Henrici Primi*, ed. L. J. Downer (Oxford, 1972). For the date of composition see ibid., pp. 34–7.
10 *Leges Henrici Primi*, p. 125 (22, 1); *Regesta Regum Anglo-Normannorum 1066–1154*, Vol. II: *Regesta Henrici Primi, 1100–1135*, ed. Charles Johnson and H. A. Cronne (Oxford, 1956), No. 1645. For a discussion of the problems concerning this charter see Christopher Brooke and Gillian Keir, *London 800–1216: The Shaping of a City* (London, 1975), pp. 207–9; Christopher Brooke, Gillian Keir and Susan Reynolds, 'Henry I's Charter for the City of London', *Journal of the Society of Archivists*, 4 (1973), pp. 558–78; C. Warren Hollister, 'London's first charter of liberties: is it genuine?', *Journal of Medieval History* 6 (1980), pp. 289–306.
11 *Borough Customs*, Vol. II, ed. Mary Bateson (Selden Society, 21 (1906)), pp. 1–2.
12 *Red Book of the Exchequer*, ed. Hubert Hall (3 vols., Rolls Series, 1897), iii. p. 1033.
13 Heinrich Brunner, 'Wort und Form im altfranzösischen Process', *Sitzungsberichte der Philosophische-Historischen Classe der Kaiserlichen Akademie der Wissenschaften*, 57 (1867–8), pp. 655–780 at pp. 700–4; *cf.* R. C. Van Caenegem, *Royal Writs in England from the Conquest to Glanvill* (Selden Society, 77 (1959)), pp. 35–6.
14 Brunner, 'Wort und Form', pp. 655–71. For passages in the *Leges Henrici Primi* which may point to English legal custom in the Anglo-Norman period adopting a similar attitude towards what was said or not said in court by litigants see *Leges Henrici Primi*, pp. 130 (28, 4), 156 (46, 6) and 162 (49, 3b).
15 Milsom, *Historical Foundations*, p. 39.
16 Milsom, *Historical Foundations*, p. 42.
17 Milsom, *Historical Foundations*, pp. 39, 42–3.
18 Brunner, 'Wort und Form', pp. 710–1.
19 *Leges Henrici Primi*, pp. 126–7 (23, 2); 154–5 (45, 1); 45, 3–5).
20 *English Lawsuits from William I to Richard I*, Vol. I, ed. R. C. Van Caenegem (Selden Society, 106 (1990)), pp. 96–7. The work is still relevant for our purposes even if composed in the second quarter of the twelfth century (as suggested by Offler) since it then reflects contemporary practice of that period: H. S. Offler, 'The Tractate De Iniusta Vexacione Willelmi Episcopi Primi', *Eng. Hist. Rev.*, 66 (1951), pp. 321–41.
21 *English Lawsuits I*, pp. 145–7.
22 *English Lawsuits I*, p. 150.
23 *English Lawsuits I*, pp. 192–3.
24 *Cf.* the similar conclusion drawn by White about the room for argument in legal proceedings in western France between 1050 and 1150: Stephen D. White, 'Inheritances and Legal Arguments in Western France, 1050–1150', *Traditio*, 43 (1987), pp. 55–103 at pp. 84–5.

Notes to Pages 5–6 163

25 White, 'Inheritances and Legal Arguments', pp. 88–9.
26 Milsom, *Historical Foundations*, p. 38.
27 On feudal courts in this period see F. M. Stenton, *The First Century of English Feudalism, 1066–1166* (2nd edition, Oxford, 1961), pp. 42–57. For the later position see F. W. Maitland in *Select Pleas in Manorial Courts* (Selden Society, 2 (1888)), pp. xxxviii–xxxix, xli.
28 Stenton, *First Century of English Feudalism*, pp. 42–4.
29 *Close Rolls, 1231–4*, pp. 588–9.
30 Stenton, *First Century of English Feudalism*, p. 77.
31 This was certainly the position in the thirteenth century: see, for example, *Close Rolls, 1231–4*, pp. 588–9. The twelfth-century position is less clear. There is evidence to suggest that the lord's tenants were simply seen as 'assisting' and 'advising' the lord (or his representative) in making judgment: see P. A. Brand, *The Contribution of the Period of Baronial Reform (1258–1267) to the Development of the Common Law in England* (Oxford D.Phil. thesis (1974)), pp. 46–8. However, in practice, this must often have meant the same thing.
32 This practice is reflected in two passages in the *Leges Henrici Primi* at pp. 136–7 (33, 1) and pp. 262–3 (86, 1). There also seems to be independent evidence of this in the record of the case of Modbert and Bath priory heard in the court of the bishop of Bath in 1121 (*English Lawsuits I*, pp. 192–3) where the case was heard not just by the bishop's barons but also by his *amici*. In the Charwelton case heard in the court of the abbot of Thorney *c*.1107–1111 we see the judgment being given by a group of named men plus the men of the saint; and the distinction seems to be between outsiders called in to make the judgment and the abbey's own tenants: *English Lawsuits I*, pp. 155–6.
33 On the hundred and its court see F. Pollock and F. W. Maitland, *The History of English Law before the time of Edward I* (2nd edition, 2 vols., Cambridge, 1898), i. pp. 556–60; H. M. Cam, *The Hundred and The Hundred Rolls* (London, 1930), chapters 2 and 10. On the pre-conquest origins of the hundred see H. R. Loyn, 'The Hundred in England in the Tenth and Early Eleventh Centuries' in *British Government and Administration: Essays presented to S.R. Chrimes* (Cardiff, 1974), pp. 1–15.
34 But see H. M. Cam, 'Early Groups of Hundreds' in her *Liberties and Communities in Medieval England* (London, 1963), pp. 91–105.
35 A meeting every four weeks is mentioned in the tenth-century Hundred Ordinance. The *Leges Henrici Primi* envisages that the hundred court will normally meet 12 times a year (p. 100 (7,4)). In 1234 it was believed that in Henry II's day hundred courts had met every two weeks: *Close Rolls, 1231–4*, pp. 588–9. If this was the case it is not clear when the change to more frequent meetings took place.
36 See the writ of William II for the abbey of Bury St Edmund's, ordering that no tenants of the abbey be forced to attend the hundred court or the county court other than those 'who had so much land that they were worthy in the time of king Edward to go to counties or to hundreds': H. W. C. Davis, 'The Liberties of Bury St Edmund's', *Eng. Hist. Rev.*, 24 (1909), pp. 417–31 at p. 424. Hence also the passage in the *Leges Henrici Primi* which mentions an especially full session of the hundred twice a year to discover whether all residents of the hundred were in tithing: *Leges Henrici Primi*, p. 102 (8, 1).
37 *Leges Henrici Primi*, p. 100 (7, 8).
38 For the link which existed in the thirteenth century between the duty of attendance and particular holdings see Pollock and Maitland, *Hist. Eng. Law*, i. p. 557; Cam, *Hundred and Hundred Rolls*, p. 172.

39 *Close Rolls, 1231–4*, pp. 588–9. For evidence that a distinction was drawn in the hundred courts of thirteenth-century Cheshire between the suitors and the judges and that it was the latter who had the main voice in the making of judgements see Robert C. Palmer, *The County Courts of Medieval England* (Princeton, 1982), pp. 59–65. These 'judges' were, however, in essence simply a superior class of suitors.

40 *Cf. Regesta Regum Anglo-Normannorum II*, No. 1812 and *Regesta Regum Anglo-Normannorum 1066–1154*, Vol.III: *Regesta Regis Stephani ac Mathildis Imperatricis ac Gaufridi et Henrici Ducum Normannorum, 1135–1154*, ed. H. A. Cronne and R. H. C. Davis (Oxford, 1968), No. 753.

41 On the county court in general see Pollock and Maitland, *Hist. Eng. Law*, i. pp. 537–56; W. A. Morris, *The Early English County Court* (Berkeley, 1926); Palmer, *County Courts*. For evidence that Derbyshire and Nottinghamshire shared a single county court before 1256 see David Crook, 'The Establishment of the Derbyshire County Court, 1256', *Derbyshire Archaeological Journal*, 102 (1983), pp. 98–106.

42 Pollock and Maitland, *Hist. Eng. Law*, i. p. 540, n. 2; Cam, *Hundred and Hundred Rolls*, pp. 10–11. But Palmer (*County Courts*, pp. 3–4) is non-committal.

43 *Leges Henrici Primi*, p. 98 (7, 2); *cf.* Pollock and Maitland, *Hist. Eng. Law*, i. pp. 545–6.

44 Davis, 'The Liberties of Bury St Edmund's', p. 424.

45 *Leges Henrici Primi*, p. 100 (7–7b), and *cf. English Lawsuits I*, p. 143 and *Regesta Regum Anglo-Normannorum II*, No. 900.

46 *Leges Henrici Primi*, p. 130 (29, 1–29, 1a).

47 Robert Palmer has recently suggested (*County Courts*, p. 129) that by the time of the composition of the *Leges Henrici Primi* 'most often the county court judges would have been, in fact, the seneschals of the barons, earls, priors, abbots and bishops of the county' but cites no evidence in support of this suggestion. The *Leges Henrici Primi* suggests that its author believed that judgment would normally be made by substantial landowners in person, rather than by their seneschals.

48 *English Lawsuits I*, pp. 37, 49; *Regesta Regum Anglo-Normannorum*, Vol. I: *Regesta Willelmi Conquestoris et Willelmi Rufi*, ed. H. W. C. Davis (Oxford, 1913), Nos. 242, 258; *Regesta Regum Anglo-Normannorum II*, No. 1511.

49 *Early Charters of the Cathedral Church of St Paul, London*, ed. Marion Gibbs (Royal Historical Society, Camden 3rd series, 58 (1939)), No. 17, p. 17.

50 *English Lawsuits I*, p. 39; an earlier reference to this plea describes the plea as heard before the commissioners '*testante vicecomitatu*': *English Lawsuits* I, p. 38.

51 *Regesta Regum Anglo-Normannorum II*, No. 651.

52 H. A. Cronne, 'The Office of Local Justiciar under the Norman Kings', *University of Birmingham Historical Journal*, 6 (1937), pp. 18–38; Doris M. Stenton, *English Justice between the Norman Conquest and the Great Charter, 1066–1215* (Philadelphia, 1964), pp. 65–8.

53 *Regesta Regum Anglo-Normannorum II*, No. 1645.

54 *Cal. Charter Rolls, 1327–1341*, p. 139.

55 *Leges Henrici Primi*, p. 168 (53, 1).

56 W. T. Reedy, 'The Origins of the General Eyre in the Reign of Henry I', *Speculum*, 41 (1966), pp. 688–724; Stenton, *English Justice*, pp. 61–5; C. Warren Hollister and John W. Baldwin, 'The Rise of Administrative Kingship: Henry I and Philip Augustus', *Amer. Hist. Rev.*, 83 (1978), pp. 867–905 at pp. 882–5; Judith A. Green, *The Government of England under Henry I* (Cambridge, 1986), pp. 108–10.

57 Paul Brand, '"Multis Vigiliis Excogitatam et Inventam": Henry II and the

Notes to Pages 8–11   165

58 Creation of the English Common Law', *Haskins Society Journal*, 2 (1991), pp. 197–222 at pp. 199–202.
58 For a particularly clear reference to the king presiding in his own court in 1086 see *Regesta Regum Anglo-Normannorum*, *I*, No. 220. But even in the king's own court it might be someone other than the king who pronounced judgment; see e.g. *Regesta Regum Anglo-Normannorum II*, No. 880.
59 See e.g. *English Lawsuits I*, pp. 29, 148.
60 See e.g. *English Lawsuits I*, pp. 128–33.
61 *Regesta Regum Anglo-Normannorum* I, No. 370.
62 For their activity in financial matters see *Regesta Regum Anglo-Normannorum II*, Nos. 1000, 1211. For evidence of them hearing 'ordinary' litigation see: ibid., Nos. 1538, 1739.
63 Hollister and Baldwin, 'Rise of Administrative Kingship', pp. 875–6, 879, 889–90.
64 *Leges Henrici Primi*, p. 162 (49, 2–49, 2a).
65 Edmund King, 'The Peterborough *Descriptio Militum* (Henry I)', *Eng. Hist. Rev.*, 84 (1969), pp. 84–101 at p. 100.
66 *Chronicon Monasterii de Abingdon*, ed. J. Stevenson (2 vols., Rolls Series, 1858), ii, pp. 132–3.
67 *The Black Book of St Augustine's Abbey, Canterbury*, ed. G. J. Turner and H. E. Salter (2 vols., British Academy Records of Social and Economic History, 1915–24), ii, pp. 462–3.
68 I. J. Sanders, *English Baronies* (Oxford, 1960), p. 109; *The Lincolnshire Domesday and the Lindsay Survey*, ed. C. W. Foster and Thomas Longley (Lincoln Record Society, 19 (1924)), pp. 118–24.
69 Sanders, *English Baronies*, p. 54; *Regesta Regum Anglo-Normannorum II*, pp. xv–xvii.
70 *Regesta Regum Anglo-Normannorum II*, pp. xi–xii.
71 *Leges Henrici Primi*, p. 156 (46, 4).
72 *English Lawsuits I*, pp. 132–3, 145–7; British Library, MS. Cotton Claudius D. XIII, f. 21r. For evidence of religious houses making arrangements to ensure that they had 'friends' to accompany them to court or be present with them in court when they had litigation see also *Black Book of St Augustine's*, ii. pp. 550–1; *Feudal Documents from the Abbey of Bury St Edmund's*, ed. D. C. Douglas (British Academy Records of Social and Economic History, 1932), pp. 126–7.
73 On the necessity for making an initial general denial see *Leges Henrici Primi*, pp. 158–9 (48, 1a; 48, 1c). That the defendant had to seek permission from the court to take counsel is indicated by the wording of the passage itself which says that the taking of counsel is by right to be denied to no one. That the defendant went apart to take such advice is indicated by another passage: *Leges Henrici Primi*, p. 158 (48, 1c).
74 *Leges Henrici Primi*, p. 156 (46, 5–6). The translation of this passage is my own.
75 Brunner, 'Wort und Form', pp. 740–76.
76 Pollock and Maitland, *Hist. Eng. Law*, i. pp. 211–2; Palmer, 'Origins of the Legal Profession', p. 134.
77 Heinrich Brunner, *Deutsche Rechtsgeschichte*, (2 vols., Leipzig, 1887–92), ii. pp. 349–53; Idem, 'Die Zulässigkeit der Anwaltschaft im französischen, normannischen und englischen Rechte des Mittelalters', *Zeitschrift für Vergleichende Rechtswissenschaft*, 1 (1878), pp. 321–83 at pp. 321–2.
78 Ludwig Lass, *Die Anwaltschaft im Zeitalter der Volksrechte und Kapitularien* (Breslau, 1891), pp. 6–8, 14–15.

79 M. T. Clanchy, *From Memory to Written Record* (London, 1979), p. 221.
80 *Anglo-Saxon and Old English Vocabularies*, ed. T. Wright and R. P. Wuelcker (2 vols., London, 1884), i. cols. 140, 183.
81 *Leges Henrici Primi*, pp. 150–1 (42, 2–3).
82 *Leges Henrici Primi*, pp. 194–5 (61, 2).
83 See e.g. *Leges Henrici Primi*, p. 194 (61, 3).
84 Brunner, 'Die Zulässigkeit der Anwaltschaft', pp. 321–83.

Chapter 2 Creating a Demand for Lawyers: the Transformation of the English Court System, 1154–1307

1 Brand, 'Henry II and the Creation of the Common Law', pp. 199–202.
2 For full references see Brand, 'Henry II and the Creation of the Common Law', p. 203. For earlier visitations of individual counties by royal justices and for the first countrywide visitation by justices but with limited powers in 1170 see ibid., p. 202. The Pipe Rolls indicate that there was also a nationwide visitation by royal justices hearing civil and criminal business in 1174/5 but it is not clear whether this was a General Eyre in the later sense: see ibid., p. 203.
3 For two exceptional final concords which also refer to others as forming part of the court where the settlement was made see Brand, 'Henry II and the Creation of the Common Law', pp. 203–4.
4 Full details and references are given in Brand, 'Henry II and the Creation of the Common Law', p. 204.
5 For discussion of the few exceptional fines which do seem to ascribe more of a role to persons other than the king's justices see Brand, 'Henry II and the Creation of the Common Law', p. 205.
6 See the literature cited in Brand, 'Henry II and the Creation of the Common Law', p. 206.
7 See Brand, 'Henry II and the Creation of the Common Law', pp. 206–7.
8 The final concords show litigation being settled in the king's court at the Exchequer at both Easter and Michaelmas sessions each year from 1179 to the end of Henry II's reign except for Easter 1180 (though there is a final concord said to have been made in the king's court at the Exchequer shortly before Easter), Easter 1184, Michaelmas 1186, Easter 1187 and Easter 1188.
9 For final concord and other evidence for the hearing of litigation at the Exchequer during the reign of Henry II see Brand, 'Henry II and the Creation of the Common Law', pp. 207–9.
10 Both terms are used in this period and seem to be interchangeable. It is only as from 1191 onwards that they are commonly described as 'justices' of the king (and only from 1196 that they are invariably so described) but they are also so described in a quitclaim made in the court as early as 1165 as well as in a final concord made there in 1177 and they are also indirectly so described in an number of other final concords of the period *c*.1170–81. No final concord directly describes them as barons but at least three final concords of the early 1180s do so indirectly and several others seem to refer to them indirectly as 'justices and barons'.
11 For examples see: *Pleas before the King or his Justices*, Vol. III, ed. Doris Mary Stenton (Selden Society, 83 (1967)), pp. lxv, lxvii, lxviii.
12 Thomas Madox, *Formulare Anglicanum* (London, 1702), p. xix; *Pleas before the King or his Justices*, III, p. lxvi.

13 For fuller details see Brand, 'Henry II and the Creation of the Common Law', pp. 211–12.
14 From 1195 a third copy of final concords began being kept in the Treasury and feet of fines survive in an almost unbroken sequence. Before 1195 copies were made only for the parties concerned and the survival rate of such copies (or later copies of them) is much lower.
15 For an attempt to demonstrate this point from surviving evidence for both the General Eyre and the Exchequer see Brand, 'Henry II and the Creation of the Common Law', pp. 213–4.
16 For a more detailed discussion of this evidence see Brand, 'Henry II and the Creation of the Common Law', p. 215.
17 On the date of this treatise see G. D. G. Hall's introduction to his edition of *Glanvill* (London, 1965), pp. xxx–xxxi. For an example of such a writ in this treatise see I, 13 (p. 9) (the writ *cape* for seizure of land into the king's hands on a default). A number of the writs issued by the court do not (as given in the treatise) order the return of the writ: see II, 15 (p. 33), IV, 4 (p. 45: but the sheriff is instructed to report on the day of seizure), VIII, 16 (p. 131). This is probably only an oversight on the part of the author or an early scribe.
18 A number of these writs (together with original writs initiating litigation) are printed by Doris Mary Stenton in *Pleas before the King or his Justices, 1198–1202*, Vol. I (Selden Society, 67 (1953)), pp. 350–418. Additional writs belonging to the same file have since been discovered and some of them are printed by Lady Stenton in *Pleas before the King or his Justices* III, pp. xi–xii.
19 Original writs returnable before the justices in eyre, however, merely instructed the defendant to appear before the justices in eyre 'at their next session in those parts'.
20 The justices of the General Eyre were also probably from the beginning limited to hearing only such other business (pleas of the crown and enquiries on the Crown's behalf) as was specifically authorized in the articles of the eyre which the justices had received when they set out on their circuit. The only such articles to survive from Henry II's reign are those drafted for the visitation of 1176: above, pp. 14–15.
21 The constant reorganization of eyre circuits may also have prevented the emergence of any kind of regional identity for groups of counties visited by eyre justices.
22 It is the close connection between the new royal courts and the 'laws and customs of England' that is reflected in the incipit of the Beta manuscripts of *Glanvill* which like its Alpha counterpart describes itself as a 'treatise on the laws and customs of the realm of England', but then goes on to say that 'it contains only those laws and customs in use in pleading in the king's court at the Exchequer and before the justices in Eyre': *Glanvill*, p. 1 and n.b.
23 *Glanvill*, XII, 25 (p. 148). The same rule is stated in slightly different terms at XII, 2 (p. 137).
24 See Brand, 'Henry II and the Creation of the Common Law', p. 217, n. 92.
25 Below, pp. 29–30.
26 *Glanvill*, XII, 7 (p. 139) and *cf.* ibid., VI, 6 (p. 61) for the availability of the same procedure in the writ of right of dower. On the origins of *tolt* see the works cited in Brand, 'Henry II and the Creation of the Common Law', p. 218 and n. 96.
27 Brand, 'Henry II and the Creation of the Common Law', pp. 220–1 and n. 107.
28 A similar procedure also applied in the case of litigation about entitlement to services. For details of the relevant procedures and references to the relevant

passages of *Glanvill* see Brand, 'Henry II and the Creation of the Common Law', pp. 218–9.
29 See Brand, 'Henry II and the Creation of the Common Law', p. 219.
30 *Glanvill*, VIII, 9 (p. 101).
31 *Glanvill*, VIII, 11 (pp. 102–3).
32 The major differences were that they were not returnable writs and did not authorize the hearing of the case on any particular day.
33 *Glanvill*, V, 1 and XII, 11 (pp. 53–4, 142–3); VI, 18 (pp. 68–9); VII, 6–7 and XII, 17 (pp. 80–81, 144); IX, 9–10 (p. 113); IX, 14 and XII, 16 (pp. 116, 143–4); XII, 12 (p. 142); XII, 13 (p. 142); XII, 14 (pp. 142–3).
34 Palmer, *County Courts*, pp. 189–98.
35 For the two forms of *pone* given in the treatise see *Glanvill*, VI, 7 (pp. 61–2) and V, 2 (p. 54). Removal might also take place if some legal difficulty arose which the county court was unable to resolve, and the position of the county court as a junior partner of the king's courts is further shown by the fact that in such cases the litigation was not returned to the county court for judgment after the difficulty was resolved: *Glanvill*, VI, 8 (p. 62). Although *Glanvill* does not specifically mention it, litigation would also be removed out of the county court into the king's court when a tenant put himself on the grand assize there.
36 The earliest direct evidence for this is of mid-thirteenth century date: *Radulphi de Hengham Summae*, ed. W. H. Dunham, jr. (Cambridge, 1932), p. 8. See also the speech of Warwick in the report of a 1290 case in British Library, MS. Stowe 386, ff. 149v–150r. This was despite the fact that by the mid-thirteenth century county courts were keeping written records of their proceedings: Palmer, *County Courts*, pp. 38–40, 153.
37 *Pleas before the King or his Justices* III, pp. lxxxi–lxxxiv, lxxxvii–lxxxix, xcii–xciv; David Crook, *Records of the General Eyre* (Public Record Office Handbooks 20 (1982)), pp. 56–63.
38 Crook, *Records of the General Eyre*, pp. 63–71.
39 Crook, *Records of the General Eyre*, pp. 86, 128.
40 Crook, *Records of the General Eyre*, pp. 71–142. In the early 1260s we even hear of a rule that no county should be visited by the eyre more frequently than once every seven years. It is possible that this reflects an otherwise unrecorded provision of the baronial reformers in 1258 or 1259. More probably it was no more than a 'customary' rule which reflects the actual practice of the recent past: R. F. Treharne, *The Baronial Plan of Reform* (2nd edition, Manchester, 1972), pp. 259–60, 398–406. In either case the rule does not in itself explain the relative infrequency of eyres during Henry III's reign as a whole.
41 *Crown Pleas of the Wiltshire Eyre, 1249*, ed. C. A. F. Meekings (Wiltshire Archaeological and Natural History Society, Records Branch, 16 (1960)), pp. 4–6; R. B. Pugh, *Imprisonment in Medieval England* (Cambridge, 1970), pp. 255–66. See also below, p. 26.
42 Meekings, *Crown Pleas of the Wiltshire Eyre*, pp. 9–12.
43 Paul Brand, '"Quo Waranto" law in the Reign of Edward I: A Hitherto Undiscovered Opinion of Chief Justice Hengham', *Irish Jurist* 14 (new series) (1979), pp. 124–72 at p. 130.
44 Crook, *Records of the General Eyre*, pp. 145–6, 171, 178–9.
45 Below, pp. 23–4.
46 This was true of the 1279–81 Yorkshire eyre, the 1281–4 Lincolnshire eyre, the 1286 Norfolk eyre, the 1293–4 Yorkshire eyre and the 1293–4 Kent eyre: Crook, *Records of the General Eyre*, pp. 148–51, 166–7, 172–3, 176–7.

47 Brian R. Kemp, 'Exchequer and Bench in the later twelfth century – separate or identical tribunals?', *Eng. Hist. Rev.* 88, pp. 559–73 at pp. 570–2; Ralph V. Turner, 'The Origins of Common Pleas and King's Bench', *American Journal of Legal History* 21 (1977), pp. 238–54 at pp. 243–4. One obvious indicator of the separation of the two institutions is whether or not the Treasurer (one of the main officials in the Exchequer) is regularly mentioned in final concords as among the justices present in the court. This was the case until Richard fitzNeal retired as Treasurer in 1196. Here and elsewhere I have used the term Common Bench for the Westminster court. The term is not a contemporary one (contemporaries used the term 'Bench' or 'king's court at Westminster') but to avoid confusion with other courts (particularly with the court of King's Bench) I will use this later name for the court.
48 When hearing ordinary civil litigation the Exchequer seems occasionally to have held sessions at other times even before the mid-1190s. The court seems, however, only to have held sessions on a regular basis in these two additional terms as from Trinity term 1195.
49 J. C. Holt, *Magna Carta* (Cambridge, 1965), p. 322. The concession was in response to clause 8 of the Articles of the Barons (ibid., p. 307). This part of clause 17 was re-enacted as clause 12 of the 1216 reissue of Magna Carta; clause 12 of the 1217 reissue and clause 11 of the 1225 reissue. For a rather different view of the significance of this clause see M. T. Clanchy, 'Magna Carta and the Common Pleas' in *Studies in Medieval History Presented to R. H. C. Davis*, ed. Henry Mayr-Harting and R. I. Moore (London, 1985), pp. 219–32.
50 The periods of suspension became steadily longer. Sessions were suspended only for three terms or less before 1234 but in 1234–5 they were suspended for one year, in 1240–1 for two years and in 1247–9 for a little over two years.
51 Thus there were no sessions of the court in Easter or Trinity terms 1264 nor in Easter term 1267.
52 Evidence as to the duration of these movements to Shrewsbury and York is derived from the court's plea-rolls. The court also moved briefly elsewhere in London during Easter term 1290 (to the London Guildhall) when parliament was held at Westminster: CP 25(1)/75/35, no. 144.
53 In 1234 orders were given adjourning all litigation then before the Common Bench to be heard before the justices in eyre in the appropriate county (*Close Rolls*, 1231–4, p. 593). Similar orders appear to have been given in 1240 and 1247. After 1250 litigation was only adjourned out of the Common Bench into the eyre after the eyre was actually summoned in the county concerned.
54 *Early Registers of Writs*, ed. E. de Haas and G. D. G. Hall (Selden Society, 87 (1970)), p. 48 (note to CC45). A similar list is given also in *Casus Placitorum and Reports of Cases in the King's Courts, 1272–1278*, ed. W. H. Dunham jr. (Selden Society, 69 (1950)), p. 37, n. 104 and in the later thirteenth-century note in *Early Registers of Writs*, pp. xxvii–xxviii (which makes plain that an additional charge is made for other writs returnable in the Common Bench).
55 Above, p. 21.
56 There was also a dramatic drop in the maximum number of justices mentioned in any fine. During Richard's reign we still find at least two fines with as many as 14 justices mentioned in them and eight with 13; in John's reign the maximum drops to ten justices (plus the king himself) in some 11 fines in 1205; by the end of Henry III's reign the largest figure encountered in a Common Bench fine in the last five years of the reign is just three. In Edward

I's reign it rose once more to a maximum of seven (in Michaelmas term 1273 and Hilary and Easter terms 1306).
57 For evidence of individual justices hearing business by themselves see e.g. CP 40/9, m. 50 (1275); CP 40/89, m. 112 (1291); CP 40/133, m. 187d (1300). For evidence of two justices hearing business by themselves see e.g. CP 40/49, m. 32 (1283); CP 40/95, m. 97 (1292); CP 40/135, m. 316 (1301). For references to the 'second bench', probably the second division of the court, in Easter term 1305 and Hilary term 1306 see e.g. CP 40/155, m. 238; CP 40/158, m. 299. There are similar references on the plea-rolls in Michaelmas term 1306 and Hilary and Easter terms 1307.
58 On the origins of King's Bench and its forerunners see Turner, 'Origins of Common Pleas and King's Bench', pp. 245–54; G. O. Sayles in *Select Cases in the Court of King's Bench*, Vol. I (Selden Society, 55 (1936)), pp. xi–xl and in *Select Cases in the Court of King's Bench*, Vol. IV (Selden Society, 74 (1957)), pp. xxvi–xxxviii.
59 Above, p. 22.
60 See C. A. F. Meekings in *Curia Regis Rolls 15*, p. xxii; G. O. Sayles in *Select Cases in the Court of King's Bench*, Vol. VII (Selden Society, 88 (1971)), pp. xlii–xliv; C. A. F. Meekings in *List of Various Common Law Records* (Public Record Office Lists and Indexes, Supplementary Series 1 (1970)), pp. 36–70.
61 *Select Cases in King's Bench*, I, pp. cxxix–cxxxiii. The numbers of justices varied between two and five.
62 *Select Cases in the Court of King's Bench*, Vol. III, ed. G. O. Sayles (Selden Society, 58 (1939)), pp. lxxxvi–lxxxvii; *Select Cases in King's Bench*, VII, pp. xliv–xlv.
63 Above, p. 20.
64 The most satisfactory treatment of these developments is that in C. A. F. Meekings's introduction to the *Calendar of the General and Special Assize and General Gaol Delivery Commissions on the Dorses of the Patent Rolls, Richard II (1377–1399)* (Nedeln, Liechtenstein, 1977), pp. 1–4.
65 Meekings, *Calendar of Commissions*, p. 4; *Cal. Close Rolls, 1272–9*, p. 52. The justices of the new circuits still received individual commissions to hear each of the assizes concerned and in practice some individual commissions were still issued to royal justices who were not among the 12 assize commissioners.
66 Meekings, *Calendar of Commissions*, p. 4; *Cal. Close Rolls, 1272–9*, pp. 135–6.
67 *Statutes of the Realm*, Vol. I, pp. 85–6.
68 *Cal. Close Rolls, 1279–88*, p. 365.
69 Meekings, *Calendar of Commissions*, p. 6.
70 Meekings, *Calendar of Commissions*, p. 5. For the 1293 ordinance see *Rotuli Parliamentorum*, Vol. I, p. 99 and *Stat. Realm I*, p. 112. The commissions are calendared in *Cal. Close Rolls, 1288–96*, pp. 319–20. The statutory provisions as to the timing of assize sessions were, however, reinstated (for reasons that are not at all clear) in May 1303 (*Cal. Close Rolls, 1302–7*, pp. 89–90) and appear to have remained in force for the rest of the reign.
71 *Stat. Realm I*, p. 29. If one of the assize justices was a cleric his colleague was to conduct the gaol delivery with the assistance of a local knight instead.
72 Pugh, *Imprisonment*, chapters 12 and 13.
73 Pugh, *Imprisonment*, p. 281.
74 Above, p. 16.
75 One obvious example is Richard fitzNeal who acted as a royal justice for over 30 years (from around 1165 to 1196). During the whole of this period he was also

acting as the Treasurer and it seems probable that it was his fiscal responsibilities that were primary. Another example is Michael Belet who was first appointed an eyre justice in 1178 and acted in every major eyre visitation to the death of Richard I (and also appeared from time to time in the Exchequer and the Common Bench) but who also acted as hereditary butler of the royal household during the same period.

76 But note that even he combined his judicial career with an appointment as sheriff and a brief period in the partly administrative post of justice of the Jews: Ralph V. Turner, *The English Judiciary in the age of Glanvill and Bracton, c. 1176–1239* (Cambridge, 1985), pp. 86, 105–6, 156.

77 A list of judges participating in Common Bench final concords of Henry III's reign was compiled by Maitland: *Bracton's Note Book*, ed. F. W. Maitland (3 vols., London, 1887), i. pp. 139–45; lists of judges participating in general eyres of the reign are contained in Crook's *Records of the General Eyre* at pp. 71–142; and lists of King's Bench justices of the reign are contained in C. A. F. Meekings's analysis of the rolls and writs of King's Bench in the *List of Various Common Law Records* at pp. 38–46.

78 They are: Martin of Pattishall; Stephen of Segrave; William de Lisle; Thomas of Moulton; William of York; William of Raleigh; Alan de Wassand; Master Simon of Walton. I am excluding three justices (master Roger of Seaton, Robert Fulks and Thomas Weyland) who began judicial careers under Henry III, as by far the largest part of their careers lay in the reign of Edward I.

79 Lists of royal justices of the Common Bench and King's Bench of the reigns of Edward I and Edward II were compiled by G. O. Sayles for Appendixes I–IV of the introduction to *Select Cases in King's Bench I*. Lists of the judges participating in the eyres of Edward I's reign are contained in Crook's *Records of the General Eyre* at pp. 142–80.

80 Ralph de Hengham, John of Mettingham, Roger le Brabazon and Gilbert of Rothbury.

81 Master Roger of Seaton; Robert Fulks; Thomas Weyland; John de Lovetot; Roger of Leicester; William of Brompton; William of Saham; master Thomas of Siddington; Solomon of Rochester; Roger of Boylund; Peter Mallore; William Howard; Lambert of Threekingham.

82 Turner, *English Judiciary*, pp. 144–6.

83 Turner, *English Judiciary*, pp. 210–1; *Rolls of the Justices in Eyre for Lincolnshire (1218–9) and Worcestershire (1221)*, ed. Doris Mary Stenton (Selden Society, 53 (1934)), pp. xvi–xviii.

84 Turner, *English Judiciary*, pp. 215–6; C. A. F. Meekings, 'Martin of Pateshull and William Raleigh', *Bull. Inst. Hist. Res.*, 26 (1953), pp. 157–80; idem, 'Martin of Pateshull of Good Memory my Sometime Lord', *Bull. Inst. Hist. Res.*, 48 (1974), pp. 224–9.

85 Turner, *English Judiciary*, pp. 216–7; C. A. F. Meekings, 'Alan de Wassand (+1257)', *Yorkshire Archaeological Journal*, 38 (1952–5), pp. 465–73 at pp. 467–8.

86 Turner, *English Judiciary*, pp. 214–5; C. A. F. Meekings, 'Six Letters Concerning the Eyres of 1226–8', *Eng. Hist. Rev.*, 65 (1950), pp. 492–504.

87 C. A. F. Meekings, 'Roger of Whitchester (+1258)', *Archaeologia Aeliana*, 4th series, 35 (1957), pp. 100–28.

88 Paul Brand, 'Ralph de Hengham and the Irish Common Law', *The Irish Jurist*, 19 (new series) (1984), pp. 107–14.

89 William of Brompton, Ellis of Beckingham, Roger of Leicester, Lambert of Threekingham, Henry of Guildford and Hervey of Stanton.

90 Ralph de Hengham, William of Saham and Ellis of Sutton.
91 Solomon of Rochester, William of Saham and John of Berwick.
92 William of Barford (Bereford), Robert of Hartforth (Hertford), William of Gisleham and William Howard.
93 Robert C. Palmer, 'The Origins of Property in England', *Law and History Review*, 3 (1985), pp. 24–46 discusses the origins of the writs of entry (writs which identified a single flaw in the tenant's title), though his explanation of the origins of these writs remains controversial.
94 But for evidence that plaintiffs were still using the writ of right and lord's courts hearing such litigation in the early fourteenth century see *Cal. Chanc. Rolls Various, 1277–1326*, pp. 145–59 (roll of those placing themselves on the grand assize in such litigation in the reign of Edward II).
95 See Paul Brand, 'Lordship and Distraint in Thirteenth-Century England' in *Thirteenth Century England III: Proceedings of the Newcastle upon Tyne Conference, 1989*, ed. P. R. Coss and S. D. Lloyd (Woodbridge, 1991) at pp. 14–15.
96 Other than the little used writ of *ne vexes* which only the tenant could bring.
97 Palmer, *County Courts*, pp. 252–62.
98 The rule received statutory form in clause 18 of the Provisions of Westminster of 1259: *Close Rolls, 1259–61*, p. 149. There is, however, reason to believe that it is much older than this.
99 Brand, *Contribution of the Period of Baronial Reform*, pp. 287–9.
100 This was the effect of restrictions on lords distraining outside their fee. Distraints outside the lord's fee were forbidden in 1259 by clause 11 of the Provisions of Westminster and again in 1267 by chapters 2 and 15 of the statute of Marlborough but the rule existed before the enactment of the legislation: see Brand, *Contribution of the Period of Baronial Reform*, pp. 154–6.
101 See *Early Registers of Writs*, CA 27, 32, 33, 36, 54, 55, 58 for the new writs. The transformed writ was the writ of replevin (see CA 21). The writ which had dropped out of the use was the one for upholding the will of deceased testator.
102 *Early Registers of Writs*, CC 121a, 142a, 147 and the various different kinds of *quod permittat* action (see CC 119a, 120, 125, 127).
103 *Early Registers of Writs*, p. cxxxii.
104 Above, p. 19.
105 *Early Registers of Writs*, CA 4, note.
106 *Radulphi de Hengham Summae*, p. 9. On the date and authorship of this treatise see Paul Brand, 'Hengham Magna: a Thirteenth Century English Common Law Treatise and its Composition', *The Irish Jurist*, 11 (new series) (1976), pp. 147–69.
107 This appears to be the implication of *Glanvill*, VI, 8 (p. 62) and certainly *Glanvill* nowhere says that such pleas cannot be removed.
108 *Radulphi de Hengham Summae*, p. 13.
109 British Library, MS. Lansdowne 564, f. 35v.
110 Palmer, *County Courts*, chapter 8.
111 Palmer, *County Courts*, pp. 169–72.
112 Palmer, *County Courts*, p. 152.
113 See J. V. Capua, 'Feudal and Royal Justice in Thirteenth-Century England: The Forms and Impact of Royal Review', *American Journal of Legal History*, 27 (1983), pp. 63–75.
114 Donald W. Sutherland, *The Assize of Novel Disseisin* (Oxford, 1973), pp. 77–81.
115 Paul A. Brand, 'Legal Change in the Later Thirteenth Century: Statutory and Judicial Remodelling of the Action of Replevin', *American Journal of Legal History*, 31 (1987), pp. 43–55 at pp. 51–4.

Notes to Pages 33—5   173

Chapter 3   Creating a Demand for Lawyers: Changes in the Process of Litigation and in the Rules Governing the Use of Legal Representatives, 1154—1307

1 Above, p. 17.
2 They were also competent to hear any of the kinds of litigation which the county court heard by writ if a litigant obtained a *pone* for the removal of the litigation: above, p. 19.
3 For the initiation of litigation without writ in the king's courts during this period see *Select Cases of Procedure without Writ under Henry III*, ed. H. G. Richardson and G. O. Sayles (Selden Society, 60 (1941)). Under Edward I there was a significant expansion in litigation brought without writ in the eyre.
4 The earliest of these probably dates from around 1210: Paul Brand, 'Ireland and the Literature of the Early Common Law', *The Irish Jurist*, 16 (new series) (1981), pp. 95—113. Some 15 others come from the period before 1275: *Early Registers of Writs*, pp. xxiii—xxv. No less than 74 belong to the remainder of the reign of Edward I: ibid., pp. xxiii—xxvi. Their evidence must, however, be used with caution. Registers of writs do not always include writs we know from other evidence to have been generally available at the time of their compilation but do sometimes include special writs which were made available to certain privileged litigants but never became generally available to the ordinary litigant.
5 But not all the original writs found in *Glanvill* are included in this register, so the number of new original writs is greater than appears at first sight. There is also a problem here and elsewhere in distinguishing between variants on a single type of writ and different types of writ, so the numbers given are no more than an approximation.
6 *Early Registers of Writs*, pp. 18—32.
7 *The Collected Papers of Frederic William Maitland*, ed. H. A. L. Fisher (3 vols., Cambridge, 1911), ii, pp. 142—8. But note that this register gives variant forms for the initiation of certain types of litigation either in the county court or directly in the king's court.
8 *Early Registers of Writs*, pp. 33—107.
9 The procedure in actions for land is spelled out in *Glanvill*, I, 7 (p. 6). *Glanvill* does not explicitly say that litigation about title to an advowson followed the same procedural rule but since in other respects the rules were the same we may assume that they were in this respect also.
10 *Glanvill*, I, 10 (p. 7) and I, 18—9 (pp. 11—12); IV, 3 (p. 45).
11 *Glanvill*, II, 1 (p. 22). *Glanvill* does not mention this possibility in connection with pleas of advowson and it was probably already the case that it was only in exceptional cases that such a view was allowed.
12 *Glanvill*, III, 1 (p. 38). *Glanvill* does not specifically mention this possibility in the case of litigation about the right to an advowson.
13 *Glanvill*, I, 7, 9 (pp. 6—7). For the requirement of personal attendance on the part of the summoners see *Glanvill*, I, 30 (pp. 17—19).
14 *Glanvill*, I, 12 (p. 8).
15 *Glanvill*, I, 12—15, 21 (pp. 8—9, 12—13).
16 *Glanvill*, I, 12 (p. 8).
17 *Three Rolls of the King's Court in the Reign of King Richard the First, 1194—5*, ed. F. W. Maitland (Pipe Roll Society, 14 (1891)), pp. 14, 29.
18 *Pleas before the King or his Justices I*, p. 156.
19 Ibid., p. 157.

20 *Bracton: On the Laws and Customs of England*, ed. George E. Woodbine and S. E. Thorne (4 vols., Cambridge, Mass., 1968–77), iv, p. 73.
21 But for examples of action being taken against 'false' essoiners in such circumstances as late as the early 1220s see *Curia Regis Rolls 8*, pp. 174–5, 186–7.
22 *Bracton*, iv, pp. 74, 89, 111.
23 On the date and authorship of the treatise see above, Chapter 2, n. 106. See also the passages in various manuscripts of another mid-thirteenth century legal work *Brevia Placitata* entitled 'Ceus sunt les delayes en la court le Rey devant Justiz en dreit del tenant' giving a brief résumé of the possible delaying tactics on an action of right in the Common Bench: *Brevia Placitata*, ed. G. J. Turner and T. F. T. Plucknett (Selden Society, 66 (1951)), pp. 4, 44 and 156.
24 *Radulphi de Hengham Summae*, p. 16.
25 *Glanvill*, II, 1 (p. 22).
26 *Bracton*, iv, pp. 180–90.
27 In 1285 c. 48 of the statute of Westminster II laid down the general rule that the view was only to be allowed where it was necessary and then discussed and specified a succession of types of factual situation where the view was in future to be excluded.
28 *Glanvill*, XIII, 38 (p. 169); *Bracton*, iii, p. 64.
29 *Glanvill*, XIII, 7 (p. 152) and *cf.* XIII, 20 (p. 161) and XIII, 25 (p. 164).
30 Above, p. 35.
31 Above, pp. 35–6.
32 *Bracton*, iii, pp. 206–8, 252–3.
33 *Bracton*, iii, pp. 259–60, 331–2.
34 *Glanvill*, IV, 9 and X, 3 (pp. 48, 117); *Glanvill*, I, 31 and V, 3 (pp. 19–20, 77).
35 *Glanvill*, I, 31; V, 31; X, 3; X, 8 (pp. 19–20, 77, 117, 122).
36 Brand, *Contribution of the Period of Baronial Reform*, pp. 308–13.
37 Ibid., pp. 313–26.
38 *Stat. Realm I*, pp. 37–8.
39 *Stat. Realm I*, pp. 78–9, 89. A variant of judgment by default (allowing for the jury to give its verdict in the absence of the defendant) was allowed in actions of admeasurement of pasture and admeasurement of dower and in the action of waste by chapters 7 and 14 of the same statute: *Stat. Realm I*, pp. 77–8, 81–2.
40 D. W. Sutherland, 'Mesne Process upon Personal Actions in the Early Common Law', *Law Quarterly Review*, 82 (1966), pp. 487, 494.
41 *Glanvill*, II, 3 (pp. 22–3); IV, 6 (p. 46); VI, 8 (p. 62). Interestingly the formulas used in the *precipe* for land and that for an advowson are quite dissimilar even for those parts of the count which in content bear a close resemblance to each other.
42 *Glanvill*, XII, 24 (p. 147).
43 See the specimen counts given by *Glanvill* both for the main writ *precipe* and for the closely related writ of *precipe* for an advowson: *Glanvill*, II, 3; IV, 6 (pp. 23, 46). It is fairly clear from the pleading in a 1208 case that the plaintiff cannot have traced the descent of the right to himself: *Curia Regis Rolls 5*, p. 282.
44 Above, n. 43.
45 E.g. *Curia Regis Rolls 2*, pp. 12, 265–6; *Curia Regis Rolls 3*, p. 184.
46 E.g. *Curia Regis Rolls 1*, p. 297; *Curia Regis Rolls 2*, pp. 188, 259; *Curia Regis Rolls 3*, p. 148.
47 But for later cases where it is omitted see *Curia Regis Rolls 7*, pp. 293–4; *Curia Regis Rolls 10*, p. 42.

Notes to Pages 39–43   175

48 *Bracton*, iv, p. 174.
49 This can be deduced from the argument in a cosinage case of 1270: JUST 1/178, m. 27.
50 *Glanvill*, II, 3 (p. 23).
51 E.g. fee and right: *Three Rolls of the King's Court*, p. 50; demesne and fee: *Curia Regis Rolls 7*, p. 334; demesne, fee and right: *Curia Regis Rolls 1*, p. 60; right and inheritance: *Curia Regis Rolls 1*, p. 69; demesne and right: *Curia Regis Rolls 1*, p. 87.
52 This is the form given by *Bracton*, iv, p. 170 and used in later formularies.
53 The following paragraph is based on my own unpublished study of the action of replevin.
54 *Casus Placitorum*, p. lxxxi/51 (a note probably dating from the 1250s).
55 *Glanvill*, II, 6 (pp. 27–8).
56 *Glanvill*, XII, 24 (p. 147).
57 The fullest discussion in the treatise is of the use of exceptions in the assize of mort d'ancestor: *Glanvill*, XIII, 11 (pp. 153–5). The discussion of possible exceptions in respect of the other assizes is much more sketchy: indeed the very possibility is not mentioned in the case of the assize utrum and the assize of novel disseisin. It is none the less certain that the possibility of making such exceptions already existed at the time he was writing and that it is probable that he discussed the possible exceptions in the assize of mort d'ancestor at such length merely by way of example.
58 *Curia Regis Rolls 7*, p. 83 (but the defendant only obtained an adjournment of the case, not its dismissal).
59 *Curia Regis Rolls 3*, p. 265.
60 *Curia Regis Rolls 13*, no. 507.
61 *Curia Regis Rolls 2*, p. 173.
62 *Bracton*, iv, pp. 245–363.
63 See the statement by Hengham in the reports of what appears to be an unidentified Common Bench case of the early 1270s in British Library, MS. Additional 31826, ff. 63r–v (and six other manuscripts). This report will be printed in a forthcoming Selden Society volume of pre-1290 Common Bench case reports.
64 *Bracton*, iv, p. 246; cf. *Radulphi de Hengham Summae*, pp. 34–5.
65 *Curia Regis Rolls 14*, no. 1427.
66 *Curia Regis Rolls 16*, no. 1750.
67 See the report of a case of 1268 in Huntington Library, MS. HM 19920, f. 40r (this report will also be included in my Selden Society volume of pre-1290 cases).
68 British Library, MS. Additional 37657, f. 68r (and cf. Lincoln's Inn, MS. Hale 188, f. 26r).
69 *Glanvill*, XI (pp. 132–6).
70 *Glanvill*, I, 12 (p. 8); I, 18–19 (pp. 11–12); III, 4 (p. 40); IV, 3 (p. 45); IV, 9 (p. 49); VI, 10 (p. 63); VIII, 5 (p. 97).
71 Hall (*Glanvill*, p. 192) accepts Woodbine's view that the *responsalis* appointed by a litigant who had been found not to have bed-sickness or at the end of a year of bed-sickness had more limited powers than the *responsalis* appointed under other circumstances. There is no warrant for this view in *Glanvill*'s text and the view seems to derive from the unjustified assumption that the position as described by *Bracton* was also the position at this time. It is, however, clear that a series of changes had taken place in the intervening period and the limitation

in the powers of the *responsalis* who had been appointed in this way were probably one of them. See further below, pp. 45–6.
72 *Glanvill*, XI, 3 (p. 134).
73 *Glanvill*, XI, 1 (p. 133).
74 *The Chronicle of Battle Abbey*, ed. Eleanor Searle (Oxford, 1980), pp. 232–5. *Cf.* also the litigation between the abbot of Battle and Alan de Beaufou where Robert the philosopher appeared on the abbot's behalf and again no such formal appointment is mentioned: ibid., pp. 244–51.
75 *Dialogus de Scaccario*, ed. Arthur Hughes, C. G. Crump and C. Johnson (Oxford, 1902), pp. 93–4.
76 The earliest final concord to contain such a reference belongs to October 1182: British Library, MS. Cotton Otho D. III, f. 29v ('per Petrum monachum et Gaufridum de Gorham quos abbas attornaverat loco suo ad lucrandum vel perdendum').
77 *Early Registers of Writs*, CC 28a, note. Elsewhere there seems to be some confusion between this restriction and the rule that an attorney could only wager law but could not make law on behalf of his principal: see *Radulphi de Hengham Summae*, p. 19; *Casus Placitorum*, p. 6/25; *Brevia Placitata*, p. 30, n. 1. They are probably wrong to suggest that the defendant could not appoint an attorney in any plea that might be determined by wager of law.
78 Sutherland, *Assize of Novel Disseisin*, pp. 44–5.
79 *Curia Regis Rolls 2*, p. 133. The appropriate writ forms are given in the register of writs belonging to the later years of Henry III: *Early Registers of Writs*, CC 28, 31, 53.
80 See the rubric to CC 28 in *Early Registers of Writs* and *Radulphi de Hengham Summae*, pp. 18–19. The earliest surviving returned writ of *dedimus potestatem* notifying such an appointment seems to be one of 1262: C 254/1, no. 2.
81 *Radulphi de Hengham Summae*, p. 18.
82 *Curia Regis Rolls 8*, p. 180.
83 *Radulphi de Hengham Summae*, p. 19.
84 Cambridge University Library, MS. Dd.7.14, f. 358r.
85 See e.g. KB 26/160, mm. 60 (before John de Wyvill), 62d (before Henry of Bratton, Peter de Percy and the Justiciar).
86 Below, Chapter 6.
87 It was now possible to appoint such an attorney only in one of two not very common situations: when a defendant had essoined himself of bed-sickness and the knights sent to view him had adjudged that he was not ill enough to merit a year and a day in bed or when a defendant had essoined himself of bed-sickness, been adjudged 'languid', stayed in bed for a year and a day and then not risen from his sick-bed: *Pleas before the King or his Justices I*, nos. 3479, 3493 and 3501; *Bracton*, iv, pp. 113, 116, 124, 139–40; *Early Registers of Writs*, J 45; *Radulphi de Hengham Summae*, pp. 9–10, 28.
88 *Bracton*, iv, pp. 139–40. As *Bracton* explains it, the defendant has little choice in the matter. If he did not send the *responsalis* then he must have defaulted and judgment would be given against him on that default: he did not have any choice as to whether or not he accepted the particular action taken by the *responsalis*. *Cf. Radulphi de Hengham Summae*, pp. 33–4.
89 *Curia Regis Rolls 4*, p. 200. For another early example see *Curia Regis Rolls 5*, pp. 96–7.
90 The earliest use of the noun *attornatus* seems to be in *Curia Regis Rolls 1*, p. 309; but in another entry from earlier in the same term the plural *attornati* is

used, though perhaps as a past participle rather than a noun: *Curia Regis Rolls 1*, p. 264. The term *attornatus* was also in use in Normandy for a similar kind of legal representative by the time of the composition of the *Summa de legibus* some time in the second quarter of the thirteenth century: see *Coutumiers de Normandie* ed. E-J. Tardif, (2 vols., Rouen-Paris, 1881–1903), ii, pp. 160–1.
91   Above.
92   British Library, MS. Cotton Otho D. III, f. 29v; *Final Concords of the County of Lincoln*, Vol.II, ed. C. W. Foster (Lincoln Record Society 17 (1920)), pp. 307–8; *Glanvill*, VIII, 2 (pp. 94–5).
93   F. Godefroy, *Dictionnaire de L'Ancienne Langue Française* (10 vols., Paris, 1881–1902), s.v. *attorner*.
94   For such counts see *Glanvill*, II, 3 (pp. 22–3); IV, 6 (p. 46); VI, 8 (p. 62).
95   *Chronicle of Battle Abbey*, pp. 232–5.
96   *Chronicle of Battle Abbey*, pp. 244–51.
97   *Chronicle of Battle Abbey*, pp. 211–21. We also find others speaking on the abbot's behalf in the dispute between him and the bishop of Chichester in 1157 at a meeting of the *curia regis* (ibid., p.197) but it is not certain whether this can really be regarded as in any sense normal litigation or as a guide to what practice in such litigation would have been.
98   For a discussion of the various terms which were used see below, Chapter 4.
99   *Curia Regis Rolls 3*, p. 161. The assize of novel disseisin in question may have been that recorded in the immediately following entry.
100 *Curia Regis Rolls 5*, p. 22. The case may be that in which Richard and his opponent reached an agreement in the following Michaelmas term: ibid., p. 72.
101 *Curia Regis Rolls 13*, no. 1194. The entry was noted by Maitland (Pollock and Maitland, *Hist. Eng. Law*, i, p. 212) and by Lady Stenton (*Pleas before the King or his Justices*, III, p. xlii). Neither noted that the count as emended was equally open to objection, for William ought to have specified that his ancestor's seisin had been on the day of Henry I's death.
102 *Curia Regis Rolls 15*, no. 1767. This was by way of preparation for making an exception to the sufficiency of the count.
103 KB 26/132, m. 6.
104 *Bracton's Note Book*, ii. pl. 131.
105 *Curia Regis Rolls 5*, p. 33. Evidence that this was a strategic disavowal comes from the fact that Richard was surety for the amercement.
106 *Curia Regis Rolls 10*, p. 203.
107 KB 26/150, m. 22 ('Et Abellus de Sancto Martino venit et narravit pro episcopo et non fuit advocatus; ideo in misericordia. Custodiatur'). Maitland (Pollock and Maitland, *Hist. Eng. Law*, i, p. 216, n.3) misinterpreted this passage, supposing that it meant either that Abel was not a member of the legal profession or that the bishop had not given him authority to plead the case: it seems certain that it simply means that the bishop disavowed what he had said.
108 KB 26/171, m. 35d: 'Et quia predictus Hugo attornatus predicti Roberti in persona sua propria posuit se in predictam assisam domini regis absque hoc quod jus vel seisinam predicti Willelmi defenderet prout moris est secundum legem Anglie ad hujusmodi breve de recto nec se ipsum potest deadvocare...'.
109 Below, p. 40.
110 Above.
111 *Brevia Placitata*, pp. 6, 20, 25, 56, 59, 60, etc.; *Radulphi de Hengham Summae*, p. 34.
112 Above, and n. 101.

113 Below, p. 67.
114 Below, p. 67.
115 For the use of the term *placitator* as an alternative to *advocatus* see the London legislation of 1244: below, p. 67. For the use of the term *causidicus* by the London chronicler Fitz Thedmar in referring to the legislation of 1259 see below, p. 67.
116 C 62/28, m. 16 (calendared in *Cal. Liberate Rolls, 1251-60*, p. 13): *Pro Laurencio de Brok'*: Rex thesaurario et camerariis suis salutem. Liberate de thesauro nostro dilecto servienti nostro Laurencio de Brock' x libras de termino Natalis domini anno etc. xxxvj de xx libris quas ei concessimus singulis annis percipiendas ad scaccarium nostrum ad se sustentandum in servicio nostro quam diu fuerit in eodem servicio nostro. Teste rege apud Thorp' ij die Januarii.' For the later use of the term 'serjeant' see below, Chapter 6.

Chapter 4   From Proto-Professional to Professional: the Emergence of the Professional Lawyer in England, 1199-1272

1 *Pleas before the King or his Justices*, III, p. xxxvi.
2 Lady Stenton noted that she had been anticipated in this conclusion by Sir Cyril Flower. A reading of the relevant passages in Flower's *Introduction to the Curia Regis Rolls, 1199-1230* (Selden Society, 62 (1944)) (at pp. 405-7) indicates that Flower did not specifically suggest that the professional attorney first appeared in John's reign but merely that his activities were already visible in the earliest surviving rolls.
3 *Pleas before the King or his Justices*, III, p. xxxvi.
4 Stephen's career is discussed by Lady Stenton at *Pleas before the King or his Justices*, III, pp. xxxvi-xxxvii; the evidence for that career is tabulated at pp. cccviii-cccvi.
5 His clients included the financial administrator and occasional eyre justice Reginald of Cornhill for whom he acted as an attorney in 1200, 1208, 1211 and 1212; the former Common Bench and *coram rege* justice Henry de Pontaudemer for whom he acted as an attorney in 1220; master Reginald of Wrotham (presumably a relative of the justice and administrator master William of Wrotham) for whom he acted as an attorney in 1208; William of Chessington (who appears to have had some kind of connection with the justiciar Geoffrey fitz Peter) for whom he acted as an attorney in 1206.
6 The main facts known about William's career in the courts are tabulated in *Pleas before the King or his Justices*, III at pp. cccvi-cccvii.
7 This is shown by a note on an 1199 plea-roll relating to an Essex mort d'ancestor case recording the fact that the names of the absent recognitors of the assize together with the original writ are in his possession. From this we can deduce that he had been the clerk responsible for the custody of writs and associated memoranda in the court from which the assize had been adjourned into the Bench, probably the Home Counties eyre circuit of Geoffrey fitz Peter and his fellows in 1198-9: *Pleas before the King or his Justices*, III, pp. cxl-cxli.
8 For details of his career see *Pleas before the King or his Justices*, III, pp. cccxi-cccxiii.
9 *Pleas before the King or his Justices*, III, p. cccxiii. Lady Stenton did not note the evidence that also connected him directly with the king's service. Numerous Close Roll entries in 1204 and 1206 are attested by him, and in 1207 the keepers

Notes to Pages 51–2   179

of the abbey of Whitby were ordered to continue payment of a pension owed by the abbey by a mandate which specifically describes him as *clericus noster*: *Rot. Litt. Claus.*, i. 83b.
10 For a summary of the main facts of his career see *Pleas before the King or his Justices*, III, pp. cccxviii–cccxix.
11 *Pleas before the King or his Justices*, III, p. cccxix.
12 Aubrec Buc's career is discussed by Lady Stenton in *Pleas before the King or his Justices*, III at pp. xl and xliii; the evidence for it is tabulated at pp. ccxcvii–ccxcviii.
13 The evidence for his career and background is assembled in *Pleas before the King or his Justices*, III at pp. cccxiv–cccxvi. There is however no real evidence to connect the Thomas de Hoc who became a property-holder in 1223 at Wheathamstead with the man who acted as an attorney and no good reason to suppose that they are the same man. Nor can we necessarily assume that the grand assize juror of that name in Middlesex in 1205 or the Cambridgeshire juror of 1206 are our man.
14 Thomas was one of Lady Stenton's 'minor professional men in the courts of justice' but she noted only those references which call him Thomas Tutadebles (or variants of that name), not those which call him by his alternative toponymic surname of Thomas of Therfield. Thomas was impleaded for one virgate at Therfield by Robert Culterweg in 1198–9 but the parties subsequently made a final concord: *Rot. Curiae Regis*, i, pp. 151, 165, 354. In 1200 he was suing Robert and then his son Ralph by action of fin fet to keep the terms of their agreement: *Curia Regis Rolls 1*, pp. 182, 355. In 1204 he was sued by the abbot of Ramsey for 20 acres of land in Therfield: *Curia Regis Rolls 3*, pp. 202, 223.
15 *Curia Regis Rolls 2*, p. 311; *Pleas before the King or his Justices, 1198–1212*, Vol. IV, ed. Doris Mary Stenton (Selden Society, 84 (1967)), nos. 4557, 4559; *Curia Regis Rolls 7*, p. 133.
16 *Curia Regis Rolls 7*, p. 337; *Curia Regis Rolls 1*, pp. 218, 232.
17 *Pleas before the King or his Justices*, III, no. 1647; *Curia Regis Rolls 3*, p. 122.
18 His career is discussed by Lady Stenton in *Pleas before the King or his Justices*, III at pp. xliii, ccxcv; the relevant evidence is tabulated at pp. ccxcviii–ccxcix.
19 *Curia Regis Rolls 13*, no. 2121.
20 *Curia Regis Rolls 5*, p. 39; *Curia Regis Rolls 5*, p. 286 (and acting in this case at *Curia Regis Rolls 6*, pp. 13, 93 and in the connected final concord in *Feet of Fines for the county of Norfolk, 1201–1215, and for the county of Suffolk, 1199–1214*, ed. Barbara Dodwell (Pipe Roll Society, new series, 32 (1958), no. 256); *Curia Regis Rolls 6*, p. 38 (and acting in this case at *Curia Regis Rolls 6*, p. 78 and in the connected final concord in *Feet of Fines for Norfolk and Suffolk*, no. 260); *Curia Regis Rolls 6*, p. 195; *Curia Regis Rolls 6*, p. 340; *Curia Regis Rolls 7*, p. 150; *Curia Regis Rolls 7*, p. 297.
21 *Curia Regis Rolls 11*, nos. 1625, 2834; *Curia Regis Rolls 6*, p. 92; *Curia Regis Rolls 9*, p. 4.
22 *Curia Regis Rolls 3*, p. 54; *Curia Regis Rolls 4*, p. 233; *Curia Regis Rolls 7*, pp. 251–2.
23 *Pleas before the King or his Justices*, III , pp. xxxvii–xxxix. For a tabular summary of the main facts of his career see pp. ccxcix–ccciii.
24 His tenure of it was reserved in a final concord of the early thirteenth century between Odo de Braimuster and Henry de Coleville: *The Feet of Fines for Oxfordshire, 1195–1291*, ed. H. E. Salter (Oxfordshire Record Society, 12 (1930)), p. 48. For proof that he had inherited it from his father, who had in

turn inherited it from his uncle Geoffrey (who had subinfeudated one and a half hides of the demesne to the abbey of Thame and more than a virgate to a junior branch of the family) see *The Thame Cartulary*, ed. H. E. Salter (2 vols., Oxfordshire Record Society, pp. 25–6 (1947–8), i. pp. 41–3, 47–50.

25 *Eynsham Cartulary*, ed. H. E. Salter (2 vols., Oxford Historical Society, 49 and 51 (1907–8)), ii. 172–4; *cf.* also the 1231 dower claim against him for land here: *Curia Regis Rolls 14*, nos. 1581, 1689. He is also known to have held a virgate or perhaps one and a half virgates at Great Kimble in Buckinghamshire which he acquired of John, son of Hugh of Kimble and then himself granted to Peter of Sonning, and a meadow at Haddenham in Buckinghamshire which he sold to Robert de Braibroc: *Curia Regis Rolls 4*, p. 147; *The Missenden Cartulary*, ed. J. G. Jenkins (2 vols., Buckinghamshire Record Society, 2 and 10 (1939–55)), ii. 154–5; 159, no. 516 (and 118, no. 450); British Library, MS. Sloane 986, f. 54v.

26 To the references given by Lady Stenton should be added: *Patent Rolls, 1216–1225*, pp. 214, 395; *Patent Rolls, 1225–1232*, pp. 349, 446, 518, 522.

27 *Patent Rolls, 1225–1232*, pp. 300, 367, 449; *Curia Regis Rolls 15*, no. 1406.

28 He was appointed to act in three cases in both 1211 and 1212, in a single case in 1213 and in as many as nine in 1214.

29 For his appointments as attorney see Lady Stenton's table of references. For evidence of the pardon granted to him in 1224 which shows him as a member of the household of Falkes see C 60/20, m. 4 (I owe this reference to the kindness of Dr David Carpenter).

30 *Curia Regis Rolls 13*, no. 1107.

31 *Curia Regis Rolls 15*, nos. 226, 1351.

32 In addition to the evidence cited by Lady Stenton see the deed of *c.*1205 in *Cartulary of Oseney abbey*, ed. H. E. Salter (6 vols., Oxford Historical Society, 89–91, 97–8 and 101 (1929–36)), iv. 175, no. 132D.

33 His career is discussed by Lady Stenton in *Pleas before the King or his Justices*, III at pp. xxxix–xl and she tabulates the references to him on the plea-rolls at pp. cccvii–cccxi.

34 G. A. Williams, *Medieval London: From Commune to Capital* (London, 1970), p. 20.

35 *Cartulary of St Mary, Clerkenwell*, ed. W. O. Hassall (Royal Historical Society, Camden 3rd series 71 (1949)), nos. 271, 272, 382; *Cartulary of St Bartholomew's Hospital*, ed. Nellie J.M. Kerling (London, 1973), nos. 319, 479, 480; *The Cartulary of Holy Trinity Aldgate*, ed. Gerald A. J. Hodgett (London Record Society, 7 (1971)), nos. 371, 372; Elijah Williams, *Early Holborn and the Legal Quarter of London* (2 vols., London, 1927), i. no. 696; E 40/1499.

36 CP 25(1)/146/2, no. 15; *Curia Regis Rolls 8*, pp. 60, 211; *A Calendar of the Feet of Fines for the County of Buckingham, 7 Richard I to 44 Henry III*, ed. M. W. Hughes (Buckinghamshire Archaeological Society, Records Branch, 4 (1942)), p. 14 (and *Curia Regis Rolls 12*, no. 1457).

37 *Rot. Curiae Regis*, i. 217; *Curia Regis Rolls 7*, p. 341; *Curia Regis Rolls 1*, pp. 156, 165, 179, 373; CP 25(1)/146/3, nos. 28, 36; *Cartulary of St Mary, Clerkenwell*, nos. 170–84; *Curia Regis Rolls 12*, no. 1457.

38 Stenton, *English Justice*, p. 195; *cf. Pleas before the King or his Justices*, III, p. xxxix.

39 *Curia Regis Rolls 3*, p. 8.

40 *Curia Regis Rolls 5*, p. 33.

41 *Pleas before the King or his Justices*, IV, no. 4075.

42 *Glanvill*, II, 3 (p. 22); IV, 6 (p. 46); VI, 8 (p. 62).
43 *Bracton*, iv. 25 (writ of entry); iv. 274 (writ of prohibition).
44 *Bracton*, iii. 319, 358, 406; iv. 169. Two of these four counts also use a Latin form of the phrase later standard for the introduction of counts ('Ceo vous mustre') which has the effect of still further increasing the distance between the speaker and the litigant for whom he is speaking. In the pleading manuals *Brevia Placitata* and *Novae Narrationes* all counts are introduced by this phrase. John Baker has noted the change from the first person count in *Glanvill* to the third person count in *Brevia Placitata* and likewise concluded from this that 'representation had become usual by the middle of the thirteenth century' but he does not discuss the various relevant passages of *Bracton*: J. H. Baker, *The Order of Serjeants at Law* (Selden Society, supplementary series 5 (1984)), pp. 8–9.
45 Above, p. 48.
46 It may, in any case, be true that the nature of the attorney's representation of his principal made the first person the appropriate form when it was the attorney who spoke. The compiler of *Brevia Placitata* does not make it clear whether or not the specimen counts and defences he gives are to be delivered by serjeants. When he goes on to give further argument which may arise out of the specimen count and defence he often attributes one or both sides of the argument to the litigants' serjeants: for examples see *Brevia Placitata*, pp. 20, 25–6, 55–6, 59, 60, 64–5, 81–3, 100, 100–2, 103–6, 129, 130–1, 143, 165, etc.
47 *Radulphi de Hengham Summae*, p. 34. On the date and authorship of this treatise see above, p. 172, n. 106.
48 *Curia Regis Rolls 9*, pp. 41–2.
49 *Curia Regis Rolls 10*, p. 203.
50 *Matthaei Parisiensis Chronica Majora*, ed. H. Luard (7 vols., Rolls Series, 1872–84), iii. 618–20. This portion of the chronicle is believed to have been compiled before 1251: Richard Vaughan, *Matthew Paris* (Cambridge, 1958), pp. 59–60. Matthew Paris again refers to this group of 'banci narratores' in a passage in his *Gesta Abbatum*. John Mansel is said to have ensured that they did not act for the abbot of St Alban's when the abbey was involved in litigation with Mansel's brother-in-law, Geoffrey of Childwick. The abbot was forced to rely on the services of his cellarer: *Gesta Abbatum Monasterii Sancti Albani*, ed. H. T. Riley (3 vols., Rolls Series, 1867–9), i. 316.
51 Above, pp. 52–4.
52 *Curia Regis Rolls 13*, no. 1194.
53 *Curia Regis Rolls 12*, no. 1309; *Curia Regis Rolls 13*, nos. 672, 960, 2413; *Curia Regis Rolls 17*, no. 956.
54 *Curia Regis Rolls 13*, no. 2785; *Curia Regis Rolls 14*, no. 1497; *Curia Regis Rolls 15*, nos. 110 (with his fellow-serjeant Richard de Hotot), nos. 135, 1561; *Curia Regis Rolls 17*, no. 2424.
55 *Curia Regis Rolls 18*, no. 1075 (= KB 26/132, m. 6).
56 *Curia Regis Rolls 12*, no. 2156; *Curia Regis Rolls 14*, no. 248 (both of these for William d'Aubigny); *Curia Regis Rolls 16*, no. 792.
57 *Curia Regis Rolls 11*, no. 935; *Curia Regis Rolls 15*, no. 110; *Curia Regis Rolls 16*, no. 715; *Curia Regis Rolls 17*, no. 1342; *Curia Regis Rolls 17*, no. 853 (on the parties reaching an agreement); *Curia Regis Rolls 17*, no. 1873 (of an unsuccessful plaintiff); *Curia Regis Rolls 17*, no. 2420; *Curia Regis Rolls 18*, no. 1811.
58 *Luffield Priory Charters*, ed. G. R. Elvey (Northamptonshire Record Society, 22 and 26 (1968–75)), ii. no. 608. Richard de Hotot also acted as a surety for a

number of baronial essoins (JUST 1/56, mm. 1, 1d, 2) and for the appearance of a number of litigants (with one of the justices of the court) (JUST 1/56, m. 26) in the same eyre. He was also appointed attorney to receive a chirograph there: JUST 1/56, m. 26. Richard also occurs together with at least one other probable serjeant (Thomas of Ramsden) among the witnesses to a undated grant belonging to the 1240s in favour of the same Robert and his wife: *Luffield Priory Charters*, ii. no. 607.

59 *Curia Regis Rolls 9*, p. 59.
60 *Curia Regis Rolls 8*, pp. 7, 114, 211, 313; *Curia Regis Rolls 9*, pp. 64, 375, 346; *Curia Regis Rolls 10*, pp. 5, 34; *Curia Regis Rolls 11*, nos. 273, 354; *Curia Regis Rolls 12*, no. 409; *Curia Regis Rolls 13*, nos. 220, 587, 1060; *Curia Regis Rolls 14*, no. 237; *Curia Regis Rolls 15*, nos. 429, 556. He was also appointed to act as an attorney in the Exchequer in 1219 and 1223: E 159/2, m.2d; E 368/2, m. 8d; E 368/5, mm. 12(2), 13(2)d (I owe these references to the kindness of Professor Robert Stacey); and acted for the master of St James's hospital at Westminster in connection with fines made in the 1219 Surrey eyre: CP 25(1)/146/5, nos. 9, 12.
61 *Curia Regis Rolls 8*, pp. 381–3; *Curia Regis Rolls 10*, pp. 83, 100; *Curia Regis Rolls 11*, nos. 1120, 1348, 2240, 2351; *Curia Regis Rolls 12*, nos. 507, 526, 1685; *Curia Regis Rolls 13*, no. 208, 1610, 2888; *Curia Regis Rolls 14*, nos. 990, 1835; *Curia Regis Rolls 15*, no. 1391 (in King's Bench).
62 *Curia Regis Rolls 16*, no. 504.
63 *Rot. Litt. Claus.*, ii. 99, 144b; *Patent Rolls, 1216–25*, p. 17.
64 *Rot. Litt. Claus.*, ii. 136–136b.
65 *Curia Regis Rolls 14*, no. 305; *Curia Regis Rolls 15*, nos. 628, 1639; *Curia Regis Rolls 16*, no. 2224; *Curia Regis Rolls 17*, no. 838. He had also served as a surety in a case of 1227 (*Curia Regis Rolls 13*, no. 208) and was surety for the essoin of the abbot of St Benet Holme in the 1241 Buckinghamshire eyre (JUST 1/55, m. 18d).
66 *Curia Regis Rolls 17*, no. 504.
67 *Curia Regis Rolls 14*, no. 305; *Curia Regis Rolls 15*, nos. 628, 1639; *Curia Regis Rolls 16*, no. 2224.
68 British Library, Additional Charter 5898.
69 *Hornchurch Priory: a kalendar of documents in...New College, Oxford*, ed. Herbert F. Westlake (London, 1923), p. 22, n. 53.
70 Although these are two different names it seems clear that a single individual is in question.
71 *Curia Regis Rolls 8*, p. 51; *Curia Regis Rolls 9*, p. 104; *Curia Regis Rolls 11*, nos. 427, 2714; *Curia Regis Rolls 12*, nos. 1196, 2374; *Curia Regis Rolls 13*, nos. 1321, 1392, 1634; 2066, 2285, 2371, *Curia Regis Rolls 14*, nos. 237, 769, 912, 1132, 1422, 1929; *Curia Regis Rolls 15*, nos. 556, 725, 1197.
72 *Curia Regis Rolls 8*, p. 109; *Curia Regis Rolls 9*, p. 79; *Curia Regis Rolls 10*, pp. 322, 338; *Curia Regis Rolls 11*, nos. 514, 923, 1353, 2351; *Curia Regis Rolls 12*, nos. 391, 526, 2028, 2593; *Curia Regis Rolls 13*, nos. 1737, 1907, 2864; *Curia Regis Rolls 14*, nos. 990, 2335; *Curia Regis Rolls 15*, no. 628.
73 *Curia Regis Rolls 15*, no. 1639; *Curia Regis Rolls 16*, nos. 856, 1221 (in King's Bench), 1305, 2632. And note that he was a surety for an appeal in the 1244 London eyre: *The London Eyre of 1244*, ed. Helena M. Chew and Martin Weinbaum (London Record Society, 6 (1970)), no. 183.
74 Canterbury Cathedral Chapter Archives, Miscellaneous Accounts I, ff. 75v–87v, *passim*.

Notes to Pages 57–8   183

75 British Library, Additional Roll 34332, m. 3.
76 *Fitznells Cartulary*, ed. C. A. F. Meekings and Philip Shearman (Surrey Record Society, 26 (1968)), pp. xxxix, xlvii.
77 'Estate Records of the Hotot family' in *A Northamptonshire Miscellany*, ed. Edmund King (Northamptonshire Record Society, 32 (1983)), pp. 1–58.
78 Ibid., pp. 17–18; 19–20.
79 Williams, *Early Holborn*, no. 1447; CP 25(1)/146/5, no. 8.
80 CP 25(1)/146/7, nos. 64, 72; CP 25(1)/146/9, no. 102; *Curia Regis Rolls 12*, no. 648; *Curia Regis Rolls 13*, no. 2733; *Curia Regis Rolls 14*, no. 853 (and see nos. 1511, 1904); *Curia Regis Rolls 15*, no. 764.
81 There are many references to his activity in this connection. The earliest are from January 1233 (*Cal. Liberate Rolls, 1226–1240*), p. 196; the latest from December 1234 (*Close Rolls, 1234–7*), p. 29.
82 E 40/3695.
83 CP 25(1)/146/10, no. 132; CP 25(1)/146/12, no. 187; *Curia Regis Rolls 16*, no. 741.
84 *Curia Regis Rolls 15*, no. 1188.
85 *London Eyre of 1244*, no. 161.
86 *London Eyre of 1244*, no. 5 (1239–40).
87 *London Eyre of 1244*, no. 3.
88 *Curia Regis Rolls 16*, no. 2354; *Curia Regis Rolls 17*, nos. 546, 1271; *Curia Regis Rolls 18*, nos. 433, 1399; *Civil Pleas of the Wiltshire Eyre, 1249*, ed. M. T. Clanchy (Wiltshire Record Society, 26 (1970)), no. 381.
89 Of the professional serjeants and probable professional serjeants whose careers began during the first half of the reign, at least two (Richard de Hotot and Peter of Bramford) had careers which extended into this part of the reign as well: above, p. 56.
90 *Cal. Patent Rolls, 1247–58*, p. 605.
91 *Curia Regis Rolls 14*, nos. 341, 962, 1365; *Curia Regis Rolls 15*, no. 25; *Curia Regis Rolls 16*, no. 2109; *Curia Regis Rolls 17*, no. 904.
92 *Curia Regis Rolls 14*, nos. 285, 336, 1041, 2242; *Curia Regis Rolls 16*, no. 744; KB 26/135, m. 8d; JUST 1/567, m. 26; *Close Rolls, 1254–6*, p. 339. For evidence that he was present in the 1247 Buckinghamshire eyre (presumably in a professional capacity) see JUST 1/56, m. 12.
93 British Library, Additional Charter 5898; *Luffield Priory Charters*, ii. no. 668; *Hornchurch Documents*, p. 22, no. 53; British Library, MS. Harley 2110, f. 34v.
94 *Brevia Placitata*, p. 4.
95 *Cal. Patent Rolls, 1247–58*, p. 617.
96 KB 26/142, m. 32; KB 26/149, m. 3d; KB 26/171, m. 72.
97 JUST 1/1193, m. 2.
98 New College Archives, no. 10709, Hornchurch 43 (calendared not altogether accurately in *Hornchurch Documents*, p. 19, n. 43.) (I am grateful to Professor Paul Hyams for transcribing the original for me). Westlake, the editor of *Hornchurch Documents*, dated the document to *c.*1237–54, perhaps because *VCH Essex* gives these two dates as those when abbot Hugh occurs. However the same source gives no reference to his successor earlier than 1272. The two royal justices named in the deed sat together in the 1262 Essex eyre, so this seems the most likely date for the deed. There is also evidence that Richard was in receipt of a second pension of half a mark from John Malegraffe, probably (though not certainly) for his legal assistance. In the 1272 Essex eyre he was suing John for six years arrears of the pension which John eventually admitted owing: JUST 1/238, m. 10.

99 Below, p. 63.
100 CP 25(1)/183/12, no. 472; KB 26/171, m. 15d; CP 40/18, m. 71d. He was also one of 12 sureties for persons appealed of ordering a murder when the appellor did not appear in the Common Bench in 1274: CP 40/4, m. 6d. A more exhaustive search of the rolls would probably uncover more instances of his activity.
101 The name is calendared as Thornbegg: *Cal. Patent Rolls, 1266–72*, p. 318. But for related deeds that give the name as Thornhegg(e) see E40/3735, 3773.
102 *Cartularium Monasterii de Rameseia*, ed. W. H. Hart and P. A. Lyons (3 vols., Rolls Series, 1884–94), iii, pp. 325–6; *Close Rolls, 1264–8*, p. 287; KB 26/200C, m. 17.
103 *Cal. Patent Rolls, 1266–72*, p. 551.
104 KB 26/193, m. 5.
105 *Cal. Patent Rolls, 1266–72*, p. 653.
106 The earliest reference I have seen is CP 40/2B, m. 7; the latest CP 40/19, mm. 10d, 41.
107 *Casus Placitorum*, p. 79.
108 JUST 1/361, m. 33; C 146/6295; CP 25(1)/214/26, no. 5; KB 26/164, m. 35.
109 *Select Cases in the Court of King's Bench*, Vol. V, ed. G. O. Sayles (Selden Society, 76 (1958)), p. cxxv; KB 26/171, m. 61; KB 26/200A, m. 17; *Close Rolls, 1268–72*, pp. 204–5.
110 *Cartularium Monasterii de Rameseia*, iii, pp. 322–6; KB 26/180, m. 20.
111 *Casus Placitorum*, pp. 57, 79, 80–1.
112 *Cal. Patent Rolls, 1266–72*, p. 67.
113 KB 26/222, m. 6; KB 26/166, m. 2d; KB 26/195, m. 19; KB 26/196, m. 15; JUST 1/1050, m. 48d.
114 Cambridge University Library, MS. Dd.7.14, ff. 387r-v (the name is given as Pag'). He may also be the *Pageman* mentioned in a report of a case heard in the 1272 Lincolnshire eyre: ibid., ff. 370v–371r.
115 KB 26/168, m. 7; E13/1C, m. 11.
116 *Cal. Patent Rolls, 1266–72*, p. 443.
117 *Cartularium Monasterii de Rameseia*, iii. pp. 322–6; *Durham Annals and Documents of the Thirteenth Century*, ed. F. Barlow (Surtees Society, 155 (1940)), p. 87.
118 *Casus Placitorum*, p. 22, T95 (Croc is misread as Crot). For Dunham's interpretation of this passage see ibid., p. xvi, n. 4.
119 *Curia Regis Rolls 17*, no. 1610.
120 *Bucks Feet of Fines*, pp. 93, 94; KB 26/137, m. 14; KB 26/139, m. 20d.
121 *Luffield Priory Charters*, ii. no. 668; *Hornchurch Documents*, p. 22, n. 53; *The Cartulary of Cirencester Abbey*, ed. C. D. Ross and Mary Devine (3 vols., Oxford, 1964–9) i. no. 54. He also acted as a surety for a champion in the 1247 Buckinghamshire eyre: JUST 1/56, m. 5.
122 His annual pension seems to have been one mark a year: *Cartularium Monasterii de Rameseia*, iii, pp. 322–5.
123 *Close Rolls, 1231–4*, p. 148; *Curia Regis Rolls 15*, nos. 926, 1730; *Curia Regis Rolls 16*, nos. 192, 403, 2011; *Curia Regis Rolls 17*, nos. 616, 1226 (for the king); *Curia Regis Rolls 18*, no. 1200 (for the king), 1553 (for Thirkleby), 1586 (for the earl of Norfolk). In 1243 he sought that the court of King's Lynn be given jurisdiction in a case on behalf of the bishop of Norwich: *Curia Regis Rolls 17*, no. 2207.
124 *Curia Regis Rolls 17*, nos. 78, 439, 654, 1203, 1441, 1563, 1791, 2069, 2239, 2391, 2473, 2501; *Curia Regis Rolls 18*, no. 276; JUST 1/55, m. 19d (1241

Buckinghamshire eyre); JUST 1/81, mm. 2, 4, 5d (1247 Cambridgeshire eyre); KB 26/135, m. 35; KB 26/136, m. 33d; KB 26/139, m. 20d; KB 26/142, m. 7d.
125 British Library, Additional Roll 34332, m. 2d; British Library, Additional Charter 5898; *Hornchurch Documents*, p. 22, n. 53. Note also that in 1239 he sought surety of the king's peace against Herbert of Burwash and his brothers William and Walter who had threatened him as he had rendered judgment by order of the justices on their brother Geoffrey who had been convicted of robbery; that in 1252 he was one of four men appointed gaol delivery justices at Bury St Edmunds; and that in 1254 a mandate was addressed to the constable of the Tower and to him about plevin of a man in Newgate gaol: *Curia Regis Rolls 16*, no. 836; *Close Rolls, 1251–3*, p. 254; *Close Rolls, 1253–4*, p. 21.
126 *Curia Regis Rolls 15*, no. 554; *Curia Regis Rolls 16*, nos. 240, 329.
127 KB 26/149, mm. 1d, 3d.
128 British Library, Additional Charter 5898; *Luffield Priory Charters*, ii, no. 607. In the 1247 Buckinghamshire eyre he also acted as surety for two baronial essoins: JUST 1/56, mm. 3d, 2d.
129 *Feet of Fines for Essex*, ed. R. E. G. Kirk, E. F. Kirk, P. H. Reaney and Marc Fitch (4 vols, Colchester, 1899–1964), i, p. 204, n. 1187.
130 *Curia Regis Rolls 17*, no. 1575; *Oxfordshire Feet of Fines*, p. 151.
131 *Curia Regis Rolls 17*, nos. 597, 2163; *Essex Feet of Fines*, i, p. 204, n. 1187; *Curia Regis Rolls 18*, no. 1759; KB 26/142, m. 32.
132 British Library, Additional Charters 5898; *Hornchurch Documents*, p. 22, n. 53; above, n. 97.
133 Below, pp. 189, 192.
134 Canterbury Cathedral Chapter Archives, Miscellaneous Accounts I, ff. 100v–116v, passim; *Cartularium Monasterii de Rameseia*, iii, pp. 323–6; British Library, MS. Cotton Roll XII. 25, m. 1d.
135 JUST 1/202, m. 17.
136 See above, p. 59 for possible evidence linking John Giffard with Westminster.
137 *Cal. Close Rolls, 1272–9*, p. 23; CP 40/18, m. 71d; CP 25(1)/147/23, no. 470; CP 40/14, m. 53; CP 40/15, m. 22.
138 *Close Rolls, 1264–8*, pp. 225–6; CP 40/14, m. 9d.
139 *Close Rolls, 1234–7*, pp. 158, 172; CP 25(1)/157/79, no. 1148; CP 25(1)/157/80, no. 1153.
140 JUST 1/567, m. 26.
141 CP 25(1)/158/83, no. 1243.
142 *Close Rolls, 1254–6*, pp. 174–5.
143 KB 26/142, m. 9d.
144 *Cal. Patent Rolls, 1266–72*, p. 318.
145 *Bucks Feet of Fines*, pp. 91, 94.
146 CP 25(1)/158/85, no. 1277; CP 25(1)/158/87, no. 1341.
147 CP 25(1)/158/91, no. 1433.
148 CP 25(1)/158/92, no. 1469.
149 CP 25(1)/214/29, no. 56.
150 CP 25(1)/159/101, no. 1678.
151 *Cal. Charter Rolls, 1257–1300*, p. 53.
152 KB 26/171, m. 63d; KB 26/200A, m. 30d.
153 CP 25(1)/85/29 no. 540: the land was at 'Munden de Fraxino' and 'Kenyton' which I have not been able to identify.
154 *Essex Feet of Fines*, i, p. 217.
155 *Cal. Inq. Post Mortem 1*, no. 585.

156 CP 40/76, m. 77d; CP 40/79, m. 9. In 1275–6 John was seeking to recover a holding of one messuage and 200 acres at Wrabness, basing his claim on the alleged seisin of his grandfather in the reign of Henry II: CP 40/11, m. 12; CP 40/15, m. 18d. The outcome of this litigation has not been traced.
157 CP 25(1)/214/27, no. 44; see also *Cal. Charter Rolls, 1257–1300*, p. 183.
158 CP 25(1)/215/32, no. 36.
159 CP 25(1)/226/20, no. 31.
160 *Curia Regis Rolls 15*, no. 1145. The following year Richard was one of the men of the court of Havering answering in the king's court for a judgment of the court: *Curia Regis Rolls 15*, no. 1458. From 1240 to 1243 he was bailiff of the manor of Havering: Marjorie K. McIntosh, *Autonomy and Community: The Royal Manor of Havering, 1200–1500* (Cambridge, 1986), p. 36.
161 *Hornchurch Documents*, p. 77, n. 331 (and p. 75, n. 323).
162 *Hornchurch Documents*, p. 22, n. 53.
163 *Essex Feet of Fines*, i, p. 194.
164 *Cal. Patent Rolls, 1247–58*, p. 617.
165 CP 40/19, m. 75; CP 40/20, mm. 21, 26 and cf. CP 40/27, m. 2d.
166 *Pedes Finium for the County of Somerset*, ed. E. Green (4 vols., Somerset Record Society, 6, 12, 17 and 22 (1892–1906)), i, pp. 169, 375. For the dower claim to the Somerset lands made by Christine in 1278–9 see CP 40/23, m. 31; /27, m. 52d; /29, m. 49d. It is these claims that show that Richard's heir was his son Wigan and that Wigan inherited from his father only a rent of five shillings and four pence in Essex. In the 1280 Somerset eyre she attempted to recover these lands as having been granted to her and Richard jointly and alienated by Richard but she was unsuccessful: JUST 1/758, m. 16.
167 CP 40/29, m. 20d; CP 40/30, m. 6d; JUST 1/876, m. 1d (the quantities mentioned vary and in the two Common Bench entries the location is erroneously given as 'Lambhurst').
168 CP 40/52, m. 9. For direct evidence that Thomas did hold at least a messuage here see *Close Rolls, 1247–51*, p. 282.
169 *Essex Feet of Fines*, i, p. 127, n. 658; p. 140, n. 739.
170 *Essex Feet of Fines*, i, p. 147, n. 776 (and for possibly related concords see ibid., p. 167, n. 934 and p. 176, n. 1009).
171 *Essex Feet of Fines*, i, p. 169, n. 948.
172 *Essex Feet of Fines*, i, p. 176, n. 1002. See also KB 26/169, m. 71d.
173 *Essex Feet of Fines*, i, p. 275, n. 1662. The Somerset lands may perhaps have been acquired by Thomas in the 1240s from the William of Berrow from whom (with his wife) he acquired Essex property.
174 CP 25(1)/85/26, no. 474.
175 Above, p. 58.
176 E 368/42, m. 3d cf. E 159/42, m. 3d. The entry is printed in T. Madox, *The History and Antiquities of the Exchequer* (London, 1711), p. 161 at n. k.
177 Above, p. 55. But for evidence that even in the reign of Edward I most of the serjeants practising in King's Bench were Common Bench serjeants see below, p. 76.
178 'Et Abellus de Sancto Martino venit et narravit pro episcopo et non fuit advocatus. Ideo in misericordia. Custodiatur': KB 26/150, m. 22 (calendared in *Abbreviatio Placitorum*, p. 137). The context makes it clear that Abel was being disavowed so that the bishop could then change his defence. Maitland considered two possible meanings for the passage, but not the one here advanced: (Pollock and Maitland, *Hist. Eng. Law*, i, p. 216, n.3). For proof that Abel was

Notes to Pages 64–5   187

the bishop's brother see *Cal. Patent Rolls, 1232–47*, p. 449; *Cal. Patent Rolls, 1247–58*, pp. 35, 168.
179   *Cal. Patent Rolls, 1232–47*, pp. 448, 449; *Close Rolls, 1256–9*, p. 309; *Cal. Patent Rolls, 1258–66*, pp. 35, 168.
180   Laurence's career is discussed by Sayles in *Select Cases in King's Bench V*, at pp. xxxii–xxxv.
181   *Cal. Patent Rolls, 1232–47*, p. 507. This grant was made on 23 August. He had already been paid twenty pounds for his expenses while on the king's service and retained by the king three days earlier: *Cal. Liberate Rolls, 1245–51*, p. 137.
182   *Cal. Liberate Rolls, 1245–51*, pp. 163, 190, 216, 241, 274, 293, 331, 361; *Cal. Liberate Rolls, 1251–60*, pp. 13, 56, 100, 142, 156, 172, 234, 263, 310, 347, 384, 420, 469, 495, 515; *Cal. Liberate Rolls, 1260–7*, p. 106.
183   KB 26/160, m. 36 (on behalf of a religious house under royal patronage); KB 26/164, mm. 1, 2; KB 26/171, mm. 9, 71; KB 26/172, m. 13d. This evidence was unknown to Sayles who believed that he had only worked in the Common Bench before being permanently retained by the king.
184   For evidence of his being described as the king's serjeant see note 116, p. 178.
185   CP 40/4, m. 28d; British Library, Additional Roll 34322, m. 3; *Cartularium Monasterii de Rameseia*, iii, pp. 322–6; *Durham Annals and Documents*, p. 87 (c. 1265–72).
186   For the inquisitions post mortem held after his death see C 133/9, no. 7 (calendared in *Cal. Inq. Post Mortem 2*, no. 110). They give a misleading impression of the full extent of those acquisitions since they do not include the Middlesex lands he had settled before his death on his younger son William; nor do they cover his lands in Cambridgeshire, Oxfordshire and Northamptonshire. For the lands settled by Laurence on William in Middlesex see CP 25(1)/147/25, no. 498. That Laurence may also have settled other Middlesex lands on William is suggested by the suit brought by Laurence's widow against William for dower in 1280 which seems to be concerned with lands other than those mentioned in the final concord: CP 40/34, m. 63. Most of Laurence's acquisitions of Middlesex lands can be traced in surviving final concords.
187   *Luffield Priory Charters*, ii, no. 668.
188   Above, p. 58.
189   British Library, MS. Additional 39758, f. 90r: 'Hoc anno statim post Pascha sederunt justiciarii itinerantes apud Lincoln' ubi dominus Gilbertus de Preston' qui fuit capitaneus itineris, dominus Ricardus de Hemington et socii. In isto itinere fuit abbas predictus ad sumptus amplos et magnas liberalitates tam justiciariis quam narratoribus et aliis de comitatu.'
190   *Casus Placitorum*, pp. 65–7 (not identified as such by Dunham but clearly identifiable as a report of JUST 1/483, m. 40d).
191   Cambridge University Library, MS. Dd.7.14, ff. 370v–371r (a report of JUST 1/483, m. 40d). For evidence indicating that the serjeant William de Thornegg' was present at the 1268 Yorkshire eyre, presumably in a professional capacity, see JUST 1/1050, m. 57.
192   Precise calculations are hindered by the poor survival of Common Bench plea-rolls at this time. To get a general view for the period of c.1260 I have looked at the surviving rolls for Michaelmas term 1258, Hilary term 1259, Hilary term 1260 (though only one membrane of attorney appointments survives from the relevant roll) and Easter term 1260.
193   KB 26/160, mm. 61, 63, 60d; KB 26/162, mm. 43d, 44; KB 26/164, m. 35d; KB 26/165, mm. 38, 38d.

194 *Essex Feet of Fines*, i, p. 229; *Close Rolls, 1254–6*, p. 447. He was also being sued in company with the abbot of Bury St Edmund's in a replevin case in Easter term 1260, which suggests he may have been in the abbot's service: KB 26/165, m. 6.
195 KB 26/160, mm. 61d, 62d, 63d; KB 26/162, mm. 44, 44d; KB 26/164, mm. 35, 35d; KB 26/165, mm. 36d, 37d, 38.
196 JUST 1/567, m. 34d; JUST 1/236B, m. 5.
197 *Cal. Patent Rolls, 1266–72*, p. 443.
198 KB 26/160, mm. 60d, 62d, 63; KB 26/162, mm. 43d, 44, 44d, 46; KB 26/164, mm. 35, 35d; KB 26/165, mm. 36d, 37, 37d, 38d.
199 *Close Rolls, 1259–61*, p. 489.
200 KB 26/160, mm. 60, 62d; KB 26/162, mm. 44, 44d; KB 26/164, m. 35; KB 26/165, mm. 36, 36d, 37, 38d.
201 KB 26/168, m. 4d; E 13/1B, m. 5d; E 13/1C, m. 9.
202 KB 26/160, mm. 61, 63; KB 26/162, m. 43; KB 26/164, mm. 35, 35d; KB 26/165, mm. 37d, 38d.
203 E 13/1C, mm. 8, 10.
204 *Lincs Final Concords II*, p. 111; *Feet of Fines for the County of York, 1246–72*, ed. J. Parker (Yorkshire Archaeological Society, 82 (1932)), pp. 116, 117, 125, 129.
205 KB 26/160, mm. 61d, 62d, 63; KB 26/162, mm. 44, 44d; KB 26/165, mm. 36d, 37, 37d, 38.
206 KB 26/208A, m. 50; CP 40/18, mm. 84d, 83d; CP 40/24, m. 79; CP 40/27, m. 201; CP 40/45, m. 75d; CP 40/46, mm. 91, 92; CP 40/47, m. 137d.
207 KB 26/160, mm. 60d, 62, 62d, 63; KB 26/162, mm. 43, 44d; KB 26/164, mm. 35, 35d; KB 26/165, mm. 37, 37d.
208 E 13/1B, m. 7.
209 KB 26/160, m. 61; KB 26/162, mm. 44, 44d; KB 26/164, m. 35d; KB 26/165, mm. 36d, 38.
210 *Somersetshire Pleas ... from the rolls of the itinerant justices, Richard I to 41 Henry III*, ed. Charles E. H. Chadwyck-Healey (Somerset Record Society, 11 (1897)), no. 1462; KB 26/171, m. 45.
211 *London Eyre of 1244*, p. 96, n. 236. The same provision also specifically forbade aldermen to play any part in the making or giving of judgment in cases where they had been of counsel with either party and had been supporters of that party.
212 *Liber de Antiquis Legibus: Cronica Maiorum et Vicecomitum Londoniarum*, ed. T. Stapleton (Camden Society, original series, 34 (1846)), pp. 42–3.
213 Below, p. 84.
214 *Liber de Antiquis Legibus*, p. 70.
215 British Library, Additional Roll 34332, m. 4.
216 *Curia Regis Rolls 13*, no. 938.

Chapter 5   The English Legal Profession in Edward I's Reign (I):
the Size of the Profession

1 Above, p. 59.
2 I am assuming here that all the serjeants of the Common Bench were professional lawyers. The reasons for making this assumption will become clear in subsequent chapters.

3 A total of 13 reports of cases identified by their editor or identifiable as having been heard in the Common Bench between 1274 and 1277 are printed by Dunham in *Casus Placitorum*. To save space in later footnotes I have omitted manuscript references to the unpublished reports: full details will be found in my Selden Society volume.
4 A total of 123 reports in all survive for the period between 1273 and 1289. Only 100 can be securely dated by reference to the corresponding plea-roll enrolment. No reports at all survive of cases heard in 1280 and the years 1273, 1281 and 1282 are represented only by a single report each. The year whose cases are best represented in surviving reports is 1284 for which 19 reports survive. Often more than one version of a reported case survives in manuscript. Both here and elsewhere I will refer to these as different versions of a single report (though sometimes they are independent of each other) and will count them as a single report.
5 (i) Adam de Arderne: retained by the bishop of Hereford as a Common Bench serjeant (*narrator banci*) in 1275: *Registrum Thome de Cantilupo, episcopi Herefordensis*, ed. R. G. Griffiths and W. W. Capes (Canterbury and York Society, 2 (1907)), p. 22; (ii) Hamon de la Barre: as (i); (iii) John of Bocking: appears in a 1275 case reported in *Casus Placitorum*, p. 103 (the surname is erroneously extended to Bockinger); (iv) Richard of Boyland: appears as the king's serjeant suing for him in the Common Bench in various cases between 1273 and 1277: CP 40/2B, m. 7; /5, m. 57; /8, m. 43d; /9, mm. 15, 26; /11, m. 59; /14, m. 35d; /15, m. 85; /17, m. 3; /18, m. 3; /19, mm. 10d, 41 (and for other references to him as the king's serjeant see *Cal. Patent Rolls, 1266–1272*, p. 653; *Cal. Inq. Misc. 1*, nos. 2221, 2157 (wrongly calendared as king's servant)); (v) Robert of Bradfield: appears in published reports of cases of 1275–6 and 1277 (and in an unpublished report of a case of 1276): *Casus Placitorum*, pp. 99 (undated here but is a report of CP 40/19, m. 31) and 122; (vi) John of Houghton: as (i); (vii) Adam of Kinsham: suspended from acting as a serjeant of the court in 1276 (CP 40/15, m. 62); (viii) John of Quy: appears in a report of a 1276 case: *Casus Placitorum*, p. 73; (ix) John of Ramsey: appears in an unpublished report of a case heard perhaps c.1274; (x) William of Stowe: as (i); (xi) Gilbert of Thornton: appears in published reports of cases of 1275, 1276 and 1277 (and in an unpublished report of a case of 1275): *Casus Placitorum*, pp. 72–3, 96, 99, 101, 104; (xii) Alan of Walkingham: appears in published reports of cases of 1275 (and in an unpublished report of a case of 1276): *Casus Placitorum*, pp. 49, 101, 103, 122.

Men who may have acted as serjeants during this period (but about whom there is some doubt) include: (xiii) Robert de Coleville, who had been a Common Bench serjeant in the latter part of Henry III's reign (above, p. 58) and who in 1277 is to be found acting as surety for a defendant who waged his law (CP 40/18, m. 71d); and (xiv) Richard of Gosfield, who is known to have been a serjeant later and appears in the Common Bench suing a case on behalf of the king in 1275: CP 40/11, m. 55.
6 (i) William of Bereford: appears in reports of cases of 1281, 1283 and 1284; (ii) John of Bocking: appears in reports of case of 1283 and 1284; (iii) Robert of Bradfield: appears in reports of cases of 1278, 1282, 1283 and 1284; (iii) Alexander of Coventry: appears in reports of cases of 1279, 1281 and 1284; (iv) William of Gisleham: appears in a report of a case of 1284; (v) Richard of Gosfield: appears in reports of cases of 1279, 1283 and 1284; (vi) Roger of Higham: appears in reports of cases of 1283 and 1284; (vii) William of Kelloe: appears in reports of case of 1283 and 1284; (viii) Adam of Kinsham: appears in reports of cases of

1283 and 1284; (ix) an unidentified Souburn appears in a report of a case of 1283 and may be the same as the Sutbur' who appears in a report of a 1284 case; (x) Gilbert of Thornton: appears in reports of cases of 1278, 1279, 1282 and 1283; (xi) Nicholas of Warwick: appears in reports of cases of 1283 and 1284; (xii) Richard of Willoughby: appears in reports of cases of 1284.

Andrew of Ely appears only in reports of three cases heard in 1283 and 1284 and in each case he is acting for the bishop of Ely. It is uncertain whether he can be classified as a professional serjeant of the court.

7 (i) William of Bereford: appears in reports of 1285, 1286, 1287, 1288 and 1289; (ii) Robert of Bradfield: appears in reports of 1285; (iii) Alexander of Coventry: appears in a report of 1288; (iv) William of Gisleham: appears in a report of 1285; (v) Richard of Gosfield: appears in reports of 1285, 1286, 1287, 1288 and 1289; (vi) an unidentified Granc' appears in a report of 1287; (vii) Robert of Hartforth: appears in reports of 1286 and 1289; (viii) Roger of Higham: appears in reports of 1284, 1285, 1286, 1287, 1288 and 1289; (ix) William of Kelloe: appears in reports of 1285, 1286 and 1287; (x) Adam of Kinsham: appears in reports of 1286 and 1287; (xi) John de Lisle: appears in reports of 1286, 1287 and 1289; (xii) Hugh of Lowther: appears in reports of 1285, 1286, 1287 and 1289; (xiii) Thomas de Playz: appears in reports of 1287, 1288 and 1289; (xiv) William of Selby: appears in a report of 1286; (xv) Henry Spigurnel: appears in reports of 1287, 1288 and 1289; (xvi) Gilbert of Thornton: appears in reports of 1285, 1286 and 1287; (xvii) John of Tilton: appears in a report of a case of 1288; (xviii) Nicholas of Warwick: appears in reports of cases of 1285, 1286, 1287 and 1289; (xix) Richard of Willoughby: appears in reports of cases of 1287.

The following serjeants appear only in unidentified reports which certainly belong to the period of Weyland's chief justiceship and probably belong to the period 1285–9: (xx) Thomas of Fishburn; (xxi) Geoffrey of Hartlepool; (xxii) William Inge; (xxiii) (?William of) Wandsworth.

8 In the compilation of the following figures I have used such reports as I have been able to identify thus far of the unprinted reports of this period, together with those reports edited by Horwood which seem to be reliably assigned to the terms and years concerned.

9 The first such entry is on m. 102 of CP 40/102, a membrane whose heading shows that it records cases heard during the return-days of three weeks and one month after Michaelmas. At first the entries do not invariably describe the individuals concerned as *narratores*, but the names given are of men elsewhere described in similar entries as serjeants and the omission seems to have no significance. The change is much more sudden and dramatic than is suggested by G. J. Turner in *YB 3 & 4 Edward II* (Selden Society, 22 (1907)), p. xv.; cf. Baker, *Order of Serjeants at Law*, pp. 12–13.

10 The fact that this is a figure covering several years must inflate the number to some extent, but this is probably counterbalanced by the effects of the imperfection of our evidence which tends to deflate the figure.

11 Below, p. 87.

12 William de Caen (de Cam and a number of variants) (appointed 65 times); Peter Child (le Child) (64) and Henry fitz William of St Edmund's (60). Henry appears under a variety of names: sometimes just as Henry fitz William; sometimes just as Henry of St Edmund's; sometimes as Henry fitz William of St Edmund's. It seems clear that only one individual is involved here.

13 Roger de la Doune (59); Robert fitzWilliam (54); William of Penkridge

Notes to Pages 73-6   191

(49); Robert de Muscegros (48); John of Attleborough (46) and John of Gisleham (42).
14 John le Botiller of Hampton and Richard of Normanby (both appointed exactly 73 times).
15 They are (with number of appointments in brackets): Thomas of Thirkleby (62); William of Easthorpe (58); William of Haddlesey (56); Peter Maunsel (55); Adam of Hopperton (52); Ellis of Swaledale (51); Robert Brun (49); John Bonet (49); John of Skelton (49); Hugh of Deepdale (40); and Stephen of Kenerthorp (40).
16 The number of recorded appointments rose by around 40 per cent between 1280 and 1300.
17 CP 40/93, m. 140d.
18 *Account of the Executors of Richard bishop of London and Thomas bishop of Exeter*, ed. W. H. Hale and H. T. Ellacombe (Camden Society, 2nd series, 10 (1874)), p. 107.
19 CP 40/156, m. 136.
20 They include one of the two busiest attorneys, Richard of Normanby, 46 of whose cases came from Lincolnshire (and a further 26 from Yorkshire). They also include William of Easthorpe, all but one of whose cases came from Yorkshire; William of Haddlesey, 46 of whose 56 cases came from Yorkshire; Adam of Hopperton, all except two of whose cases came from Yorkshire; Peter Maunsel, all except two of whose cases came from Yorkshire; Ellis of Swaledale, 43 of whose 51 cases came from Yorkshire; Thomas of Thirkleby, 56 of whose 62 cases came from Yorkshire; John Bonet, 43 of whose 49 cases came from Yorkshire; Hugh of Deepdale, 39 of whose 40 cases came from Yorkshire; and Stephen of Kenerthorp, 38 of whose 40 cases came from Yorkshire.
21 They include two out of the three attorneys with over 60 appointments to their credit (Peter Child and Henry fitzWilliam of St Edmund's) for both of whom appointments to act in Suffolk cases constituted a majority of their business.
22 Six out of the seven attorneys concerned are exclusively appointed in Norfolk cases; the seventh in Gloucestershire cases.
23 *Radulphi de Hengham Summae*, p. 18.
24 Almost invariably these were appointments of three attorneys, but in one instance in 1300 four attorneys were appointed.
25 There are three versions of this report, which is of an assize of novel disseisin. The versions in Cambridge University Library, MS. Dd.7.14 (at ff. 370r-v) and British Library, MS. Royal 10.A.V (at ff. 92r-v) give the names of the serjeants involved as Bereford (the Bench serjeant William of Bereford) and (H)ernesby (the Eyre serjeant Richard of Arnesby); the version in British Library, MS. Additional 5925 (at f. 13v) as Bereford and Warwick (the Bench serjeant Nicholas of Warwick).
26 British Library, MS. Egerton 2811, ff. 82r-v.
27 *Select Cases in King's Bench I*, pp. xcviii-c.
28 For evidence that as late as 1298 an attorney in King's Bench might make a defence in court on behalf of his client see KB 27/155, m. 2. The defence was, however, challenged for being formally defective and the case adjourned for judgement. The enrolling clerk was careful to note that the defence was made 'by his own mouth' (*per os proprium*).
29 *Select Cases in King's Bench I*, pp. 67-8, 80-1.
30 *YB 32 & 33 Edward I*, ed. A. J. Horwood (Rolls Series, 1864), pp. 193-5; *YB 33-35 Edward I*, ed. A. J. Horwood (Rolls Series, 1879), pp. 37-43, 55-63 (and

British Library, MS. Additional 31826, f. 325v), 577–87 (and British Library, MS. Egerton 2811, ff. 97v–98r); British Library, MS. Egerton 2811, ff. 42v–43r (and Lincoln's Inn, MS. Hale 188, ff. 63r–v), 87r–v, 88r, 125v–126v (and British Library, MS. Additional 5925, ff. 90r–v and Holkham, MS. 754, ff. 45v–46r); British Library, MS. Stowe 386, ff. 82r–v (and British Library, MSS. Additional 37657, ff. 96r–97r and Additional 31826, ff. 385v–386r and Lincoln's Inn, MSS. Miscellaneous 87, ff. 112v–113r and Hale 174, ff. 58v–59r); British Library, MS. Additional 35116, ff. 11r–v, 26v, 21r (and Holkham, MS. 754, f. 53r); British Library MS. Additional 31826, ff. 274v and 279r; British Library MS. Hargrave 375, f. 162r.

31 They are: East; Friskney; Harle; Hartlepool; Howard; Huntingdon; Inge; Kinsham; Mablethorpe; Mutford; Scotter; Scrope; Spigurnel; Sutton; Tilton; Tothby; Warwick; Westcote; and Willoughby.

32 Roger Querdeliun and Robert of Ashbourne.

33 Richard Dalimond of Oxwick (46); William of Cave (43); Walter of Graffham (43); Gervase of Derby (40); Roger Querdeliun of Cirencester (40).

34 They include the busiest King's Bench attorney, Geoffrey of Lakenham, 63 of whose 69 appointments came from Norfolk as also the next busiest Richard Dalimond of Oxwick, 41 of whose 46 appointments came from the same county. Thirty-six of the 43 appointments of William of Cave also came from Yorkshire.

35 They are: Richard of Arnesby; William of Bereford; Robert of Bradfield; Alexander of Coventry; Thomas of Fishburn; Robert of Hartforth; William Howard; William Inge; William of Kelloe; John de Lisle; William Pageman; John of Ramsey; Roger of Scotter; William of Selby; Henry Spigurnel; and Gilbert of Thornton.

36 An unidentified Cave; Walter of Friskney; Roger of Higham; John of Milton or Middleton; Robert of Swillington; Gilbert of Tothby; and Nicholas of Warwick.

37 Thus William of Kelloe and John de Lisle both appear in reports of cases from the 1281–4 Lincolnshire eyre, the 1284 Leicestershire eyre, the 1285 Warwickshire eyre, the 1285 Northamptonshire eyre, the 1286 Buckinghamshire eyre, the 1286 Cambridgeshire eyre and the 1287 Gloucestershire eyre. William of Selby is not mentioned in any identified reports of the 1281–4 Lincolnshire eyre or of the 1286 Buckinghamshire eyre but otherwise appeared in the same eyres together with the earlier 1279–81 Yorkshire eyre.

38 William of Bereford seems only to have acted as a serjeant at the 1281–4 Lincolnshire eyre; Robert of Bradfield only at the 1284 Leicestershire and 1285 Warwickshire eyres; and Robert of Hartforth only at the 1279–81 Yorkshire and 1281–4 Lincolnshire eyres.

39 The only eyre serjeants not to appear among the serjeants of the Common Bench are Arnesby, Howard, Scotter and Pageman. Of these both Howard and Scotter appear as Common Bench serjeants after 1290. Of the seven possible eyre serjeants Higham and Warwick appear as Common Bench serjeants before 1290; Friskney, Milton and Tothby only after 1290.

40 John of Bocking; Robert of Bradfield; Robert of Copdock; William of Gisleham; Richard of Gosfield; Robert of Hartforth; Roger of Higham; William Howard; Ralph of Huntingdon; William Inge; John de Lisle; John of Mutford; William of Ormsby; John of Ramsey; Henry Spigurnel; (?William of) Wandsworth; and Nicholas of Warwick.

41 Bradfield; Hartforth; Howard; Inge; Lisle; Ramsey; and Spigurnel are the known serjeants; Higham and Warwick the possible serjeants.

42 They are John of Walcot and Stephen of Bonnington: for the litigation see CP 40/75, m. 126; CP 40/80, m. 72d.
43 Thomas of Fishburn; Walter of Friskney; Geoffrey of Hartlepool; John of Haverington; Roger of Higham; William of Harle (Herle); (William) of Hartforth (Hertford); Ralph of Huntingdon; William Inge; William of Kelloe; John de Lisle; Middleton; Roger of Scotter; Henry le Scrope; Thomas de Playz; John of Tilton. The Hamond mentioned in the reports is probably either Hamon de la Barre or Hamon Gruscy, both of them Common Bench serjeants. The men named in these reports who were not Bench serjeants are Brom' (unless this is John of Bromholm); Colney; Methele (but note that T. de Methelay does occur once in Trinity term 1299 in the Common Bench as a serjeant authorizing a final concord); and Sherloc.
44 For the eyres of Herefordshire, Shropshire and Staffordshire these separate collections of reports are printed in the Rolls Series edition of the *Year Books of Edward I*. For the Kent eyre of 1293 there is an unpublished collection of reports at ff. 67v–79v of British Library, MS. Additional 37657. The Rolls Series edition of the *Year Books of Edward I* also includes a collection of cases ascribed to the 1294 Middlesex eyre, but many of these cases demonstrably belong to other years and to the Common Bench: the only cases that do seem to belong are in *YB 21 & 22 Edward I*, ed. A. J. Horwood (Rolls Series, 1866) at pp. 301–9, 317–37 and 339–53.
45 William Aubyn; Richard of Coleshill; William of Goldington; William Grymet; William Howard; Ralph of Huntingdon; Adam of Kinsham; Hugh of Lowther; William de Mareys; Middleton; John of Mutford; Roger of Southcote; Henry Spigurnel; John of Tilton; and Nicholas of Warwick. The men named in these reports who were not Common Bench serjeants are: Beaufou; Beufrond (?the same); Richard of Arnesby; Hurste; Pain; and Preston.
46 Ralph of Huntingdon; John of Tilton and perhaps Middleton (though there were three Common Bench serjeants of this name and it may well be that the two men who practised on the two circuits were different).
47 The 1299 Cambridgeshire and Ely eyre is reported in British Library, MS. Stowe 386, ff. 99r–108r (and in British Library, MS. Additional 31826, ff. 155r–156v, 241r–242v, 245r, 248r). Reports from the Cornwall eyre are printed in the Rolls Series edition of Edward I Year Books.
48 William Aubyn; William Batayle; William of Goldington; Ralph of Huntingdon; William Inge; Adam of Kinsham; John of Middleton; John of Mutford; Robert Norman of Hedon; Roger of Scotter. The others are: Beaufou and Sampson (but note that Ralph Sampson occurs once in the Common Bench in 1305 as authorizing a final concord).
49 R. of Hopton; Ralph of Huntingdon; Adam of Kinsham; Simon of Kinsham; Nicholas of Laver; Middleton; John of Mutford; John of Westcote; Richard of Willoughby. The other is: Poleyn.
50 Thomas Trussebut (112); William Dareyns (100); Thomas Goscelin (100). Thomas of 'Hoton' may also belong here if he is to be identified with Thomas of Hawthorne.
51 Thomas of Hoton (92 appointments) (but if he is also to be identified with Thomas of Hawthorne this would raise his total to 119 appointments); Thomas of Thirkleby (87); Ralph of Selby (67); Ralph of Appleby (55); William Arlet of Pontefract (56) (but if he is also to be identified with William of Pontefract this would raise his total 90); John de Cort (56); William of Ellerton (44); Robert Harald (44); William of Malton (44); Richard of Pontefract (43).

52 Walter de Blaunkenay (12); William of Kilvington (11).
53 Nine men were appointed in three cases each (and these nine include two men who were each appointed 37 times as attorneys in the Yorkshire eyre); three men in four; three men in five (including a man appointed 67 times as attorney in the Yorkshire eyre); three men in six (including a man appointed 24 times in the Yorkshire eyre); three men in seven (including one man appointed 44 times in the Yorkshire eyre and another appointed 15 times in the Common Bench in 1280); three men in eight.
54 Poleyn was appointed in only 11 cases in the Dorset eyre and in only 15 in the Hampshire eyre but in 37 in the Somerset eyre.
55 De la Hele was appointed in 44 cases in the Somerset eyre and in eight in the Hampshire eyre; Denston in 13 in the Dorset eyre, 12 in the Somerset eyre and 15 in the Hampshire eyre.
56 Ten of these 37 (between them accounting for around 6 per cent of all appointments) were appointed only in a single eyre on this circuit; a further 16 (between them accounting for around 13 per cent of all appointments) only in two eyres (and in the pattern of appointments of each of these 16 men there is a marked bias towards one of the two eyres); and only 11 (between them accounting for around 12 per cent of all appointments) were appointed in all three eyres.
57 R. C. Palmer, 'County Year Book Reports: the Professional Lawyer in the Medieval County Court', *Eng. Hist. Rev.*, 91 (1971), pp. 776–801; Palmer, *County Courts*, pp. 97–110. Palmer's own estimate is that the reports show 13 or 14 serjeants (he calls them pleaders) practising in the court. Re-examination of the relevant reports, however, suggests that of these only Crompe, Sutham, Heyford, Boydin, Payn and Alne can be safely regarded as serjeants practising there. Stamp' is clearly serjeant pleading in a local court: but there is no proof that this is the Warwickshire county court. The opinions recorded as being given by Stoke, Schereman, Attemere, Wolleward, Adam des Okes and Hoke(le) do not seem to have been given by them as serjeants. Many look like the opinions of third parties not actively engaged on either side (and one of the arguments ascribed to Adam des Okes is in a case to which he was himself party). The one report to mention H. de Hurst shows him challenging an essoin; and could well show him as either a litigant or an attorney. I am grateful to Professor Palmer for making available to me a transcript of the relevant reports.
58 British Library, MS. Stowe 386, f. 153r (serjeants: Madingley and Burwell); Lincoln's Inn, MS. Hale 188, f. 42v and British Library, MS. Additional 31826, ff. 150r–v (reports of same case) (serjeants: Madingley, Burwell and Grantchester).
59 They are to be found in the following county courts: (i) Cheshire: *Two Compoti of the Lancashire and Cheshire Manors of Henry de Lacy, Earl of Lincoln, 24 and 33 Edward I*, ed. P. A. Lyons (Chetham Society, 102 (1884)), p. 51; (ii) Cornwall: Palmer, *County Courts*, p. 93; (iii) Leicestershire: ibid., p. 95; (iv) Lincolnshire: 'Early Trailbaston Proceedings from the Lincoln roll of 1305', ed. Alan Harding in *Medieval Legal Records edited in honour of C. A. F. Meekings*, ed. R. F. Hunnisett and J. B. Post (London, 1978), p. 155; (v) Norfolk: N. Denholm-Young, *Seignorial Administration in England* (Oxford, 1937), p. 38, n. 3; (vi) Sussex: *Herriard v. Vilers*: CP 40/162, m. 43d; (vii) Westmorland: Palmer, *County Courts*, p. 96.
60 Palmer, 'Origins of the Legal Profession', p. 135.
61 Palmer, 'Origins of the Legal Profession', pp. 136–7.
62 See below, chapter 7.
63 *Calendar of Letter-Books of the City of London: Letter-Book A*, ed. R. R. Sharpe

Notes to Pages 84–7   195

(London, 1899), p. 205: Richard of Kirkham; Hugh de Hertweyton; William de Mareys and Richard of Wilton. Kirkham's name appears with that of Berewik' as pleading in a case heard in the court of the warden of the city reported in British Library, MS. Harley 2183, ff. 5r–5v.

64 *Calendar of Letter-Books of the City of London: Letter-Book C*, ed. R. R. Sharpe (London, 1901), pp. 147–8: Robert of Kelsey; Robert of Sutton; Reginald of Oundle; William of Grafton; and Richard de Honewyk.

65 It is moreover certain that Robert of Sutton and Robert of Kelsey, two of the five serjeants who were 'admitted' in 1305, had been practising as serjeants in the city courts prior to that date: *Calendar of City Letter-Book A*, p. 192 (1291); *Calendar of City Letter-Book C*, pp. 185–7 (1300). To judge from this last case Gilbert of Tothby, the Common Bench serjeant, was also practising as a serjeant in the city courts in 1300 though no memorandum of his admission survives. It is possible that liberty to practise in the city courts went with his admission in 1298 as 'counsel' to the city of London at a salary of four marks a year: *Calendar of Letter-Books of the City of London: Letter-Book B*, ed. R. R. Sharpe (London, 1900), p. 215.

66 Below, chapter 7.

67 *Calendar of City Letter-Book A*, p. 205. Of the men named Richard Gladewyn, Geoffrey of Roding (Rothinge) and Ralph Peverel appear regularly as attorneys on the surviving rolls of the city courts. Note also that in 1298 among the *interlocutoria* recorded for the session of 9 June there is a reference to the 'order' of serjeants, attorneys and essoiners: 'Loquendum est de ordine narratorum servientum attornatorum et essoinatorum': Corporation of London Records Office, Common Pleas Roll 24, m. 25.

68 *Calendar of City Letter-Book C*, pp. 147–8.

69 *Ringstead v. prior of Coxford*: CP 40/108, m. 94 (1295).

70 *Select Bills in Eyre, 1292–1333*, ed. W. C. Bolland (Selden Society, 30 (1914)), pp. 3–4.

71 *Placita Coram Domino Rege: Pleas of the Court of King's Bench, Trinity term, 25 Edward I (1297)*, ed. W. P. W. Phillimore (British Record Society, Index Library, 19 (1898)), pp. 139–40.

72 Oxford City Archives D/17/1 (b). I am grateful to Dr David Postles of the Department of English Local History in the University of Leicester for drawing my attention to this roll and lending me his microfilm copy of it.

73 'De Ricardo de Sancto Martino quia deadvocatus est per se ipsum in narracione quam narravit pro Johnanne le Pestur versus Johannem de Boxore': ibid., m. 5d.

74 *Select Pleas in Manorial Courts*, pp. 155–6, 159–60; *Select Cases Concerning the Law Merchant*, Vol. I, ed. C. Gross (Selden Society, 23 (1908)), pp. xxxiv, 30–2, 35.

75 In the Earl of Oxford's court of Castle Camps in Cambridgeshire: CP 40/100, m. 98d; in the earl of Gloucester's court of Clare in Suffolk: Palmer, *County Courts*, pp. 95–6.

76 In the Oxfordshire hundred of Chadlington: *FitzNeal v. abbot of Bruerne*: CP 40/118, m. 59d.

77 Such an assumption is made by Palmer: 'Origins of the Legal Profession', pp. 127–8.

Chapter 6   The English Legal Profession in Edward I's Reign (II): the Profession at Work

1 For examples see CP 40/91, m. 296d (1291); /95, m. 79d (1292); /103, mm. 70d, 159d (1294); /105, m. 59d (1294); /108, m. 6d (1295). Confusingly, the same

term was also sometimes used in a somewhat different sense, to refer to an attorney appointed to represent his principal not in a single piece of litigation but in all litigation brought during a particular eyre (by virtue of clause 10 of the statute of Westminster II) or in any litigation in any court while his principal was out of the country. But the context normally makes clear which kind of 'general attorney' is being referred to.

2 For examples see CP 40/89, m. 26d (1291); /90, m. 57d (1291); /95, m. 61d (1292); /92, m. 109 (1292) [=*Select Cases in King's Bench*, V, pp. cxxv–cxxvi].

3 *Select Cases in the Court of King's Bench*, Vol.II, ed. G. O. Sayles (Selden Society, 57 (1938)), pp. 39–41.

4 *Radulphi de Hengham Summae*, pp. 16, 28. This treatise is of particular value as a guide to procedure in the Common Bench since it was probably the work of John Blundel and reflects his experience as keeper of rolls and writs in the court between 1257 and 1262: Brand, 'Hengham Magna', pp. 147–69.

5 This appears from a case of 1294 (*Gernun v. Gernun*) in which the jurors empanelled to try a case complained about the conduct of the plaintiff's attorney. Although he had been told by his client that the defendant had died he had still had the jurors called and the case respited for lack of sufficient jurors: CP 40/103, m. 70d. Other references to the 'suing' of defaults by attorneys may refer to this but may simply refer to the attorney ensuring that the opponent's default was entered on the plea-rolls of the court: see e.g. *Skipsea v. Carleton* (CP 40/93, m. 140d) or *Le Clerk of Burton Fleming v. prior of Bridlington* (CP 40/92, m. 186d).

6 *Radulphi de Hengham Summae*, p. 20. To be on the safe side the plaintiff's attorney would need to be in court on the actual day appointed for his client's appearance or his opponent might have his client's case dismissed for want of prosecution: see e.g. *Huse v. Otford*: CP 40/83, m. 85d (Trinity 1290). He would not, however, be able to secure judgment on the default of his client's opponent until three days later.

7 The only specific references to this practice are to litigants present in person doing so: see CP 40/104, m. 75d (1294) (=*YB 4 Edward II*, ed. G. J. Turner (Selden Society, 42 (1925)), p. lxiii) ('cum ... stetisset hic ad barram ad placitandum cum quodam adversario suo') and JUST 1/985, m.2 (1292 Westmorland eyre) ('cum ... stetisset hic ad barram ad prosequendum jus suum'). But there can be little doubt that this was also the normal practice in the case of attorneys.

8 British Library, MS. Additional 31826, f. 322r: *Fresel v. prior of Barnwell* (a subsequent stage of this case is recorded on the Bench plea-roll for Easter term 1298: CP 40/123, m. 23); Lincoln's Inn, MS. Miscellaneous 738, ff. 16v–17r (ascribed to Hilary term 1303).

9 See further below, p. 98. Note also that according to one report of a case of 1296 when a serjeant made a disclaimer on behalf of his client, the justice (in this case Bereford) could make the attorney not merely affirm what the serjeant had said but actually repeat the disavowal himself: Inner Temple, MS. Miscellaneous 1, ff. 3r–3v (report of case enrolled on CP 40/115, m. 108).

10 British Library, MS. Additional 37657, f. 18v ('Vous atorne, acertet le eveske de soen fet [de]mene, a queu fet nous donom fey e avum graunt regard. E parlet de pes entre cy e la seint John'). The plea-roll enrolment of this case is on CP 40/133, m. 12. See also the report of a debt case of 1299 (enrolled on CP 40/130, m. 204d) where Bereford held that the plaintiff should not recover as his deed was usurious and the court apparently instructed the attorney to

tell his client that he was a usurer ('Et dictum fuit attornato rei quod diceret domino suo quod erat usurarius'): British Library, MS. Additional 31826, f. 102v.

11 For an instance of a serjeant giving such advice see *YB 33–35 Edward I*, p. 215.
12 For a report of a case where an attorney was seeking judgment on a default but was then unexpectedly faced with a serjeant seeking cognizance of the case for the liberty of St Peter's York, who then attempted to challenge the form of words used by the attorney in seeking judgment see British Library, MS. Additional 31826, f. 119r. The plaintiff's attorney also had the power to waive a default. Robert of Wiggenhall is said to have punched Henry of Thurston in Westminster hall in 1290 because he refused to do this ('Convictum est ... quod idem Robertus in aula ista ante bancum, quia predictus Henricus noluit consentire ad relaxandum quandam defaltam quam quidem clyens ipsius Roberti fecerat percussit ipsum Henricum pugno suo sub audito') (CP 40/87, m. 87); and William of Brockhall was advised by his attorney, John of Upton, in 1291 that he could take money for remitting a default (CP 40/91, m. 191d).
13 See, for example, *de la Haye v. Boulton*: CP 40/89, m. 143 (1291) (though here it is not entirely clear that the attorney is a professional and it appears that a previous writ had been obtained by the client herself); *Dunstable v. Bayfield*: CP 40/90, m. 57 (1291); *le Sok v. Beauchamp*: CP 40/158, m. 156d (1306). See also *Cal. Patent Rolls, 1281–92*, p. 518.
14 For evidence of messengers going to chancery to obtain writs see *Select Cases in King's Bench II*, p. lxxxvii and *Early Registers of Writs*, p. cxxv, n. 7.
15 See e.g. *Grey v. Huish* at CP 40/28, m. 57 (1279) which incorporates the following note: 'Et sciendum quod ista defalta inrotulata fuit in crastino Purificacionis Beate Marie per preceptum Thome de Weylaund pro predicto Rogero quia pauper eo quod attornatus predicti Rogeri cognovit quod per oblivionem suam non fuit intrata ad quindenam sancti Martini'. See also *Hunt' v. Tykesore*: CP 40/108, m. 70d (1295).
16 See e.g. *Balingale v. Runham* (1292) where an attorney got into trouble because he had enrolments of defaults made but had then failed to sue out the appropriate judicial writs: CP 40/92, m. 186d. For a more detailed account of what happened see *Suthmere v. bishop of London*: CP 40/91, m. 210 (1291).
17 This appears from the judgment of chief justice Mettingham in a case of deceit reported in British Library, MS. Additional 31826 at f. 7v. In it he held that the client's attorney 'est charge ceyns a fere la syute pur vus e nent aylors, einz enverra vo brefs a vus a loutel, e vus le devez la syure en due manere'.
18 See the proceedings against John Sturmyn who handed over a schedule with a note of such an adjournment ('quandam cedulam de quodam prece parcium intrandum') to the senior clerk, Henry of Lichfield, in a case where he claimed to be the attorney of the plaintiff but was not: CP 40/103, m. 159d (1294).
19 *Pollard v. Welleby*: CP 40/126, m. 63d (1299); *Le Sok v. Beauchamp*: CP 40/158, m. 156d (1306). Another possible instance occurs in the 1292–3 account roll of the bursar and cellarer of Worcester cathedral priory where we find payment of one mark to Roger Chaperun (perhaps the attorney of the priory) and a further payment of four shillings to him for a serjeant: *Early Compotus Rolls of the Priory of Worcester*, ed. J. M. Wilson and C. Gordon (Worcester Historical Society, 1908), p. 12. For later evidence of the same practice see *YB 15 Edward III*, ed. L. O. Pike (Rolls Series, 1891), pp. 345–7.
20 British Library, MS. Additional 31826, f. 380r (probably a report of a case heard in 1305): in this case the defendant's serjeant alleged that one of the

plaintiffs in the case was dead. The plaintiffs' serjeant is reported to have 'examined his client' and then said that he was alive ('Westcote examina sun client e dit qe il fut en pleine vie").
21   *Select Cases in King's Bench I*, pp. 80–1.
22   British Library, MS. Lansdowne 467, f. 115r. For other evidence of written communication between attorney and client see *Gernun v. Gernun*: CP 40/103, m. 70d (1294).
23   *Calendar of City Letter-Book C*, pp. 115–16.
24   CP 40/90, m. 13d; CP 40/103, m. 127d.
25   CP 40/155, m. 67.
26   For examples see *Burne v. Echyngham*: CP 40/147, m. 34d (1303) and *Torksey v. St Elena*: CP 40/148, m. 125 (1303).
27   For examples see *Dakeny v. Hokewald*: CP 40/80, m. 135 (1289); *Crioll v. Crioll*: CP 40/125, m. 75d (1298).
28   'quendam Willelmum hominem Henrici de Hales clerici predicti justiciarii etc. ad custodiam rotulorum ibidem deputatum verbis contumeliosis et vilibus reprobavit eo quod inspeccionem rotulorum predictorum ad voluntatem suam habere non potuit': CP 40/124, m. 22d. In 1291 another professional attorney, Robert de Greshope, had readily gained access to the plea-rolls to check some enrolments and had then taken the opportunity to remove part of a membrane from the roll: CP 40/90, m. 57d.
29   *Prudomme v. Pottone* (1292) printed in *Select Cases in King's Bench V*, pp. cxxv–cxxvi.
30   *Morewy v. Frome*: CP 40/108, m. 6d.
31   See also *Huntingdon v. Tykesore*: CP 40/108, m. 70d (1295); *Elyot v. Lupi de Tylio*: CP 40/82, m. 13d (1290).
32   Above, Chapter 3, p. 45.
33   CP 40/21, m. 112.
34   For examples see JUST 1/1068, mm. 34d, 35 (Loveday); m. 36 (Mettingham); m. 37 (Siddington); m. 35d (Saham).
35   CP 40/161, mm. 544, 559, 570, 571, 549d, 536d, 534d, 528d.
36   *Tew v. Wade*: CP 40/15, m. 33d; CP 40/17, m. 88d.
37   Justices of King's Bench: Roger Brabazon chief justice: CP 40/133, m. 197; /134, m. 216; /131, m. 386; William of Ormsby: CP 40/131, m. 386; Gilbert of Rothbury: CP 40/132, m. 224d; CP 40/133, m. 199. Exchequer: before Walter of Langton, the treasurer: CP 40/134, m. 211d; before John de Lisle, one of the barons: CP 40/132, m. 221; /134, m. 209d; /131, m. 373; before Peter of Leicester, one of the barons: CP 40/132, m. 226; /133, m. 200; /131, m. 378; before William de Carleton, one of the barons: CP 40/133, m. 195d; before John de Kirkby, a remembrancer: CP 40/131, m. 373. Assize Justices: before William Inge: CP 40/132, m. 230; before John of Battisford: CP 40/133, m. 198d; before Adam de Crokdayk: CP 40/133, m. 196d; before John de Lythegreyns: CP 40/134, m. 213; before William of Amersham: CP 40/131, m. 392.
38   CP 40/158, mm. 304, 321d; CP 40/161, mm. 528, 530, 531, 537, 568, 562d.
39   *Stat. Realm I*, p. 215.
40   CP 40/164, mm. 360, 366, 374, 361d, 359d.
41   See *Daubeney v. Brunnolvesheved*: CP 40/89, m. 13d (1291); *in re Skynner*: CP 40/106, m. 13 (1294); *Paunton v. Bokeland*: CP 40/118, m. 51 (1297) (bill for removal of attorney). See also the references cited by Sayles in *Select Cases in King's Bench I*, p. xcii, n. 3.
42   CP 40/38, m. 75.

Notes to Pages 91–4   199

43 CP 40/89, m. 13d.
44 CP 40/155, m. 165d.
45 Even where the client in a particular case successfully denied the existence of any such agreement as that alleged by the attorney we are, I think, entitled to assume that agreements of the kind alleged to have been made did indeed exist, if only between other attorneys and their clients.
46 *YB 5 Edward II*, ed. G. J. Turner (Selden Society, 33 (1916)), pp. 1–9. John of York appears as a professional attorney of the Common Bench in 1300 and became a serjeant in 1309.
47 *Calendar of City Letter-Book B*, p. 216; *Calendar of City Letter-Book C*, p. 26.
48 CP 40/152, m. 158d (1304). For an action of debt in 1338 in which an attorney sued on an agreement to serve the defendant as his attorney for ten years at the rate of 20 shillings a year see *YB 11 & 12 Edward III*, ed. A. J. Horwood (Rolls Series, 1883), p. 587.
49 CP 40/141, m. 17. Thomas appears as a professional attorney on the Common Bench plea-rolls in 1300, mostly acting in Yorkshire cases.
50 CP 40/158, m. 156d.
51 *Calendar of City Letter-Book C*, pp. 115–16.
52 *Calendar of City Letter-Book C*, p. 116. In April 1298 William of Asthall (Esthalle) had been appointed to act as the city's attorney in both the Exchequer and the Common Bench. The terms of his appointment are not recorded: *Calendar of City Letter-Book B*, p. 215.
53 CP 40/156, m. 136.
54 CP 40/62, m. 27d: the litigation was probably heard in the 1281–4 Lincolnshire eyre.
55 KB 27/94, m. 42d. For Richard's career as an attorney in the court and subsequently as marshal and king's serjeant there see *Select Cases in King's Bench I*, pp. lxxxix–xc, xcviii–xcix, cxii–cxiii.
56 CP 40/90, m. 13d. This was perhaps an inclusive sum covering all the legal costs of the case.
57 CP 40/102, m. 160.
58 CP 40/153, m. 375.
59 JUST 1/758, m. 71.
60 Such agreements were subsequently made illegal: see below, p. 121.
61 JUST 1/915, m. 39.
62 CP 40/126, m. 63d (1299). In earlier related litigation in 1291 William Pollard had claimed that the agreement had been made only in 1289 but the daily rate to be paid was exactly the same: CP 40/87, m. 146d.
63 CP 40/183, m. 344d.
64 CP 40/147, m. 122. Accounting is also mentioned in a case of 1301. Here Agnes widow of Abraham son of Rannulf of Grantham claimed she had handed over eight marks to John Morice of Easton on 20 December 1299 to acquire writs for her and to pay all the costs of all pleas involving her, including the cost of serjeants, but conditionally on his rendering account of the money he spent at the following Easter. He denied there had been any attached to the delivery of the money: CP 40/138, m. 28d. Here, however, there seems to be no suggestion that John Morice was also to act as her attorney.
65 CP 40/102, m. 93d.
66 *Carswell v. rector of Britwell*: above, n. 58.
67 *Le Sok v. Beauchamp*: above, n. 50.
68 *Brampton v. Somerton*: above, n. 63.

69 *Pollard v. Welby*: above, n. 62.
70 *le Hansere v. community of city of Lincoln*: above n. 48.
71 *Marske v. Applegarth*: above, n. 53.
72 *York v. Swinburn*: above, n. 46.
73 *Hayton v. Castello:* above, n. 49.
74 CP 40/108, m. 70d.
75 *Stat. Realm I*, p. 214.
76 Ibid., p. 139.
77 Above, p. 49.
78 See e.g. JUST 1/832, m. 4d (association of Matthew of the Exchequer with 'dilecto serviente nostro' William of Gisleham to act as the king's serjeant in the Suffolk eyre of 1286); E 159/66, m. 26: admission of Roger of Higham on 27 May 1293 in the Exchequer 'ad officium servientis regis' to sue for the king in the Yorkshire and other eyres. But for a reference to the *narratores regis* in 1278 see *Rot. Parl. I*, p. 7.
79 CP 40/92, m. 162d.
80 The earliest use of the term seems to be in a report of a Common Bench case of 1284, where the term is used by Chief Justice Weyland: Cambridge University Library, MS. Dd.7.14, f. 375r.
81 *Britton*, ed. F. M. Nichols (2 vols., Oxford, 1865), i. 93.
82 *Stat. Realm I*, p. 34.
83 *Fleta*, Vol. II, ed. H. G. Richardson and G. O. Sayles (Selden Society, 72 (1953)), p. 139.
84 Baker, *Order of Serjeants at Law*, pp. 21–7.
85 On vicarious liability *cf.* T. F. T. Plucknett, *Concise History of the Common Law* (5th edn., London, 1956), pp. 472–5 and for the verdict in a trespass action of 1300 which specifically describes a lady whose servant had committed a wrong as '*deadvocans*' the servant after the deed by removing him from her service see CP 40/134, m. 151.
86 Baker, *Order of Serjeants at law*, p. 27, n. 3.
87 See the reports of the replevin case of *Bastard v. de la Torre* in British Library, MS. Additional 5925, ff. 36r–37r, British Library, MS. Additional 37657, ff. 80r–82v and Lincoln's Inn, MS. Hale 188, ff. 31v–32v (the plea-roll record of the case is on CP 40/112, m. 91). However a fourth report of the case in Lincoln's Inn, MS. Miscellaneous 87, ff. 12v–13r mentions only two of these five serjeants as acting for him.
88 For examples see Lincoln's Inn, MS. Miscellaneous 87, ff. 13v–14r (Lowther); British Library, MS. Additional 31826, f. 399r (Harle 'non pars stans a latere'); *YB 21 & 22 Edward I*, p. 243 (Warwick 'qui non fuit ex una parte nec ex alia'); *YB 33–35 Edward I*, p. 477 (Willoughby 'non existens cum aliquo parcium').
89 e.g. Cambridge University Library, MS. Dd.7.14, f. 405v: 'Scotere dyst hors de la barre'.
90 British Library, MS. Additional 31826, ff. 372v–373r: 'Item sciendum quod in consilio narratorum demande fut si W. la Zouche poeit point entrer le fee la persone pur la verte cyre; item sil en le lyu de cel marche fut seisi de agistement ou enparka ou approva ou meynovera etc.' This note is not to be found in the report of the same case in *YB 32 & 33 Edward I*, pp. 51–3.
91 Bodleian Library, MS. Rawlinson D 913, ff. 111r–v. The otherwise fuller report of this case in *YB 32 & 33 Edward I*, pp. 249–55 does not mention this private session or what was said there.
92 British Library, MS. Hargrave 375, f. 135r: 'Warr' dixit in consilio. Jeo pos qe

jeo suy le heir mon pere e quant mon pere devie jeo suy outre mer. Le chief sengnur entre les tenemenz etc. Vent le frere mon pere e se profre com heyre apparaunt apres son frere. Le chief sengnur li livere la seisine sur condision etc. E il devie seisi. Son fiz entre. Tut veyne joe en tere jeo sui forclos a touz jours a demander ces tenemenz pur la apparance. Et alii assentirent ei.' For evidence of what Mablethorpe had said *in consilio* about a case heard in Easter term 1302 see British Library, MS. Additional 31826, f. 138v ('sed prius dixit Malm' in consilio qe quele veye qe lem doune si avera il merveile qc si de parcele dunke ij seignurs inmediate de un tenement, si de lenter dunk serra lur contumacie prejudiciel a ly e eus de tant rien perdant').

93   Lincoln's Inn, MS. Miscellaneous 738, f. 42v: *prior of Hospitallers v. William Latimer senior*. There is a report of a related case in *YB 30 & 31 Edward I*, ed. A. J. Horwood (Rolls Series, 1863), pp. 23–7.
94   Lincoln's Inn, MS. Hale 174, f. 12v. The plea-roll record of the case is CP 40/105, m. 29. Other material relating to this case will be found in the pleading manual *Novae Narrationes: Novae Narrationes*, ed. E. Shanks and S. F. C. Milsom (Selden Society, 80 (1963)), B 32C–D; C 32–32A, 37.
95   Lincoln's Inn, MS. Miscellaneous 87, ff. 19v–20r: it may have been disallowed because Tilton concluded the 'evidence' by seeking judgment of the writ, a form of words inappropriate to such a speech.
96   Lincoln's Inn, MS. Miscellaneous 738, f. 51r. The report of the same case in *YB 33–35 Edward I*, pp. 167–9 is complementary to this report. The plea-roll enrolment of this case is CP 40/153, m. 241d. For a report of an unidentified assize of novel disseisin in which the serjeant Huntingdon made 'un evidence' to the assize and the assize then gave its verdict word for word as Huntingdon had spoken to them see British Library, MS. Additional 37657, f. 30v.
97   Lincoln's Inn, MS. Miscellaneous 87, ff. 108v–109r.
98   Cambridge University Library, MS. Dd.7.14, ff. 269r–v.
99   See the brief description of the levying of a final concord contained in the *Modus Levandi Fines: Stat. Realm I*, p. 214. This must belong to a date before 1290 since it appears to envisage a grant in fee simple by way of subinfeudation.
100 British Library, MS. Additional 31826, f. 350v.
101 Lincoln's Inn, MS. Miscellaneous 738, ff. 64v–65r.
102 Above, pp. 47–8.
103 CP 40/100, m. 46d. In a report of a debt plea of uncertain date we find the defendant's serjeant asking if the count was avowed as a preliminary to seeking a hearing of the writ and then challenging the count for seeking a debt for failure to fulfil a contract: British Library, MS. Harley 25, ff. 180v, 182r.
104 Lincoln's Inn, MS. Hale 188, f. 33r.
105 British Library, MS. Egerton 2811, ff. 98v–100r.
106 Above, p. 87.
107 British Library, MS. Hale 25, ff. 13ov–131v.
108 Lincoln's Inn, MS. Hale 188, f. 26r.
109 CP 40/92, m. 185d.
110 CP 40/92, m. 42.
111 Palmer, 'County Year Book Reports', 797; Palmer, *County Courts*, p. 92.
112 The text is printed by Palmer in 'County Year Book Reports' at pp. 800–1.
113 Above, pp. 58–60. Much of this evidence is only of the payment of retainers and we cannot be certain that the retainers were payable for life, but it seems probable that most, if not all of them, were.
114 Nigel Ramsey has suggested that it was only judges and their clerks and canon

lawyers who were commonly retained before 1300, but he was unaware of the plea-roll and other evidence which shows that serjeants were commonly retained prior to that date: Nigel Ramsey, 'Retained Legal Counsel, c.1275-c.1475' in *Trans. Roy. Hist. Soc.*, 5th series 35 (1985), pp. 95–112.

115 Above, p. 58.
116 *Registrum Thome de Cantilupo*, p. 22. The register suggests that at the same time almost identical deeds were also made in favour of four other Common Bench serjeants.
117 British Library, MS. Cotton Faustina B. I, f. 104r.
118 *Select Cases in King's Bench I*, p. cxliii.
119 JUST 1/207, m. 2d.
120 John Hodgson, *A History of Northumberland* (3 parts in 7 volumes, Newcastle, 1820–58), Part III, Vol. ii, pp. 28–9 (n. 7): a deed of 1278 by John de Lisle in favour of William of Swinburn printed from deeds then in the possession of the Swinburne family. I have not attempted to trace the original.
121 *Select Cases in King's Bench I*, p. cxliii: but note that the 18 'clerici' to which Sayles refers in his footnote (and whose names he does not print) include another five men known to have been serjeants (Ashby, Coleshill, Gosfield, Milton and Scotter).
122 Canterbury Cathedral Chapter Archives, Miscellaneous Accounts I, ff. 122r–272r *passim*: showing pensions paid to Walkingham, Giselham and Bereford.
123 *Documents Illustrating the Rule of Walter de Wenlok, abbot of Westminster, 1283–1307*, ed. Barbara F. Harvey (Camden 4th series 2 (1965)), pp. 30–3: the serjeants (not specifically identified as such by Miss Harvey) are de la Barre, Bereford, Coventry, Gosfield, Higham, Inge, Kelloe (Kellawe), Adam of Kinsham (Kingsmead), Spigurnel, Thornton and Warwick.
124 British Library, MS. Cotton Tiberius E. VI, f. 129v (Fishburn, Hartlepool, Lisle).
125 W. Hudson, 'The Camera Roll of the Priory of Norwich in 1283, compiled by Bartholomew de Cotton', *Norfolk Archaeology*, 19 (1917), pp. 268–313 at p. 281.
126 *Extracts from the Account Rolls of the Abbey of Durham*, Vol. II, ed. J. T. Fowler (Surtees Society, 100 (1899)), pp. 492 (pensions to unnamed clerks, serjeants and others in 1292), 502 (pension to Fishburn in 1298).
127 *Records of the City of Norwich*, ed. W. Hudson and J. C. Tingay (2 vols., Norwich, 1906–10), i. 31, 32, 36 (pension to John of Mutford); i. 32, 34, 35, 36, 37 (pension to Simon East).
128 Palmer, 'Origins of the Legal Profession', p. 132 is in error in saying that they 'normally ranged between one mark and 20 shillings', at least so far as this group of serjeants is concerned.
129 CP 40/33, m. 52; CP 40/36, m. 58d. But note that in neither case is it absolutely clear that the annuity was granted for legal assistance.
130 *Select Cases in King's Bench I*, p. cxliii. But by this date Roger was already a royal assize justice.
131 For examples of retainers payable wholly in kind (in the form of one or two robes) see CP 40/59, m. 49d; CP 40/122, m. 85; CP 40/17, m. 53; CP 40/158, m. 129d.
132 For examples see CP 40/73, m. 5; CP 40/141, m. 143d.
133 CP 40/104, m. 102d and JUST 1/1306, m. 11; CP 40/144, m. 345; CP 40/153, m. 268d.
134 CP 40/145, m. 304d.
135 CP 40/80, m. 72d.

Notes to Pages 101–3   203

136 CP 40/127, m. 122.
137 For evidence showing that Inge and Spigurnel were paid separately for their services in two pleas in 1297–8 while they were also in receipt of annuities from Westminster abbey see *Documents ... Walter de Wenlok*, pp. 194–5.
138 The term *patrocinium* is commonly used for the service performed by an advocate in the ecclesiastical courts for his clients.
139 CP 40/105, m. 15d.
140 CP 40/158, m. 129d.
141 Above, n. 117.
142 Above, n. 120.
143 CP 40/104, m. 102d.
144 CP 40/90, m. 107. This case is discussed by Palmer in 'Origins of the Legal Profession', pp. 129–30.
145 CP 40/108, m. 94.
146 CP 40/143, m. 113.
147 CP 40/162, m. 43d. This is the case inadequately reported in *YB 33–35 Edward I*, pp. 403–5. It was on the basis of this last report that Robert Palmer erroneously speculated that 'Default of service ... and perhaps even hostile action was no sufficient defence if the grant had been made in consideration of services already performed as well as to be performed. The condition of the annuity in that situation had been sufficiently fulfilled already at the time of the grant': Palmer, 'Origins of the Legal Profession', pp. 130–1.
148 *Walcot v. Bardolf*: CP 40/75, m. 126 (1288: in the 1286 Norfolk eyre); *Bonington v. Roscelyn (rector of Field Dalling)*: CP 40/80, m. 72d (1289: in a plea before the official of the bishop of Norwich and in a case in the 1286 Norfolk eyre); *Osmund v. Say*: CP 40/100, m. 98d (1293: in a plea in the Earl of Oxford's court of Castle Camps and elsewhere); *Calveley v. (Roscelyn) rector of Field Dalling*: CP 40/105, m. 15d (1294: in a plea before the official of the bishop of Norwich and in the 1286 Norfolk eyre); *Fitz Neal v. abbot of Bruern*: CP 40/118 m. 59d (1297: in a plea in the Oxfordshire hundred of Chadlington); *Pakeman v. Staunton Harold*: CP 40/121, m. 146d (1297: in a plea in the county court of Leicestershire) (this case is reported in Lincoln's Inn, MS. Hale 188, f. 13v); *Angot v. prior of Bromehill*: CP 40/129 m. 120 (1299: in the Clare honour court of the earl of Gloucester).
149 Palmer, 'Origins of the Legal Profession', pp. 129–30. A further example of the working of this rule is *Walcote v. Bardolf*: CP 40/75, m. 126, a case of 1288 where the defendants attempted to bar a claim for four years of arrears by assistance to an opponent in the 1286 Norfolk eyre. It is less clear that Palmer has correctly explained the rule whether in terms of the action being 'based so strictly on the original written contract' ('Origins of the Legal Profession', p. 129) or in terms of an analogy between such agreements and the feudal relationship between lords and their men and escheat for feudal felony (*County Courts*, p. 95). It may be that the rule was an accidental byproduct of the fact that a living annuitant could only bring an action that asserted his right to a continuing annuity as well as to arrears of that annuity: there was therefore no way in which he could recover arrears of an annuity that had been terminated by his own misconduct.
150 *Calendar of City Letter-Book B*, p. 215.
151 Above, p. 91.
152 The earliest recorded admission of two king's serjeants to their office in 1293 specifically records that they have been admitted toooo sue for the king *ad*

voluntatem regis: Select Cases in King's Bench I, p. clii. The point is not made in the writ to one of the groups of justices in eyre (Hugh of Cressingham and his fellows in the Yorkshire eyre) before whom Roger of Higham was to act ordering them to admit him to his office: JUST 1/1090, m. 1.
153 *Select Cases in King's Bench V*, p. xli.
154 *Rot. Parl. I*, p. 7.
155 *Select Cases in King's Bench V*, p. xlii and n. 6. For evidence of Walkingham acting for the king in litigation in the Common Bench before 1278 see e.g. CP 40/21, mm. 16d, 95 (1277).
156 Above, p. 64.
157 Above, pp. 58–9 (William of Thornegg'; John of Houghton; Richard Boyland; John Giffard).
158 It was probably envisaged from the beginning that Thornton would act for the king on the northern eyre circuit and Gisleham on the southern. Although the third serjeant (Walkingham) did join Thornton for the eyre of his own home county of Yorkshire, it was perhaps intended that he should act mainly in the Common Bench.
159 *Select Cases in King's Bench V*, p. xlii.
160 *Select Cases in King's Bench V*, pp. xlii–xliv. There is no evidence that William of Selby, who acted in place of Thornton in 1285 while the latter was on the king's business in Ireland, was ever paid for his work. Nor is there any evidence for the payment of Matthew of the Exchequer who was assigned to assist Giselham in the eyres of the southern circuit by a writ of 11 November 1286 (JUST 1/832, m. 4d) and who can be seen at work in the Hertfordshire eyre of 1287 (*Placita de Quo Warranto*, pp. 287, 288, 289, 291), though as a member of the king's household he may have been paid from household sources. There is evidence for the payment in 1283 of Richard of Coleshill for assisting Giselham in the Somerset and Dorset eyres of 1280 (C 62/59. m. 2). For evidence of his work in the Somerset eyre see *Placita de Quo Warranto*, pp. 689, 695, 700, 703–4. Only one serjeant was paid in respect of the period 1287–90 though two were paid again from 1290 (even though the eyres were in suspense between 1290 and 1292).
161 *Select Cases in King's Bench V*, pp. xxxvi–xxxviii; *Select Cases in King's Bench I*, pp. cxii–cxiv.
162 *Select Cases in King's Bench V*, pp. xliii–xliv, cix–cxi.
163 Above, p. 96.
164 British Library, MS. Harley 25, ff. 130v–131v. This is not noticed in other reports of the same case, though these do show Howard making an avowry that supersedes a defective one made by a different serjeant.
165 *YB 33–35 Edward I*, p. 291. For another case, perhaps of 1302, where the plaintiff's original serjeant (Hampton) makes a tactical error in pleading and the litigant is only rescued from this by a second serjeant (Harle) coming up (*superveniens*) and taking over from him see British Library, see MS. Additional 31826, f. 144v.
166 G. J. Hand, *English Law in Ireland, 1290–1324* (Cambridge, 1967), p. 49; Paul Brand, 'The Early History of the Legal Profession of the Lordship of Ireland, 1250–1350' in *Brehons, Serjeants and Attorneys: Studies in the History of the Irish Legal Profession*, ed. Daire Hogan and W. N. Osborough (Dublin, 1990), pp. 15–50 at p. 19. By the last quarter of the fourteenth century, there is evidence of English serjeants being assigned to litigants in the same way, though the serjeant might still decline to act for the client if he thought his case a bad

one: see *Burton v. Pope* (CP 40/472, m. 443) (I owe this reference to the kindness of Professor Robert C. Palmer).
167 SC 8/42, no. 2070: printed in *Select Cases in King's Bench I*, pp. cxliv–cxlv. For another complaint alleging that Brompton had ordered all the serjeants of the Bench not to act for a particular litigant see *State Trials of the reign of Edward I, 1289–1293*, ed. T. F. Tout and Hilda Johnstone (Royal Historical Society, Camden 3rd Series, 9 (1906)), pp. 18–21.
168 *Select Bills in Eyre*, p. 21. Another complainant in the 1293 Staffordshire eyre thought it relevant to mention that he is to poor to pay for the services of a serjeant and may have been asking for similar treatment: ibid., p. 47, n. 72.
169 E. W. Ives, *The Common Lawyers of Pre-Reformation England* (Cambridge, 1983), p. 295. Ives found that it was then still the sum commonly, though not invariably, paid to serjeants: ibid., pp. 295–307.
170 *The Early Rolls of Merton College Oxford*, ed. J. R. L. Highfield (Oxford, 1964), p. 135; CP 40/126, m. 63d; CP 40/158, m. 156d. It also occurs once as the sum payable to a serjeant practising in the London city courts: *Calendar of City Letter-Book C*, pp. 185–7.
171 *Documents ... Walter de Wenlok*, pp. 92, 126.
172 *Documents ... Walter de Wenlok*, p. 92 (Inge and Spigurnel paid two marks between them for their activity in a plea about Burlingham on behalf of Westminster abbey in 1298); F. F. Giraud, 'Municipal Archives of Faversham, A.D. 1304–1324' in *Archaeologia Cantiana*, 14 (1882), pp. 185–205 at p. 187 (John Tilton paid one mark by Faversham in 1304).
173 *Documents ... Walter de Wenlok*, pp. 125, 126.
174 SC 6/1132/10, m. 14 (but we cannot be certain that the total of four pounds and ten shillings paid to the three unnamed serjeants here was evenly distributed between them; the serjeants were paid to appear for pleas touching the bishopric of Ely during the vacancy in the see and for a plea concerning the king's claim to custody of the priory of Ely during vacancies of the see at the 1299 eyres of Ely and Cambridge).
175 *Boldon Boke*, ed. W. Greenwell (Surtees Society, 25 (1852)), Appendix II, p. xxxv (William of Harle's payment by bishop Bek for his activity on the bishop's behalf apparently in litigation heard at Easter 1307).
176 CP 40/127, m. 86; *Boldon Boke*, Appendix II, p. xxxv (Gilbert of Tothby paid for his services to bishop Bek probably in litigation heard at Easter 1307).
177 *Select Cases in King's Bench I*, pp. 80–1 (agreement by William of Wells in 1281 to act as the serjeant of the men of South Petherton in the court of King's Bench). Note also that in 1278–9 four named serjeants were paid a total of seven pounds, six shillings and eight pence by the priory of Durham, possibly for their services in the 1279 Northumberland eyre (but we are not told how much each received or in how many pleas they had acted for the prior): *Extracts from the Account Rolls of Durham II*, p. 488; that in 1280–1 five named serjeants were paid 70 shillings and eight pence in all for their services to the countess of Aumale in a particular case probably before the justices in eyre (but again we are not told how much each of them received): SC 6/824/12.

Chapter 7 The English Legal Profession in Edward I's Reign (III): Training and Entry into the Profession

1 Baker, *Order of Serjeants at Law*, pp. 14–17, 28–43, 94.
2 Below, pp. 123–8.

3 Baker, *Order of Serjeants at Law*, p. 11.
4 CP 40/92, m. 162d.
5 Richard Newman had probably been present in the court as a litigant and had been at the bar for his own litigation. In Trinity term 1291 he had been the plaintiff in litigation brought against the prior of Ely, Mark Pannecak and others: CP 40/90, m. 120d.
6 Below, pp. 114–17.
7 Above, p. 71.
8 Above, p. 72.
9 Baker, *Order of Serjeants at Law*, pp. 10, 14.
10 The serjeants who began practising as such late in 1293 or early in 1294 and who in most cases can be traced being appointed as attorneys up to 1292 or 1293 are: Robert of Ashill; William Aubyn; Richard of Hampton; Ralph of Stallingborough; Richard of Stapleford; Gilbert of Tothby; Richard of Willoughby (and possibly Simon of Kinsham). The serjeants who began practising late in 1299 or early in 1300 are: Thomas de Cailly; William of Harle; Robert of Haydock; Robert of Mablethorpe; Edmund of Pashley; Gilbert of Singleton; and John of Westcote.
11 Baker, *Order of Serjeants at Law*, pp. 136–7.
12 As Professor Baker notes, this is clearly observable by 1293. The career of Adam of Kinsham suggests that complete separation may still not been achieved in the 1280s.
13 Below, p. 110.
14 Baker, *Order of Serjeants at Law*, p. 11.
15 Baker, *Order of Serjeants at Law*, p. 14.
16 Thus the Robert Norman mentioned as appearing only once on the plea-rolls in 1306 (ibid., p. 14, n. 1) is clearly the serjeant normally known as Robert of Hedon: for on the Common Bench plea-roll for Michaelmas term 1300, when he was still an attorney, he is to be found being appointed by clients to act in cases under the name Robert Norman of Hedon.
17 There is no reason on the available evidence to suppose that the Nicholas Rolond retained by Westminster abbey between 1295 and 1307 (cited by Baker, *Order of Serjeants at Law* at p. 14, n. 2) was ever a serjeant in the Common Bench. He could easily have been a serjeant of one of the county courts of counties where Westminster abbey held lands.
18 Above, pp. 76, 79–80.
19 The first reference to any part of them seems to be in a 1329 manuscript report referring to the first argument of two of the newly created serjeants 'after the giving of gold': British Library, MS. Additional 41160, f. 40v.
20 Baker, *Order of Serjeants at Law*, Chapter 3.
21 *Munimenta Gildhallae Londoniensis*, ed. H. T. Riley (4 vols., Rolls Series, 1860–2), ii, part i, p. 280.
22 This rigid separation of groups had been foreshadowed in 1264 when the hustings established the rule that no serjeant (here called *advocatus*) was to act as an essoiner in the hustings court or in the other courts of the city: *Liber de Antiquis Legibus*, p. 70.
23 Above, p. 84.
24 JUST 1/1286, m. 15: they are here described as 'duo aprenticii de Banco'.
25 In the 1292 ordinance concerning attorneys (above, p. 115); in the case of *Barnwell v. le Vineter of Sproughton* (below, n. 61); and in the 'Statute of Conspirators' which mentions 'aprentifs' as among those engaged in champarty: *Stat. Realm I*, p. 216; *YB 21 & 22 Edward I*, pp. 147–51 (at p. 149) (case

ascribed to Easter term 1293 but can be identified as one heard in Michaelmas term 1292: interjection reported in Latin of '*quidam apprentis*').
26 JUST 1/1095, m. 1 (presentment made against William Cok, bailiff of Tickhill and his son William 'apprenticius de Banco' in the 1293–4 Yorkshire eyre for being common conspirators and maintainers of false pleas).
27 CP 40/122, m. 153: complaint of Roger of Wells, door-keeper of the court, that certain malefactors calling themselves apprentices of the court ('*qui se faciunt apprenticios hic*') had assaulted him at night; the jury indicted Richard of Thorp and Nicholas of Ingarsby of Leicestershire of this trespass.
28 In *re Thomas Torel*: below, p. 114.
29 British Library, MS. Stowe 386, ff. 125v–126r: report of a case heard in Trinity term 1302 with a note at the end of what chief justice Hengham had said by way of explanation to the apprentices ('Nota par Rauf de Hengham e dist en avantage des aprentiz').
30 CP 40/148, m. 163d: *Nicholas of Wylye v. Henry Lysewy*: complaint against an attorney for continuing to act in a plea after removal and making a damaging admission. The jury tells of the plaintiff's removal of the defendant and how he told him that 'ipse fuit homo de curia regis et apprenticius de Banco et placita sua propria in eadem curia regis prosequi voluit'.
31 *YB 33–35 Edward I*, pp. 63–5: comment by chief justice Hengham in a case of Michaelmas term 1305: 'mes jeo vous dy qe un de ceux aprentiz fist le purchaz pur fere quel jugement nous freoms sur ceo bref'.
32 *YB 21 & 22 Edward I*, p. 446: note of what 'les uns aprentiz deseint' given at end of a case ascribed by the editor to the 1294 Middlesex eyre but which does not belong to that eyre (and the comment may well be later than the case reported in any case); *Fleta II*, p. 139.
33 Plucknett wrote that 'the use of the word "apprentice" suggests that the student was attached to a practising lawyer whom he assisted in minor matters in return for instruction': *Concise History*, p. 218. There is, however, no evidence that these apprentices were ever 'apprenticed' to existing practitioners in this kind of way: they were apprenticed to the court, not to particular serjeants.
34 The earliest direct evidence for apprentice lawyers doing this is in letters of attorney issued for Robert de St Michael on 28 June 1287, appointing an attorney to represent him in Ireland for one year. Robert is said in the enrolment to be staying by the king's licence 'causa addiscendi in Banco regis apud Westm'': C 66/106, m. 11 (calendared in *Cal. Patent Rolls 1281–92*, p. 269). Robert was presumably in fact if not in name an apprentice of the Bench. I owe this reference to Dr David Higgins.
35 SC 8/189, no. 9409, printed by Turner in *YB 3 & 4 Edward II*, p. xlii. For another early reference to the 'crib' see *YB 2 & 3 Edward II*, ed. F. W. Maitland (Selden Society, 19 (1904)), pp. xv–xvi.
36 British Library, MS. Stowe 386, ff. 125v–126r: 'Nota par Rauf de Hengham, e dist en avantage des aprentiz'. For later references to other justices doing the same thing see Paul Brand, 'Courtroom and Schoolroom: the Education of Lawyers in England prior to 1400', *Historical Research*, 142, (1987), pp. 147–65 at p. 151, n. 15.
37 *YB 3 Edward II*, ed. F. W. Maitland (Selden Society, 20 (1905)), pp. x–xvi.
38 For indirect evidence of the part played by senior apprentices and perhaps more junior serjeants in the teaching of the junior apprentices see Brand, 'Education of Lawyers', pp. 158–60.
39 Above, p. 96.

40 For an example see Brand, 'Education of Lawyers', p. 158.
41 For a particularly clear example see Brand, 'Education of Lawyers', p. 158.
42 See Brand, 'Education of Lawyers', pp. 160–2.
43 To the manuscripts cited in Brand, 'Education of Lawyers', 160, n. 69 should be added Gonville and Caius College Cambridge, MS. 715/721 (at f. 43r); Cambridge University Library, MS. Mm.1.30 (at ff. 14r, 38v–39r) and probably Philadelphia Free Library, MS. LC 14.3 (at ff. 15v, 22v). See also Baker in *Readings and Moots at the Inns of Court in the Fifteenth Century*, Vol. II, ed. S. E. Thorne and J. H. Baker (Selden Society, 105 (1990)), pp. xxi–xxii and (for some examples) pp. cxxxii–cxxxvii.
44 In a minority, however, we are given only one side of the argument. There is also in British Library, MS. Royal 10.B.VIII (at f. 29v) what looks like a collection of factual situations appropriate to the posing of *questiones* but without the actual *questiones* and without any subsequent argument.
45 Justice Bereford appears in one of these *questiones* (Cambridge University Library MS. Mm.1.30, f. 14r) arguing against the serjeant Gilbert of Tothby but he does not seem to speak with quite the authority of a justice in court.
46 Compare for example the *questio* in British Library, MS. Harley 408, ff. 176v–177r with the argument in *YB 33–35 Edward I*, pp. 495–7.
47 Lincoln's Inn, MS. Hale 174, ff. 40r–v.
48 The main difficulty here is that even where names are attached to the individuals putting forward arguments there is no way of dating when the arguments themselves had taken place. Thus although we are told in two quite separate *questiones* that it is Pashley (Passelewe) who has put forward some of the arguments, we have no way of knowing for certain whether he was speaking before or after he had become a serjeant: Lincoln's Inn, MS. Hale 188, ff. 49r, 49v (in the latter report arguments are also ascribed to the Bench serjeants Harle and Claver). We cannot wholly exclude the possibility that the argument took place after he had become a serjeant. But for an argument made by an otherwise unknown Ford' who never became a serjeant see British Library, MS. Additional 31826, f. 119v.
49 British Library MS. Additional 31826, f. 223v.
50 Brand, 'Education of Lawyers', p. 163.
51 Brand, 'Education of Lawyers', p. 163 and notes.
52 *Novae Narrationes*. Another similar collection which has not been edited is to be found in British Library, MS. Hargrave 375, ff. 15r–21v.
53 *Cf.* Hall in *Early Registers of Writs* at p. cxxix, n. 1. The treatise also occurs in many other manuscripts.
54 Manuscripts which include this treatise include: British Library, MSS. Additional 18600 (at ff. 171r–178v), Harley 1120 (at ff. 148r–152v), Harley 1208 (at ff. 125v–133r), Lansdowne 467 (at ff. 173v–176v); Bodleian Library, MS. Additional C 188 (at ff. 126v–133v); Cambridge University Library, MS. Ll.4.17 (at ff. 181v–186r); Harvard Law Library, MS. 24 (at ff. 88–91r).
55 See below, pp. 118–19. The treatise has been edited by George Woodbine in *Four Thirteenth Century Law Tracts* (New Haven, 1910), pp. 163–83.
56 William of Goldington, for example, seems only to have acted as an attorney between 1285 and 1288: see CP 40/58, mm. 57, 57d; CP 40/59, mm. 87, 90; CP 40/61, mm. 75d, 76; CP 40/62, mm. 70, 72; CP 40/70, m. 100d; CP 40/75, mm. 195, 201d, 203d.
57 Richard of Stapleford, for example, can be shown to have been active as an attorney with many clients between 1276 and 1289; and the future royal justice

William of Barford (Bereford) seems to have been an attorney from at least 1269 to 1280.
58 Above, p. 88.
59 Above, p. 87.
60 This legislation is discussed further below at p. 115.
61 CP 40/95, m. 61d: *Isabel of Barnwell v. John le Vyneter of Sproughton.*
62 CP 40/139, m. 106.
63 For the careers of Thomas of Sutham, John of Heyford, Thomas Boydin of Stretton and Nicholas Crompe of Coventry see Palmer, *County Courts*, pp. 101–6.
64 British Library, MS. Stowe 386, f. 153r.
65 Harvard Law Library, MS. 162, ff. 174r–187v; Cambridge University Library, MS. Ee.2.19, ff. 133r–140r; British Library, MS. Royal 9.A.VII, ff. 219v–227r; British Library, MS. Egerton 656, ff. 188v–192v; and probably Bridport Corporation MS. 2644, pp. 329–368 (which I have not seen). The two British Library manuscripts contain one version; the Cambridge University Library and Harvard Law Library manuscripts the second.
66 Harvard Law Library, MS. 162, f. 184v.
67 Cambridge University Library, MS. Ee.2.19, f. 138r.
68 *Rot. Parl. I*, p. 84 (no. 22), which has to be read in conjunction with a subsequent royal mandate of 2 June 1292 enrolled on CP 40/95, m. 71d. The latter is printed by Robert Palmer in 'Origins of the Legal Profession' at p. 139, n. 71. The original ordinance belongs to the Epiphany parliament of 1292; the royal writ was issued during the next parliamentary session.
69 On the interpretation of this passage see above, p. 114.
70 'Se de negociis in eadem curia intromittant.' The precise meaning of this phrase is made clear by its use as the standard form in prohibitions delivered to professional attorneys convicted or professional misconduct, warning them against attempting to practise in the court in future e.g. CP 40/90, m. 57d: release of Robert de Greshope after imprisonment for a year and a day 'et curia regis hic et alibi per justiciarios hic ei est inhibitum, ne decetero in eadem de aliquibus negociis se intromittat etc., quousque etc.'.
71 For this royal mandate see above, n. 68.
72 *Select Cases in King's Bench V*, p. lxiii.
73 *Cf.* the commission of June 1292 to Gilbert of Thornton and William de St Quentin to enquire into the activities of William of Kelsey and other men of the county of Yorkshire who 'induce people without either the right or the will, to go to law; who sometimes with their assent, sometimes without it, sometimes entirely without their knowledge, cause writs to be made out and fines to be made thereupon in the Chancery, and obtain other writs under the names of persons in the nature of things not existing, whereby they may cause disherisons, grieve and disquiet others and extort money': *Cal. Patent Rolls, 1281–1292*, p. 518 (I am grateful to Professor Paul Hyams for drawing my attention to this commission).
74 Pollock and Maitland, *Hist. Eng. Law*, i, p. 216.
75 Plucknett, *Concise History*, pp. 218–9.
76 Above, p. 75. It should also be noted that only a small minority of attorneys drew all their business from a single county, though a majority took the major part of their business from just one: above, p. 75.
77 Above, p. 84.
78 Above, p. 84.
79 Above, p. 84.

80 See Brand, 'Education of Lawyers', pp. 151–2.
81 Cf. Brand, 'Education of Lawyers', p. 152.
82 *Modus Componendi Brevia* is edited by Woodbine in *Four Thirteenth Century Law Tracts* at pp. 143–62.
83 For some of the manuscripts which contain this treatise see Brand, 'Education of Lawyers', p. 154, n. 38.
84 Hence for example at one point the author says that 'cestes variaunces et plusors altres peount estre assignetz entre ceux deux brefs' and then later adds 'Et unquore altre variance'.
85 The history of this textual transmission is complicated by evidence from the section which is concerned with the action of wardship that indicates that most, if not all, manuscripts of this treatise are descended from an archetype which went to Ireland and was altered there to incorporate material appropriate only to the legal custom of the lordship.
86 This is edited by Dunham in *Radulphi de Hengham Summae*, pp. 51–71.
87 See Brand, 'Education of Lawyers', pp. 155–7.
88 Above, p. 88.

Chapter 8   The English Legal Profession in Edward I's Reign (IV): Regulation

1 *Stat. Realm I*, p. 34.
2 Certain infelicities in the drafting of this clause suggest that it may originally have been concerned solely with serjeants and that it was only at a fairly late stage that it was rather clumsily amended to cover other professional lawyers practising in the king's courts as well.
3 This clause is free floating in the text and could be interpreted as authorizing the king to impose a stiffer penalty if necessary on serjeants. The context, however, suggests that the intention was only to allow such a penalty to be imposed in the case of those other than serjeants who were already subject to heavier penalties than other offenders.
4 But for evidence from the code of professional conduct enacted for lawyers practising in the courts of the city of London in 1280 that the provisions of the statute were also thought to be applicable in the city courts (and to cover negligence as well as conscious deception) see below, pp. 122–3. For evidence of a royal writ of 1291 which likewise assumed that the legislation was applicable in the city courts in London see below, p. 137.
5 The London regulations of 1280 are discussed below, pp. 122–3. There may have been similar regulations in other cities and towns but none are known to survive.
6 *Stat. Realm I*, p. 34.
7 In the 1293–4 Yorkshire eyre John of Cave of Middleton, who was probably a local serjeant, was described in the verdict of a jury on conspirators as '*narrator et manutentor Thome de Middelton contra Johannem de Thorni injuste et aliarum parcium quandoque injustarum*' (JUST 1/1095, m. 2); while in the 1292 Herefordshire eyre John Lightfoot, probably another local serjeant, was described in a similar verdict as one who '*manutenet partem dominorum suorum tam juste et injuste*' (JUST 1/303, m. 67). In both cases, all the serjeant seems to have been doing was speaking for his client in court.
8 See *OED* s.v. barrator; *The Chronicle of Jocelin of Brakelond*, ed. H. E. Butler (London, 1949), p. 12 and n. 3.

Notes to Pages 121–5   211

9   *Stat. Realm I*, p. 216.
10 Above, p. 115.
11 *Select Cases in the Court of King's Bench*, Vol. III, ed. G. O. Sayles (Selden Society, 58 (1939)), p. lix.
12 *Rot. Parl. I*, p. 96.
13 *Stat. Realm I*, p. 139.
14 The authors of the statute seem to to have ignored the close connection between 'conspiracy' and 'champerty' made by the authors of the 1293 Ordinance and thus the extent to which such behaviour was already banned under the earlier legislation.
15 *Munimenta Gildhalle Londoniensis*, ii, part ii, pp. 280–2. Restriction of practice in the city courts to a closed group of professional serjeants also formed part of the same ordinance. This is discussed above, p. 110.
16 This part of the code was not, however, new and merely re-enacted legislation of 1259: *Liber de Antiquis Legibus*, p. 43.
17 This part of the code built on, but modified, one of the provisions of the legislation enacted in the 1244 London eyre which had prohibited any *advocatus* or *placitator* making or rendering judgment or being involved in making or rendering judgment in any case in which he had acted in either capacity: *London Eyre of 1244*, p. 96, n. 236.
18 This clause is particularly puzzling for it suggests that the statute was applicable not just in the king's courts but also in London's city courts. It also suggests that the chapter covered negligence as well as intentional misbehaviour on the part of professional attorneys, not something readily apparent from the statute nor perhaps intended by it.
19 JUST 1/832, m. 4d; *Placita de Quo Warranto*, pp. 287, 288, 289, 291.
20 N. Denholm-Young, 'Who wrote Fleta?' and 'Matthew Cheker' in *Collected Papers of N. Denholm-Young* (Cardiff, 1969), pp. 187–204. Matthew's authorship is, however, still doubted by G. O. Sayles: see *Fleta*, Vol. IV, ed. G. O. Sayles (Selden Society, 99 (1984)), pp. xxiv–xxv.
21 Both cases are recorded on CP 40/83, m. 168. The first began with a petition to the king and his council at the Easter parliament of 1290 but was then referred to the justices of the Common Bench (who were afforced by outside members for the hearing of this case). The second seems to have been brought directly before this specially afforced court. Towards the end of the two years it was alleged that he had been allowed out of gaol by his gaolers on a number of occasions and adjudged that the two-year term should begin all over again: *Select Cases in King's Bench II*, pp. cliv–clv; *Select Cases in the Exchequer of Pleas*, ed. Hilary Jenkinson and Beryl E. R. Fermoy (Selden Society, 48 (1932)), pp. 141–2. For other proceedings of 1292 in which it was adjudged that Matthew be sent to gaol during the king's pleasure for misconduct, see CP 40/92, mm. 32–32d.
22 For evidence of the punishment of attorneys for misconduct in their own litigation see below, pp. 134–5.
23 *Select Cases in King's Bench I*, pp. 80–1.
24 British Library, MS. Harley 2183, ff. 79r–v.
25 Lincoln's Inn, MS. Miscellaneous 87, ff. 80r–80v: 'Mut' fust chalange pur ceo qe einz ces houres en mesme ceo cas si fust il pur Johan de Byland devant le roy, issint qe a cele houre si fust il de son consail e seet touz lour privetez e agarde fust quil alast a Johan'. The case is enrolled at CP 40/96, m. 79. The judgment is a little surprising because it might have been supposed that he was also now privy to the 'secrets' of the Earl.

26 British Library, MS. Lansdowne 467, f. 115r. It is enrolled on CP 40/104, m. 37.
27 'et il diceunt qe co fut le maundement lor seignour'.
28 *YB 33–35 Edward I*, pp. 461–3. The case is enrolled on CP 40/162, m. 163d.
29 Robert reappears in reports of the following term: *YB 33–35 Edward I*, pp. 475, 511, 513, 515.
30 *YB 32 & 33 Edward I*, pp. 447–9. The case is enrolled on CP 40/155, m. 105d.
31 British Library, MS. Stowe 386, f. 132r. The plea-roll record of the case is in CP 40/143, m. 58. There is no mention of this episode in a second report of the same case in British Library, MS. Additional 31826, f. 142v.
32 British Library, MS. Additional 31826, f. 375r.
33 CP 40/15, m. 62. Part of the relevant entry is printed in Palmer, 'County Year Book Reports', p. 797, n. 1.
34 Palmer, 'Origins of the Legal Profession', p. 133.
35 *Hawise de la Haye v. William of Bolton*: CP 40/89, m. 143. For other litigation less certainly involving professional attorneys in the 1292 eyres of Herefordshire and Shropshire in which clients alleged the payment of money for the purchase of writs from chancery and the defendants' failure to do this see JUST 1/303, m. 77d (*Walter Haklute v. Gilbert de Seyntefey*) and JUST 1/739, m. 37 (*Robert de Dovil v. John le Teynturer of Ludlow*).
36 *In re John Sturmyn*: CP 40/103, m. 159d. The case is discussed in Palmer, 'Origins of the Legal Profession', p. 137.
37 *In re John of Upton*: CP 40/91, m. 191d.
38 For a second case in which the statutory punishment was inflicted on a clerk who practised as an attorney in the court of King's Bench see JUST 1/541B, m. 45d. A puzzlingly different version of the same case appears on m. 41d of the same roll. For other proceedings against attorneys for failure to sue litigation with due diligence for the interests of their clients (but in which the eventual outcome of the proceedings has not been traced) see *In re William of Kelsey*: CP 40/90, m. 60d; *Isabel of Barnwell v. John le Vyneter of Sproughton*: CP 40/95, m. 61d (this case is discussed by Palmer in 'Origins of the Legal Profession' at pp. 138–9).
39 JUST 1/579, m. 69d.
40 Simon of Cley occurs as an attorney, mainly for litigation from Norfolk, between 1278 and 1285. He had previously been in trouble in 1279 for acting as if he was the duly appointed attorney of a litigant when there was no record of his appointment, but on that occasion all that is recorded as happening is that he was then bailed by six men, some of whom are recognizable as fellow-professional attorneys: CP 40/28, m. 79. For other proceedings against professional attorneys alleging similar kinds of misbehaviour see *Ilger of 'Talighidyon' v. Simon Crucoyl*: CP 40/101, m. 60d (where all that is recorded is that Ilger has asked and received permission to sue against Simon in his own name and that of the king); *John Marshal of Heckington v. John of Stamford*: CP 40/131, m. 62d (where only the plaintiff's plaint is recorded).
41 *Roger Deye v. Simon of Stowe*: CP 40/95, m. 79d.
42 'nec Simon per ignoranciam se potest in hoc casu excusare, eo quod generalis attornatus dudum extitit et sufficienter eruditus ad premissa exequenda si volebat'.
43 For a complaint of similar misbehaviour made in 1299 against the very busy Common Bench attorney John de la Haye of Hereford (in which an order was issued for John's arrest but no further proceedings are then recorded) see *de la Grene v. de la Haye of Hereford*: CP 40/127, m. 81d.
44 British Library, MS. Stowe 386, f. 99v.

Notes to Pages 130–7 213

45 For cases in which he was appointed attorney by litigants see CP 40/64, mm. 148d, 149d; CP 40/66, m. 84d; CP 40/69, m. 171d; CP 40/75, mm. 198, 198d, 200d, 204; CP 40/79, m. 112.
46 CP 40/90, m. 146d: printed by Sayles in *Select Cases in King's Bench V*, pp. cxviii–cxix.
47 Above, p. 120.
48 *William le Tyeys v. Walter le Walur et al.*: CP 40/91, m. 303d.
49 *In re Simon of Downham and Gerin le Lyndraper*: CP 40/91, m. 210.
50 *The King and Walter Morewy v. William of Frome*: CP 40/108, m. 6d.
51 *Cecily widow of William Clerk of Oswestry v. John Wynel of Great Wenlock*: CP 40/110, m. 41.
52 British Library, MS. Additional 31826, f. 67v.
53 *Simon la Veille of Dunstable v. master Matthew of Dunstable*: CP 40/89, m. 26d; CP 40/90, m. 57.
54 The record mentions payment of a 40-shillings fine as the intended punishment but notes that this is subject to the king's agreement. It is not clear why he was not given the statutory term of imprisonment. Perhaps he merely claimed to be a professional attorney of the court but was not. However, the 12 men who stood surety for him until the arrival in court of the chief justice and one of his colleagues in Michaelmas term 1291 do all seem to have been professional attorneys: CP 40/91, m. 64.
55 CP 40/103, m. 70d.
56 For examples see CP 40/27, m. 4d; CP 40/17, m. 59d; CP 40/66, m. 66. In a case of 1291 the challenge was to the alleged appointment of an attorney by a minor but the attorney claimed his principal was of age: CP 40/89, m. 118. In a case of 1295 two men were sent to gaol for attempting to act as attorneys after they had been removed: CP 40/110, m. 178.
57 *In re Roger del Plat*: CP 40/125, m. 236d.
58 'et inhibitum est ei quod decetero non stet in curia hic in officio attornati nec aliquo alio officio nisi inde habeat specialem graciam domini regis'. C. J. Mettingham certified the cause of his imprisonment to chancery in answer to a writ of 20 December 1298: C 260/11, no. 12.
59 *Martin Bone v. Robert de Scales et al.*: CP 40/89, m. 112.
60 British Library, MS. Stowe 386, f. 174r.
61 CP 40/92, m. 109: printed in *Select Cases in the Court of King's Bench V*, pp. cxxv–cxxvi.
62 CP 40/90, m. 57d.
63 C 260/6, no. 14.
64 CP 40/92, m. 190d. This was presumably some kind of proclamation about the end of term and the latest times for the doing of business.
65 CP 40/93, m. 140d.
66 *In re Walerand Asshe* and *In re Hugh of Cottleby*, both enrolled on CP 40/92, m. 186d.
67 *In re William Balliol*: CP 40/105, m. 59d.
68 For proof of this relationship see JUST 1/14, m. 9; JUST 1/1276, m. 18.
69 CP 40/91, m. 296d. For an apparently related plaint see E 175/File 1, no. 7, m. 2.
70 CP 40/96, m. 100; CP 40/104, m. 22d.
71 CP 40/91, m. 191d.
72 Above, pp. 122–3.
73 Corporation of London Records Office, Common Pleas Roll 19, m. 4d.
74 H. T. Riley, *Memorials of London and London Life in the Thirteenth, Fourteenth*

and *Fifteenth Centuries* (London, 1868), pp. 27-8; *Calendar of City Letter-Book A*, p. 192.
75 *Calendar of City Letter-Book C*, pp. 185-7.
76 Corporation of London Records Office, Pleas of Land Roll 21, m. 8d.
77 *Select Bills in Eyre*, pp. 3-4.
78 *Select Bills in Eyre*, pp. 52-3.
79 JUST 1/303, m. 67.
80 JUST 1/1095, m. 2d.
81 JUST 1/744, mm. 5d, 2d.
82 JUST 1/306, m. 6.
83 For other possible professional lawyers indicted for ambidexterity at the same sessions see JUST 1/306, m. 5 (John Lyghtfot), m. 6 (John Love, Nicholas de Hakeleye, John le Graunt of 'Mershton', and John of Bradfield).
84 JUST 1/744, m. 5d.
85 JUST 1/744, m. 2d.
86 JUST 1/306, m. 6.
87 Ibid.
88 JUST 1/303, m. 67.
89 JUST 1/1095, m. 2d.
90 Ibid.

Chapter 9   The Other Legal Profession: Canon Lawyers in England before 1307

1 Professor James A. Brundage of the University of Kansas is working on a history of the legal profession in Western Europe as a whole. I should like to record my thanks to him for giving me access to a number of his unpublished papers on aspects of that history of particular relevance to this chapter as well as for allowing me see a number of papers now published in advance of publication. I am also grateful to him for his comments on an earlier draft of this chapter.
2 Professor Brundage has argued in an unpublished paper ('The Professionalization of Canon Lawyers in the Thirteenth Century') for a division of that development for canon lawyers in Western Europe as a whole into four separate stages. A three-stage scheme seems to me to make more sense in the English context, nor are the dates of my stages quite those of Professor Brundage's schema, but I remain indebted to his overall vision of the development of the canon lawyers as a professional group.
3 Stephan Kuttner and Eleanor Rathbone, 'Anglo-Norman Canonists of the Twelfth Century: An Introductory Study', *Traditio*, 7 (1949-51), pp. 279-358 at pp. 292-6; Leonard E. Boyle, 'The Beginnings of Legal Studies at Oxford', *Viator*, 14 (1983), pp. 107-31 at p. 107.
4 Kuttner and Rathbone, 'Anglo-Norman Canonists', pp. 282-4; Boyle, 'Beginnings of Oxford Legal Studies', p. 107.
5 Kuttner and Rathbone, 'Anglo-Norman Canonists', pp. 321-7; Boyle 'Beginnings of Oxford Legal Studies', pp. 113, 117-26. For rather different views on Vacarius and the teaching of Roman law at Oxford see Richard W. Southern, 'Master Vacarius and the Beginning of an English Academic Tradition' in *Medieval Learning and Literature: Essays presented to Richard William Hunt*, ed. J. J. G. Alexander and M. T. Gibson (Oxford, 1976) at pp. 257-86; P. Stein, 'Vacarius and the Civil Law' in *Church and Government in the Middle Ages: Essays presented to C. R. Cheney on his 70th birthday*, ed. C. N. L. Brooke et al. (Cambridge, 1976) at pp. 119-37.

Notes to Pages 144–9

6 Below, p. 145.
7 Kuttner and Rathbone, 'Anglo-Norman Canonists', pp. 284–90, 304–16.
8 Above, chapter one, p. 2.
9 Boyle, 'Beginnings of Oxford Legal Studies', pp. 109–10.
10 Professor Brundage (in the unpublished paper cited above at n. 2) divides this period up into two separate stages at around 1235 and extends the terminal date to 1275: but the division makes little sense in a specifically English context and I think that the general regulation of professional canon lawyers by the Council of Lyons is better regarded as marking the beginning of a new era in the history of the profession than as the culminating point of the previous era.
11 On the emergence of the university see Richard W. Southern, 'From Schools to University' in *The History of the University of Oxford, vol. I: The Early Oxford Schools*, ed. J. I. Catto (Oxford, 1984), pp. 1–36, especially pp. 12–17.
12 Boyle, 'Beginnings of Oxford Legal Studies', pp. 108–13; Leonard E. Boyle, 'Canon Law before 1380' in *History of the University of Oxford I* pp. 530–52 at pp. 530–3.
13 This reorganization and its effects are discussed by Boyle in *History of the University of Oxford I* at pp. 533–42.
14 M. B. Hackett, *The Original Statutes of Cambridge University: The Text and its History* (Cambridge, 1970) at pp. 41–63, 131; James A. Brundage, 'The Cambridge Faculty of Canon Law and the Ely Consistory Court' (unpublished paper), pp. 1–8.
15 James A. Brundage, 'Perceptions of Propriety: The Discipline of the Canonical Bar in Late Medieval England' (unpublished paper), esp. pp. 2, 6–8; Brundage, 'The Lawyer as his Client's Judge: The Medieval Advocate's Duty to the Court' (unpublished paper), pp. 11–12; Brundage, 'When Did Lawyers become Professionals? The Case of the Canonical Bar' (unpublished paper), pp. 10–11. See also Brundage, 'The Medieval Advocate's Profession', *Law and History Review*, 6 (1988), pp. 439–64 at pp. 449–50.
16 *Councils and Synods with other documents relating to the English Church, II*, ed. F. M. Powicke and C. R. Cheney (2 vols., Oxford, 1964), i. pp. 258–9. It should be noted that Professor Brundage ('Medieval Advocate's Profession', p. 449) interprets this legislation somewhat differently.
17 *Councils and Synods II*, i, pp. 314–15, 386, 465.
18 *Councils and Synods II*, ii, p. 773.
19 *Councils and Synods II*, i, p. 435.
20 *Councils and Synods II*, i, p. 493.
21 *Concilia Magnae Britanniae et Hiberniae, A.D. 446–1718*, ed. David Wilkins (4 vols., London, 1737), ii. 27.
22 *Councils and Synods II*, i, pp. 107, 120.
23 *Councils and Synods II*, i, pp. 275, 332, 387, 466, 521, 567, 622, 723; ii, pp. 849, 1058.
24 *Councils and Synods II*, i, p. 259.
25 *Councils and Synods II*, ii, pp. 917–18.
26 Wilkins, *Concilia*, ii, p. 205. The purpose of the year's attendance at the court is spelled out in the regulations of archbishop Stratford for the same court of c. 1342: Wilkins, *Concilia*, ii, p. 688.
27 Wilkins, *Concilia*, ii, p. 688.
28 Wilkins, *Concilia*, ii, pp. 690–1. But note that in 1334 the bishop of Lincoln required that no proctor be admitted to practise in the Lincoln consistory court unless he had studied civil and canon law for a minimum of four years: Wilkins, *Concilia*, ii, p. 572.

29 Wilkins, *Concilia*, ii, pp. 204, 206. For some discussion see Irene J. Churchill, *Canterbury Administration* (2 vols., London, 1933), i, pp. 435–6, 450–1; ii, p. 208.
30 Wilkins, *Concilia*, ii, p. 207.
31 CP 40/123, m. 40.
32 For other litigation between master John Lovel and a client (Thomas Doynton) about an annual pension granted for master John's service, though this time not expressly for his service in the Court of Arches, but in which none the less the client claimed the pension had been forfeited when master John failed to act for him in a suit in that court see CP 40/60, m. 15.
33 E 13/16, m. 9. For previous litigation between the same two parties in the 1288 Sussex eyre about the same pension which does not mention the limitation on where master Peter is obliged to serve see JUST 1/929, m. 19d. Nor is any such limitation mentioned in the pension litigation brought by master Peter against the abbot of Bayham, though the abbot's defence makes plain that the pension was granted for his services in a particular suit: CP 40/73, m. 102.
34 Wilkins, *Concilia*, ii, p. 410. The same statutes also imposed a quota of six on the number of notaries allowed to practise there.
35 E.g. British Library, MS. Additional 15668, f. 9v (1282 agreement between master Robert of Lech' and the prior of Newent); JUST 1/622, m. 28d (agreement between master Alan of Whixley and the prior and convent of Luffield); JUST 1/739, m. 19 (1289 agreement between master Richard Bernard and the abbot and convent of Lilleshall); British Library, MS. Harley 662, f. 114v (1303 agreement between master Robert of Malling and the prior and convent of Dunmow). But for a pension specifically granted for assistance in one particular plea and apparently contingent on success in that plea see CP 40/104, m. 105d (1282 agreement between master John of Bures and master Andrew Avenel); for a pension granted only for service in the Court of Arches see CP 40/123, m. 40 (1283 agreement between master John Lovel and Roger bishop of Coventry and Lichfield); for a pension granted for service as an advocate either in person or through a suitable substitute in the city of Norwich, but only for service through counsel in litigation outside the city see CP 40/147, m. 157d (1271 agreement between master John of Bures and Robert rector of Foxley).
36 E.g. CP 40/105, m. 112 (claim by the abbot of Quarr that master Henry de la Rode has forfeited his pension for failure to appear for the abbot before the dean of Chichester at Chichester and before the commissary of the official of the bishop of Winchester at Winchester, met by master Henry's claim that he had subsequently accepted his service in a cause at St Martin le Grand in London before the commissary of the conservator of the privileges of the Hospitallers); CP 40/121, m. 13 (claim by master Michael rector of Cropthorne that master Peter of Pirton had forfeited his pension for failure to appear for him before unspecified judges in Wells and Worcester cathedrals).
37 Clearly in some senses archdeacons and ecclesiastical judges of various kinds remained full-time professional canon lawyers after their appointments since they made regular use of their legal expertise and owed their appointments to that expertise; but no attempt was made to bar them from benefices with the cure of souls.
38 *Councils and Synods II*, i, pp. 314–15.
39 *Register of archbishop William Wickwane (1279–1285)*, ed. William Brown (Surtees Society, 114 (1907)), pp. 208–9. The order was repeated by archbishop William Greenfield in 1308 and again in 1315: *Register of archbishop William Greenfield (1306–1315)*, Vol. I (Surtees Society, 145 (1931)), pp. 116, 157.

40 Wilkins, *Concilia*, ii, p. 205.
41 *Councils and Synods* II, ii, p. 1031.
42 E.g. *Select Cases in King's Bench V*, pp. cxxiii–cxxv (agreement between master Bernard Cornish and the abbot and convent of Evesham); British Library, MS. Lansdowne 402, f. 32r (1279 agreement between master William of Pickering and the abbot and convent of Selby); JUST 1/622, m. 28d (agreement between master Alan of Whixley and the prior and convent of Luffield); JUST 1/739, m. 19 (1289 agreement between master Richard Bernard and the abbot and convent of Lilleshall); CP 40/102, m. 239 (*c.*1263 agreement between master Alan of Frieston and the prior and convent of Barnwell); British Library, MS. Harley 645, f. 254v (1263 agreement between master Alan of Frieston and the abbot of Bury St Edmund's); CP 40/142, m. 48d (1276 agreement between master Richard of Sigglesthorne and the abbot and convent of Meaux); CP 40/161, m. 358 (1287 agreement between master William of Henhow and the prior and convent of Monk's Kirby).
43 For discussion of this legislation see Brundage 'Medieval Advocate's Profession' at p. 450. See also Brundage, 'Perceptions of Propriety: The Discipline of the Canonical Bar in late Medieval England', pp. 8–9 where Brundage notes that William Durandus was author of this canon and secured its adoption but that the Roman consistorial advocates objected so bitterly to its implementation that it was omitted from the *Liber Sextus* of Boniface VIII.
44 *Register of William Wickwane*, pp. 208–9.
45 *Councils and Synods II*, ii, pp. 1030–1.
46 Wilkins, *Concilia*, ii, p. 204
47 Wilkins, *Concilia*, ii, p. 418.
48 Wilkins, *Concilia*, ii, p. 205–6.
49 *Conciliorum oecumenicorum decreta*, ed. G. Alberigo, P. Joannou et al. (2nd edition, Basel, 1962), pp. 300–1.
50 Wilkins, *Concilia*, ii, p. 410.
51 Wilkins, *Concilia*, ii, p. 418.
52 On this professional obligation and its enforcement see James A. Brundage, 'Legal Aid for the Poor and the Professionalization of Law in the Middle Ages', *Journal of Legal History*, 9 (1988), pp. 169–79.
53 Wilkins, *Concilia*, ii, p. 418.
54 Wilkins, *Concilia*, ii, p. 206.
55 Turner, *English Judiciary*, pp. 36–8.
56 Turner, *English Judiciary*, p. 96.
57 Turner, *English Judiciary*, p. 233.
58 *Cartulary of Oseney Abbey*, iii, pp. 42, 1176. For evidence that the king initially employed him as canon lawyer see *Cal. Patent Rolls, 1232–47*, pp. 173, 261, 265. For another royal justice of the period, William Bonquer, who was also a learned lawyer see Brand, 'Education of Lawyers', p. 162 and n.
59 *Registrum Palatinum Dunelmense*, ed. T. D. Hardy (4 vols., Rolls Series, 1873–8), i, pp. 336–7. For evidence that his colleague master Ralph of Farningham, a justice of the Common Bench between 1274 and 1278, was also trained in the learned laws see Brand, 'Education of Lawyers', p. 162, n. 81.
60 Above, p. 150.
61 *Select Cases in King's Bench I*, p. cxlix.
62 *YB 33–35 Edward I*, p. 471.
63 But for other evidence of Pashley's knowledge of Roman law see the reports in British Library, MS. Egerton 2811, ff. 101v–102r and Holkham, MS. 754, f. 58v.

64 See British Library, MS. Hargrave 375, f. 147v.
65 For a report which shows him exchanging Roman law-tags with Pashley see British Library, MS. Egerton 2811, ff. 101v–102v; and for his quotation of the tag 'minor et ecclesia pari passu ambulant' see British Library, MS. Additional 31826, f. 91v.
66 See Lincoln's Inn, MS. Miscellaneous 738, f. 62r; Holkham, MS. 754, f. 51v.
67 See British Library, MS. Hargrave 375, ff. 42v–43v; Cambridge University Library, MS. Ee.6.18, ff. 11r–v; *YB 2 & 3 Edward II*, pp. 173–8 at p. 176; British Library, MS. Harley 25, f. 186v; British Library, MS. Stowe 386, f. 115r.
68 See British Library, MS. Additional 31826, f. 116r; British Library, MS. Stowe 386, f. 115r.
69 British Library, MS. Additional 5925, f. 76r.
70 CP 40/105, m. 15d. William claimed Nicholas had actually acted for his opponent in the case before the official.
71 CP 40/105, m. 135.
72 In 1283 he was in receipt of an annual fee of one mark a year from the prior of Norwich: Hudson, 'Camera Roll of Norwich priory', p. 281. For evidence of his presence at, and activity in, the 1286 Norfolk eyre see JUST 1/578, m. 3 and British Library, MS. Stowe 386, ff. 94r–95r (report of case enrolled on JUST 1/578, m. 47).

Index

Abingdon abbey, 9; abbot of, 7
abuse of opponents, 122, 153
admission oath, required of advocates in late antiquity, 146; required of canon lawyers in England, 146–7, 152–3; required of canon lawyers in France, 146; required of London city serjeants under 1280 ordinance, 110, 122; revival of practice of requiring from advocates, 146; taken by serjeants at law in late fourteenth century, 106
advocates, in mid-twelfth century England, 2; *see also* professional advocate
advocatus, 11–12, 48–9, 67
ambidexterity, 122, 123–4, 130, 139–40
Ambrose, master, 2
Amcotts, Nigel of, 110
amicus curie, 96
annual oath, required of professional canon lawyers, 152
annuity *see* pension
Anstey case, 1–2, 10, 12
Anstey, Richard of, 1, 10, 12, 144
Appleby, Ralph of, 193
apprentices of the Common Bench, their activity as attorneys, 113–14, 115–16; early references to, 110; education and training, 110–14; encouragement of by the court, 110–11; later development of, 158; significance of term, 110
Arderne, Adam de, 189
Arlet, William, of Pontefract, 193
Arnesby, Richard of, 191, 192, 193
Articuli qui narrando indigent specificari, 113
Ashbourne, Robert of, 192
Ashbourne, unidentified serjeant, 76
Ashby, Richard of, 97, 202
Ashill, Robert of, 206
assessors, professional serjeants acting as in Common Bench, 54, 185; restrictions on in London city courts, 67, 122
assize *see* grand assize; petty assizes
Asthall, William of, 199
attachment, in mesne process, 37–8
Attleborough, John of, 191
attornatus, 46, 86, 176–7
attorner, attornare, 46
attorneys, advantages of use, 43; methods of appointment, 43–6, 89–91, 132–3; multiple appointment of, 75–6, 78, 81, 83; powers of, 43, 48, 84–5; restrictions on use of, 12–13, 43–5; restrictions on use of under thirteenth century French customary law, 13; terms used for, 46; *see also*

non-professional attorneys, professional attorneys; proto-professional attorneys
Aubyn, William, 193, 206
Avenel, master Andrew, 216
avowal of serjeant, circumstances where might be requested, 98–9; nature of, 99–100; *see also* disavowal

Badeschawe, Agnes daughter of Richard of, 140
Baker, John H., 95, 107, 108, 109
Balliol, Gilbert de, 47
bar of the court, 87, 96, 107
Bardfield, Ralph of, 55
baretour, 121
Barlings, abbot of, 100, 101
Barnwell, prior and convent of, 217
Barre, Hamon de la, 100, 189, 193, 202
Barre, Richard, archdeacon of Ely, 155
barrister, 158
Barwe, John de la, 140
Batayle, William, 193
Bath, Henry of, 27
Bath, prior and monks of, 5
Battle, abbey chronicle, 44, 47; abbot of, 4, 44, 47; Osbert monk of, 44, 47
Bayham, prior of, 216
Beauchamp, Roger de, 92
Beaufou, unidentified serjeant, 193
Beaufou, Alan de, 47
Beckingham, Ellis of, 28
Belet, Michael, 171
Bench *see* Common Bench; King's Bench
Bereford (Barford), William of, 28, 97, 98, 126, 155, 189, 190, 191, 192, 202, 208, 209
Berewyk, unidentified serjeant, 195
Bernard, master Richard, 216, 217
Beufrond, unidentified serjeant, 193
Bigod, Roger, 4; *see also* Norfolk, earl of
Bigstrup, Matthew of, 52
bills, recording appointments of attorneys, 90
Binham, master Stephen of, 161
Blaunkenay, Walter de, 194
Blundel, John, 196

Bocking, John of, 189, 192
Bologna, university of, 143, 144, 155
Boncretien, Stephen, 51
Bonet, John, 191
Bonnington, Stephen of, 193
Bonquer, William, 217
Botiller, John le, of Hampton, 191
Boyland, Richard of, 29, 58–9, 189; property acquisitions of, 61–2
Boyland, Roger of, 59–60; his origins, 61
Boyle, Leonard E., 144
Bracton, 35, 36, 37, 39, 42, 54, 113, 123
Bradfield, Robert of, 189, 190, 192
Bramford, Hubert of, 57; Rose wife of, 57
Bramford, Peter of, 56, 57
Brampton, Thomas of, 93
Bratton, Henry of, 28, 67
Breaute, Faukes de, 53
Bretteville, Richard de, 92, 103
Brevia Placitata, 48, 54, 58
Britton, 113
Britwell Salome, Oxfordshire, 94; Roger rector of, 92
Brok, Laurence del, 49, 60, 64–5, 94
Brom', unidentified serjeant, 193
Bromholm, John of, 100, 193
Brompton, William of, 104
Brun, Robert, 191
Brundage, James A., 146
Brunner, H. C., 3, 4, 11
Buc, Aubrey, of Barking, 51–2
Buckingham, William of, 51
Buckland, Hugh de, sheriff of Berkshire, 7
Bucuinte, John, 48, 53–4
Bungay, Reyner or Reynold of, 56–7; his wife Philippa, coheiress of Nicholas Duket, 57
Bunny, Nottinghamshire, church of, 97
Bures, master John of, 216
Burgate, Philip of, 93
Burgh, Hubert de, 55, 64
Burne, Henry of, 93
Burton, Robert of, 74, 134
Burwell, unidentified serjeant, 194
Bury St Edmund's, abbot of, 59, 217;

court of abbot of, 59; tenants of abbey of, 6; see also St Edmund's
Caen, William de, 190
Cailly, Thomas de, 206
'calls' of serjeants, in 1293 and 1299, 108; in 1329, 206; in later fourteenth century, 106
Calveley, Nicholas of, 101, 155–6
Cambridge, university of, foundation, 145–6; foundation of faculty of canon law at, 146
Cambridgeshire, county court, serjeants of, 83, 114
canon lawyers see advocates; professional canon lawyers
Canterbury, abbey of St Augustine's, 10; archbishop of, 1, 4, 64; cathedral priory of, pensions paid by, 57, 60, 100
Cantilupe, Thomas de, bishop of Hereford, 100
Cantilupe, Walter de, bishop of Worcester, synodal statutes of, 151
Carswell, John of, 92
Castleacre priory, 58
Casus Placitorum, 59, 65
causidicus, 11, 49, 67
Cave, John, of Middleton, 141
Cave, unidentified serjeant, 76, 192
Cave, William, 192
champerty, oath against, 147; legislation prohibiting, 67, 121, 122; presentments alleging, 140; see also contingency fee
chancery, defect in writ obtained from, 135; function in appointment of attorneys, 45, 89; treatise allegedly based on instruction given by senior clerk of, 118; see also writs
Chanu, John le, 134; Wymund le, 134
Chapele, John de la, executors of, 102
Charles, Thomas, 88
Chateau-Gontier, canons of provincial council at, 146
Chester, John of, 104
Chichester, dean and chapter of, 59; Hilary bishop of, 155; see also Jocelin

chief justiciar, 25; see also Glanville; Lucy
Child, Peter, 190, 191
Cirencester, abbey of, 59
Clanchy, Michael T., 169
Claver, John le, 208
clerical privilege, claimed by professional attorney, 133
clerks of chancery, receiving appointment of attorneys, 90; giving instruction, 118–19
clerks of Common Bench, agreeing to cross through enrolment, 133; entering adjournment 'at the request of the parties', 128; receiving appointment of attorneys, 89–90; writing writ to secure appearance of jury, 131
clerks of courts, activity as proto-professional attorneys in reign of John, 51; appointment as justices, 28–9
Cley, Simon of, 129
Coffer, Thomas le, 137–8
Colchester, abbot of St John's, 65
Colchester, Richer or Richard of, 65
Coleshill, Richard of, 193, 202, 204
Coleville, Robert de (of Westminster), 58, 60–1, 189; assault on Robert of Fulham, 63–4
collusion, by professional lawyers, punishment of, 120
Colney, unidentified serjeant, 193
Common Bench, beginnings of four annual termly sessions of, 22; complement of justices, 23, 25; crier of, 87; division into separate sections, 23; effect of reduction in frequency of General Eyre on, 21; expansion in amount of business, 23–4; importance of long-serving justices in, 28; jurisdiction of, 23; keeper of rolls and writs in, 87, 131, 155, 196; location of, 22; origins of, 15; relationship to Exchequer, 15, 22; sessions suspended during General Eyre, 22; as source of demand for legal services, 32; suspension under John, 22; see also apprentices of the Common Bench;

assessors; clerks; serjeants of the Common Bench; professional attorneys of the Common Bench
communis attornatus, 87, 132, 133
communis serviens, 94, 107
consilium (litigation strategy), 124, 138
consilium narratorum (preliminary meeting for briefing and planning strategy in litigation), 96; *see also* counsel
contingency fee, payment through, 93, 130; *see also* champarty
Cookham, William of, 48
Copdock, Robert of, 192
Cornhill, Stephen of, 99
Cornish, master Bernard, 217
Cornwall, earl of, 61
coroner, beginnings of office of, 20
Cort, John de, 193
Cottenham, William of, 74–5
counsel, in Anglo-Norman legal proceedings, 10; *see also* consilium
le countour, 94
counts, 3–4, 38–9, 95; development of, in action of right for land, 38–9; development of, in action of replevin, 39; in first and third person, 47, 54; mistakes in, 59, 98; in thirteenth century French customary law, 3–4; *see also* avowal; disavowal
county courts, duty of attendance at, 6–7; frequency of sessions, 6; judges in, 7, 19; professional attorneys in, 83–4; professional serjeants in, 83, 114–15, 121; subordinate position of, 19; transfer of litigation into, 18; transfer of litigation out of, 18, 19, 30–1; transformation under Henry II, 19; viscontial writs initiating litigation in, 19, 30
Court of the Arches, admission requirement for advocates in, 149; code of professional conduct for lawyers practising in, 153, 154; oath for canon lawyers practising in, 147, 152; preference for university-educated proctors in, 149; quotas on numbers of advocates and proctors allowed to practise in, 149–50; statutes of archbishop Winchelsey regulating, 149–50, 152, 153, 154
courts *see* Common Bench; county courts; Exchequer; gaol delivery; General Eyre; hundred and wapentake courts; King's Bench; local justiciar; petty assizes; royal courts; seignorial courts; town courts
Coutances, bishop of, 7
Coventry, Alexander of, 189, 190, 192, 202
Coventry and Lichfield, Roger bishop of, 216
Coxford, prior of, 102
'crib' (enclosure for apprentices), 110–11
Criol, Peter de, 47
Croc, Andrew, 59, 61
Cropthorne, master Michael rector of, 216
Crowland, abbey of, 53, 125
le cuntur, 48
Curia placitata (*Chescun manere de trespas*), 114–15

Dalimond, Richard, of Oxwick, 192
Dareyns, William, 193
deception of court, by professional lawyers, 120, 124, 125–6
Decretals, 145
decretals, collection of, in England, 144
Decretum of Gratian, compilation, 143; English academic interest in, 144, 145; glossed by Oxford teachers, 145; supplementation by collections of decretals, 144; use in Oxford as basic academic text, 145
deeds, attorneys entrusted with in connection with litigation, 88; recording agreements between attorneys and litigants, 91–4; recording pension agreements between advocates and clients, 151, 216; recording pension agreements between serjeants and clients, 100; *see also* penal bond

Deepdale, Hugh of, 191
defamation of justices, punishment of professional attorney for, 135
default, failure to sue process on, 134; fraudulent conduct leading to recovery by, 129; fraudulent failure to ensure recovery by, 128–9; fraudulent recovery by, 132
defences, in the Anglo-Norman period, 4, 11; in the late twelfth century, 40; in the thirteenth century, 41–2; in thirteenth century French customary law, 4; serjeant's responsibility in making for client, 95; *see also* avowal; disavowal; exceptions
Denham, Thomas of, 104
Denstone (Denardestone), Peter of, 82
Derby, Gervase of, 192
Devon, Amice countess of, 60
Dialogue of the Exchequer, 44
diligence, duty of professional attorney in conducting client's business, 122–3, 128–30; *see also* negligence
disavowal, attorney's function to disavow serjeant for client, 87, 113; inability of attorney to disavow self, 48, 85; of serjeants in early thirteenth century, 47–8, 53–4, 64; *see also* avowal
disclaimer, attorney has to avow, 99
discourtesy to opponents, prohibition of, in the Court of Arches, 153; in London city courts, 122
distraint, in mesne process, 37–8
Doncaster, John of, 112
Doune, Roger de la, 190
Doynton, Thomas of, 216
Dublin, serjeants of Common Bench in, 104
Ducket, Richard, 51
Duffhus, Robert, 102
Dunmow, prior and convent of, 216
Durham cathedral priory, 59, 64, 100

East, Simon, 125, 192, 202
East Somerton, Norfolk, 94
Easthorpe, William of, 191

Easton, John of, 65–6
Eaton Socon, Bedfordshire, 94
ecclesiastical legislation *see* Lyons; provincial legislation; synodal legislation
Ellerton, William of, 193
Ely, Andrew of, 190
Ely, bishop Eustace of, 146
Enfield, Terry of, 138
English law and custom, national courts create, 17; need for expert assistance when dealing with, 32; product of legislation, 17
enrolments, duty of attorney to check, 89; duty of attorney to ensure made, 88, 128; fraudulent alteration of, 130; opposing attorneys agree to crossing out of, 133; *see also* plea-rolls
Erdington, Giles of, 29
Essex, Swein of, 7
essoin, alteration of enrolment relating to, 130; *de malo lecti*, 34, 36; *de malo veniendi*, 34–5; fraudulent suing of default when opponent essoined, 131–2; limitations on use in petty assizes, 36–7; professional attorney's function to arrange for clients, 89; warranting of, 35
essoiners, 35; London legislation relating to, 67, 110, 117; responsibility for essoins, 35–6
Everingham, John of, 66
Evesham, abbot of, 7; abbot and convent of, 217
Excepciones ad cassandum brevia, 113
Excepciones contra brevia, 113
exceptions, in the action of right, 41–2; in the Anglo-Norman period, 4, 11; of bastardy, 41; encourage use of multiple serjeants, 96; encouragement to make, 42; to jurisdiction, 41; in the later twelfth century, 40–1; of law do not require avowal, 99; obligation of canon law advocates not to advance false, 147; peremptory and dilatory, 42; in the petty assizes, 41; punishment of serjeant for false, 137; rules about

when to make, 42; rules about order of making, 42; of villeinage, 41
Exchequer, attorney of city of London in, 92; barons or justices of, 8, 15; as forum for civil litigation, 15; official of involved in litigation elsewhere, 44; officials receiving appointment of attorneys for Common Bench litigation, 90; separation of Common Bench from, 22
Exchequer, Matthew of the, 123, 200, 204
excommunication, as punishment for canonical advocates, 147
Exeter, bishop of *see* Quinel; cathedral school at, 144

false judgment, action of, as mechanism for challenging judgments in local courts, 18–19, 31
false proofs, oath not to use, 147; punishment of subornation or use of, 148, 153
Farnham, Nicholas of, bishop of Durham, synodal statutes of, 147
Farningham, master Ralph of, 89, 217
Faucunberg, master Eustace de, 28
Felipper, Godwin le, 137
Field Dalling, Norfolk, William rector of, 101, 155–6
final concords, attorneys mentioned in, 15, 44; entries recording proffer and acceptance of fines to make, 71, 107–8; responsibility of serjeant for form of, 98; role of serjeants in making, 97–8
fines, for permission to make final concords, 71; as punishment for professional misbehaviour, 128, 129, 131, 133, 136
Fishburn, Thomas of, 190, 192, 193, 202
fitzAucher, Thomas, 60
fitzNeal, Richard, treasurer, 169, 170–1
fitzThedmar, Arnulf, London chronicler, 67
fitzWilliam, John, 66
fitzWilliam, Robert, 190
Fleet gaol, London, imprisonment in, as punishment for professional misconduct, 123, 128, 129, 130, 131, 132, 133, 135
Fleta, 94, 113, 123
forespeca, 11–12
forgery of deeds, 139, 153
Fox, Richard, of Shrewsbury, 93
Foxley, Robert rector of, 216
France, English students of canon law in, 144; English teachers of canon law in, 144
Francheville, Mabel de, 1
Fraunceys, Hugh, of Eynesbury, 93–4
Frescheville, Ralph de, 96
Frieston, master Alan of, 217
Friskney, Walter of, 126, 192, 193
Fulham, Robert of, 58, 63–4

Gaddesden, John of, 59, 60
gaol delivery justices, appointment of, 20, 27; emergence of circuits of, 27; merger of circuits with assize circuits, 27
Gaunt, Gilbert of, 97
General Eyre, beginnings of, 14–15; business of, 14–15, 20; circuits, 14–15, 20, 21; end of, 20–1; frequency of visitations, 15, 20, 168; justices of, 15, 16, 20, 21; length of individual sessions, 21; length of visitations, 20; nature of individual sessions, 17; position of justices of, 15, 21; presentments of conspirators at, 139–41; relationship to Common Bench, 20, 21, 22, 23; *see also* professional attorneys in the General Eyre, professional serjeants of the General Eyre
generalis attornatus, 87, 132
Giffard, John (of Westminster), 59, 60
Ginges, Ralph of, 60
Gisleham, John of, 191
Gisleham, William of, 123, 189, 190, 192, 200, 202, 204
Gladewyn, Richard, 195
Glanvill, 16, 17, 18, 19, 30, 31, 33, 34, 35, 36, 37, 38, 39, 40, 41, 43, 44, 45, 47, 54
Glanville, Gilbert de, bishop of Rochester, 144

Glanville, Ranulf de, 161
Glastonbury abbey, 64
Gloz, Reiner de, 52
Goldington, William of, 193, 208
'good faith', warnings to serjeants to answer in, 126
Goscelin, Thomas, 193
Gosfield, Richard of, 189, 190, 202
Graffham, Walter of, 192
Grafton, William of, 195
Grainthorpe, Walter of, 92
Granc', unidentified serjeant, 190
grand assize, creation, 18; effect on seignorial courts, 18; exception to use of, 40; serjeant addresses jurors of, 96–7
Grantchester, William of, 75
Grantchester, unidentified serjeant, 194
Grantham, Lincolnshire, 94
Grantham, William of, 91
Gratian, 143
Great Yarmouth, Norfolk, 88
Gregory IX, pope, 145, 151
Greshope, Robert of, 133
Gruscy, Hamon, 193
Grymet, William, 193
Guildford, Henry of, 88

habeas corpus, in mesne process, 37
Haddlesey, William of, 191
Hakebech, Robert of, 125
Hales, Henry of, 89; assault on his servant, 89
Hamo *dapifer*, 10
Hampton, Richard of, 204, 206
Hansere, Eustace le, 91
Harald, Robert, 193
Harle (Herle), William of, 126, 192, 193, 200, 204, 205, 206, 208
Harpley, John of, 66
Hartforth (Hertford), Robert of, 190, 192
Hartforth (Hertford), William of, 193
Hartlepool, Geoffrey of, 99, 190, 192, 193, 202
Havering, Richard (de Ulmis) of, 56, 58, 59, 60, 62, 65, 100; Christine wife of, 63

Havering, Richard of (another), 62
Haverington, John of, 193
Hawthorne, Thomas of, 193; *see also* Hoton
Haydock, Robert of, 206
Haye, William de la, 140
Hayton, Thomas of, 92
Heacham, Richard of, 61
Hedon *see* Norman
Hele, Hugh de la, 82
Hengham, Ralph de, 28–9, 111, 119, 126
Hengham Magna, 31, 36, 48, 54, 75, 172
Hengham Parva, 118–19
Henhow, master William of, 217
Henry I, king of England, writ of, 7
Henry II, king of England, 1; creation of General Eyre by, 14; supposed creation of Common Bench by, 15; policy in keeping core group of royal justices, 16
Hereford, bishop of, 140
Hereford, Roger of, 140
Herriard, Robert of, 102–3
Hertford see Hartforth
Hertweyton, Hugh de, 195
Higham, Roger of, 98, 100, 101, 155, 189, 190, 192, 193, 200, 202, 204
Ho, Thomas de, 52
Honewyk, Richard de, 195
Honorius, master *see* Kent
Hopperton, Adam of, 191
Hopton, R. of, 193
Hornby, Bertram of, 47
Hoton, Thomas of, 193; *see also* Hawthorne
Hotot, Richard de, 48, 56, 57, 60; his son Thomas, 57
Houghton, John of, 58, 60, 189
Howard, William, 80, 99, 126, 155, 192, 193, 204
hundred and wapentake courts, duty of attendance at, 6; frequency of sessions, 6; judges in, 6; presiding officers of, 6; professional serjeants in, 85
Hunmanby, Yorkshire, manor of, 97
Huntingdon, master Nicholas of, 94

Huntingdon, Ralph of, 80, 192, 193, 201
Hurste, unidentified serjeant, 193

imprisonment, as punishment for champerty, 121; as punishment for insulting clerk of sheriff of London, 137; as punishment for professional misconduct, 120, 122–3, 129, 130, 131, 132, 133, 134, 135, 136; *see also* Fleet gaol
incompetence, punishment for professional, 127, 132
infamia, 155
Inge, William, 112, 155, 190, 192, 193, 202, 203, 205
Inland, Richard of, 54
Inns of Court, 158

Jesmond, Adam of, 59
Jocelin, master, archdeacon of Chichester, 155
John, king of England, concession relating to Common Bench, 22; effect of political conditions of reign on General Eyre, 20; suspension of Common Bench by, 22
judicial writs, attorney's responsibility for ensuring court clerks write, 88, 131, 134; attorney's responsibility for ensuring reached client, 88; being written in church of St Andrew's York in 1298, 89
jurors, challenging of, 89, 133, 138; fraudulent attempt to change, 131; royal monopoly of power of compulsion to serve as, 30; professional attorneys serve as for trials of fellows for misconduct, 130, 131, 136; suing of process against after death of litigant, 132
jury trial, role of serjeants at, 96–7
justices *see* royal justices

Kelloe, William of, 97, 189, 190, 192, 193, 202
Kellow, Richard de, bishop of Durham, regulations of (1312), 153–4

Kelsey, Robert of, 137–8, 195
Kelsey, William of, 209
Kenerthorp, Stephen of, 191
Kent, master Honorius of, archdeacon of Richmond, 144, 145
Kernyek, Reginald de, 89
Kilvington, William of, 194
Kilwardby, Robert, archbishop of Canterbury, regulations of (1273), 147
King, Edmund, 57
King's Bench, appointment of professional serjeant as chief justice of, 29; creation of, 24; forerunners of, 24; jurisdiction of, 24; justices of receive appointment of Common Bench attorneys, 90; numbers of justices, 25–6; *see also* professional attorneys in King's Bench and professional serjeants of King's Bench
King's Lynn, town court at, 84, 102; *see also* Lynn
king's serjeant(s), beginnings of regular retaining of, 64–5, 103–4; reservation in favour of king in pension agreement of private client with, 101; *see also* Boyland; Bretteville; del Brok; Giffard; Houghton; Pakenham; Thornegg; Thornton; Walkingham; Warwick
Kinsham (Kingeshemede), Adam of, 80, 100, 101, 107, 126, 189, 190, 192, 193, 202, 206
Kinsham (Kingeshemede), Simon of, 193, 206
Kirkham, Richard of, 195
Kneton, Alexander of, 141
knights, sent to see man essoined *de malo lecti*, 34, 35; make presentment against professional attorney, 129
Kuttner, Stephan D., 144
Kylot, Alice, of Shrewsbury, 138

Lakenham, Geoffrey of, 77, 192
Lambeth, legislation of provincial council at (1281), 149
Lamport, Roger of, 133
Lancaster, John of, 102
Lass, Ludwig, 11

Laton', little Michael of, 140
Laver, Nicholas of, 193
law reports, compiled by apprentices, 111–12; as evidence of functions performed by serjeants, 95; as evidence for preliminary sessions of serjeants, 96; use in legal education, 111–12
law reports from the Common Bench, earliest surviving, 70; as source of information on serjeants of court in reign of Edward I, 70–1
law reports from county courts, 83, 114
law reports from the General Eyre, from 1272 Lincolnshire eyre, 65; of reign of Edward I, 79–80
law reports of King's Bench, from reign of Edward I, 76
Lech', master Robert of, 216
lectures, in education of apprentices, 112; in education of local court serjeants, 114–15; in education of future attorneys, 117–19
legal education, attendance at court as part of, 110–11; of apprentices, 110–13, 116; of future attorneys, 117–19; connexion with treatises, 113, 118–19; role of disputations in, 112; role of law reports in, 111–12; practice in court room technique as part of, 112; role of lectures in, 112, 114–15, 117–19; role of private reading in, 112–13; *see also* apprentices of the Common Bench; lectures; training and university education
legal expertise, absence of demand for in Anglo-Norman period, 5; creation of demand for, 32; required when choosing writs, 34; required in connection with legal process, 36, 38; required in making counts, 40; required in making and rebutting exceptions, 42
legal experts, absence of in secular courts in mid-twelfth century England, 2; absence of in secular courts in Anglo-Norman period, 2–3; appointed as justices, 22, 27–9, 32; royal courts

develop own, 16; royal courts provide for seignorial courts, 19
legal profession, working definition used, viii
legatine legislation *see* London
Leges Henrici Primi, 3, 9, 10–11, 12
legislation *see* ecclesiastical legislation; London city courts; Magna Carta; statutes
l'Estrange, John son of John, 100
Lewes, prior of, 150
Lexington, Robert of, 27, 56
Liber Pauperum, 145
life-grants of land, to retain serjeants, 101
life-retainers, of professional attorneys, 91; of professional serjeants, 100–3
Lightfoot, John, 141
Lilleshall, abbot and convent of, 216, 217
Lincoln, agreement made at, 94; teaching of canon law in cathedral school at, 144; *see also* Hansere
Lincoln, bishop of, 8, 65
Lisle, John de, 98, 99, 190, 192, 193, 202
Lisle, master Godfrey de, 28
litigants, ability to conduct litigation without leaving home county, 94; attorney makes initial contact with in home county, 94; attorney's role in engaging and paying serjeants for, 88, 104; attorney's role in making appearances for, 87; attorney's role as channel of communication between court and, 87; contracts with professional attorneys, 91–4; expansion in choice of remedies open to, 29, 34; responsibility for judicial writs reaching sheriffs, 88; in written communication with attorneys, 88
Littlebury, master Peter of, 161
local courts *see* county courts; hundred and wapentake courts; seignorial courts; town courts
local justiciar of the Anglo-Norman period: judges in his court, 8; his role in his court, 7–8
London, bishop of, 7
London, city of, attorney of in

Exchequer *see* Whitwell; attorneys of in King's Bench *see* Grantham, Palmer; mayor of, 57; serjeant retained by *see* Tothby; suspect royal writ in favour of, 7

London city courts, legislation of 1244 referring to serjeants in, 49; legislation of 1259 referring to professional serjeants in, 67; legislation of 1264 referring to professional serjeants in, 49, 67; legislation (ordinance) of 1280 creating monopoly of regular paid employment for specially admitted serjeants and enacting code of conduct for professional lawyers in, 84, 109–10, 122–3, 136–8; number of professional attorneys practising in after 1280, 84; number of professional serjeants practising in after 1280, 84; professional lawyers in during reign of Henry III, 67; restrictions on numbers of professional attorneys allowed to practise, 84, 117; restrictions on professional lawyers acting as assessors in city courts, 122

London, Fleet Street in, 115; Holborn in, 115; legislation of 1237 legatine council at, 146; location for lectures aimed at serjeants of local courts, 114–15; quota of canonical advocates practising in, 150; tavern near Woolchurchhaw in, 94; *see also* Court of Arches; Fleet gaol; Inns of Court

Longespee, Roger, bishop of Coventry and Lichfield, executors of, 150
Loveday, Roger, 63
Lovel, master John, 150, 155, 216
Lowther, Hugh of, 102, 190, 193, 200
loyalty to clients, as duty of professional attorneys, 128–30; as duty of professional canon lawyers, 146, 147, 152; as duty of professional serjeants, 123–5, 137–8; *see also* ambidexterity
Lucy, Godfrey de, 155
Lucy, Richard de, 1, 162
Luffenham, Peter of, 130
Luffield, prior and convent of, 216, 217

Lynn, Nicholas of, 57–8, 61; his wife Margery, 61
Lyons, Second Council of (1274), legislation of, 151, 152, 153, 154

Mablethorpe, Robert of, 192, 201, 206
Madingley, unidentified serjeant, 194
magister, 144–5, 146
Magna Carta, effect on Common Bench, 22; effect on King's Bench, 24; and frequency of meetings of county court, 6
'maintenance' of litigation, 121, 141
Maitland, F. W., 111, 116
Malling, master Robert of, 216
Mallore, Peter, 134
Malton, William of, 193
Mareys, William de, 193, 195
Marshal, Thomas, of Oxford, 84–5
Marske, John son of Robert of, 75, 92
Maunsel, Peter, 191
Meaux, abbot and convent of, 217
Meleti, master Peter de, 2
Merk, Maud de, 102
mesne process, attorney's functions in respect of, 87; in actions for land and advowsons, 34–5; in personal actions, 37–8; *see also* attachment; distraint; habeas corpus; summons; outlawry
Methelay, T. de, 193
Methele, unidentified serjeant (?same), 193
Mettingham, John of, 87, 88, 112, 113, 125, 132
Middleton, Adam of, 193
Middleton, Robert of, 193; *see also* Milton
Milsom, S. F. C., 3–5
Milton or Middleton, John of, 192, 193, 202
miskenning, 3
Modbert, 5
Modus Componendi Brevia, 118
Modus Levandi Fines, 94
Monk's Kirby, prior and convent of, 217
Monnington, John of, 140
Motekan, Osbert, 92

Moyne, Thomas le, 130; his father William, 130
Muscegros, Robert de, 191
Mutford, John of, 96, 97, 124–5, 126, 155, 192, 193, 292

narrator, 48, 85, 94
Natura Brevium, 118
negligence, punishment of professional attorneys for, 122–3, 134, 138; of professional serjeant for, 127; *see also* diligence
Newent, prior of, 216
Newman, Richard, of Suffolk, 107
non-professional attorneys, appointed in Common Bench in 1280 and 1300, 73; appointed in King's Bench in 1280 and 1299, 77; appointed in eyres c. 1280, 80–2; continuing possibility of use, 46
non-professional serjeants, of the reign of king John, 54; of the reign of king Henry III, 55; of the reign of Edward I in King's Bench, 76; possible survival in lower courts, 85
Norfolk, earl of, 59, 124–5
Norman, Robert, of Hedon, 98, 126, 193, 206
Normanby, Richard of, 191
Northampton, meeting of king and council at (1176), 14–15
Northampton, Warin of, of St Neot's, 93–4
Norwich, bishop of, 4, 87, 156
Norwich cathedral priory, pensions paid to serjeants by, 100, 218
Norwich, city of, possible payment to serjeants in court of (in 1242), 67; payment of pensions by city to serjeants, 100
Novae Narrationes, 113
novel disseisin, used to challenge judgments in lower courts, 31–2; restriction on use of attorneys by defendants in, 45; resulting from disseisin advised by serjeants, 98; *see also* petty assizes

oath *see* admission oath; annual oath
opponent of client, obligations of professional attorneys to, 130–2; obligations of canon law advocates to, 146–8
ordinance *see* London; statutes
Organ, John, of Newcastle under Lyme, 139
original writs, absence of forms for initiating litigation in seignorial courts about services, 29–30; attorney's functions in acquiring or advising client on choice of, 88, 119, 128, 138; expansion in number during thirteenth century, 33; forgery by professional attorney, 134–5; *pone* for removal of litigation from county court, 18, 19, 31, 33–4; required to initiate litigation about title to free land, 18; removal of, from files of court, 131; returnable used in connection with litigation, 16–17; variety available for recovery of land, 34; viscontial, 19, 33–4; writs of entry, 29
Ormsby, William of, 156, 192
Osney, abbey of, 155
Oundle, Reginald of, 195
outlawry, in mesne process, 38; of professional attorney involved in misconduct, 135
Otto, papal legate, 146
Ottobuono, papal legate, 147
Oxford, city court of, 84–5; legislation of council of Canterbury province at (1222), 147; as place to engage canon lawyers, 144; professional lawyers active in, 84–5
Oxford, university of, beginnings of education in canon law at, 145; and foundation of university of Cambridge, 145–6; reorganisation of law syllabus at, c. 1234, 145; teaching of canon and Roman law in Oxford prior to foundation of, 144
d'Oylly, Nigel, 9–10

230   Index

Pageman, William, 192
Pain, unidentified serjeant, 193
Pakenham, John of, 59, 65; property holdings of, 62
Palmer, Robert C., vii, 31, 83, 99, 103, 127, 162, 164
Palmer, Thomas, of Cornhill, 88, 92
Paris, Matthew, St Alban's chronicler, 55
Pashley, Edmund of, 96, 97, 155, 206, 208
patrocinium, 101
Pattishall, Martin of, 28
Pattishall, Simon of, 27
payment, of canon lawyers, regulation of, 147, 153, 154; of professional attorneys, 91–4; of professional serjeants, 100–5; *see also* pension(s)
Pecche, Hamon, 44, 47; Geoffrey his son, 44, 47
Peckham, master Peter of, 150, 216
penal bond, use of, 93
Penkridge, William of, 190–1
pension to professional attorney, 91
pensions to professional canon lawyers, envisage mobility of advocates in service of clients, 151; envisage presentation to ecclesiastical benefice, 152; litigation about, 150, 151, 155–6
pensions to professional serjeants, amounts paid to serjeants in king's courts, 100–1; amounts paid to serjeants in lower courts, 101; form of payments, 101; litigation about, 100; payments in addition to, 101; in reign of Henry III, 57, 58, 59, 60, 64; in reign of Edward I, 100–4; secured on land, 101; service owed in return for, 101–3; written bond of serjeant for service due in return for, 100
Penskawen, Nicholas of, 134
Peterborough, abbey of, 9, 65, 100, 101
petty assizes, procedural rules in, 36–7; use of exceptions in, 41
petty assize justices, commissions to, 20, 26–7; creation of circuits of, 26; given additional responsibility for gaol delivery, 27; limitations on times of sessions of, 26–7; receive appointments of attorneys for Common Bench litigation, 90
Peverel, Ralph, 195
Pickering, master William of, 217
Picot son of Colswain, 9–10
Pirton, master Peter of, 216
placitator, 2, 49, 67
plaints, used to initiate suits alleging professional misconduct, 136
Planaz, John de, 48, 56, 57
Playssh', Walter son of Reginald de, of Egerton, 140
Playz, Thomas de, 190, 193
plea-rolls, access by attorneys to, 89, 133; appointments of attorneys recorded on, 90; beginnings, 16–17; expansion in size of, in Common Bench, 23–4; infrequency of mentions of serjeants on, 95; *see also* enrolments
pleader, in early medieval European legal custom, 11; in England in reign of Henry II, 46–7; in French thirteenth century customary law, 11; supposed use in Anglo-Saxon England, 11–12; *see also* serjeant
pledour, 139
Plucknett, T. F. T, 116
Poleyn, unidentified serjeant, 193
Poleyn, William (?same), 82
Pollard, William, of Fulbeck, 93
pone see writs
ponere, positus, 46
Pontefract, Richard of, 193
Pontefract, William of, 193; *see* Arlet
poor and disadvantaged clients, duty of serjeant to provide gratuitous service to, 104, 205; enforcement of duty of advocates and proctors to act for, 154; privileges of advocates providing service to, 146, 151–2
Prat, Alan, 132
Preston, Gilbert of, 27
Preston, unidentified serjeant, 193
professional advocate, acting also for client in secular courts, 156; admission oath required of, 146–7, 152–3;

Index

barriers to beneficed clergy practising as, 151–2; ethical standards, 147–8; maximum fees regulated, 153–4; as members of international legal profession, 154; mobility expected of, 151, 154; movement towards more localised, 151; qualification for practice as, 146, 149; quotas in particular courts, 149–50; requirement of clerical orders for, 152; *see also* advocates

professional attorney, criteria for distinguishing from non-professional, 50–1; difficulties in distinguishing from semi-professional and non-professional, 73–5; education of, 117–19; ethical standards enforced on those in king's courts, 128–36; ethical standards for, 120–3; views of Lady Stenton on date of emergence, 50; terms used for in reign of Edward I, 71, 87

professional attorneys in the Common Bench, absence of comprehensive lists of, 71; apprentices acting as, 113–14; contracts with clients, 91–4; degree of specialisation in business from single county, 69, 75, 78, 132; county quotas proposed, 115–16; functions performed by, 87–9; misconduct by, 115–16, 128–36; multiple appointments of by individual litigants, 75–6; numbers and identities c. 1260, 65–7; numbers in 1280 and 1300, 71–6; ordinance of 1292 limiting numbers of, 115–17; reasons for comparatively late emergence, 69

professional attorneys in county courts, 83–4

professional attorneys in the General Eyre, numbers in eyres of c. 1280, 80–3

professional attorneys in King's Bench, absence of comprehensive lists of, 77; multiple appointments of by individual litigants, 78; numbers in 1280 and 1299, 77–8; retainer of, by city of London, 88, 92; retainer of, by king, 103–4

professional attorneys in town courts: numbers practising in city of London, 84, 117; practising in Shrewsbury town court, 84

professional canon lawyers, comparison with development of professional common lawyers, 157; stages in history of development in England, 143

professional lawyer, working definition of, vii

professional proctors, beginning of recognition of membership of professional group, 148, 154; beneficed clergy prohibited from acting as, 151; maximum fees regulated, 153–4; oath required of, 147, 152; quota on numbers in Court of Arches, 149; required to employ advocates, 150

professional serjeants, acting as *amici curie*, 96; *ad hoc* engagement, 104; advantages in using several, 96; assignment to service of litigants, 104; attorney briefs for client, 88; attorney engages for client, 88; attorney pays for client, 88; difficulty in distinguishing from non-professional serjeants in lower courts, 85; ethical standards, 120, 123–8; in fair courts, 85; functions performed by in reign of Edward I, 95–8; gain monopoly of judicial appointments after 1307, 158; life retainers of, 100–4; reasons for early emergence in the Common Bench and London city courts, 68–9; of the reign of king John, 52–4; role in making of final concords, 97–8; role as legal advisers, 98; in seignorial and hundred courts, 85; terms used for, in reign of Edward I, 94–5; in town courts outside London, 84–5; training and education, 110–5, 116

professional serjeants in county courts, 83

professional serjeants in London city courts, attempt to reduce need for, 67; monopoly for group of under 1280 ordinance, 84, 109–110; numbers after 1280, 84; prohibited from acting as

essoiners, 67; prohibition of champerty by, 67
professional serjeants of the Common Bench, closed group by end of thirteenth century, 106–9; employed by king, 104; freedom from compulsion to serve litigants, 104; numbers in reign of Edward I, 70–1; overlap with serjeants of the General Eyre, 79–80; payment of, 104–5; possessing expertise in Roman and canon law, 155; practise also in King's Bench, 76; of reign of Henry III, 55–64; significance of stability in numbers, 108; special status of regular practitioners, 107; *see also* 'calls'
professional serjeants of the General Eyre, assignment to service of poor clients, 104; numbers in reign of Edward I, 79–80; overlap with serjeants of the Common Bench, 79–80; in reign of Henry III, 65; retained by king, 103
professional serjeants of King's Bench, in reign of Henry III, 64–5; in reign of Edward I, 76
proof, methods of, used in civil litigation in the Anglo-Norman period, 4; *see also* false proofs
proto-professional attorneys of reign of king John, distinguishing characteristics of, 51; three different types of, 51–4
provincial legislation *see* Chateau-Gontier; Lambeth; Oxford; Reading and Rouen
Pucelle, Gerard, 144
Purdeu, Arnold, 88

quaestiones of teachers of canon law, 145
Quarr, abbot of, 216
Querdeliun, Roger (of Cirencester), 192
questiones (disputate), used in teaching of common law, 112
Quinel, Peter, bishop of Exeter, synodal statutes of (1287),152

quotas, for advocates and proctors in provincial courts, 149–51; for attorneys in the Common Bench, 115–17; for serjeants in the Common Bench, 106–9; for serjeants in London city courts, 109–10
Quy, John of, 66, 189

Ragon, John, 140
Raleigh, William of, 28
Ramsden, Thomas of, 56, 58, 59, 60, 62; his wife Isabel, 56, 58, 59, 60, 62; property holdings of, 63
Ramsey, abbey, 57, 58, 59, 60, 64, 67; abbot of, 52
Ramsey, John of, 60, 189, 192; property holdings of, 62; Agnes wife of, 62
Rathbone, Eleanor, 144
Reading, provincial legislation enacted at (1279), 148
reading, as part of education of apprentices, 112–13
'readings' (lectures on statutes), forerunners of, 112
register of writs, as evidence of expansion in number of original writs, 33; as subject of organised educational course, 119
repleading, of case already pleaded to issue, 126, 133; of matter already subject of previous litigation, 125–6
replevin, use of action of, to challenge judgments of lower courts, 32; development of count in action of, 39
reportationes (student notes) on glosses of Oxford canon law teachers, 145
representation of litigants, extension of availability, 43–8; limitations on, 10–13
responsalis, 43, 46, 175–6
retainer *see* pension
Richmond, Yorkshire, 94
right, action of, defences in, 40–1; development of count in, 38–40; only land action available in seignorial courts, 29; process in, 34–6
Ringstead, Robert of, 102

Index 233

Risley, Walter of, 124
Rivers, Baldwin de, 59
Robert the philosopher, 47
Rochester, Solomon of, 90
Rockingham, Robert of, 51
Rode, master Henry de la, 216
Roding (Rothinges), Geoffrey of, 195
Rokele, Richard de la, 66
Roman law, Common Bench serjeants' knowledge of, 155; purpose of studying, 145; teaching of, 145
Ross Hall, Stephen son of Alan of, 93
Rouen, canons of provincial council at, 146
royal courts of the Angevin period, characteristics of, 15–17, 32; continuity of sessions, 16, 21; record-keeping by, 16–17; requirement of specific royal authorisation, 17; role of justices in, 16; *see also* Common Bench, Exchequer, gaol delivery, General Eyre, King's Bench; petty assize justices
royal courts of the Anglo-Norman period, judges of, 7, 8–9; presiding officers of, 7, 8–9
royal justices, appointment of, 16, 27–9, 155, 158; functions of, 16; length of tenure of judicial office by, 16, 27–8; require avowal of serjeants, 99; role in appointment of attorneys, 89–90
Rue, Adam de la, 138

St Alban's, abbey school at, 144
St Alban's, master Laurence of, 55
St Alban's, Reginald or Roger of, 66
St Calais, William of, bishop of Durham, 4
St Edmund's, Henry fitz William of, 190, 191; *see also* Bury St Edmund's
St Ermine, William de, 62
St Ives, fair court at, 85
St Martin, Laurence de, bishop of Rochester, 64; his brother Abel, 64
St Martin, Richard de, 85
Sackville, William de, 1

Sampson, ?Ralph, 193
Sayles, G. O., 103, 115, 121
Scotter, Roger of, 96, 192, 193, 202
Scrope, Henry le, 155, 192, 193
Seaton, master Roger of, 155
seignorial courts, different types of, 5; entitlement to hold, 5; frequency of sessions, 5; judges in, 6; limitations imposed on jurisdiction, 18, 29–30; presiding officers of, 5–6; privileges of lord in, 13; procedural constraints on, 30; removal of litigation from, 18, 19; royal control of, 18–19, 29–30; serjeants in, 85
Selby, abbot and convent of, 217
Selby, Ralph of, 193
Selby, William of, 97, 190, 192, 204
Semon, Lovekyn, of Stafford, 139
serjant, 94
serjeant contour, 94
serjeants, avowal and disavowal of, 47, 53, 54, 85, 98–100; beginnings of evidence for use in king's courts, 47–8, 52–5; briefing of, 89, 96, 113; terms used for, 48–9, 95; use of serjeants in king's courts in reign of Henry III, 54–5, 64; *see also advocatus; causidicus; le countour; le cuntur*; king's serjeant(s); *narrator*; non-professional serjeants; *placitator*; pleader; professional serjeants; *serjeant; serjeant contour; serviens; serviens narrator; serviens regis*
serjeants at law, order of, 106
serviens, 49, 94
serviens narrator, 94
serviens regis, 94
Shap, abbot of, 102
Shardlow, master Robert of, 155
Sherloc, unidentified serjeant, 193
'shrews', 134
Shrewsbury, movement of Common Bench to, 22; professional attorney acting in town court at, 84, 138–9
Sigglesthorne, master Richard of, 217
Singleton, Gilbert of, 206
Skelton, John of, 191

Skip, Laurencia widow of John, 137
Skutterskelfe, William of, 66
Smith, John, of Monnington, 140
Sok, Thomas le, 92
solicitors, 158
Souburn ?alias Sutbur', unidentified serjeant, 190
South Petherton, men of, 123
Southcote, Roger of, 193
Southwell, dean and chapter of, 96–7
Southwell, Simon of, treasurer of Lichfield, 145
Spalding, priory of, 53
Spigurnel, Henry, 80, 90, 97, 155, 190, 192, 193, 202, 203, 205
Stallingborough, Ralph of, 206
Stanton, Hervey of, 155
Stapleford, Richard of, 206, 208
'State Trials' (1289–93), complaints made in, 104
statutes and ordinances: Provisions of Westminster (1263), c. 7, 38; Statute of Marlborough (1267), c. 12, 38; Statute of Westminster I (1275), c. 25, 121; Westminster I, c. 29, 94, 120–1, 123–36, 137; Westminster I, c. 33, 121; Westminster I, c. 45, 38; *Districciones Scaccarii* (1275), 125; Statute of Gloucester (1278), 118; Statute of Westminster II (1285), 38; Westminster II (1285), c. 30, 26–7; 1292 Ordinance restricting numbers of attorneys allowed to practise, 114, 115–17, 121; Statute of Conspirators (1292), 121; 1293 Ordinance of Conspirators, 121; Statute of Fines (1299), c. 3, 27; *Articuli super Cartas* (1300), c. 11, 94, 121–2; Statute *de Finibus et Attornatis* (1307), 90; *see also* Magna Carta and 'readings'
Stenton, D. M., 50
Stephen, king of England, 7–8
steward, as lord's representative in litigation, 12–13, 43
stewards of the royal household, in King's Bench, 25–6; in marshalsea court, 26

Stowe, William of, 189
Stradbroke, John of, 61
Strand, Stephen of the, 56, 57
Stratford, abbey of, 58, 60, 65, 100
Stuteville, William de, 58
Sudbury, Robert of, 55
Summa de multiplici iuris divisione, 144
Summa Omnis qui juste, 144
summons, attested by summoners, 35; denial of, 35; number in land and advowson actions, 34–5; number in personal actions, 37
supporters accompanying litigants to court, 2, 10
suspension from benefice as punishment for professional misconduct by canonical advocate, 148
suspension from practice, permanent, as punishment for professional misconduct, 120, 122, 130, 133, 134, 135, 136, 153; temporary, as punishment for professional misconduct, 122, 126, 127, 128, 130, 134, 136, 137, 148, 152, 153; threatened by justices, 125, 126
Sutton, Henry of, 192
Sutton, Robert of, 137, 195
Swaledale, Ellis of, 191
Swillington, Robert of, 192
Swinburn, John of, 91
Swinburn, Northumberland, 94
Swinburn, William of, 102
synodal legislation, imposing admission oath on advocates, 146–7; *see also* Cantilupe; Farnham; Quivel

Tattershall, Robert of, 97
tavern, agreement between litigant and attorney made in, 94; regular attendance in, forbidden to advocates and proctors of the Court of Arches, 153
Tebaud, William, 92
terms, for hearing business, 21, 22
Thetford, monks of, 4
Thirkleby, Roger of, 27, 28, 59
Thirkleby, Thomas of, 191, 193

Thornborough, Robert of, 56, 58, 59, 60, 65
Thornegg, William de, 58, 61
Thorni, John de, 141
Thornton, 113
Thornton, Gilbert of, 29, 65, 90–1, 100, 101, 189, 190, 192, 202, 204, 209
Tilton, John of, 97, 190, 192, 193, 205
tolt, 18
Tony, Ralph de, 101
Tony, Robert de, 140
Torel, Thomas, 114
Tothby, Gilbert of, 96, 97, 103, 138, 192, 195, 205, 206, 208
town courts *see* Great Yarmouth; King's Lynn; London city courts; Norwich; Oxford; Shrewsbury
trailbaston sessions, presentments at, 139–41
Trussebut, Thomas, 193
Tutadebles, Thomas, of Thurfield, 52
Tykesore, William of, 94
Tynemouth, John of, archdeacon of Oxford, 145
Tynemouth, priory of, 100

Ugley, John of, 138
university education in canon and Roman law, appointment of men possessing as royal justices in England, 155; beginnings in England, 145–6; no evidence of formal requirement of, prior to 1274, 146; imposition of requirement of, for advocates, 149; priority for proctors with, in Court of Arches, 149; serjeants with, 155
unjust causes, duty of canon lawyers to relinquish and not to accept, 146–7, 152
usury, 196–7

Vacarius, master, 145
Valoines, Gunnora de, 130
Vere, Aubrey de, 7
Vezano, master Giffred de, 99
view of property in dispute, 34; restrictions on availability, 36
Vilers, Robert de, 102–3

wager of law, gesture appropriate to, 99
Walcot, John of, 193
Walkingham, Alan of, 103, 189, 202, 204
Walton, master Simon of, bishop of Norwich, 155
Wandsworth, John of, 66
Wandsworth, William of, 60, 190, 192
wapentake *see* hundred
warranty, voucher to, in the Anglo-Norman period, 4; in land actions, 35; in petty assizes, 36–7
Warwick, Nicholas of, 96, 99, 104, 155, 190, 191, 192, 193, 200, 202
Warwickshire, serjeants of county court of, 83, 114
Welby, William of, 93
Wells, William of, 76, 123–4
Westcote, Alard of, 47
Westcote, John of, 192, 193, 206
Westminster, abbot of, 52, 100, 101
Westminster, Common Bench sessions at, 22; Exchequer sessions at, 15; temporary movement of Common Bench away from, 22
Westmorland, county court of, 102
Weyland, John, Common Bench clerk, 56, 58, 60
Weyland, John, son of chief justice Thomas, 124–5
Weyland, Thomas, 104
White, Stephen D., 5
Whitchester, Roger of, 28
Whitwell, Harsculph of, 92
Whixley, master Alan of, 216, 217
Wickwane, William, archbishop of York, 151, 152
Willenhall, John of, 140
William, Abel son of, 48, 54
William II, king of England, 6–7
Willoughby, Richard of, 96, 190, 192, 193, 200, 206
Wilton, Richard of, 195
Winchelsey, Robert, archbishop of Canterbury, statutes of, for Court of Arches, 149–50, 151, 152, 153, 154
Winterton, Norfolk, Bartholomew rector of, 156

Wolmersdon ('Wolmereston'), Robert of, 66
Worcester, bishop of, 7
Writtle, Essex, 7
writs *see* chancery; judicial writs; original writs; registers of writs
year-books *see* law reports

York, agreement made at, 94; church of St Andrew's in, 89; movement of Common Bench to, 22, 23, 73, 133
York, archbishop of, consistory court of, 151, 152, 153
York, John of, 91
York, William of, 28